Society Scottish Historical

**Diary of Sir Archibald Johnston, Lord Wariston. 1639,**

The Preservation of the Honours of Scotland, 1651-52

Society Scottish Historical

**Diary of Sir Archibald Johnston, Lord Wariston. 1639,**
*The Preservation of the Honours of Scotland, 1651-52*

ISBN/EAN: 9783337021429

Printed in Europe, USA, Canada, Australia, Japan

Cover: Foto ©ninafisch / pixelio.de

More available books at **www.hansebooks.com**

PUBLICATIONS

OF THE

# SCOTTISH HISTORY SOCIETY

VOLUME XXVI

WARISTON'S DIARY AND OTHER PAPERS

December 1896

*This Volume is presented to the members of the Scottish History Society by T. and A. Constable*

*December* 1896

ARCHIBALD JOHNSTON, LORD WARISTON

*From the portrait by Jamesone in the possession of Sir James Gibson-Craig, Bart.*

# DIARY OF
# SIR ARCHIBALD JOHNSTON
## LORD WARISTON
### 1639

## THE PRESERVATION OF
## THE HONOURS OF SCOTLAND
### 1651-52

## LORD MAR'S LEGACIES
### 1722-27

## LETTERS CONCERNING HIGHLAND
## AFFAIRS IN THE 18th CENTURY
### BY MRS. GRANT OF LAGGAN

## EDINBURGH
Printed at the University Press by T. and A. Constable
for the Scottish History Society
### 1896

# EXTRACT FROM THE MINUTES OF THE COUNCIL OF THE SCOTTISH HISTORY SOCIETY
## February 1896

'The Secretary read a letter . . . making offer on behalf of Messrs. T. and A. Constable to print at their own cost, and to present to the Society, in October next, a volume of Miscellanies, in commemoration of the Tenth Anniversary of the Society's institution. The offer was cordially accepted, and the Chairman was requested to convey to Messrs. Constable the Council's appreciation of the generous gift.'

T. G. L.
*Hon. Sec.*

# CONTENTS

                                                  PAGE

I. FRAGMENT OF THE DIARY OF SIR ARCHIBALD JOHNSTON, LORD WARISTON, 1639,    *Edited by* GEORGE M. PAUL    1

II. PAPERS RELATIVE TO THE PRESERVATION OF THE HONOURS OF SCOTLAND, IN DUNNOTTAR CASTLE, 1651-1652,
   *Edited by* CHARLES R. A. HOWDEN    99

III. THE EARL OF MAR'S LEGACIES TO SCOTLAND, AND TO HIS SON, LORD ERSKINE, 1722-1727,
   *Edited by* The Hon. STUART ERSKINE    139

IV. LETTERS WRITTEN BY MRS. GRANT OF LAGGAN CONCERNING HIGHLAND AFFAIRS AND PERSONS CONNECTED WITH THE STUART CAUSE IN THE EIGHTEENTH CENTURY,
   *Edited by* J. R. N. MACPHAIL    249

FRAGMENT OF
# THE DIARY OF
# SIR ARCHIBALD JOHNSTON
## LORD WARISTON

MAY 21-JUNE 25

1639

Edited from the Original Manuscript with
Introduction and Notes by
GEORGE MORISON PAUL
M.A., F.S.A. SCOT.

# INTRODUCTION

WODROW relates[1] that Mr. Ridpath[2] informed him that he had been 'imployed by Secretary Johnstoun to goe throu his 'father, my Lord Wariston's papers, and put them in order; 'which he spent severall dayes and weeks upon. That amongst 'other papers of the greatest value to the Church of Scotland, 'he fell upon my Lord Wariston's Dyary, which he sayes he read 'over. There is a great deal of it, and all bound up in differ-'ent boundels. It conteans many valuable passages with 'relation to the history of these times, noe where else to be 'found.' Secretary Johnston lived during the latter years of his life at Twickenham, and died in May 1737. What became of his papers after his death is not known; and probably his father's Diary is irretrievably lost. A fragment has fortunately been preserved in a separate manuscript volume. It covers the short period of thirty-six days, from the 21st of May to the 25th of June 1639, and contains the details of the negotiations which ended in the pacification of Berwick, and the conclusion of the first Bishops' War.

The manuscript was submitted to this Society by its owner, Mr. Maxtone Graham of Cultoquhey and Redgorton, the nephew and heir of the late Mr. Robert Graham of Balgowan,

---

[1] *Analecta*, ii. 218.

[2] Mr. George Ridpath was a well-known political writer in the reigns of King William III. and Queen Anne. He was the translator from the Latin MS. of Sir Thomas Craig's *Treatise against the Right of the Crown of England to Homage from the Kingdom of Scotland*, 1695, which he dedicated to Secretary Johnston; and he was the author of an *Account of the Rights and Powers of the Parliament of Scotland*, 1703, to which Secretary Johnston is said to have written the Preface.—Atwood's *The Scotch Patriot Unmasked*, 1705; Wodrow, *Analecta*, ii. 267. See also Carstares' *State Papers*, 216.

in whose library it was found. Nothing is known of its history prior to its discovery in Mr. Graham's library. It is contained in a small folio which is bound in white vellum, eleven and a half inches long, by eight and three quarters broad, and has attached to it the roots of four vellum strings or ties. The volume is written from both ends—the Diary being written from one end, and some interesting miscellaneous notes and papers from the other. On the front page of this end is written in Wariston's handwriting, 'The names of the books q$^h$. I taik to the airmee with me.' Then follow: 1. 'Memorandum of paperis takine with me to the Campe in 'July 1640.' 2. 'The new and constant plote of planting 'the whole kirks of Scotland penned to be presented to the 'Kinge and the estaits in anno 1596.' This extends to eleven and a half closely written pages. 3. 'Ane schort note 'of the decisiones and interloquitors given be the Lords of 'Counsell since the moneth of Januar 1619.' The latest date is 30th July 1646. The cases are arranged in alphabetical order according to the subjects, and are reported very briefly. There are sundry markings on the margin in Wariston's handwriting. This digest occupies ninety-seven pages. 4. Notes from 'the books of the register of Session beginning 4th February 1531,' and ending on 1st February 1545. This occupies sixteen pages. 5. Papers relating to the scheme for 'the erecting of a comon fishing' for England and Scotland in 1630. They contain notes upon the Fishery Laws of some of the Continental nations. 6. Some notes entitled 'Avisandum anent the Union.' 7. Acts and orders of the Commissioners for administration of justice in Scotland, 27th June 1655 to 8th November 1656.

The Diary, which is the only writing from the other end of the book, is written in a small but neat and legible seventeenth century hand. It is not that of Wariston, but it is abundantly clear from internal evidence that the Diary was his.

During the whole of the eventful period, from the uprising

# INTRODUCTION

of the Scottish people against the Service Book and the Bishops in 1637 until the Restoration, Sir Archibald Johnston of Wariston (Lord Wariston) was in the very front rank of the Presbyterian party. He was perhaps the most remarkable Scotsman of that very troubled period of British history.

The family to which he belonged seems to have been an offshoot from the noble house of Annandale.[1] He has been described as a son of James Johnston of Beirholm in Dumfriesshire, but that was not so. In 1608 James Johnestoun, who is described as 'of Beirholme,' was served heir of Gavin Johnestoun 'in' (*i.e.* tenant of) 'Kirkton of Kirkpatrick Juxta' in Dumfriesshire, his grandfather, and heir of his father, 'James Johnestoun, in' (*i.e.* tenant of) 'Midilgill.'[2] Neither grandfather nor father is described as 'of Beirholm.' How or when James Johnston became possessed of Beirholm does not appear, but it seems clear that he did not inherit it from either of them. And from what follows it will be seen that he was not Wariston's father, although he may have been a relation.

Archibald Johnestoun (Wariston's grandfather) was a native of Kirkpatrick Juxta. By his will[3] he left 'ane hundreth 'merks to help the repairing and completing of ye kirk callit 'Kirkpatrick Juxta, where my predecessors' bonis lyes.'

This Archibald Johnestoun was an eminent merchant and leading citizen of Edinburgh during a considerable part of the reign of James VI. On 22nd April 1589 the King wrote to Archibald Douglas, thanking him 'for his services in behalf of 'Archibald Johnestoun, son-in-law of the Provost of Edin-'burgh';[4] and on 31st May 1595, he wrote to Queen Elizabeth

---

[1] He, as well as his uncle Johnston of Hilton in Berwickshire, carried the principal arms of the Annandale family, but for a difference engrailed the saltier.—Nisbet, i. 144 ; *The British Herald*, by Robson, vol. ii. *voce* Johnston.

The Editor unfortunately did not see *The Annandale Family Book*, by Sir William Fraser, K.C.B., until this Introduction was written. Portions of Wariston's family history which follow, and which have been collected from the original sources, will be found in that work.

[2] *Printed Special Retours*, Dumfriesshire, 28th April 1608, Nos. 51, 52.

[3] *Register of Confd. Test.*, Edinburgh, 28th April 1619.

[4] *Historical Manuscripts, Hatfield Collection*, iii. 407.

soliciting her good offices with reference to a suit in which Archibald Johnestoun was engaged before her Council.¹ Bishop Burnet, his great-grandson, described him as 'the greatest merchant' of his time, and said that he left to his wife an estate of £2000 a year, a large fortune in those days, 'to be disposed of among his children as she pleased.'² By his will he bequeathed a legacy to the University of Edinburgh, which still has a bursary of £11, 2s. 2d. sterling, a year, bearing his name.³ His wife was Rachel Arnot, a daughter of Sir John Arnot of Birswick, who was Lord Provost of Edinburgh from 1587 till 1589, and for some years Treasurer-Depute, and a Privy Councillor. Sir John Arnot is said by Burnet to have been 'a man in great favour.'⁴ Rachel Arnot died on 20th March 1626.⁵

Archibald Johnestoun and Rachel Arnot had three sons and two daughters, viz.: 1. James, a merchant burgess of Edinburgh, who married Elizabeth Craig, second daughter of Sir Thomas Craig of Riccarton, the most eminent lawyer of his time, and author of the very learned Latin treatise on Feudal Law.⁶ 2. Samuel, who was an advocate, succeeded on the

---

¹ *Historical Manuscripts, Hatfield Collection*, v. 223.
² Burnet's *History of his own Time*, 8vo. vol. i. p. 31.
³ *Register of Confd. Test., ut supra*; *Edinburgh University Calendar*, 1895-6, pp. 329-333.      ⁴ Burnet, *ut supra*.
⁵ *Register of Confd. Test.*, Edinburgh, 23rd August 1626.
⁶ Her mother's name was Helen Heriot. Tytler and others, following the Biography of Craig prefixed to the third edition of the *Jus Feudale*, have erroneously described her as daughter of Heriot, Laird of Trabroun. She was second daughter of Robert Heriot of Lumphoy or Lymphoy, an estate in the parish of Currie, near to Craig's estate of Riccarton. The mansion-house of the old estate is now in ruins, and is called Lennox Tower. Robert Heriot was also rentaller under the Archbishop of Glasgow of the lands of Ramshorn, Meadowflat, and Cardarroch. Helen Swinton, his wife, was probably the eldest daughter of John Swinton of that Ilk (Douglas *Baronage*, p. 130). Heriot's eldest daughter and heiress was Agnes, wife of James Foulis, Baron of Colinton. Helen Swinton, after Robert Heriot's death, married Edward Henryson, a learned Doctor of Laws, to whom she had a son, Sir Thomas Henryson, Lord Chesters in the Court of Session. See *Reg. Eccl. Colleg. Sancte. Trinit. Edinburgh*, pp. 118-132; *New Statist. Account,* 'Currie,' 546; also *Diocesan Register of Glasgow*, Grampian Club, vol. i. pp. 161-172; Brown's *Monumental Inscriptions in Greyfriars Churchyard*, Edinburgh (Henryson), p. 76.

death of his mother to the property of Sheens (Sciennes), now part of Edinburgh, and to the estate of Dunglass in Berwickshire. 3. Joseph, who succeeded to the estate of Hilton in Berwickshire, was founder of the family of Johnston of Hilton in that county.[1] 4. Rachel, married (first) John Jaksone,[2] and (secondly) Sir William Bruce of Stenhouse, whom she survived.[3] 5. Jonet, married (first) Sir James Skene of Curriehill, Lord President of the Court of Session from 1626 till 1633; and (secondly) James Inglis of Ingliston.[4]

James Johnston, the eldest son,[5] and Elizabeth Craig had eight children, of whom four seem to have died in infancy. The four who survived their grandfather were: one son, the celebrated Archibald Johnston of Wariston, and three daughters,[6] of whom the eldest, Rachel, married Robert Burnet, Advocate (afterwards Lord Crimond in the Court of Session), the editor of the first edition of Craig's *Jus Feudale*; and Beatrix, the youngest, married, in 1639, Patrick Congalton of that Ilk.[7] Of the other daughter, Margaret, nothing has been discovered.

In the beginning of the seventeenth century Edinburgh was a comparatively small town. It was then as now 'the metropolis of law,' as Jedediah Cleishbotham termed it, and its leading citizens were, consequently, mostly connected with the Law Courts. Wariston's grandfather was Sir Thomas Craig, the eminent feudal lawyer; his wife's grandfather was Sir John Skene of Curriehill, who had been one of the Octavians, Lord Clerk Register, and a Lord of Session; and her father was Sir Alexander Hay, Lord Foresterseat, also a Lord of Session.[8]

---

[1] There was, and still is, another family of Johnston of Hilton in Aberdeenshire.
[2] *Register Confd. Test.*, Edinburgh, 28th April 1619.
[3] *Register Great Seal*, Printed Abridg., 5th July 1627, No. 1101.
[4] *Ibid.* 13th March 1637.
[5] Died 24th April 1617. *Reg. Confd. Test.*, Edinburgh, 2nd July 1618.
[6] *Reg. Confd. Test., supra.*
[7] Douglas *Baronage*, p. 523. It is there said that she was a daughter of Wariston, but that is obviously a mistake.
[8] *Register Great Seal*, Abridg., 1169, 11th July 1642.

Wariston's great-aunt, Marion Arnot, was the wife of (first) James Nisbet, a brother of Patrick Nisbet, Lord Eastbank, and uncle of Sir John Nisbet of Dirleton, Lord Advocate and a Lord of Session in the time of Charles II.;[1] and (secondly) Sir Lewis Stewart, the famous Advocate, who was a loyal adherent of Charles I., and legal adviser of the Royal Commissioner at the General Assembly of 1638. Margaret Craig, his mother's eldest sister, was the wife of Sir Alexander Gibson, the first Lord Durie, and mother of Sir Alexander Gibson, the second Lord Durie.[2] His uncle, Samuel Johnston of Sheens, married Helen Morison, a sister of Lord Prestongrange,[3] and granddaughter of John Preston of Fentonbarns, Lord President of the Court from 1609 till 1616; and his aunt, Jonet Johnstoun, was, as has been mentioned, the wife of Sir James Skene of Currichill, Lord President of the Court.[4] Wariston was thus closely related to, and from his childhood must have been intimately acquainted with, the leading men of Edinburgh.

His nearest relations were probably all Presbyterians; some of them at least were zealous for the cause. Of his grandmother, Rachel Arnot, Burnet[5] wrote that being a very rich woman, and much engaged to the Presbyterian party, she was most obsequiously courted by them. 'Bruce lived concealed 'in her house for some years: and they all found such advan-'tages in their submissions to her, that she was counted for 'many years the chief support of the party. . . . My father' (Lord Crimond), 'marrying her eldest grandchild, saw a great 'way into all the methods of the puritans.' She was, no doubt, the friend referred to by Kirkton,[6] at whose house at Sheens, in the year 1621, the Presbyterian ministers, who had been ordered to depart from Edinburgh for refusing to observe the Five Articles of Perth, met to spend in fasting and prayer the day on which these Articles were to be ratified by Parliament

---

[1] *Dirleton Writs.*      [2] Tytler's *Life of Craig*, p. 323.
[3] *Reg. Confd. Test.*, Edinburgh, 6th March 1627.
[4] *Ibid.* 28th April 1619.    [5] Burnet, vol. i. p. 31.    [6] P. 16.

# INTRODUCTION 7

—the Black Parliament as it was called. When Sir James Skene, President of the Court, failed, notwithstanding the King's orders, to be present at the Kirk of Edinburgh on Easter Day 1619 to receive the Communion kneeling as prescribed by one of the Articles of Perth, his absence was ascribed by some 'not to conscience, but to dissuasions of his mother-in-law' (Rachel Arnot) 'and her daughter, his wife' (Jonet Johnstoun), 'a religious gentlewoman.'[1] The other daughter, Rachel, was no doubt of the same way of thinking. Her eldest son, Sir William Bruce of Stenhouse, was a ruling elder in James Guthrie's separate Presbytery, which was composed of the most extreme or Remonstrant members of the party.[2] And Burnet wrote of his own mother, 'Guthry, the 'chief of their preachers, was hid in my mother's house, who 'was bred to her brother Waristoun's principles, and could 'never be moved from them.'[3] The steadfastness of some of Wariston's own children to his principles will be afterwards noticed.

Wariston was born in 1611, probably in the month of March, as he was baptized on the 28th of that month.[4]

He was educated at the University of Glasgow, and received the degree of Master of Arts from that University. The year when he went to College is nowhere stated, but the College books note the receipt 'fra Archibald Johnstoun for his buird for the spaice of five moneths III$^{xx}$ lib.,'[5] and on 1st March 1630 he was matriculated as a student in one of the higher classes.[6] The muniments of the University contain a list of books, which 'Archibaldus Jonstonus laurea donandus Accademiae

---

[1] Calderwood's *Hist. MSS.* viii. 838.     [2] Baillie, iii. 257.
[3] Burnet, vol. i. p. 434.
[4] '1611, 28 Martii, James Johnestoun, Merchant, Elizabeth Craig a s(on) 'n(amed) Archibald, w(itnesses) Archibald Johnestoun, David Johnestoun.' *Fyft Register of Baptisme Ministrat in the Kirks of Edinburgh after the First Reformation*, 2nd September 1610-11th December 1621, General Register House.
[5] *Munimenta Universitatis Glasguensis*, iii. 530.     [6] *Ibid.* 82.

Glasguensi donavit in εὐχαριστίας τεκμήριον,' but the year is unfortunately not stated.[1] He passed through his College classes under Baillie (afterwards Principal Baillie) as regent. Baillie, whose mother was one of the Gibson of Durie family (Letters I. XXII.), was connected with Wariston, whose aunt, Margaret Craig, married Sir Alexander Gibson of Durie. They maintained a close friendship for many years. In a letter to James Sharp (afterwards Archbishop of St. Andrews) about Wariston, Baillie[2] wrote of the friendship professed by him 'to me constantly since he was a child and my scholler.'

Wariston passed Advocate at the Scottish Bar on 6th November 1633.

His marriage with Lord Foresterseat's eldest daughter, Helen Hay, must have taken place soon after he passed, as at least one child had been born to them before 1636.[3]

They had a large family. Lady Wariston, in petitioning the King, in 1660, for a pardon for her husband, stated that she 'and her 12 children were reduced to a poore and desolate condition,'[4] and at least two of her daughters were then married.[5] The following were their children, but probably not their whole family :

1. ARCHIBALD, the eldest son. He was alive in 1643, but must have died young.[6]

2. JAMES, first of that name, died in infancy.[7]

3. ALEXANDER, who, in 1672, was 'eldest son and apparent heir' of his father.[8] He was, at least at one time, the black

---

[1] *Munimenta Universitatis Glasguensis*, iii. 412.  [2] Baillie, iii. 336.
[3] See p. 12.  [4] British Museum Addl. MSS. 23, 114.
[5] Wariston died deeply in debt. It was ascertained after his death that his debts exceeded the value of his estate by 12,361 merks Scots.—*Acts of Parliament*, vii. 621.

After his death Kirkton wrote of him : 'He left his lady and numerous family 'in mean estate, tho' afterward the Lord provided better for many of them than 'if their father hade stood in his highest grandeur,' p. 174.

[6] *Reg. Great Seal*, Abridg., 20th November 1643, No. 327.
[7] Wodrow's *Analecta*, ii. 219.  [8] *Acts of Parliament*, ix. 213.

sheep of the family. Brodie[1] wrote of him, '1671, Nov. 17th,
'I heard that Alexander, Waristoun's son, had brok, and
'through cheating, lying, wrong ways. My brother and
'others had suffered much by him.' He married Francisca
Cuninghame, daughter of Captain James Cuninghame of
Ballichan, in Ireland, son of Sir James Cuninghame of Glengarnock and Lady Catherine Cuninghame, daughter of
James Earl of Glencairn. Her sister, Penuel, married Sir
James Colquhoun of Balvie, afterwards of Luss.[2] Alexander
seems to have been bred a lawyer, but for some time he made
a livelihood by buying and selling tallies at the Treasury,
Exchequer, etc., equivalent to Exchequer bills. This he afterwards gave up, and devoted himself to secret service under
William III., and the discovering of the plots which were then
being hatched for the assassination of that King and the
return of King James.[3]

4. JAMES (2nd) born 9th September 1655.[4] His father
recorded in the lost Diary that this 'was to be the stay and
support of his family.'[5] After his father's death he was sent
to Holland where he was educated. 'He had the character
'of the greatest proficient in the civil law that ever was in
'Utrecht.'[6] He was introduced into political life through his
cousin-german Bishop Burnet, and was from time to time
employed on important political missions. He was Secretary of
State for Scotland from 1692 till 1696. In the latter year he
married as his second wife, Catherine, daughter of John, second
Baron Poulett.[7] In writing to Carstares he spoke of his first
wife as having been related to Adam Cockburn of Ormiston,
the Lord Justice Clerk, but who she was has not been dis-

---

[1] *Diary*, p. 322.
[2] *Printed General Retours*, 29th April 1682, No. 6385; Fountainhall's *Historical Notices*, vol. ii. pp. 778-9; Douglas *Baronage*, p. 26.
[3] See Carstares' *State Papers*, 200-225. [4] Brodie's *Diary*, 155.
[5] Wodrow's *Analecta*, ii. 218.
[6] Macky's *Memoirs*, 204. Macky described him as 'a tall fair man.'
[7] Collins's *Peerage*, iv. 12.

covered. He had a son by that former marriage.¹ He was Lord Clerk Register in the reign of Queen Anne 1704-5. After retiring from public business he resided at Orleans House, Twickenham. Mr. John M'Claurin said of him to Wodrow that 'he keeps out a very great rank, and frequently 'has Mr. Walpool and the greatest courtiers with him at his 'country house near London; and the King sometimes does 'him the honour to dine with him.'² He was a great favourite with Queen Caroline, 'who was much entertained with his humour and pleasantry.'³ He is described as 'a person of 'learning and virtue, perfectly sincere, but,' like his father, 'hot and eager, too soon possessed with jealousy, and too 'vehement in all he proposed.'⁴ 'The freedom of his manners 'was rather disgusting to King William.'⁵ He died at Bath in 1737, and was buried at Twickenham on the 11th of that month.⁶ The *Scots Magazine* of the time stated that he died at the age of ninety-five, but that is impossible, as Brodie of Brodie who was present at his baptism has noted in his Diary that he was born on 9th September 1655.⁷ His son James Johnston was served as heir-general to him on 13th March 1744.

5. ELIZABETH, married Thomas, eldest son of Sir Adam Hepburn of Humbie⁸ to whom she had one child Helen, who married Walter Scott of Highchester, Earl of Tarras.⁹ Elizabeth married, secondly, General William Drummond of Cromlix, created Viscount Strathallan in 1686. She died in 1679, before her husband's elevation to the peerage, and was buried in St. George's Church, Southwark.¹⁰

6. RACHEL married the noble Robert Baillie of Jerviswood—

---

[1] Carstares' *State Papers*, 155-6.    [2] Wodrow's *Analecta*, iii. 206.
[3] Carstares, 93.
[4] *The Jerviswood Correspondence*, Bannatyne Club. Preface.
[5] Carstares, *ut supra*.
[6] Lysons's *Environs of London*, vol. iii. pp. 563, 594.    [7] Brodie's *Diary*, 155.
[8] *Act. Par.* vii. 20-64; *General Retours*, 25th Jan. 1659, Nos. 4415, 16, 17.
[9] Douglas *Peerage*, vol. ii. p. 588.    [10] *Ibid.* 552.

the Scottish Sidney, as he has been called—who after suffering cruel imprisonment by order of the King and Privy Council, was executed on 24th December 1684 on the groundless charge of compassing the death of the King and his brother the Duke of York. Rachel died before 18th September 1707.[1]

7. HELEN married George Home of Graden, in the parish of Earlston. Her husband and she were both warm supporters of the principles of the Covenanters. In the last days of her brother-in-law Robert Baillie, when his wife, owing to feeble health, was unable to attend him, she devoted herself to the alleviation of his sufferings in prison, where she remained with him in close confinement. She accompanied him to the place of execution, and with a courage truly heroic remained on the scaffold 'till all his body was cut in coupons,' and she went with the hangman to 'see them oyled and tarred.'[2] She died before 11th September 1707.[3]

8. MARGARET married (first) Sir John Wemyss of Bogie,[4] (secondly) Benjamin Bressey.[5] During her father's close confinement in the Tower prior to his being brought to Edinburgh for execution in 1663, she was on her petition permitted to live with him there.[6] She was imprisoned by the Privy Council for taking part in the gathering of Presbyterian ladies in the Parliament Close on 4th and 11th June 1674 to present a Petition to the Council for liberty to their ministers to perform divine service according to the Presbyterian forms.[7]

9. JANET married Sir Alexander Mackenzie of Coul, Baronet.[8]
10.         married Mr. Roderick Mackenzie.[9]

---

[1] *Register of Confd. Test.*, Edinburgh, 18th Sept. 1707.
[2] Fountainhall's *Historical Notices*, ii. 594. See an interesting account of her in *The Ladies of the Covenant*, by the Rev. James Anderson, p. 373.
[3] *Register of Confd. Test.*, Edinburgh, 11th Sept. 1707.
[4] Douglas *Baronage*, p. 562.
[5] *Register of Confd. Test.*, Edinburgh—Margaret Johnston, Lady Bogie, 16th August 1707.      [6] Historical MSS., Duke of Leeds, 6.
[7] Law's *Memorials*, p. 67 ; *Ladies of the Covenant*, p. 221.
[8] Brodie's *Diary*, p. 397 ; Burke's *Peerage*.     [9] Brodie, *ut supra*.

11. EUPHAN died unmarried, May 1715.[1]

In the year 1636 Archibald Johnston acquired the property of Wariston in the parish of Currie, seven miles from Edinburgh, and adjoining his grandfather's estate of Riccarton. Lord Foresterseat, his father-in-law, had bought it in 1620;[2] and his son Alexander Hay sold it in 1636 'to Elizabeth Craig, 'relict of the late James Johnstoun, merchant burgess of 'Edinburgh in liferent and Mr. Archibald Johnstoun her son, 'Advocate, and Helen Hay his spouse, and the longest liver of 'them in conjunct fee,' and to their heirs *born* and to be born.[3] Sir John Scot[4] says that its annual value was (in Johnston's time) 1000 merks Scots, about £55 sterling. The farm of Wariston, which now belongs to the Earl of Morton, is valued at £400 a year.[5]

Wariston's town residence was situated in the High Street of Edinburgh, on the east side of what is now known as Wariston's Close, and was probably entered from the close. Here on the night before the first sitting of each General Assembly the leading members used to meet to consider 'about 'the choising of the Moderator, Committees, and cheife points 'of the Assemblie.'[6] The windows of the house looked upon the Market Cross, close by which, amid scenes of intense popular excitement, Wariston, in 1638, read on several occasions from extemporised platforms protestations against the Royal Proclamations; and where, twenty-five years afterwards, he was himself hanged on 'ane gallous of extraordiner heicht,' surrounded by the King's Life Guards on horseback, 'with thair 'carabynes and naikit swords, and trumpettouris and kettill 'drum and ane gaird of the toun of Edinburgh with thair 'cullouris displayed.'[7] It is narrated that when Robert Baillie of Jerviswood was being carried to the place of execu-

---

[1] *Register of Confd. Test.*, Edinburgh, 11th July 1715.
[2] *Reg. Great Seal*, Printed Abridg., 6th July 1620, No. 715.
[3] *Ibid.* 1636, No. 511. [4] *Staggering State*, p. 127.
[5] Valuation Roll, Edinburgh, 1895. [6] Baillie's *Letters*, iii. 53.
[7] Nicoll's *Diary*, pp. 394-5.

tion at the Market Cross, accompanied by his sister-in-law, Lady Graden, they passed the house of her father; and 'in pass-
' ing it, Baillie looked up to the chamber where Lord Wariston
' usually sat, and a multitude of associations connected with
' the past vividly rushing into his mind, he said to her, "Many
' " a sweet day and night with God had your now glorified
' " father in that chamber." "Yes," she replied, and thinking
' of his cruel death she added, "Now he is beyond the reach
' " of all suffering, equally free from sin and sorrow; and the
' " same grace which supported him is able to support you."'[1]

Wariston was a man of great energy and unwearied application, with an extraordinary memory and great quickness of thought.[2] He could seldom sleep above three hours in the twenty-four. He was very learned in the Law of Scotland, particularly in Constitutional and Church law, in which he had become proficient at an early period of life.

It must be borne in mind that he was a young man during the most important and successful period of his career. Between the year 1637 when, at the age of twenty-six, he first appeared in public life as the trusted adviser of the Covenanting leaders,[3] and the year 1649 when, still a comparatively young man, he was appointed to the office of Lord Clerk Register, then the most lucrative and highly prized office under the Crown in Scotland, he had occupied positions of the highest honour and responsibility in Church and State; and it seems clear from the way Baillie wrote of him that he had secured the entire confidence of his friends. He was Clerk to the Tables;[4] he was the contriver, and, with Alexander Henderson, the framer of the National Covenant of 1638; in the same year he was appointed clerk and legal adviser to the great General Assembly held at Glasgow; in 1639 he was one of the Scots Commissioners

---

[1] See Wodrow's *Analecta*, iii. 78-80. *Ladies of the Covenant*, p. 388.
[2] Burnet, vol. i. p. 49.
[3] Rothes' *Relation*, 43; Baillie, i. 48.
[4] Large Declaration, 239.

who arranged with the king the pacification of Berwick; in 1640, when the army was about to march into England, he was directed by Parliament, as the person 'best acquaint,'—who had a greater grasp than any one else of the questions in dispute between the King and the Scottish nation,—to attend the General and the Committee and advise with them in such matters as the framing of treaties and public declarations,[1] and he was afterwards one of the Scots Commissioners who concluded with the English the treaty of Ripon. In 1641, at the age of thirty, he was appointed a Lord of Session by the title of Lord Wariston, and received the honour of knighthood; in 1643 he was sent as one of the small group of Scots Commissioners to the Assembly of Divines at Westminster, where he is said to have taken part in the debates with much ability and learning against the most distinguished ecclesiastical lawyers of the time; in 1644 he was chosen one of the joint committee of both nations for managing the war against the King; in 1646 he was appointed Lord Advocate, and in 1649 Lord Clerk Register. Such early and continuous success could only have been achieved by a man of conspicuous ability and eminent business habits. In writing of him on 8th July 1645 Baillie described him as ' one of the most faithful, and diligent, ' and able servants that our Church and Kingdom has had all ' the tymes of our troubles.' [2]

As regards his creed in the affairs of Church and State, he had an extraordinary zeal for Presbyterianism. It 'was to him more than all the world,' . . . 'he looked on the Covenant as the setting Christ on His throne.'[3] Presbyterianism, he firmly believed, was of divine institution, therefore the nation must be soundly Presbyterian; no other form of church government should be tolerated, nor any doctrine taught except what was approved by the General Assembly. Schismatics and heretics should be punished, and all such as refused to take the Covenant

---

[1] *Acts of Scots Par.* v. 284 b.   [2] Baillie, ii. 297.   [3] Burnet, vol. i. p. 50.

should be disqualified from places of profit and trust.¹ He
was withal a sincere upholder of the monarchical principle.
On 24th April 1646 Baillie wrote, 'All the Royalists in Scot-
' land could not have pleaded so much for the Crowne and the
' King's just power, as the Chancellour and Wariston did for
' many dayes together.'² And according to an informant of
Wodrow, before Wariston went up to Cromwell he was a
violent Royalist and used to say that, sooner than submit to
the English 'he would take his wife and ten children and
begg.'³ But then his sovereign must be a Presbyterian king,
ruling a Presbyterian people, with powers greatly restricted
from those which King James VI., in his later years, and his
son Charles, had ventured to assume. This restriction of the
prerogative, he maintained, was nothing but a return to the
ancient constitution of Scotland—a restoration to Parliament
of the powers which of right belonged to it, but of which it
had been deprived through recent royal encroachments. This
subject of the powers and rights of Parliament was one which
he had deeply studied, and it was without doubt he who, in
1641, submitted the constitutional principle, which was enforced
in Parliament by Argyll, that appointments to the great offices
of state are made by the King and Parliament jointly, not
by the King alone, as was maintained by Charles. The lost
Diary contained an interesting passage on this subject, the
purport of which Wodrow received from Mr. Ridpath and
related as follows⁴: 'After the treaty of Wilks [? Birks],
' when the King came a litle into Scotland, there wer many
' conferences among the prime of the Covenanters and the
' King, at all which Wariston was. The Scots Lords insisted
' much that the King would allou them the liberty of chusing
' the Officers of State in the Parliament. The King was
' very peremptory against it. They pleaded that it had
' been anciently alloued by the Kings of Scotland, and
' alledged the Records. The King denyed ther was any

---

¹ Principal Lee's *Lectures*, ii. 303, 304.   ² Baillie, ii. 368.
³ Wodrow's *Analecta*, ii. 145.   ⁴ *Analecta*, ii. 219.

'such thing, and told them he kneu in his father's time, any-
'thing with relation to these was lost. After their insisting,
'the King required to see the Records. They told him they
'wer yet extant, though not among the Records of the nation.
'After the King had given his oath to them he would not call
'for them out of their hands, some two or three on the King's
'side, and as many on the other side, all upon oath, wer lett
'into the secret; and the King and they went over to Dum-
'fermline, where they wer, and discovered by my Lord
'Wariston. It seems that King James vi., throu the advice
'of some that wer for inslaving the liberty of the subject, and
'it may be to please England, had ordered Hay of Dumferm-
'line, in whoes hand then they wer, to destroy them. It seems
'he laid them up in his Charter Chest, which was not opned
'till Wariston upon some civil process was called to look throu
'his papers, and there found them. The King had them laid
'before him. It may be supposed that thir papers wer the
'plan of many things the Covenanting Lords then did, and
'gave them both courage and light hou to act.'[1]

Wariston was not merely a learned Church lawyer and theologian, he was moreover deeply religious. Kirkton[2] wrote of him that he spent more time in prayer, reading, meditations, and observing his providences than any man he ever knew in the world. He continued in prayer many hours a day,[3] and three hours at a stretch was pretty frequent with him.[4] On one occasion, which has been recorded, his grace after meat lasted for an hour.[5] While engaged in prayer he became entirely absorbed in it, and lost all consciousness of what was passing around him. One day, intending to spend an hour or two in prayer, he continued his devotions from six in the

---

[1] Wariston had unusual good fortune in discovering lost registers. Three years before this he had presented to the General Assembly of 1638 five volumes of its registers, extending from 1560 to 1590, which were believed to have been lost.—Peterkin's *Records of the Kirk*, 133; Baillie, i. 129.

[2] 173.    [3] Burnet, vol. i. p. 49.    [4] Wodrow's *Analecta*, ii. 159.

[5] Kirkton, 171. Note by Mr. Kirkpatrick Sharpe.

morning till, to his surprise, the bells began ringing at eight in the evening. On another occasion, while he was engaged in prayer, Lady Wariston, who was at the time in delicate health, swooned away beside him, but he went on to the end unconscious of that or of the servants raising her up and laying her on a bed in the room.[1] In those days they used to 'wrestle' in prayer as Jacob wrestled with the angel at Peniel. Wariston, on the baptism of his son James (the secretary), recorded in the lost Diary the great lengths he had win-to[2] in wrestling anent him.[3] During a dangerous illness of Mr. James Guthrie, some of his friends met to pray for his recovery. Wodrow quaintly tells the story.[4] 'All that 'prayed before Wariston wer conditionall in their petitions for 'his life. When he came to pray, he was mighty peremptory, 'and would not at all take a refusall, and said, "Lord, thou '"knouest this Church cannot want him!"' He had the conviction that he had close communion with God,—that he saw God face to face. Kirkton has recorded of him[5] that on the night before his execution Wariston said to him 'that he 'could never doubt of his own salvation, he hade so often seen 'God's face in the house of prayer.' 'He was a great observer 'of providences, and, according to the rule, mett with very 'many remarkable providences himself.'[6] And Ridpath said to Wodrow, with reference to the lost Diary, 'as to his soul's 'state, it's not possible to conceive what atteanments, what 'elevated exercise, that man has been under! He records hou 'it's with him in prayer, and the answers and returns made 'to his prayers, which are astonishing.'[7]

He possessed in a high degree the *perfervidum ingenium* of his countrymen, but the zeal of his youth for the cause to which the nation had so deeply committed itself passed in the later years of his life almost into fanaticism. He had a ready,

---

[1] *Analecta*, ii. 135.   [2] Reached.   [3] *Analecta*, ii. 218.   [4] *Ibid.* ii. 158.
[5] Page 171.   [6] Kirkton, 173.   [7] *Analecta*, ii. 218.

vehement style of eloquence characteristic of himself,[1] but by his irritating mode of speaking he seemed to have the misfortune to make his political opponents his personal enemies.[2] Of these failings he was himself conscious. In his dying speech he said, 'My natural temper (or rather distemper) hath been 'hasty and passionate, and in my manner of going about and 'prosecuting of the best pieces of work and service to the Lord 'and to my generation, I have been subject to many excesses 'of heat, and thereby to some precipitations, which hath no 'doubt offended standers-by and lookers-on, and hath exposed 'both me and the work to their mistakes.'[3] Kirkton[4] wrote, 'He studied Christ's honour more than man's, and was a man 'that used argument more than complement.' He was wanting in tact and in the courtly graces which find favour with kings, and his manner and bearing seem to have excited an extraordinary antipathy towards him in the Charleses (father and son) and their adherents. Charles I. cordially disliked him. Charles II. hated him, not only for the position which, as leader of the Remonstrants, he took up against him and his party, but also for personal reasons. Wariston, with apparently considerable plain speaking, had reproved the king for his dissolute conduct while in Scotland. Charles seemed to take it in good part at the time, but he never forgave Wariston,[5] and this personal hatred of the king was said to have been the real cause of Wariston's death.[6]

But he must have had many qualities which commanded esteem and even love from those who knew him well. For many years the kindly and genial Baillie had a sincere affection for him. He had been his instructor in Glasgow University, and in after-days when Wariston was a great man he did not hesitate to write unreservedly to him as to the regulation of his ambition and the conduct of public business.

---

[1] Burnet, i. 50; Kirkton, 172.  
[2] Baillie, iii. 64.  
[3] *Scots Worthies*, vol. ii. 76.  
[4] P. 173.  
[5] Wodrow, *Analecta*, ii. 145.  
[6] Kirkton, 173.

One of his letters began formally with 'My Lord,' and concluded 'My service to my Cumer (gossip) and all friends, Your Master, R. Baillie.'[1] He also referred to him as 'the good Advocate' and 'Good Wariston.'[2] Brodie[3] and Kirkton[4] have testified to the love which his friends bore to him. He was closely associated with Argyll in public life and seems to have been on intimate terms with him privately. In 1647 he bought from Argyll the Island of Suna in the old parish of Kilchattan,[5] and in the following year, when it was thought advisable that he should go into retirement for a short time he withdrew to Kintyre on a visit to Argyll.[6] But after he joined the extreme party of the Protesters many of his old friends withdrew from him, and some even of those who were favourably inclined to the Protesters thought that he went too far.[7] In writing to Spang on 19th July 1654, Baillie said, 'Wariston lives privilie, in a hard enough condition, much 'hated by the most, and neglected by all, except the Remon-'strants to whom he is guide.'[8] Although Baillie and he had come to differ widely as regarded public affairs, Baillie remained, throughout his distresses, one of his fastest friends.[9] His old friends did not forget him on the day of his execution. They attended him to the scaffold, and afterwards to his 'buriall in thair murning apperrell';[10] and Kirkton wrote that 'he 'rendered up his spirit into the Lord's hand with much com-'fort of mind, and much bemoaned by all that knew him.'[11]

The crowning error in his career was his acceptance of employment from Cromwell. He was regardless about money matters and spent his patrimony in the promotion of his views. Consequently, upon the loss of his office when Cromwell came to Scotland, he was reduced to great pecuniary straits, which

---

[1] Baillie, ii. 106. [2] Baillie, iii. 53, 64. [3] *Diary*, 322.
[4] Kirkton, 172. [5] *Great Seal Reg.*, Printed Abridg. 1647, No. 1863.
[6] Baillie, iii. 64. [7] Brodie, 1655, October 2, 160.
[8] Baillie, iii. 249. [9] Baillie, iii. 338. [10] Nicoll's *Diary*, 395.
[11] Kirkton, 172.

were aggravated by his having had to restore considerable sums which certain individuals had paid to him or his wife for offices in his gift.[1] His inability to provide for his large family without an income has been pleaded in extenuation of his ratting, but he was ever after 'afflicted and sad, never prosperous, because he hade made himself a trespasser,'[2] and he regretted to his last day the false step he took in accepting office. In his dying speech he spoke of it pathetically as follows: 'I must withal confess, that it doth not a little
' trouble me, and lie heavy upon my spirit, and will bring me
' down with sorrow to the grave that I suffered myself through
' the power of temptations, and the too much fear anent the
' straits that my numerous family might be brought into to be
' carried unto so great a length of compliance in England with
' the late usurpers, which did much grieve the hearts of the
' godly, and make these that sought God ashamed and con-
' founded for my sake, and did give no small occasion to the
' adversary to reproach and blaspheme. And my turning aside
' to comply with these men was the more aggravated in my
' person that I had so frequently and seriously made profession of
' my adverseness from, and abhorrence of that way, and had
' shown much dissatisfaction with these that had not gone so
' great a length; for which, as I seek God's mercy in Christ
' Jesus, so I desire that all the Lord's people, from my
' example, may be more stirred up to watch and pray that
' they enter not into temptation.'[3]

The occurrences and, in particular, the discussions on ecclesiastical affairs, related in the Diary, may be elucidated by the following short preliminary statement.

Since his accession to the Crowns of England and Scotland in 1625, Charles I. had shown himself singularly wanting in tact

---
[1] Scot's *Staggering State*, p. 127.  See also Baillie, iii. 249.
[2] Kirkton, 173.  [3] *Scots Worthies*, vol. ii. 76, 77.

and good judgment in his interference with ecclesiastical affairs in Scotland.  Like his father he had exalted notions of the kingly office and the Royal Prerogative.  He believed, as his father had done, that the Episcopalian form of church government was, in its nature, better suited for a monarchical establishment than the more republican parity of Scottish Presbyterianism.  James had had to endure, in his early days, much plain speaking in the pulpit and out of it—sometimes even personal indignities—from the Presbyterian ministers of Edinburgh, and such treatment must to him and his family have contrasted unfavourably with the courtly manners and pleasant speeches of the churchmen of England.  Moreover, the imposing services of the Church of England and its stately ritual appealed to their senses, if not to their higher natures, in a way which it seemed to be impossible for the plain and comparatively rude services of the Church of Scotland to do.  Charles frankly admitted this : ' Our father of blessed memorie
' immediately after his comming into England, compared the
' decencie and uniformitie of God's worship here, especially in
' the Liturgie of the Church, with that diversitie, nay deformitie,
' which was used in Scotland, where no set or publike forme
' of prayer was used, but Preachers or Readers and ignorant
' Schoolmasters prayed in the Church, sometimes so ignorantly
' as it was a shame to all Religion to have the Majestie of God
' so barbarously spoken unto, sometimes so seditiously that
' their prayers were plaine Libels, girding at Soveraigntie and
' Authoritie ; or Lyes, being stuffed with all the false reports
' in the Kingdome.' [1]

All these considerations contributed to make these Sovereigns desire to impose upon Scotland what they admired so much in England, that is to say, to establish Episcopacy and to provide for the Church an order of service identical, as nearly as might be, with what was in use in England.  ' As became a

---

[1] Large Declaration, 15, 16.

'Religious Prince,' James bethought himself seriously 'how
'his first reformation in that Kingdome might begin at the
'publike worship of God, which hee most truely conceived
'could never be happily effected, untill such time as there
'should be an unitie and uniformitie in the publike prayers,
'liturgie, and service of the Church, established throughout
'the whole Kingdome.'[1]

James had made a considerable advance towards the attainment of his ends although his methods had been high-handed. He had obtained the introduction into the Church of the order of Bishops, and was gradually vesting them with the powers of government which the Presbyterian Church Courts had previously possessed. The preparation of a Book of Common Prayer, which it should be obligatory on the clergy to use in the public worship of the Church, was also being proceeded with, and certain religious observances (known as the Articles of Perth) had been enjoined. But these innovations were highly unpopular, and many refused to obey the King's injunctions. Knowing the people with whom he had to deal, and being conscious of the risk of pressing his reforms further against their determined objections, he thought it more prudent to allow some of the prescribed observances to fall into abeyance.

But James died, and Charles speedily began to take an active personal charge of the administration of Scottish affairs. He, however, had not lived in Scotland since his childhood—he had been brought up amidst widely different surroundings from those of his father in his youth—and neither he nor the statesmen and churchmen who were his advisers seemed able to understand the peculiar temperament of the Scottish people or to comprehend the depth and pertinacity of the national character.

He had the misfortune to make himself unpopular with one

---

[1] Large Declaration, 16.

class or another of the community by everything he did, even when it was well done. He excited the animosity of the great nobles by his threatened revocation of all his father's grants of Church lands, whereby they had acquired so large an accession of influence and power; by his admirable arrangement for putting a stop for ever to the intolerable burden of the drawn teind, and for making a competent provision for the clergy; and by promoting the Prelates to high offices in the state, which the nobles thought belonged rightly and almost constitutionally to their class. Many petty jealousies also seem to have been aroused by the manner of distribution of honours at his coronation.[1] The great nobles whom he might have counted upon to support him were thus alienated and driven to make common cause with the large party in the kingdom who resented his interference with the government and form of worship of their Church. The powerful combination thus formed came to be directed wholly against the king's ecclesiastical policy.

The settlement throughout the kingdom of one common form of divine service and church government[2] was to be achieved by introducing into the Church of Scotland the mode of worship and rules of government which were established in England. This was to be done by an exercise of the Royal Prerogative —the Sovereign was to command and his subjects were to obey. Charles seemed to be unaware that his project would meet with resistance,[3] and in this to have been misled mainly by the reports as to the state of the national feeling which he received directly, or through Laud, from the younger generation of Bishops. Of these men, the High Treasurer (Traquair) wrote to the Marquis of Hamilton on 27th August 1637, that 'their 'rash and foolish expressions, and sometimes attempts, both 'in private and publick, have bred such a fear and jealousie in 'the hearts of many, that I am confident, if His Majesty were

---

[1] Large Declaration, 11.    [2] *Ibid.* 44.    [3] *Ibid.* 19.

'rightly informed thereof, he would blame them, and justly
'think, that from this and the like proceedings arises the
'ground of many mistakes amongst us.'[1] Experienced men
foresaw the troubles that would arise. On 2nd January 1637,
after the issue of the Royal Proclamation commanding the
use of the Service Book, Baillie wrote, 'I am affrayit sore that
'there is a storme raisit which will not calme in my dayes.
'It's a pitie that we should have none to give our gratious
'Prince deu information.'[2]

While the ferment was general throughout the nation, the
first overt act of opposition to the introduction of the Service
Book was the riot of the serving maids in St. Giles Cathedral
on 23rd July 1637. 'No sooner was the Book opened by the
'Deane of Edinburgh, but a number of the meaner sort, who
'used to keep places for the better sort, most of them women,
'with clapping of their hands, cursings, and outcries, raised
'such a barbarous hubbub in that sacred place, that not
'any one could either heare or be heard.' The Bishop of
Edinburgh, in an attempt to appease the tumult, 'was enter-
'tained with as much irreverence as the Deane, and with more
'violence; insomuch, that if a stoole, aimed to be throwne at
'him, had not by the providence of God beene diverted by the
'hand of one present, the life of that Reverend Bishop, in that
'holy place, and in the Pulpit, had beene indangered if not
'lost.'[3]

After that Sunday the new Service Book was never read in
Edinburgh. In the course of the following week the Privy
Council approved of a report by the Archbishop of St. Andrews
on behalf of the Bishops that there should be a surcease of the
Service Book till the King's pleasure was known, 'and that
'neither the old Service nor the new established Service be
'used in this interim.'[4] The King, in an angry letter to his

---

[1] Burnet's *Memoires of the Hamiltons*, p. 31.   [2] Baillie, i. 2.
[3] Large Declaration, 23.
[4] The Clergies' Report anent the Service Booke.—Peterkin, 52.

Council, reproved them for their faint-hearted conduct, and commanded that every Bishop should cause the Service Book to be read within his diocese,[1] but the Council did not dare to put this order in force. The people seemed 'possessed with a bloody devill.'[2]

The first wild and unregulated outbreaks of the mob gradually gave place to an orderly and, to the King, more dangerous attack upon his innovations, led by the greater part of the nobility, gentry, and other influential classes. Four men stood out conspicuous as their leaders, Rothes, Loudoun, Alexander Henderson of Leuchars, and the youthful Wariston—who fought the King and the Prelates with remarkable ability and skill, checkmating every move. For success against the powerful influences which the King and his adherents could bring to bear in order to secure their ends, it was essential that Scotsmen should stand shoulder to shoulder, and speak with one voice. For the attainment of the first of these objects, Wariston is said to have bethought him of a renewal of the old National Covenant of 1580, by which King James and his subjects swore to defend against Popery the true reformed religion as expressed in the Confession of Faith, and to maintain the King's Majesty, his person and estates;—'the true worship of God and the 'King's authoritie being so straitly joyned, as that they 'had the same friends and common enemies, and did stand 'and fall together.'[3] Wariston's suggestion was adopted and the famous National Covenant of 1638 was thereupon framed by him and Henderson jointly. To suit the oath of 1580 to the altered circumstances of the time, and secure united action against the innovations which in the interval had been introduced into the Church, an addition was made to it, whereby the subscribers swore to adhere to and defend the true religion and forbear the 'practice of all novations, already introduced in

---

[1] Peterkin, 54.  [2] Baillie, i. 23.
[3] Preamble to National Covenant of 1638.

'the matters of the worship of God, or approbation of the
'corruptions of the publick government of the Kirk, or civill
'places and power of Kirkmen, till they bee tryed and allowed
'in free Assemblies, and in Parliaments.' They further swore to
defend the King, his person and authority in the defence of
the true religion; 'as also to the mutuall defence and assist-
'ance everie one of us of another, in the same cause of main-
'taining the true Religion, and his Majestie's Authoritie,
'against all sorts of persons whatsoever, so that, whatsoever
'shall be done to the least of us for that cause, shall be taken
'as done to us all in generall, and to everie one of us in par-
'ticular. And that we shall, neither directly nor indirectly
'suffer ourselves to be divided or withdrawn, by whatsoever
'suggestion, combination, allurement, or terrour, from this
'blessed and loyall Conjunction, nor shall cast in any let or
'impediment that may stay or hinder any such resolution, as
'by common consent shall be found to conduce for so good
'ends.'[1] This Covenant was virtually a solemn obligation by
the individuals composing the nation that they would faithfully and for ever stand by each other in their resistance to the
hated innovations. The circumstances attending its subscription are well known. It was acknowledged by the King that
'the fire of this seditious Covenant flamed throughout all
'the corners of the kingdome, and that to such an unexpected
'height and violence, as it was past both the skill and power
'of our Councell to quench it.'[2] The enormous body of
people so banded together was represented by small committees selected from each class of the community, and these
again were for executive purposes represented by a General
Committee, or General Table as it was called, composed
of the ablest men of the party, which sat permanently
in Edinburgh with Wariston as Clerk. 'What they of

---

[1] National Covenant of 1638; Large Declaration, 64, 65.
[2] Large Declaration, 75, 76.

'the General Table resolved on, was to be put in practice
'with a blinde and Jesuiticall obedience.'[1]  Charles and his
advisers at once saw what a powerful engine had been devised
and perfected to baffle their schemes.  In referring to it in
his Declaration, the King wrote, 'And now began the most
'unnaturall, causlesse, and horrible rebellion that this or
'perhaps any other age in the world hath been acquainted
'with: for now these Protesters begin to invest themselves
'with the supreme Ensignes and Markes of Majestie and
'Soveraigntie by erecting publike Tables of advice and
'Councell, for ordering the affaires of the Kingdome, without
'our Authoritie, and in contempt of Us and our Councell
'established by us there, and by entring into a Covenant
'and most wicked Band and combination against all that
'shall oppose them, not excepting Our owne Person, directly
'against the law of God, the law of Nations, and the munici-
'pall lawes of that Our Kingdome.'[2]  In view of the gravity
of the situation, the King, after much consultation with his
advisers, resolved to send down the Marquis of Hamilton as
his High Commissioner with instructions to examine into the
alleged grievances, and to calm the commotions by giving the
nation all just satisfaction.

The line of action taken by the Covenanters was to profess
to absolve the King personally from all responsibility in connection with the innovations.  They laid before the Privy Council
a formal complaint against the Bishops[3] as 'the contryvers,
introducers, and urgers upone' the nation of the Service Book
and book of Canons, and as the authors of the other innovations.
For this, they maintained, the Bishops should be brought to trial
and should not be allowed to sit as judges till the matter was
determined.[4]  But this the King would not accept.  He was
proud of the part which he had personally taken in the pre-

---

[1] Large Declaration, 54.   [2] *Ibid.* 53, 54.
[3] *Relation*, 49.   [4] Declinator; Rothes' *Relation*, 51.

paration of the Service Book, and at once stated in reply that it was he who had ordered it to be compiled, and that he had in the framing of it taken great care and pains, 'so as 'nothing passed therein but what was seene and approved by 'Us before the same was either divulged or printed.'[1]

In all the numerous long and able papers issued by the Covenanters, one desire was kept prominently in the front, viz., that the King should call a free General Assembly and Parliament as the only means by which the great disorders of Church and State could be redressed: 'All the Desires of the Suppli-'cants resolves on ane Generall Assemblie and Parliament, these 'being the meanes to cognosce and redresse the whole parti-'culars.'[2] A mere withdrawal of the Service Book, Book of Canons, and High Commission would not remedy the evils nor prevent their recurrence. The Church, they urged, must be secured in time to come against any alteration in points of doctrine, divine worship, and church government, but such as should be agreed on in lawful free General Assemblies,[3] *i.e.* such assemblies as should be constituted according to the laws of the pure reformed Church of Scotland, not the packed and corrupt assemblies which had carried out the commands of King James in the later years of his reign.

Much discussion took place between the Commissioner and

---

[1] Proclamation.—Large Declaration, 48.

In the sale catalogue of the Duke of Hamilton's library, p. 25, the following entry occurs: '316, Booke of Common Prayer, R. Barker 1637—Psalmes in 'Meeter, with music,' 1635, black letter, Charles the First's copy with numerous 'alterations and additions in his autograph—small 4to. Prefixed to the Order 'for Morning Prayer, Charles I. has written with his own hand: "Charles R. I '" gave the Archb<sup>p</sup> of Canterbury comand to make the alteracons expressed '" in this book and to fit a Liturgy for the Church of Scotland and wheresoever '" they shall differ from another booke signed by us at Hamp<sup>t</sup> Court, Septemb<sup>r</sup> '" 28th, 1634, our pleasure is to have these followed rather than the former; '" unless the Archb<sup>p</sup> of St. Andrews and his Brethren who are upon the place '" shall see apparent reason to the contrary. At Whitehall, April 19th, 1636." 'The above note proves beyond a doubt that the alterations made in the folio 'edition of 1637, usually termed Laud's Scotch Liturgy, emanated from Charles I. 'himself, and that his emendations were adopted with scarcely a variation.'

[2] Rothes to Hamilton, *Relation*, 184. [3] *Relation*, 96.

the Covenanting leaders. Before agreeing to indict a General Assembly, the Commissioner demanded that the Covenant should be abrogated. This the Covenanters rejected without hesitation. He further asked for an undertaking that the Covenanters should not at the Assembly 'goe about to deter-'mine of things established by Acts of Parliament, otherwise 'than by remonstrance or petition to the Parliament.'[1] But such an undertaking they declined to give. The introduction of the Service Book, although the immediate cause of the outbreak, was only one of the innovations of which they complained. Their object was to strike at what they conceived to be the root of the evil, and to restore the Church to its purity as it existed at the end of the previous century before the introduction of Episcopacy by the King and Parliament against what the Covenanters believed was the will of the people. They insisted that the Church, acting through its Supreme Court legally constituted, had alone the cognisance of matters of doctrine, church government, and forms of worship. The King had no power to regulate such matters, and although Parliament might, for the fortification of the resolutions of the Church Courts, give them formal ratification, its power to legislate upon ecclesiastical subjects went no further. A ratifying Act of Parliament had no force, independently of the resolution of the Church Court which it confirmed, but at once became of no effect on the abrogation of the resolution by a subsequent duly constituted Assembly. An Assembly being supreme, it was impossible, they urged, that private individuals could bargain on its behalf that certain subjects should be excluded from its consideration.

The other point upon which a vital difference was manifested was the constitution of General Assemblies. The Commissioner, as representing the King and the Episcopal party, maintained that the practice which had been followed since

---

[1] Large Declaration, 123.

the introduction of Episcopacy should be continued, that is that Archbishops and Bishops, and constant (perpetual) Moderators of Presbyteries, should be members by virtue of their offices. The Covenanters would not admit this, and contended that only those persons could lawfully be members who were sent up as Commissioners from presbyteries or burghs. A further question arose as to the rights of ruling elders, or lay elders,[1] as the Episcopalians called them, to be members of Church Courts. The Episcopal party, who drew a broad distinction between clergy and laity, denied that ruling elders were members of Church Courts, although they might be called in by presbyteries 'for their assistance in discipline 'and correction of manners, at such occasions as they stood in 'need of their *godly concurrence*.'[2] Not being members they could neither vote in the election of ministers as commissioners from presbyteries nor be sent up as Commissioners themselves. On the other hand, the Covenanters declared that the rule of the Church was that each kirk-session should send up to its presbytery, as constituent members, the minister and one ruling elder. A presbytery would thus be composed of an equal number of ministers and ruling elders. As to the mode of election of Assembly Commissioners they founded on the instructions sent down to presbyteries by the Dundee Assembly on 7th March 1597, whereby three ministers and one ruling elder were directed to be sent up by each Presbytery as Commissioners to each Assembly.[3]

---

[1] 'Some reproachfully, and others ignorantly, call them Lay Elders. But the 'distinction of the Clergie and Laity is Popish and Antichristian. The name of 'Clergie, appropriate to Ministers, is full of pride and vaine glory, and hath 'made the holy people of God to be despised, as if they were prophane and 'uncleane in comparison of their Ministers.'—*Assertion of the Government of the Church of Scotland in the Points of Ruling Elders*, etc., Edinburgh, 1641, p. 3.

[2] Bishop's Declinator.—Large Declaration, 252.

[3] 'Elders are of three sorts (1) Preaching Elders or Pastors, (2) Teaching Elders or Doctors, (3) Ruling Elders. All these are elders, because they have voice in Presbyteries and all Assemblies of the Church, and the Government of the Church is incumbent to them all.'—*Assertion, ut supra*, p. 8.

These differences were not arranged, but the King, nevertheless, resolved to call an Assembly. By way of clearing the ground, and as a substantial bid for the support of the mass of the people, who might be supposed not to care much about such matters as the Royal Prerogative and theories of church government, provided the recent innovations were removed, Charles issued a Proclamation expressing his detestation of Popery; virtually sweeping away all the innovations; declaring that Bishops who had abused their powers should be subject to trial by the General Assembly; and directing that a free Assembly should be held at Glasgow on 21st November 1638.[1]

The famous Assembly met in the great Cathedral on the appointed day amid scenes of intense excitement, Baillie's vivid description of which[2] recalls Macaulay's well-known picture of the opening of the impeachment of Warren Hastings in Westminster Hall. The ministers and elders who had been sent up as Commissioners were, almost to a man, enthusiastic Covenanters, eager to condemn the innovations and to sit in judgment on the Prelates. Henderson was elected Moderator, and Wariston Clerk[3] and afterwards Procurator or Legal Adviser. Hamilton speedily foresaw what the result would be if an Assembly so constituted were allowed to proceed to business, and therefore, on the plea that ruling elders had no right to be members, he, on 29th November,[4] declared the Assembly dissolved and departed. The Assembly, however, after his departure, passed a formal resolution that it was a lawful Assembly, and might continue to sit till its business was despatched. It accordingly sat till 20th December, and in the interval it swept away the whole fabric of Episcopacy, rejected and condemned, as unlawful innovations, the changes in the forms of church government and worship introduced by the King, deposed and excommunicated both

---

[1] Large Declaration, 137.
[2] Baillie, i. 123 *et seq.*
[3] 'A nonsuch for a clerk.'—Baillie, i. 122.
[4] Peterkin, 44.

the Archbishops and six of the Bishops, and deposed without excommunicating six more of the Bishops.

The cup was now full. Charles felt that he had been defied and insulted before the world, and at once proceeded to hasten on the preparations which he had for some time been quietly making[1] for punishing his rebellious subjects. On 26th January 1639 he summoned his English nobility to meet him at York on 1st April, each with a suitable following, on the plea, absolutely without foundation, that the Scots might invade England. His real intention undoubtedly was to reduce the Scots to obedience by force of arms. To that end he had planned landings of troops on the shores of the Clyde and the coast of Argyllshire; the north was to be secured by the Marquis of Huntly; Hamilton with a fleet was to enter the Firth of Forth; and the King with his army was to advance to the Tweed. While at York he published a Proclamation promising to grant an act of oblivion to all such as should within eight days lay down their arms, declaring such as should not obey rebels, and ordering their vassals and tenants not to acknowledge them, nor pay them any rent, but to reserve one half of it to the King's use, and the other half to their own use. But the projected landings on the west coast did not take place; the Earl of Montrose disposed of Huntly and the town of Aberdeen; Hamilton's fleet, which entered the Forth on 1st May, could not effect anything beyond the taking of a few ships; and the Covenanters would not allow the Proclamation to be read. The Royal army was assembled at the Birks near Berwick early in May, and the King himself arrived there about 30th May,[2] nine days after the commencement of Wariston's Diary. His army had no heart for the war. Sir Ralph Verney wrote to his son on 1st May, 'I dare say ther was never . . . soe unwilling an army brought to fight.' And on 5th May he wrote, 'This

---

[1] See Letters, the King to Hamilton: Burnet's *Memoires*, pp. 55, 59.
[2] Verney Papers, 241.

'daye I spake with an understanding Scottishman, and one
'that is affected the moderate waye. Hee is confident noe-
'thing will sattisfye them but taking awaye all bishopps, and
'I dare saye the King will never yeelde to that, soe wee must
'bee miserable.'[1]

The Covenanters were determined to resist to the utmost. They composed the great majority of the nation, and were thoroughly organised. Alexander Leslie, the hero of the defence of Stralsund, who had learned the art of war under the great Gustavus, was appointed general in chief, and the Nobles served under him as Colonels of their respective regiments. Large supplies of arms and ammunition had been imported from the Continent. The great strongholds of the country had been captured, and Leith had been fortified. A force had been sent under the command of Montrose to overawe Aberdeen and the north-east; and considerable bodies of men had been stationed along the shores of the Forth to watch the English fleet. The main army which was to oppose directly that of the King was quartered in the villages of East Lothian, when Leslie, with his colonels, set out to take the immediate command on the 21st of May, the day when the Diary was begun.

The Society desire specially to express their acknowledgments to Mr. Maxton Graham for his kindness in placing the manuscript of the Diary at their disposal, and to Sir James Gibson Craig of Riccarton, Baronet, for allowing his unique portrait of Wariston by Jamesone to be photographed as a frontispiece.

GEORGE M. PAUL.

---

[1] Verney Papers, 228, 231.

# JOHNSTON OF WARISTON'S DIARY

Upon Tuesday the 21 of May 1639, my Lord Generall with sundrie of his Colonells, the Earle of Rothes, my Lord Lindsay, my Lord Loudon, my Lord Yester, my Lord Montgomerie, my Lord Dalhusie, with five and fourtie peece of canon marcht from Ed$^r$ to Haddingtoun wher my Lord Rothes and my Lord Montgomeries regiments wer lying.[1]

Upon Wednesday the 22 May the Lord Generall went to Dumbar wher my Lord Lindsay and my Lord Loudon, my Lord Yester, and my Lord Muntros regiments wer lying ther and ther abouts.

This night eighteene ships which wer lying above Inchcome came downe to the rode of Leeth.

This day ane letter from the noblemen, with sundrie Articles was taken in to the Comissioner by Mr. Wm. Cunynghame.

Upon Thursday the 23 May[1] twentie of the English ships went from the rode of Leeth to the May, the guards of both coasts of Louthian and Fyfe following them.

The Generall went from Dumbar to see Tantallan.[2]

*Ane letter sent to the whole Shyres.*

'RIGHT HONORABLE, These are to desire the Noblemen within your shyre with all possible diligence to send hither to

---

[1] '21 May 1639. Twysday. This day Generall Leslie, Erl Rothes, and Lord Lyndsay, tuik journey to the bound rod.'

'23 May 1639. *Item*, Mr. Alexander Henrysoun, with Mr. Archibald Johnstoun, raid to the bound Rod.'—*Diary of Sir Thomas Hope* (Bannatyne Club), 97. Henderson and Wariston no doubt accompanied the army as the official representatives of the Church, having been respectively Moderator and Clerk of the last General Assembly.

[2] This castle, now a ruin, was then a place of great strength. It was taken by Cromwell in 1651, 'after he had battred at the for wall 12 dayes continually with grate canon.'—Balfour, iv. 249.

the borders at the least the two part of the horses and horsemen both of Gentlemen and yeomans who will readylier come out with them nor[1] without them, conforme to Instructions befor sent to Shyres theranent, if they be not already come away befor this advertisement. The king's armie especially of horsemen lying now close upon our borders in despight of all foot companies may and will assuredly ravage all the country, and ryde into the heart of the kingdom w$^{ch}$ our footmen cannot imped, bot we both remaine useles to other pairts bot q$^r$ they are guarding and be in hazard of the enemies horse in the feilds except the horse come to us and that w$^t$ all possible expedition, lest they mak our foot armies to ly still heere spending our victuals, q$^r$as having the horsemen we might both march to the borders, gett assurance either of present peace or warre and stay the enemie from spoyling the countrie; let not any man now either linger or think it sufficient to send any unworthy body or a bachling naig[2] in his stead, seeing our enemies strength consists in ther horse, Bot as they love the standing of Gods cause and liberties of this kirk and kingdome, let them use extraordinarie diligence in this extraordinarie exigent to come themselves and hasten others to come, either w$^t$ carrabeins, hagbuts, pistols, or jacks and lances, or swords and lances, or any other fensible weapon. Lykeas we most earnestly requyre the noblemen and gentlemen in everie paroch that whosoever steales away from this armie home w$^t$out ane passe from us or his owne Colonell be presently putt in yrons and sent back to the armies to suffer exemplary punishment. Your affectionat freinds

*Dumbar* 24 *of May* 1639.

Upon Fryday the 24 May ther come two Commissioners with ane supplication from the Colledg of Justice to my Lord Generall, desyring not to be tyed to march all on foot from Ed$^r$ presently, wherunto the Generall condescended and desyred them to make up ane troup of horse, and to report this his desyre to them that sent them.

This night Captaine Winnercom brought alongs with him from Ed$^r$ one of his Ma$^{ties}$ trumpeters who came from my

---

[1] than.  [2] A shambling nag.

Lord Holland[1] through Kelso with one letter to the noble men of Scotland and with one to the Earle of Argyle.

My Lords—As it hath beene my fortune to have receaved great expressions from yow of the disposition of your Loyalty and dueties to his Matie, so is it now to give your L^op ane occasion to shew it by your obedience to this his Maties proclamation which asking bot civile and temporall obedience from his naturall kingdome having beene borne in the bowels of it, I most beleeve by the earnest professions of love and duty to him and lykwyse by the eminence of your qualities, that so justly ought to serve what created them:

Your L^ops will most joyfully and readily submitt to that which in this sacred and powerfull way is thus demanded from you, by which meanes you may not onlie avoyd that name yow professe so litle to deserve, but lykewyse shunne in all your particulars the inconveniences of it with those others of the publick threatned in the distraction of these kingdomes which are so intressed in the safety and prosperity of each other as their differences will appear as unnaturall toward ourselves as it may prove unfortunate. The fulness of my heart upon this occasion maks me say more then is propper for me, since I am rather to obey in this office then to advyse. —My Lords I am your L^ops humble servant    HOLLAND

*From my quarter this*
    *20 of May.*

My Lord—I have receaved a civilitie that challenges a reall returne of it unto your L^op, and truelie I can in nothing expresse it so much as in my letter and freindlie persuasions to your L^op that ye wold upon this occasion advyse as you professe that your religion and Lawes being safe ther is no undutiefulnes or violence intended, I am confident neither of them will justifie the disobeying of such a comand as the retiring of those forces that hath beene raised without them, And my Lord in the freedome and sinceritie of my heart and conscience give me leave to say It most appeare strange to our Soveraigne Lord and Master thus to be faced with ane Armie

---

[1] The Earl of Holland was General of the Horse in the King's Army.

that hath covered us all so many yeares under the wings of peace, when all other princes have beene laid open to the rage and calamities of warre; if this deserve not, with so many other blessings of his personall vertues, the retiring to such a distance as the least motione of his Ma/ just sword may not fall upon you I leave it to your conscience, w^ch can never enquire to find any so guilty of the moving of any thing towards such distractions as these must be, that may with ther honour and duety thus remove to preveine them, All thus my Lord wer I your brother I should offer unto you, which is the best and truest expression of my being your L^op most humble servant

*From my quarter*  HOLLAND
*22 May.*
### By the King [1]

Charles by the Grace of God, King of Great Britaine,[2] Scotland, France and Ireland, Defender of the Faith. To all our loving subjects whom it shall or may concerne; Greeting. Wheras we ar thus farr advanced in our Royall person with our armie, and the attendance of our nobility and gentry of this kingdome, and intend to be shortly at our good towne of Barwicke, with purpose to give our good people of Scotland all just satisfaction in Parliament, as soone as the present disorders, and tumultuous proceidings of some there, ar quieted: and will leave us a faire way of comming lyke a gracious king to declare our good meaning to them: But finding some cause of impediment and that this nation doth apprehend (that contrarie to their professions) ther is ane intention to invade this our kingdome of England, We doe therfor to cleare all doubts, that may breed scruples in the mynds of our good subjects of either kingdome, reiterate this our just and reall protestation: That if all civile and temporall obedience be effectually and tymely given and shewen unto us we doe not intend to invade them with any hostilitie, But, if they shall without our especiall authority and command raise any armed troupes, and draw them downe within ten miles of our border of England,

---

[1] This Proclamation was issued at Newcastle on 14th May 1639. An original print has been preserved at Queen's College, Oxford, which Mr. Firth has been good enough to collate with this copy. Peterkin's copy is inaccurate and misleading.    [2] *England* in original print.

we shall then interpret that as an invasion of our said *Kingdome of England*,[1] and in that case doe expressly command the Generall of our armie and our superiour officers of the same, respectively to proceede against them as Rebells, and Invaders of this our kingdome of England, and to the outmost of their power to sett upon them and destroy them, In which they shall doe a singular service both to our honour and safety.

Given at our Court at Newcastle the fourteenth day of May, in the fifteenth yeare of our raigne.

God Save the King.

Imprinted at Newcastle by Robert Barker printer to the Kings Most Excellent Majestie: and by the assignes of Jhon Bill 1639.

Upon the 25 May being Saturday we sent away with the trumpeter Sir Jhon Hume of Blacader Knight with our answer to my Lord Holland and with privat instructions to himself.

OUR NOBLE LORD—As nothing can be more acceptable to us then to heare that his Matie is pleased to give just satisfaction unto us and to all his good people, so shall we ever be willing with all due respect to remember and honour all such as shal be so happie as to be mediators to procure the same, w$^{ch}$ we acknowledg to be yours at this tyme, And for our part shall to the outermost of our power render all civile and temporall obedience unto his Ma/ as tymely and effectually as may be with the preservation of our Lyves and safety of the Countrey, And therfor as we doe humblie intreat and certainely expect that his Ma/ is willing to cleare all doubts that may bread scruples in the mynds of the good subjects of either kingdome, will in his justice recall all his forces by sea which are lying heere within our bosome to our great hinderance, will release our Ships arrested in his Ma/ other dominions, will remove his armies from the borders for our securitie, and will be graciouslie pleased to give signification of his Ma/ will for accomodation of affaires in such a peaceable way whether by the conference of some pryme and well affected men of both

---

[1] The italics were omitted in the Diary. See original print.

nations or any other meane (which we presume not to prescryve) as may prove more powerfull then those already assayed hath done, So doe we resolve in all humilitie presently to doe his Ma/ will in keeping our armies within the bounds of his Ma/ limitation, and to performe all things we can conceave may conduce for our common peace, The speedy effectuating of this on both sydes, as your Lo/ knowes to be his Ma/ honour, So doe we know it to be the well of this his Ma/ kingdome now in armes whose present condition is such that it cannot indure longer delay, and all men who looke upon us will perceave to be the scattering of that dark clouds which hingeth over the two kingdomes, This blessed work if your Lo/ who hath begunne so happily shall bring to passe which from the knowledg of his Ma/ justice and goodnes we suppose to be facible by your Lo/ and others who hath accesse And therfor intrust this Gentleman Sir Jhon Hume of Blacader Knight with further information, Then shall we yet be further obliedged to prove       Your lo/ humble servants

Lochend the 25 May 1639.

### Instructions

Ye shall shew my Lord Holland

1. The true estate of the question whether we shal be governed by generall assemblies in matters ecclesiasticall and by parliament in matters civile unto whose decision we have ever submitted ourselves, our person our cause and our proceidings; albeit proclamations be wrapt up in generals of religion and Law, yet the grounds of both ar condemned in particular, as our covenant with God and the generall assemblie wherof we cannot obtaine ane ratification in parliament.

2. That we never had any intention either to diminish his Ma/ authority and Monarchie or invade our neighbour kingdome bot only to defend ourselves in the mantenance of our religion and liberties.

3. That we have hitherto used all possible meanes by supplications, informations etc both to cleare our intentions to his Ma/ and our neighbour nation.

4. That, to show the greatest testimony of our civile

obedience after by proclamation[1] we wer declared rebells and traitours, we most humblie renewed our Supplications wryte to sundry noblemen of England and most heartily consented to the prorogation of the Parliament.

5. That the English Navie hes now lyen this fourthnight in our Firth stopping all trade and commerce betwixt this and any other natione, taking our ships, boats, barks, their victuals, goods, geire and moneyes detaining the men both mariners and passengers or forcing them to sweare oathes contrare to our religion and lawes.

6. That manifestoes and relations of our foul conspiracies (as they call them) ar published to the world against us and yet never one of them suffered to be sent home to lett us know our accusations, that our estates be disponed to our tennents and our lyves subjected to all wold be rewarded for the taking them.

7. That albeit it be strange that ane forraigne armie after threatning our destruction shall march to our borders ready to come in upon us at their pleasure, and we who intended and professe not to send any bot defend ourselves should be discharged from the bounds so lyable to their invasion, yet to give full satisfaction in everie poynt, we ar content to stay our armies upon assurance of the present removing of the navie from our firth and armies from the borders.

8. That it is not lykely that matters of so great importance as is now to be treated upon can so shortly be broght to a conclusion as necessitie requyreth by interchange of letters and intercourse of mesḡres etc., doth therfor seeme convenient that a conference wer appointed betwixt some of the nobility of Ingland and some of our nobilitie in some convenient place upon the march so speedily as may be which doubtles will prove the best way to accommodat bussines shortlie.

This day Mr. Wm. Cunynghame broght back the Comissioner his answere and tooke a new letter back with him.

This day order was sent to Crowner Muntroe[2] to march

---

[1] York Proclamation. See p. 32.
[2] Colonel Munro was in command of a force then quartered at Dumfries.

hither seeing we heard the troupes of Carleel wer come towards Berwick.

Upon the Sabboth the 26 May my Lord Generall heard sermon in Dumbar church wher Mr. Alex<sup>r</sup> Henderson did beginne to preach upon the fight of the Israelites with Amalek.

Afternoone we had intelligence by one come from the armie that the Kings Matie with his armie had marcht to Gozik[1] with ten regiments twelve colours in everic regiment, a hundreth men under everie colour, and of the blacknes of the bread wherwith they wer intertained.

This night the Kings ships chast a litle barge into the Sketerraw, and my Lord Generall rode away to Kelso to order my Lord Louthian and my Lord Askins[2] regiments and the Shirreffe of Tividailes horse troupe.

Upon Munday the 27 May the Laird of Blacader, returning from my Lord Holland, desyred ane alteration of ane mitigating interpretation of the letters sent to my Lord which we sett downe in some articles and sent away with Blacader.

'The noblemen who did direct and subscryve the answer to my Lord Hollands letter ar not heere for the present to enter upon any new deliberation, neither can they be broght together so soone as that the bearer may keepe the dyet appointed by his Lo/, we who are heere understanding the right and loyall meaning of all the particulars contained in the same may be answerable to his Lo/ and to those of our owne who ar absent for saying so much as may be a remedie against all mistaking.

'My Lord knoweth how great reason we have to apprehend ane invasion, for his Maties proclamations threaten no lesse, all preparations for warre ar used, all supplications and means assayed by us ar rejected: Manifestoes ar published against us and keeped up from us, our lands and estates disponed to our vassals and tennents,[3] the fleet lyeth heere to our great and dayly hinderance, the armies ar now come to the borders; matters so standing, how necessary it is that we see to

---

[1] Goswick lay nearly opposite the north point of Holy Island.
[2] Erskine's.    [3] York Proclamation.

ourselves, and doe and labour for all things conducing for our lawfull defence My Lord and all wyse men can judge, and more then defence we have not intended.

'His Lo/ wold be pleasd to consider that we have undertaken to give present obedience to his Ma/ will in keeping the distance of place designed, and doe not capitulat that his Ma/ should remove his armies to the lyke distance, bot doe earnstly begg and humblie supplicat that his Maties armies by sea and land may be so farr removed or in his Maties justice so disposed upon that we may be secured from invasion and that our commerce and country now blocked up may be made free, What urgent necessity there is that this be granted althogh cravd by way of supplication as beseemeth humble subjects we desyre his Lo/ will take to consideration.

'The earnst desyre we have of pacification and to give both his Matie and the whole nation just content may be kent by our proposition for a meeting of some pryme and well affected men, and by our readines to accept any the lyke meane which shal be prescryved to us and serving most for the Kings honour and our common peace, and this way of pacification in the generall is that which is meant in our answer wher we spake of a speedy effectuating, and q$^r$ we say that it is begunne happily by his Lo/ who knowth that both for his Maties honour and for the estate of both kingdomes now in armes a speedy accomodation is most necessarie.'

This day the pay of the regiments at Dumbar and Haddingtoun was changd from mony unto victual, and because sundry souldiers wer not content with their quarters my Lord Lindsay and my Lord Loudon quartered them in the feilds.

Upon Tuesday the 28 of May upon advertisement that some Englishmen had proclaimed the proclamation at Haymouth and Aytoun, other some had taken in Ethringtoun, and others had slaine some scores of sheepe pertaining to the Laird of Blacadder, and all had pitched their tents up and downe the water of Tweid, there was ane letter writen in to the Committee of Ed$^r$ with ane commoun advertisement for the whole shyres, and ane other letter to the ministers of Ed$^r$ to be sent to the whole presbyteries.

*For the Committe at Ed<sup>r</sup> and from thence to be sent to the whole Shyres.*

Wheras it was formerly appointed that if the Kings armie should approach to the border with any great force that upon warning all should be ready upon the first call to march with what armes they could horse and foot, this is therfor to warne all that loves the good of this cause and their owne safetie to come in all haste once this week, and bring what they can of a months provision, and let the rest follow them: for if ther come a competent number together we shal be able to hold them up from breaking in unto the country, which if once they get fitting[1] it will not be easie to bring them to a stand, and upon the guard of thir parts depends the safetie of the whole kingdome, they that shal be found wanting now ar enemies to this cause and their country, Stirre up one another and remember that all your charter kists ar lying at the border: We shall beare them witnes, bot let none stay at home when strangers ar hyred for three shillings a week to make us all slaves, they are not worthy to be freemen that will stay at home and neglect their country, which is now ready to bleed for their neglect, some of the enemies ar come over the border, Ethringtoun is taken, Haymouth is feared to be taken this night, wher is a great magazin of victuals; if horse and foot haste not we can hardly here hold them up; be not wanting to yourselves, and be confident God will send ane outgate to all these difficulties: So in haste looking for all dispatch at your hands whom it alyke concernes I rest.

My Lord—Receave the generall directions to call up all the kingdome in armes, take the gentlemen of several shyres where they ar in towne and send them in post hast through all the shyres to call them all up with what armes they gett, The Kings armie is about Berwick, places ar saised upon the borders Haymouth is feared to be taken this night where is the magazin of our victual, if they see not speedy help the border wil be lost, we have no horsmen at all, ther is no provision of victuals and money; if that everie one set not up

---

[1] footing.

his rest upon this and come presently it will be difficult to draw to ane head, Let everie one pray to God and putt to his hand and God will send us releife; for the six companies about Leeth I have sent order to requyre them to march hither, since many of the souldiers ar out of the ships the town of Ed$^r$ and Leeth may guard the shoare: what other encouragments ar fitting to be given to all I doubt not bot ye will make use of them, I will wryte to Argyle and ye must doe the lyke from the table that he bring all along with him, They that comes upon this call most bring provision with them for few dayes and the rest most follow of the months provision.

My Lord send a coppy of this warning, direct to you, to all the Shyres; adde a letter of your owne to enforce the same from the Table.

*Lochend* 28 *May* 1639.

REVEREND AND BELOVED IN THE LORD—Yee will perceave by the warning given to the Shyres what great need ther is of assembling all forces that may be had toward the borders; we neid not make any new representation of the present danger unto you, We will only intreat you as ye love Christ and your own peace, and as ye wish that yourselves and the people committed to your charge may be saved from spirituall and bodyly slaverie, that ye will now bestirre yourselves in your severall places and in the most powerfull way ye can conceave; stirre up all betwixt sixty and sixteen both horse and foot to march forward to the border neither staying upon armes bot bringing such weapons with them as they have, nor one company staying upon another bot comming as they themselves ar in readines with what provision they can have in haste in victual or money or can have to follow them upon carriage horses, for ther is no other meane left unto us now for peace or for victory under God, who wold be entreated by fasting and prayer in publick and private by all who ar not able to come on, that this his owne cause and work, to which his Matie hath called us and which he hath countenanced and carried on so farr by so many evidences of his gracious and powerfull presence, be not now when it is come to the shock deserted and forsaken by himself. We ar yet confident in our Lord that if the people at home be exercised in prayer, and so many as are able to come on linger not, the event shal be a matter of praise to our God and of Christian and civile peace to this land, for which we also who ar marching on shall joyne as beecometh

    Your loving freinds and brethren in the Lord
*Dumbar May* 28.

 Let the first to whose hands these shall come send them presently to his nearest neighbour and see y$^t$ all be advertysed tymously.

 Ane other letter to the Earle of Argyle to that same purpose, a letter to the Earle of Marshall and to the Earle of Muntrose to stirre up the North to that same purpose, ane letter to the Laird of Blacader to complaine to my Lord Holland of these wrongs done during the treatie.

 Ane preceise order written to Crowner Muntroe to march night and day to Jedburgh, ane letter to my Lord Jhonstoun to hasten all their horsmen and what foot may be spared hither, ane letter to the Earle of Louthian my Lord Ker and Sheirife of Tividaile to gather ther horse and foot together to remove their victual and cattels, and keep themselves in the feilds, ane letter to the Earle of Hume to draw his people together both horse and foot at Dunse and to bring away all victual and cattels from the border, ane letter to my Lord Dalhusie to march presently to Dumbar, Many other letters written to sundrie Noblemen both West and North to stirre them up.

 This night my Lord Generall went to Coberspeth.[1]

 Upon Wednesday the 29 May my Lord Muntros and my Lord Lindsayes regiments marched with the canon to the leaguer a little bewest Dunglas and encamped there wher we learned of the people of Haymouth and Aytoun applauding to the proclamation and sent them the warning following:[2]

 Lykeas finding great deficiency of victuals and appearance of greater in tyme comming for want of care and good order in the Commissērs we gave many orders to Dumbar, Haddingtoun for continuall baking and brewing and sending to the

---

[1] Cockburnspath.      [2] See next page.

camp, we wrote sundry advertisements to Ed$^r$ for sending the baken briskatt they had, for baking and brewing in Dalccath, Mussilburgh and all other places and sending it by shillops, boats or cariag horses, to Haymouth, Cauringhame, Coldstreame, Dunce to transport all ther victuals to the camp toward Coberspeth, we used all meanes and yet found litle supplie, praying God to give us greater wisdome to direct, and men greater diligence to execute, and be his providence he furnished us lest for want we dissolved, which we trust in God he will prevent and albeit a naturall mind might presently despaire for this want, yea the want of all the necessares of warre, men, horses, victual, money, munition, comanders, order and dicipline, yet we know in q$^m$ we trust, that in his providence as he lives he will most certainly crowne this work with his grace with the capstone of a glorious successe

*Ane warning from the Armie to the people of Haymouth and Aytoune.*

'We cannot wonder enough neither ar we a litle greived that ye should be so simple as to suffer yourselves to be deceaved with the faire promises of that late declaration which is even now published amongst you : have ye forgotten for what necessary causes we have taken armes, how often we have petitioned for our religion and liberties and all in vaine, what meanes have been assayed against us to work division, and that this is the last temtation for the same end ; will ye be perjured against God, losse all your former labours, and by your defection or wavering now losse your country, religion, liberties, and lyves : Ar we not heere in armes ready to take part with you to the last dropp of our blood ; is not the whole kingdome obleiged to stand for yours and there owne defence, shall ye dreame to yourselves to be free of invasion of both hands. Our Religion and Lawes in the general ar promised, Bot when we supplicat for them in particular as we have them established they ar refused Assure yourselves that hopes of gaining lands and moneyes this way will but deceave you ; may not Aberdeene and the places about be a present example unto you, God forbidd that so base and unchristian thoughts as we heare of you should harbour in true Scottish and Christian hearts.'

Upon Thursday the 30 May ther was ane order and warrant given to the mariners of Fyfe and Louthian to help and defend all boats and barks from the invasion of the English ships and catches; order also given to Ed$^r$ and Leeth to guard by three companies Newheaven and Leeth, and to lett my Lord Foster's regiment, the Colledg of justice and other companies that was guarding that coast to march.

We receaved Blacaders letter anent my Lord Hollands answer, whereof the tenour is in the next page.

My Noble Lords—I was at my Lord Holland yesterday, and this morning was on horseback to come to your Lo$^{ps}$, bot befor I had ridden a mile I tooke such a pain in my back about my cares that I was scarce able to return home so that I am constrained to write to your Lo$^{ps}$ my Lord Hollands answer which is that the king was pleased with the obedience given to his Ma/ proclamation of keeping the armie ten myles from the borders, bot wheras your Lo$^{ps}$ desyred a meiting of some Noblemen on both sydes for a treatie, the kings Ma/ having now come this farr with his royall armie and being ingaged in his honour and reputation by taking of his Castles and ornaments of his Crowne, and having the eyes of all men upon these actions, his Maties will was that his Castles and crowne should be delivered back to him without which he could neither keepe a parliament, nor have a place to lodge in at a parliament which as it was ane obedient and peaceable way so it was the most handsome way of obedience; and as for byegones his Ma/ wold remitt all; w$^{ch}$ in effect seemes to me to be the verie tenour of the proclamation; my Lord said also that the King seeing the uncleanlines of the places of divyne worship even on the borders of England and also in Scotland wold have helped that one wold have wished things of that kynd to have beene reformed in a more comelie manner, bot seeing this nation so willfully bent for matters of religion the King was purposed to give them their will in these things y$^t$ concernes religion, and if his Matie wer obeyed he wold come to Ed$^r$ in quyet and peaceable manner and hold a Parliament for setling of all disorders; this is all in effect y$^t$ I could conceave or remember of my Lord Hollands discourse which I desyred he might wryte and give me to carry bot he refused and said if your Lo$^p$. had any further to wryte to him he wold answer it in wryte. Concerning the lambs taken at Fishwick they wer nyne and twentie of them only by some unruly souldiers, and their commanders sent to offer satisfaction either in punishment of ther bodyes or pryce of the goods, and concerning Ethringtouns house it was a vaine conceat of a idle man young Westnisbitt. I am sorry that I was not able to come to your Lo/ and if your Lo/ have any more to wryte to my Lord Holland send it to me if your Lo/ please and I shall either goe with it if I be able or send my sonne, I am sorrie of my unability at this tyme w$^{ch}$ hes hindered to speak with your Lo$^p$, for the common people are all in such a feare y$^t$ lyes upon the border neare the Inglish Camp that they can scarce be kept from yeilding and some ar found to have done it already—rests your Lo$^p$. humble servant JHON HUME.

*Blacader* 30 *May* 1639.

I was informed by a man [who] told the colours that the first night the English encamped ther was threescore colours, and sensyne ther is some moe come which it is thoght came out of the ships w$^{ch}$ some calls two some three thousand men.

Upon Friday the 31 May in the morning we had ane alarme by sundrie bearers alledging that the whole English armie was marching to Dounce, therafter we learned the truth of it that ther was ane thousand English horse with my Lord Holland who came to Dounce in the morning to preveene the Earle of Humes conveening of the regiment of the Merse at Dounce, did ther read the proclamation and tooke away the Laird of Rentons charter kist out of the Castle of Dounce and retired therafter home againe, We wer advertised that sundrie in the Merse had yeelded already and farr moe was to yeeld, wherupon we send the third warning or summonds to raise the country betwixt sixty and sixteen and sent it to the Committee of Ed$^r$ to be sent to all the Shyres.

D

'RIGHT HONOURABLE AND LOVING FREINDS—We have done our part first in requyring you to be ready upon advertisement to come to the border when necessity should urge; we have next given warning that the necessity presseth sore and that ye should come forward horse and foot without staying of one company upon another; and now we tell you and give you the third summonds that as ye love your country, your conscience, your lyves and liberties, and wold be delivered from the destruction threatned against us ye wold haste haste hither, and be not deceavd with further hopes of peace except by this meane, neither be ye detained any longer by the apprehension of the particular invasion of the pairts of the country wher any of you have your residence, for all the souldiers that wer in the ships ar landed at Barwick to help the armie there. Shall our enemies be more forward for invasion against the truth and for our slaverie, then we for our defence, for the truth, and for our libertie? In end they have neither Christian nor Scottish hearts who will expose their religion, their countrie, ther neighbours and themselves to this present danger without taking part with them, and stand out for any respect under Heaven against this warning of

YOUR ASSURED FREINDS.

*From the Camp besyd*
*Dunglas, 30 May.*

Since the wryting of this the Kings horsmen came this morning 31 May to Dounse, therfor haste haste hither with q$^t$ provision of weapons and victual ye can bring and let the rest of your months provision follow you with all diligence.

MY NOBLE LORD—These ar to show you the Kings horsmen ar this morning come to Dounse, therfor in all haste haste send away this letter to the shyres with ane assured bearer. We have neither seene your horsemen, nor of any other shyre, so they may ryde wher they please without any possible impediment from us, We have receaved no spades, nor howes, no swyne feathers wherby we may intrinch ourselves. Let their danger and ours both stirre up greater diligence in us all or we will all repent it; see yesterdayes directions anent supplying us with bread and drink, obey it in haste or else we will dissolve for want of baking and brueing, and if the few people heere be cutt of for want of materiall to intrinch ourselves or dissolve for want of intertainement, or the horsmen ryde into y$^r$ bounds for want of horsemen it is not our fault who gives warning on warning bot the fault of your Lordships in Ed$^r$ and gentry in the shyres.

Sent in haste haste.

31 *May from the Camp*
   *besyd Dunglas.*

At Dunglas 31 May.

One Jhon Oliphant a youth of North Berwick was taken at the passe, being a servant to Sir Henry Vane.

After great enquirie he told us at last that his M$^r$. desyred that he should try wher Generall Leslie lay and what forces he had and by his discourse.

One M$^r$ Tuesden putt him on this imployment.

Ther was ane letter writen to my Lord Hume mentioning these things that had past in the Merse that day and desyring his Lo/ to come to Dunglas the next day where they might advyse concerning the safetie of the country; this letter was given to Wetherburne to be sent to him.

Ther came letters also from Kelso from my Lord Askin to informe of their estate. Captain Hume was sent from Munroe to shew the regiments comming to Jeddard according to former orders.

Upon this ther was order sent to my Lord Louthian, to Colonell Munroe, and ane order to my Lord Phleeming that was marching thither that they should all draw together at Kelso and ther make the place fast against the English horsmen, that they should keep diligent watch and have good intelligence of the enemie that when they beganne to dislodge they might make ready also and come and march towards the armie that was lying besyd Dunglas.

Upon Saturday the 1 of June ther came a letter from Selchrig sent by my Lord Phleeming telling of his four companies and some few horse that wer with him, and of the hinderance that Lambingtoun had made to that leavie, and of the want of amunition ; his order was renewed to joyne with the rest at Kelso and ther to attend ther common direction.

Ther was another letter sent to the Proveist and Bailzeis of Ed$^r$, ane answer that they requyred of the guard from Newheaven to Cramont that Midlouthian should guard, this was recommended to my Lord Balmirrinoc that he should see it performed, in which letter also he was forwarnd as befor of all the necessityes of the armie.

Ther was another letter written to the Committee of warre in Fyfe by the Generall subscryved by my Lord Rothes Lindsay taxing ther negligence in sending out of horsmen, and suffering so many to stay at home besydes these that guarded the coast, when the necessity was so great at the border they wer ane evill example to others in sending out all betwixt sixty and sixteen that had armes.

This day also ther come letters from my Lord Kircubright and others and a petition from the towne of Dumfrise complaineing of the taking away from them Colonel Munroe and his regiment and of laying them open and ther country to the malice of their enemies the Maxwells and their adherents at home and to the invasion of any forces from England.

This day ane English catch chased in the ship of Kirkadie unto the Scatterraw, shott sundrie peaces at her, bot was impeded from taking her. She had twenty carrabeins, twentie paire of Franch pistoles, fourscore muskett, and nyne hundreth weght of pouder.

This day ane English gentleman either really or fainedly a foole who was sent back as he came.

This day the Erle of Hume came to the camp and cleared himself to the Generall from all misreports.

There was the same day directions given to Wauchton and S$^r$ Patrik Murray That Wauchton and S$^r$ Patrik Murray conveane the gentlemen of East Louthian and two of the most understanding yeomen in each paroch, who may by common consent appoint in each paroch a gentleman to receave directions and oversee the carriages and other bussines of victuals etc. in each paroch who may have under him two yoemans to be Constables to asist the execution and see directions done, and to represent that on the furnishing of victuals and drawing of the canons consists the safetie of this land, for without neither can we stand a day. And therfor to intimate that whosoever disobeyes the ordinance, it shall forfeit his horse at least and hazard his lyfe to bring all our lyves thus in hazard.

Coberspeth and Allhamstoks is to attend the ordinance till Sunday, on which day Waughtone and S$^r$ Patrik most come hither to the armie, most make report of the diligence of each paroch, and the stent be made according to the number contained in this list, which we conjecture to be just, but ye may make it perfect and exact, and bring then the fourth pairt of the horse of ilk paroch to releave those of Coberspeth and Auldhamstoks on Sunday to remaine 48 houres till you send by turnes everic forty eight houres ane fourth part of each paroch to releive another fourth part, and everic fourth part as they come to bring the provision of victuals with them.

| THE PRESBITERIE OF DUMBARR. | Horses. | Quarter. | HADDINGTOUN PRESBITERIE. | |
|---|---|---|---|---|
| Auldhamstoks, | 250 | 60 | Norberwick, | 100 |
| Innerwick, | 250 | 60 | Dirltoun, | 200 |
| Coberspeth, | 150 | 40 | Elsinfoord, | 040 |
| Dumbarr, | 350 | 80 | Norhame [Morham], | 60 |
| Spott, | 040 | 10 | Barra, | 50 |
| Stentoun, | 040 | 10 | Boutin [Bolton], | 50 |
| Whittingtoun, | 100 | 25 | Heddingtoun, | 350 |
| Tinninghame, | 080 | 20 | Abberlady, | 80 |
| Whytekirk, | 040 | 10 | Trenent, | 300 |
| Prestonkirk, | 200 | 50 | Saltoune, | 100 |
| | — | — | Pencaitlen, | 100 |
| | 1500 | 365 | Humbie, | 150 |
| | | | Bothens, | 60 |
| | | | Garvitt [Garvald], | 50 |
| | | | | 1690 |

The same day ther came ane Petition from the towne of Dumfreis to my Lord Generall desyring that Colonel Munroe with his regiment might stay still there, which is heere answered.

'RIGHT HONORABLE AND LOVING FREINDS—We have receaved your letter and the petition of the toune of Dumfreis shewing your regraite of our sending for Colonell Munroes regiment, and desyring their returne to defend you against threatned invasion, and perfect your begunne work in Dumfreis for your defence, ye wold consider that seeing the Kings Mātie hes gathered together all his forces both of sea and land hither to march with ane royall armie through the heart of this country, for preservation of the whole we ar necessitat to conveane all the regiments even from everie particular shyre qlk hes their owne feares and dangers as Fyfe, Louthian, the west coast, and now from the north, because being divyded we can defend no part sufficiently bot wold losse all, bot being united and making head to the Kings maine forces, neither is it lykely they will sett on any other part lest it provoke our principall armie, and if they did invade any particular ye might defend yourselves for a tyme the best way ye could, and when ye ar overmastered stryve by all meanes to joyne yourselves to our armie, and we might soone repaire your losses; if the King prevaile heere none will be saife, if God make us to prevaile all may be safe and all losses soone repaired, especially seeing it is declared that whatsoever losse or præjudice any shyre or person shall sustaine in this cause præferring the welfare of the country to the safetie of their owne particular shall be repute and repaired by the whole kingdome as being the common interest and losse of all; and that ye may perceave sensibely that we ar not negligent of your particular interest, we have appointed the Earle of Galloway, the Lord Kirkcubright, the Lord Drumlandrick, the Lord Jhonstoun, James Crechtoun, Laird Lag, Campsfeild, Closeburne, and Aplegirth and remanent gentlemen to conveane ther whole forces and freinds in armes and to joyne together and ly at Dumfreis for defence of that country, against all plotts and invasion from the Erle of Nidsdaile or any other be his instigation and how soone the forces we expect from the rest of the Kingdome shortly shall come to the armie, and that we find ourselves of sufficient power to oppose the maine royall armie, upon the advertisement of your condition and danger we shall send (if then it be necessare) Colonel Monroes regiment or some other as steadable to you, and it may be moe as ye have adoe and we may spare ; in the meanetyme both ye will be carefull to have ane ey upon my Lord Nidsdailes wayes, and give proofe of your valour and affection for defence of your covenant with God which tyes you and us all simplie, and we shall have care to see that regiments charges defrayed to the towne of Dumfreis, and doe desyre you to defend the Minister of Carlaveroke from the violence of those who ar within the house, as also to gather your victuals into Dumfreis as your magazin for your intertainement ther.'

Upon Sunday the 2 June thir orders wer given :

To send out two or thrie out of everie regiment to the severall quarters of the country to asist the Commissars in taking up of victuall, baiking and brueing and sending it in to the generall proviant master that he may charge it in his bookes and distribute the same conforme to the proportions efter specified viz. to everie souldier two pound weght of aite bread in the day and twentie eight ounce of wheat bread and ane pynt of aile in the day, and what the sojours wints in one day shall be payd them so soone as it comes in to the magazin.

*Item* that ane list of the number of everie regiment be given to the generall proviant master that he may distribute the bread and drink accordingly to ane quartermaster in everie regiment, who shall keepe compt and give his note to the said generall proviant master.

*Item* that the souldiers bring back the towne barrels and puncheons, otherwyse they shall pay the triple of the pryce of them, and deliver them to the sayd proviant master at the place of the magazine.

The quarters of the countrie wher the regiments shall take paines are as followes, viz. : My Lord Lowdons regiment hes Tinninghame, Whytekirk, and Prestonkirk parochin.

The Erle Muntrose regiment hes North Berwick, Dirletoune, and Abberladdie.

The Earle of Rothes regiment and Lord Sinclares and Lord Montgomeries Prestonpans and Trenent.

The Erle of Dalhoussies regiment, Mussilburgh, Fisherraw, and Dalkeith.

The Lord Yester Saltoun, Humbie, Ormestoun, Pencaitland, Bothans, Barra, Garvitt, Norhame, Stentoun and Whittinghame.

The whole provision most be direct to the general proviant master and booked in his bookes.

To wryte in to Ed$^r$ to the Committee there and towne of Ed$^r$ for money to be sent to the armie with all haste, And in the meane tyme everie Colonell shall pay his whole regiment two shillings in the day everie man for fyfeteene days qlk most be repayed be the Commissars so soone as money comes in, or be the country in case the Commissars doe not pay it.

That everie Colonell or gentleman who hes charge of the horse troupes give up ane list of the number of everie troupe that they may be quartered and corne and straw provyded for them.

That everie horse troupe be appointed to carry their owne corne and straw from such places as the Commissars shall desyne.

It is thoght fitt that everie man give in his silver and gold work to the coine house to be striken in money for supplying of the present urgent necessity in entertaining the armie.

*Item* that Captaine George Phanles be adjoyned to the present M$^r$ Conzier to asist him in receaving the said silver work, weighing it and causing stryke it in money, and delivering it to the Commissars or to the Provest of Ed$^r$ or these whom the estates hes secured be bond and these who getts the said bond shall give their notes to the pairties who shall give in the said silver work for repayment so soone as they shall receave the same be vertue of the said band, or by any other way as may best be found out for payment therof from the saids estates.

*Item* that any who hes money to lend be dealt withall for it upon any kynd of securitie they please. And if they refuse, to be reputed as men careles of religion and liberties of the country and ther moneyes to be confiscate.

It is recommended to the Erle of Rothes that he represent to the Committee at Ed$^r$ and Provest and Bailzeis there the extreme necessity to have money answerd for payment of the armie, and therfor to use all possible meanes to lift it and coyne all silver work.

*Item* to appoint men to gett reports from the burghs anent the money they should lend to the comon cause with all diligence.

*Item* to advertise all noblemen, gentlemen and burgesse and others to send in their whole silver work to the coyne house with all expeditione.

*Item* whatever money is presently ready to cause send it out with all haste.

*Item* to cause send ane Comissare to Kelso with all haste for furnishing the regiments who are there, if spades and howes be not sent shortly we may smart for want of them.

The performance of all which is recommended to the Committee at Ed$^r$, who we hope will enact the same and sie it putt in executione without delay, for on it dependeth the keeping together or disbanding of the armie.

This day S$^r$ Jhon Stewart of Caudinghame came to Aytoun and Caudinghame to read the proclamation but could not gett the people gathered againe, therafter he came to Haymouth, railed upon the minister who had red in the kirk to the people the warning from the armie, and against the Laird of Wetherburne, tooke their dinner in the streete, drank their fill of wyne and aile without paying anything for it, brake ane honest man's head because he refused to bring them intelligence, threatned to returne and take all their victuals, to hang ther minister over the jockstooles if he did not preach for the proclamation.

Upon Munday the 3 of June the letters direct from my Lord Louthian the rest of the noblemen wer together at Kelso with Colonell Munroe wer answered they should stay together make the place fast against any horsmen; if the King's armie of foot did move towards them, they should not ingage themselves to be overmastered bot should march to be nearer to the rest of the armie, that my Lord Louthian should give orders whyle they wer together that regiments should march be turnes and that my Lord Louthian in all things should follow the advyce and Counsell of Colonell Munroe in all things who was a skild and experienced man; that, concerning the three cheife mutinires of Colonel Munroe's regiment whom they had declared be the sentence of the Counsell of warre to be worthy of death and had deferred the execution till the General's pleasure was knowne, The Generall declared by his Letters that they had proceided orderly thogh they wer worthy of death yet he had the solicitation of these noble men, he pardoned them for that tyme in hope that no such thing should fall out therafter by them or any other, besydes this the provision for their victuals was recommended to my Lord Louthian, my Lord Ker and the Shirreffe of Tividaile in the interim untill the Commissars came from Ed$^r$ and order was sent from thence for money to the sojours; it was told them what course was taken according to the order of the 2 of June.

This day we heard that some English gentlemen had offered and casten gold amongst the people of Dunse.

This day M$^r$ Alex$^r$ Henderson, M$^r$ David Dickson, M$^r$ Robert Meldrum [1] and M$^r$ Archibald Jhonston have bethoght and better bethoght the whole afternoone upon the present necessities of the armie the wants of money, munition, victual, order and discipline, the naturall impossibilities either to retire, remaine or goe on, the manifold perplexities of our intentions q$^n$ we ar at the borders; we wer forfoghten with the consideration heerof on the one part and yet considering the Lord's providence casting us in thir straites and his delivering us from the lyke befor, in a despaire of all the secondary causes we acknowledged ther was no way nor meane under heaven apparent to naturall reason to beare through, who did cast the cause the present straites and the saincts therin over upon God himself, wherupon M$^r$ David Dickson tooke instruments in my hand and attested befor God that whensoever God should give us a glorious outegate, none, even those that wer thoght to have the greatest hand in the work should or could claime any part of it, bot as now we ar emptie and annihilated all our wits and judgments and broght so low as to acknowledg ther was no appearance nor possibilitie under heaven, so heerafter we might more and more admire and adore his wonderfull manifestation of himself in building so high ane edifice upon so low ane fundation in bringing so great ane

---

[1] Meldrum was General Leslie's secretary.

ebb to so great a tyde, and drawing so great aboundance out of so great want. I pray God, and doe certainely expect in despyte of the devill and all our straites yet to have occasion really to give out ane extract of this instrument.[1]

The same day at night we heard that the English was come over to make ane trench betwixt Paxton and Huton a myle and ane halfe from Tweid neare unto Quhitteter, and that they had sent three thousand men the most part horse towards Kelso to plant their canon on the other syde of Tweid wherof we advertised the Erle of Louthian.

This night also we sent a party of two hundreth musketers and two hundreth horsemen to Caudinghame for to preveene Jhon Stewarts taking away of the victuals there bot they saw no body, as upon the Fryday at night befor a partie had gone out and broght in a hundreth bolles.

This night we receaved letters from my Lord Balmirrinoe shewing that my Lord Durie and my Lord Naper had beene in at the Commissionar but had gotten ane harsh answer that he would not leave his navie for such generell propositions, shewing also that my Lord Argyle was to be at Stirling with six hundreth men; with this letter he sent us the coppies of the letters following w^ch had past betwixt the King's Commissionar and Bruntiland.

### For Captaine Watsone

LOVING FREIND—Being commanded by his Maj/ to signifie unto the port Townes his grace and goodnes to all merchants, and seafaring men, yours being one of the principall I have sent my boat and this letter to them which I as his Maj/ High Commissioner doe require yow to see delivered unto them, that both you and they may see his tender care of yow which I hope wilbe so thankfulie receaved, as befitt obedient subjects which no man shall joy more in then your good freind

HAMILTOUN.

*From abord the Rainebow*
*in Leithroad the 1 Junii* 1639.

### For the Towne of Bruntiland

GOOD FREINDS—His Maj/ being full of compassion and

---

[1] See note p. 96.

tender care of his good and loving subjects of this kingdome and particularlie considering the great dammage w^ch all merchants and seamen suffer by their stopp of trade and hinderance of going out of their vessels, and not intending that his loyall subjects (such as he understands many of you ar) should be ruined for the fault of others Hath beene graciouslie pleased to command me to signifie his pleasure unto you and the rest of the port Townes that such of you as ar traffiqueris by sea (yeilding such obedience as is fitting for loyall subjects to his Maj/) should have free egresse and regresse in their trade, and to that effect shall have a passe port from me not to be molested by any of the King's fleet or officers, this I thoght good to lett you know, not doubting bot ye will joyfully accept of this his Maj/ grace, and redeim your selfs from that miserie w^ch by others disobedience you ar broght unto.—So I rest your good freind                HAMMILTOUN.

*From abord the Rainebow
in Leithroad, the* 1 *Junii* **1639.**


### *A Coppie of their Answer*

PLEASE YOUR GRACE—The proofe of his Maj/ royall favour to these of our trade, mentioned in the letter sent unto us by your Grace, can challenge no more from us then what is due from his most loyall subjects sensible of his fatherlie compassions over his auncient native people who doe heartily pray for his Maj/ prosperitie and happie reigne. Bot because the proposition concerneth not onlie these seafaring men indwellers in this Towne, bot all those of other port Townes in this kingdome, and hath annexed to it some conditiones which are so wrapped up in generals y^t they transcend our reach, We humblie begg your Graces favour to condescend more speccallie upon these conditiones required of us, and to grant us some short competent tyme for advysing therupon, that neither we may trench upon our oath to God and our covenant or be pressed with oathes contrarie to the lawes of our Kirk and Kingdome, nor yet ommitt any temporall duety of civile obedience which we most heartily will deferr to our Gracious

Soveraigne, wherin we humbly begg your Graces favor, which we shall recompense with our blessing and these best services which may proceid from

     your Graces humble servants.

Upon Tuesday 4 June my Lord Louthians letters to the Generall did shew that the Erle of Holland did come with ane number of horsemen and foot, y$^t$ upon their approach they drew out their regiments from Kelso and finding they wer lyke to have that resistance they did not expect from these in Kelso they retired in great disorder; while they wer neare one another ane Trumpetter came towards Colonell Munroe qr he was standing with his Regiment and cald that they had not obeyed the proclamation, who commanded to gett him back for the English had broken first; amongst other advertisements that had past that Monday befor, my Lord Louthian wrytes that notwithstanding any other information had been made, he beleived he should be forced soone either to retire to Jeddard or to join with the Generall if it wer possible, and together with this the Generall was informed from another hand that the English wer marched with fyfteen hundreth horse, four thousand foot, and ten peice of canon towards Kelso to repaire that affront they had gotten the day befor, upon this straite the Generall gave present order to my Lord Louthian that he should come and joyne with the rest of the armie at Dunse whether he intended to march that nyght, that in case of my Lord Louthians retiring to Jedburgh, w$^{ch}$ he did not expect because that had beene to make ther meiting more doubtfull and dangerous, yet in that case he should retire by the way of Lader, and this order was dispatcht in all haste upon Tuesday afternoone by my Lord Phleemings brother.

This fornoone befor we receaved Louthians letters M$^r$. Robert Meldrum and I being with my Lord Generall discoursed two houres upon the present difficulties and impossibilities wherwith the Generall was extreamly perplexed, was broght low befor God indeid, and acknowledged ther was no appearance of any naturall meane or ordinarie way either of our conveening or subsisting together remaining or retiring or going on for want of victuals, money and horses especially, and that we had no ground of confidence except in the providence of our God who had led us in thir straites and certainly contrare to all appearance was to lead us out of them, thus the Lord was emptying everic heart and annihilating everie spirit, for to prepare us as we hope to receave some greater subsequent blinks of his favour.

This afternoone we did wryte in to the Committee of Ed$^r$ and other shyres ane new letter.

Noble Lords and worthie Gentlemen—We found it necessarie to tell you that we ar to remove this night from this place toward Dunse, upon information of the march of the English forces, 4000 foot 1500 horses and ten peices of great ordinance, to Kelso this morning, upon the repulse they received yesternight there, And having told you so much we think not onlie your selves bot all others who shall heare and beleive what we ar now doing on both sydes, will easilie determine what is incumbent for you and them to doe in this extremitie: All possible advertisements have beene given already: The sword was drawne befor, now it is at the throat of religion and libertie if it have not given a deepe wound already; we might say, upon confidence of ane extraordinarie providence in this extraordinarie exigent, that God shall provyde, if the Lord had not putt power in our owne hands which might give a re-encounter to our enemies. Bot our unexcusable fault is that the power committed to us we have not used although we have sworne and subscryved to do it. It wold seeme that people ar either rewing what they have beene doing and will subject their necks to spirituall and bodily slaverie that they and their posterity may be desperatly miserable heere and for ever (which we ar loath to conceave) or that some Spirit of slumber hath overtaken and possessed them, which maketh them to think that the fyre is not kindled when the flame may be seene and all is in a burning: We can say no more bot we resolve under the conduct of our God, to whom we have sworne, to goe on without feare and in a lyvelie hope, if our countrie men and fellow covenanters equally obleiged with us shall either withdraw themselves, or come too late it may be to the burying of our bodies,[1] which with the cause itself might be safe by their speid horse and foot, Let them answer for it to God, to whose Grace commending both ourselves and you we continue,

Your loving freinds

*Dunglas* 4 *June* 1639.

Let coppies of this goe to all places with your advertisements

Upon Wedensday the 5 of June the armie marched from Dunglas, when the canon wer drawne over the passe, the armie was drawne up in the moore befor Allhamstoks, and after prayers said through all the regiments, some Troupes of horse four hundreth commanded musketers, four peice of small Canon wer sent out in a partie befor and the Generall went with them ; as he was upon his march he receaved word from my Lord Louthian that he was to obey the orders, that he hoped to be at Dunse that fornoone or die be the gate.

About one afternoone my Lord Generall came to Dunse and made Dunse Law his Leaguer wherunto the regiments of Kelso came also.

This day the Erle of Hume and Dumferling spake with the Erle of Mortoun, S$^r$ Patrik Hammiltoun and Mr. Adam Hebroun spake with the Erle of Haddingtoun, and about eight a clock Robin Leslie came to the Generall, all running to one purpose that we wold supplicat the King to appoint ane present conference betwixt some of the English and some of ours, and to intreat the English Councell and nobility to asist our Supplication.[2]

This day, as we had learned by the intercepting of my Lord Southasks letters, so by Mr. Borthrik from the

---

[1] 'We returned to our former resolution of present fighting; and sent posts athort all the countrey, to haste on our friends for that end. The last of our advertisements was so peremptor, inviteing to come to the buriall of these who were like to be deserted, that the hyperbolies of Meldrum, the Secretar, did offend manie.'—Baillie, i. 210.

[2] Baillie's account was somewhat different. He wrote that the fear of an attack by the Scots made the English army anxious to conclude a treaty. ' The way of the procedure was this : Robin Leslie one of the old pages, being come over to Dunce Castle, made, as it were, out of his own head, ane overture that we should be pleased yet to supplicate.'—*Letters,* i. 215.

Commissionar we heard that the King yet wold never quyte Bishops with limitation bot wold quyte his Crowne before he quyte them all.

Upon Thursday the 6 of June Robin Lesly returned in the morning to the Camp and urged the supplication wherupon we sent my Lord Dumferling with the supplication unto the Kings Ma$^{tie}$, and ane gentleman with ane letter to the Erle of Holland, the Nobility and Councell of England, for to asist the said Supplication.

*To the King's most Excellent Ma$^{tie}$ the Supplication of His Ma$^{tie's}$ Subjects of Scotland humbly Shewing—*

That wher the former meanes used by us have not beene effectuall for recovering your Ma$^{tie's}$ favour and the peace of this your Ma$^{tie's}$ native kingdome, we fall downe againe at your Ma$^{tie's}$ feete, most humbly supplicating that your Ma$^{tie}$ wold be graciously pleased to appoint some few of the many worthy men of your Ma$^{tie's}$ kingdome of England who ar well affected to the true Religion and to our common peace, To heare by some of us of the same disposition our humble desyres, and to make knowne to us your Ma$^{tei's}$ gracious pleasure, That as by the providence of God we ar joyned in one Iland under one King, so by your Ma$^{tie's}$ great wisdome and tender care all mistakings may be speedily removed, and the two Kingdomes may be keept in peace and happynes under your Ma$^{tie's}$ long and prosperous raigne, for which we shall never cease to pray as it becommeth your Ma$^{tie's}$ most humble subjects.

MOST NOBLE LORDS—Although we have beene labouring this long tyme past by our Supplications, Informations, and Missives to some of your Ll// to make knowne to his Ma$^{tie}$ and the whole Kingdome of England the loyalty and peacableness of our intentions and desyres and y$^t$ we never meant to deny unto his Ma// our dread Soveraigne and Native King any poynt of temporall and civile obedience, yet contrarie to our expectation and hopes, maters to this day growing worse and worse, both Kingdomes ar broght to this dangerous and deplorable condition wherin they now stand in the sight of the world.  In this Extremitie we have sent to his Maj/ our humble supplication (besyde which we know no other meane of pacification), and doe most earnestly entreat that it may be asisted by your Ll// that, if it be possible by a meeting in some convenient place of some pryme and well affected men to the reformed religion and our common peace, maters may be accomodate in a faire and peacable way and y$^t$ so speedily and with such expedition as that through further delayes, which we see not how they can be longer endured, our evils become not uncurable, We take God and the world to witnesse that we have left no meanes unassayed to give his Maj/ and the whole Kingdom of England all just satisfaction and that we desyre nothing but the preservation of our religion and lawes.  If the fearfull consequents shall ensue w$^{ch}$ must be very neare, except they be wysely and speedily prevented We trust they shall not be imputed unto us who till this tyme have beene following after peace and who doe in every ducty most ardently desyre to shew ourselves his Māties faithfull subjects and          Your Ll// humble servants.

My Lord Dumferling was broght into the Kings tent, gott ane kiss of his hand and after presenting the supplication was removed to another roume till the Councell of England had consulted with his Ma$^{tie}$ the space of three or foure houres, therafter was broght in againe, gott another kiss of the King's hand who declared that he had receaved no supplication of that kynd befor, and that he wold send his answer w$^t$ S$^r$ Edmond Vermar Knight Mershall of his house.[1]  Sir Edmond came to Dunse w$^t$ my Lord Dumferling this night and desyred that the noblemen might be conveened the morrow morning.

About eleven a clock at night upon some watcher shooting his muskett or pistole the alarm went through the whole armie and the whole souldiers in an instant with a wonderfull speed and resolution wer in armes and in order, some dancing, some singing psalmes.

---

[1] Sir Edmund Verney of Middle Claydon, co. Bucks, Marshal of the King's Palace (*Verney Papers*, Camden Club)—'A gentleman who was known to be a lover of our nation.—Baillie i. 215.

Upon Friday the 7 of June in the morning the whole noblemen and pryme Barrons being conveened about the Generall S$^r$ Edmond Vernar delivered his commission[1] by word and therafter shewed his memoer and warrant in wryte as followes: 'The King's Ma$^{tie}$ having redd and considered the humble supplication presented unto him by the Erle of Dumferling hath commanded me to returne this answer: "That Wheras his Maj/ hath published a gracious proclamation to all his subjects of Scotland, wherby he hath given them full assurance of the free enjoying both of the religion and lawes of that Kingdome, as lykewyse a free pardon upon their humble and duetifull obedience, which proclamation hath beene hitherto hindered to be published to most of his Ma$^{ties}$ said subjects, therfor his Ma$^{tie}$ requyres for the full information and satisfaction of them that the said proclamation be publicly redd; that being done his Maj/ will be graciously pleased to heare any humble supplication of his subjects."'

Wherunto the noblemen after sundrie reasonings to and fro gave ther direct answer, wherof he being desyrous to have some memorandums gott these that followes; and the Erle of Dumferling was sent away againe with the former supplication without any alteration except the addition of the word YET.

'His Ma/ proclamation which I desyred in his Ma/ name to be published was called for by the noblemen and others conveaned to here his Ma/ gracious desyre, and with all due reverence was redd and heard, unto which as I conceave these answers wer made:

'That they ar most willing in all humility to receave his Ma/ just commandement as becommeth loyall subjects, that the Estats being conveaned for holding the parliament called by his Ma$^{tie}$ had receaved from the Magistrats of the Towne of Ed$^r$ a coppy of this proclamation w$^{ch}$ his Ma/ High Commissionar had commanded them to publish; and the said Estats considering therof seriouslie, had returned ther reasons to his

---

[1] 'Upon theyr petition to the Kinge I was sent by his Majesty with a message to them, wherin, thoughe I had a hard parte to playe, yett I dare bouldly say I handled the business soe that I begatt this treaty.—Sir Edmund Verney to Ralph Verney.—*Verney Papers*, 249.

Ma/ Commissionar why it could not be published, which they doe conceave war represented to his Maj/ by his Commissionar and wherunto they still adhere.

'Ane of the reasones which I did heare from them was that this proclamation did not come in the ordinarie and legall way by his Maj. Councell, qch both is the law and hath beene the perpetuall custome of this kingdome as was acknowledged by the whole Councell since the beginning of this commotion in presence of his Maj/ Commissioner. It was remembered also that both his Ma$^{tie}$ Councell and Senatours of the Colledg of Justice being divers tymes since conveened had testified their dislyke therof.

'Another reason was that they found it to be most prejudiciall to his Ma/ honour whose desyre is to governe according to law.

'A third was, that it was destructive of all ther former proceidings as traiterous and rebellious which notwithstanding they maintain to be religious and loyall.

'A fourth was that wheras the meanest subject cannot be declared a traitour by proclamation, nor his estate forfault but after citation and conviction in parliament, or the Supreme Justice Court, yet heerin the whole body of the Kingdome, without any citation or conviction, are declared rebels and traitours, and ther estats disponed to their vassals and tennents.

'A fyfth was that they wer persuaded this did not flow from his Ma/ royall disposition, bot from men evill affected to the peace of the Kingdome, and that this was so farr from giving satisfaction to his Ma/ subjects that it so dissolved all the bonds of union betwixt his Ma/ and this his native Kingdome that ther could be no hope of accomodation of affaires therafter in a peacable way, which hath ever been ther desyre, and that they wer confident that his Ma; wold take to his royall consideration, how illegal in manners and prejudiciall in matters this is both to his Ma/ honour and the well of this Kingdome, and especially to the intended pacification. And that his Maj will now be pleased to send a gracious answer to ther humble Supplication sent by my Lord Dumferling.'

Upon Saturday the 8 of June my Lord Dumferling returned with this answer to our petition.

'*At his Ma/ Campe the eight of June* 1639

'His M/ having understood of the obedience of the Petitioners in reading his proclamation as was comanded them is graciously pleased so farr to condescend unto ther petition, as to admitt some of them to repaire to his M/ campe upon Munday next at 8 a clock in the morning at the Lord General's Tent; wher they shall find six persons of honour and trust appointed by his Ma/ to heare ther humble desyres.

'IHON COOKE.

And did shew us that in his judgment S$^r$ Edmond Vermar had not showne our memoers unto the Kings Ma/; we had long reasounings against the narrative of the answere and sent back againe my Lord Dumferling with sundrie copies of our memoers to be spred amongst the English Noblemen for clearing of ourselves y$^t$ we had neither published nor acknowledged the proclamation and w$^t$ the draught of ane safe conduct to those q$^m$ we should send.

'Wheras the subjects of our Kingdome of Scotland have humbly supplicated that we may be graciously pleased to appoint some of this our kingdome to heare, by such as shall be sent from them, ther humble desyres and to make knowne to them our gracious pleasure, unto which supplication we condescend so farr as to admit some of them to repaire to our campe upon Munday at eight houres in the morning and because they may apprehend danger in ther comming, abode or returning, we doe offer them upon the word of a Prince that the persons sent from them shall be safe and free from all trouble and restraint, wherof these shall be a sufficient warrant.'

This day we intercepted ane letter of the Marques of Hamiltons to my Lord Oggilvie.

'MY LORD,—Would God I had receaved your letter a few dayes sooner and then I wold have beene the messenger myself, for not having any hopes of a partie in those quarters I had sent 3500 of my best men to Barwick for a present desine that is intendet by his Ma/, so it will be now some dayes before these troupes returne to me. In the interim if ye cannot secure yourself wher ye ar, ye shall be welcome to me, Bot for the sending of any ships to you at this present I cannot, thogh shortly it may be you sie some in those quarters; I darr not write what I would for feare it should not come safe to your hands, only this, Rest assured that it will not be long before his Ma/ himself declare himself in that way w$^{ch}$ will not please the Covenanters, and power he hath to crubb their insolencies if they continue in them, your M$^r$ hath been such that you may expect that reward w$^{ch}$ a deserving servant and a loyall subject justly deserves and merits, q$^t$ I can contribute therto looke for it from your L/ faithfull freind and servant,

'HAMMILTOUN.'

Upon Sunday the 9 June my Lord Dumferling returned with ane refusal of a safe conduct unto us qrupon after long reasoning we resolved to send none bot sent back this answer:

'We trust his Ma$^{tie}$ will favorably construct this our humble requyring a safe conduct since upon our confidence in his gracious Ma/ we desyre no further bot assurance under his royall hand, albeit by the statutes of England w$^{ch}$ wer befor cited to the Lord of Dalzell all assurances and conducts ar declared to be null if they have not passed the Great Seale of England.

'The proclamation published throughout the paroch churches of England and these later sent to be published in Scotland, declaring us his Ma/ subjects to be rebells and our proceidings to be treacherous, forfaulting our estates and threatning to destroy us, lay a necessitie upon us, who desyre to cleare ourselves, to crave ane safe conduct of his Ma$^{tie}$.

'The former refusall of safe conduct to his Ma$^{ties}$ Councell and Session when they craved libertie to goe up to informe his Ma/ of the true estate of our bussines, and to ourselves when we desyred libertie to cleare our proceidings and intentions to his Ma/, showes the greater necessitie of our craving the same, for to give ane full and free information of our affaires.

'This refusing of ane safe conduct being knowne to the

armie maks them more unwilling then befor, that any should goe there.'

Upon Munday the 10 June the Erle of Dumferling broght back the former answer which was subscryved by Cooke, now subscryved by the King himself with ane verbal assurance of the King befor his Councell that he wold never wrong any that is sent, he wold rather quyte his Crowne and wer worse then ane infidell and ther armie might fall on them without mercie, and therupon delayed the meiting till Tuesday. We chused my Lord Rothes my Lord Loudon and the Shirreffe of Tividaile to go there to present our humble desyres q'rof we drew up this draught.

'*The humble desyres of his Ma$^{ties}$ subjects of Scotland*

'First, it is our humble desyre that his Ma$^{tie}$ wold be graciously pleased to assure us that the acts of the late assemblie at Glasgow shall be ratified by his Ma$^{tie}$ in the ensewing Parliament to be holden at Ed$^r$ July 23 since the peace of the kirk and kingdome cannot endure further prorogation.

'Secondly, That his Ma$^{tie}$ from his tender care of the preservation of our religion and lawes will be graciously pleased to declare and assure that it is his royall will that all maters ecclesiasticall be determined by the Assemblies of the Kirk, and maters civile by Parliament, which wil be for his Ma$^{ties}$ honor and keiping peace and order amongst the subjects in the time of his Ma$^{ties}$ personall absence.

'Thirdly that a blessed pacification may be speedlie broght about and his Ma$^{ties}$ subjects may be secured, our humble desyre is that his Ma/ ships and forces by land be recalled, that all persons ships and goods arrested may be restored, the losses which we have sustained by the stopping of our trade and negotiating be repaired and we made safe from violence and invasion, and that all excomunicate persons, all incendiaries and informers against the kingdome who have out of malice caused these commotions for ther owne private ends, may be returned to suffer ther deserved punishment, and the proclamations and manifestoes sent abroad by them under his Ma$^{ties}$ name to the dishonouring of the King and defaming of the Kingdome may be suppressed.

'As these ar our humble desyres, so is it our greife that his Ma^tie should have been provoked to wrath against us his most humble and loving subjects, and shall be our delight upon his Ma^tie's assurance of the preservation of our religion and lawes to give example to others of all civile and temporall obedience which can be requyred or expected of loyall subjects.'

This morning I gott ane sight of the Kings manifestoes[1] the most bitter invective false peice that can be against the whole proceidings and blasphemous against our covenant with God which God will revenge in his own tyme on the informers and wryters.

Upon Tuesday the 11 of June in the morning our Comissioners wer conveyed to the English camp wt ane hundredth horse and went to the Erle of Arundels[2] tent q^r q^n they had begunne to clear ther proceidings to the English Lords the King's Ma^tie himself came in without giving them ane kiss of his hands bade them proceid and told them he had come on suddenty because he was calumniated never to heare ther desyres, and q^n they begouth to justifie ymselves in ther proceidings, he had no will of that but bade them propone their desyres, my Lord Loudon in repetition of the state of the bussines justified all our proceidings and shew that all our desyres wer to enjoy our religion and liberties qrupon the King taking hold bade them tell ther desyres which they gave in as is befor said with only this alteration in generall termes of meanes of accomodation in stead of the reparation of losses and recalling of manifestoes which the King receaved dyted unto them this direction following.

That our desyres are only the enjoying of our religion and liberties according to the ecclesiasticall and civile lawes of this his Ma^ties Kingdome.

---

[1] 'A Large Declaration concerning the late tumults in Scotland from their first originalls: together with a particular deduction of the seditious practices of the Prime Leaders of the Covenanters, collected out of their owne foule Acts and Writings. BY THE KING.'
It was written for the King by Dr. Balcanqual, Dean of Durham.

[2] Thomas Lord Howard, Earl of Arundel and Surrey, premier Earl and Lord Marshal of England, was Commander-in-Chief under the King of the Royal Army. He was a Roman Catholic.

To cleare by sufficient grounds y$^t$ the particulars w$^{ch}$ we humbly crave ar such, and shall not insist to crave any poynt w$^h$ is not so warranted, and y$^t$ we humbly offer all civile and temporall obedience to his Ma/ w$^{ch}$ can be requyred or expected of loyall subjects.[1]

This day I had sent some memorandums both anent our desyres and anent y$^r$ cariage with my Lord Rothes and my Lord Loudon.

In generall to urge that this Kirk may be governed by generall and subordinate assemblies in all ecclesiasticall maters, and by Parliaments and other subordinate judicatories in maters civile under his Ma/ authoritie.

In speciall to desyre first that the late generall assemblie holden at Glasgow be approven in the next parliament, and all the generall printed acts therof ratified expreslie et specifice.

2. That all the censures of the late generall assemblie be followed with the civile punishments according to law, and all excomunicat persons may not only be declared Rebels, Bot also in respect of their obstinacie be banished his M/ dominions, and, in respect of their treason against this kirk their king and countrey, they may be punished exemplarie and extremelie.

3. For the stabilitie of maters of religion y$^t$ the King's Ma/ and Councell now declare and y$^r$after the Parliament, that the King and his Councell shall not heerafter meddle with any maters of religion in their proclamations (w$^{ch}$ hath beene the cause of all this combustion) bot leave the samine to the yearly generall assemblies, qlk for y$^t$ end must be holden without faile.

4. That as we tooke not up first armes and now hes them but only for our owne defence so not onlie they who threatned invasion most lay them first doune, Bot also both the King and the English must give us assurance that heerafter they will not invade or wrong us any maner of way.

5. That seeing the countrie, what by the treacheries of some of our owne nation stirring up the King and the English to this warr, what by the English navies stopping of all trade, is extremelie poverished, that if the Englishe refund not our losse suffered from them, yet y$^t$ the estats of papists and

---

[1] A full note of the first day's proceedings will be found in the *Hardwicke State Papers*, vol. ii. p. 130.

other traiterous incendiaries be disponed to the publick use, at leist that Bishopricks (the cause of all this trouble) be disponed to comon and pious uses for releife of the poore, maintenance of ministers and schollers and other such lyke publick uses.

6. That the only way both of preserving the Kings honour and for assuring the people of his reall intentions of peace is to punish ignominiouslie and exemplarlie those firebrands who by their misinformations hes broght him to this extremitie against his people, doe declare his former manifestoes and proclamations to have proceided from their misinformation And therfor to recall and repeale and punish the misinformers.

7. To render all persons, ships, goods and geare taken from us and to assure all those in England who have beene favourers to Christs cause in our hands and to restore them in safetie to ther families and estats, as also to declare $y^t$ none heerafter in England for their conformitie with us either in judgment or practise anent religion either in doctrine or discipline shall be troubled or molested, wherby Christs governement and puritie of worship will be enlarged.

8. That the King's Ma/ may show himself reconciled even to those whom he thoght by misinformation to be most rebellious, That the King's Ma/ being fullie assured that there is no intention to change his monarchicall governement, he will assure to heare and redresse the greivances of the countrie in parliament, And seeing in his owne absence by his under officers many disorders ar comitted, for remedie *stata parliamenta* once in two or three yeares be keiped.

9. That the King giving assurance now to doe thir or such lyke things in parliament and making some declaration in that kynd, both the armies may be dismissed, the castles put in some moderate mans hand in keiping till the parliament have ended all, and then the King with honour and safetie may come in a peacable way.

10. That heerafter the castles may be putt in the custodie of any the King and Estates shall name according to the old custome of this Kingdome.[1]

11. And because all mischeifes and abuses hes flowed (next

---

[1] See Introduction, p. 15.

unto the prelats) from the corruptions of Councell and Session, q$^r$in men are placed at everie courtiers desyre, only to serve the courts pleasure without regaird to kirk or kingdome, Therfor as it was of old y$^e$ Councellors and Sessioners be chosen by the Kings Ma/ and Estates *in statis parliamentis* and by themselves in the interim betwixt those.[1]

12. That no stranger lest of all any forraigne prelate meddle with the affaires of our Kirk, nor forraigne statesman with the affaires of our estate, bot that we may be governed by our owne church men and statesmen in lawfull judicatories ecclesiasticall and civile respective.

To remember first to cleare the mistaking of the English That ye have neither published nor acknowledged the proclamation, And if they ground their treatie upon that proclamation and your acknowledgment y$^r$of, to carrie yourself as becommes your cause and covenant for religion croune and country.

To present the printed Acts of the generall assemblie that the King's Ma/ may declare his resolution to ratifie the samine in the subsequent parl. specifice and expreslie.

To cleare the great mistaking of the English from their not considering the differences of our reformation *contradicente magistratu*, and of theirs by the Magistrats concurse, of ours restoring Christ unto his owne place, and of theirs changing *papam sed non papatum* seing they put the King in the Popes place, and from not considering the differences betwixt our assemblies and their convocations, betwixt our lawes and their statutes.

To show that this church is als free and als independent as any other and is no more lyable to give ane account of our actions to them nor they unto us, Yet of superabundance we offer them all satisfaction in reason.

To show that nationall commotions either in Church or State can only be tryed in nationall judicatories of kirk and kingdome, as in generall assemblies and parliaments, so that heere this bussines cannot be decided.

Let your discourse be ay relative to your former actions, as your supplica$^o$ns to his Ma$^{tie}$ informa$^o$ns and remonstrances

---

[1] See p. 15 of Introduction.

unto England, wherby may cleared your former actions and present intentions.

To show that no proclama°n can be a suretie to the Leiges, far lesse a proclama°n in generall termes of maintaining religion and law, seeing in the same proclama°ns the essentiall particulars of both, as your covenant, assemblie, abjura°n of Episcopacie, reception of ruling elders, defence of your selves ar condemned as irreligious and rebellious.

Take heede no wayes either to exclude the civile greivances of any other his Ma$^{ties}$ subjects, or shyres, who are neither heere nor hes given comisson for the particulars of a treatie, neither prelimitate the parliament, whose freedome in civile bussines should be preserved als well as the libertie of assemblies from prelimitation either of members or maters ecclesiasticall; desyre what ye will, but doe not exclude any other petitions.

Eschew all questions wherof the answere wold either be unpleasant to them or prejudiciall to us (as anent the King's negative voyce)[1] upon pretext y$^t$ they ar not in your comission, and y$^t$ the parliament can only judge such questions, bot whatsoever they propone to you tell ye must only heare and report and therfor in q$^t$soever overture they propone albeit it please your judgment at the first glance, neither declare unto them your approbation y$^r$of, neither ingadge your promise of your endeavour to obtain the samine, bot both keepe your owne mynd free from prejudice and leave that freedome to the rest

---

[1] This seems to have been an unsettled point. James VI., in a characteristic speech upon the question of Union with Scotland made on the adjournment of the English Parliament on 31st March 1607, explained how he cut that knot: ' It hath likewise beene objected as an other impediment, that in the Parliament ' of Scotland the King hath not a negative voice, but must passe all the Lawes ' agreed on by the Lords and Commons. . . . I can assure you, that the forme ' of Parliament there is nothing inclined to popularitie. . . . Onely such Bills as ' I allow of are put into the Chancellor's hands to bee propounded to the Parlia- ' ment, and none others; and if any man in Parliament speake of any other matter ' then is in this forme first allowed by me, The Chancellor tells him there is no such ' Bill allowed by the King. Besides, when they have passed them for Lawes, ' they are presented unto mee, and I, with my Scepter put into my hand by the ' Chancellor, must say, *I ratifie and approove all things done in this present* ' *Parliament*. And if there bee anything that I dislike, they rase it out before. ' If this may bee called a negative voyce, then I have one, I am sure, in that ' Parliament.'—*His Majesties Speech*, etc., 1607. London: Robert Barker.

of your number, that without partialitie the expediencie or inexpediencie of the overture may be agitate heere, and ye not be forced to plead heere for what ye have consented there, or to be offended q$^n$ it is refused. Insinuate to the English the substance of that remonstrance q$^{lk}$ ye have already prefaced in some articles to your owne shyres, and q$^{lk}$ ye intend to manifest to England at an up giving.

Remember whether warre or peace follow, your cariage in this act will be remarkable in historie, and let it never be said of you as yourselves hes many tymes said of some nobles in the land, and that when the[y] parlied anent the tithes and the revocation that everie one looked so to his owne particular accomodation of the King as everie one betrayed another and all betrayed the publick.

Upon Wednesday the 12 of June after ther reports we drew up the grounds of our desyres and appointed M$^r$ Alex$^r$ Henderson and Mr. Archibald Jhonston to ther former Comissioners to goe over to the King and with these grounds of our former desyres to seeke the totall abolition of Bishops both from Kirk and State both for benefites and office, after long reasoning betwixt my Lord Argyle and my Lord Durie S$^r$ Thomas Nicholson and me in law.

*Reasons and grounds of our humble desyres*

We did first humbly desyre a ratification of the acts of the late assemblie in the ensuing parliament, first because the civile power is keiper of both Tables and q$^r$as the kirk and kingdome are one body consisting of the same members, ther can be no firme peace nor stabilitie of order, unles the ministers of the kirk in their way presse the obedience of the civile lawes and magistrate, and the civile power add ther sanction and authoritie to the constitutions of the kirk. Secondly because the late generall assemblie indicted by his M/ was lawfully constitute in all the members y$^r$of according to the institutions and order prescryved by acts of former assemblies. Thirdly because no particular is enacted in the late assemblie, w$^{ch}$ is not grounded upon the acts of preceiding assemblies and is either expresly contained in them or by necessarie consequence may be deduced from them. That the parliament be keiped without proroga$^o$n his M/ knowes how necessarie it is, since the peace of the kirk and kingdome call for it without further delay.

We did secondly desyre that his Ma/ wold be pleased to declare and assure that it is his royall will that all maters ecclesiasticall be determined be the assemblies of the kirk, and maters civile by the Parliament and other inferiour judicatories established by law, because we know no other way for the preservation of our religion and lawes and because maters so different in ther nature ought to be treated respective in ther owne proper judicatories. It was also desyred that Parliaments might be holden at sett tymes as once in two or thrie yeares, by reason of his M/ p'sonall absence q$^{ch}$ hindereth his subjects in ther complaints and greivances to have immediate accesse unto his Ma/ presence.

And wher his M/ requyres us to limite our desyres to the enjoying of our religion and liberties according to the ecclesiasticall and civile lawes respective, we are heartily content to have the occasion to declare that we never intended further then the enjoying of our religion and liberties, and that all this tyme past it was farr from our thoghts or desyres to diminish the royall authoritie of our native King and dread Soveraigne or to make any invasion upon the Kingdome of England q$^{ch}$ ar the calumnies forged and spred against us by the malice of our adversaries and for which we humbly desyre that in his Ma/ justice they may have ther owne censure and punishment. Thirdly, we desyred a blessed pacification and did expresse the most readie and powerfull meanes q$^{ch}$ we could conceive for bringing the same speedily to passe, leaving other meanes serving for that end to his Ma/ royall consideration and greater wisdome.

Upon Thursday the 13 of June in the morning we went over to the English Camp, to the Lord Arundel's tent presented unto the King the grounds of our desyres. The Kings Ma/ craved y$^t$ my Lord Rothes wold condescend what petitions of the subjects were concealed from him as he had affirmed the day befor, qlk poynt the Marqueisse of Hamiltoun pressed hard for his exoneration. My lord Loudon remembered the petitions w$^{ch}$ wer refused by the Councell and y$^t$ no petitions wer formerly answered bot by way of proclamation. The King urged his proclama"n was satisfactorie, especially y$^t$ given to the Assemblie, wherupon I redd those passages of the protestation Decemb. 18 clearing y$^t$ it was no wayes satisfactorie, neither in maner or matter.[1]

The King's Ma/ proponed and urged y$^t$ no assemblie could meddle with y$^t$ w$^{ch}$ once was established by law, q'unto we gave many answers, especiallie y$^t$ as ane parliament could not make ecclesiastick constitutions originallie bot only added ane civile sanction therunto to give obedience to the ecclesiastick constitution, which being taken away cannot be obeyed, so that the ratificatorie act must fall *cum principali*, especiallie seing the parliament cannot judge, bot only the subsequent assemblie, whether the former assemblie was lawfull or not, and if the former be declared to have been null *ab initio*, the act of Parliament can no more subsist nor [*than*] if it had made an ecclesiastick constitution of itself, even as the parliaments confirmation of a false charter does fall when the charter is reduced or declared null.

Thereafter we fell under dispute of the independancie of the assemblie from the parl. in maters ecclesiasticall, as of the parl. from the assemblie in maters civile, with this difference only, that the King or parl. might call the assemblie, bot the assemblie could not call the parliament.

The King urged that no ecclesiastick constitution could have force till it was ratified in parl: We cleared y$^t$ it had ane ecclesiasticall force of the censure of the Kirk even to excommunication albeit not of civile punishments whilk behoved to be added by the civile law. Thereafter the King alleadged the passage *Soli Deo peccavi*, and y$^t$ the assemblie could not judge him, the Erle of Rothes answered y$^t$ if he wer king and had comitted David's fault y$^t$ the kirk might excomunicate him, bot that he knew the King's Ma/ wold never fall in such transgressions.

---

[1] See Protestation in Large Declaration, 387 *et seq.*

At this time we gave the king one of the Acts of Assemblie, one of the Remonstrances, and one of our answers to the declinatour.

The Marquess of Hamiltoun his declaration was produced and the Bishops declinatour, the one shewing that Bishops ar of apostolick Institution the other that they are of Christs Institution.

In this conference the king allowed his manifestoe and said $y^t$ it was against his will $y^t$ it was not published to the leiges. He declared also that nothing could be said against the Service booke of Scotland bot it behoved to reflect against $y^t$ of England for they wer all one, $y^t$ he had hand himself in the differences betwixt them,[1] $y^t$ he wold not suffer any to be punished albeit they had broght in the Alcoran.

Mr. Alex$^r$ Henderson told the king of three things $y^t$ stirred up the peoples hearts, first the pressing of such books so full of innovations of religione and superstitions. 2. Their hearing of the prelats and their adherents at home to mantaine in schooles and preach in pulpits many Armenian and popish tenets. 3. The reading of manyfold bookes printed in England *cum privilegio*, all full of poperie and Armenianisme.

The king fell on upon his authoritie to change all things $y^t$ wer not *de fide* as maters of discipline and government. Mr. Alexr. cleared $y^t$ albeit they wer not *de fide* as articles of the creede yet they wer *de fide* as *credenda* being warranted by the word of God, and as in fundamentall poynts *ignorantia in superfundamenta error in circafundamenta, obstinacia* against the light of the word is a great sinne,[2] and as my Lord Rothes instanced the denyall of David's cutting of Goliaths head and we shew $y^t$ by the booke of discipline and acts of assemblie the government of this kirk by pastors, doctors, elders, and deacons was grounded on Gods word and unchangable.

After that we wer removed a whyle the King's Ma/ gave us this generall answere:

---

[1] See note, p. 28 (Hamilton Library).

[2] This seems to have been a favourite subject with Henderson. He discussed it in answering Dr. Balcanqual at the Glasgow Assembly. See Peterkin's Records, 142: 'I thought the moderator took too much libertie to discourse (of that he professed had been his late studie) of poynts fundamentall and preter-fundamentall.' Baillie I. 140. See also Large Declaration, 274.

'That wheras his Ma/ the 11 of June received a short paper of the generall grounds and limites of ther humble desyres his Ma/ is graciously pleased to make this answere:

'That if their desyres be only the enjoying of their religion and libertie according to the ecclesiasticall and civile lawes of his Ma/ kingdome of Scotland, his M/ doth not only agree to the same, but shall alwayes protect them to the outermost of his power. And if they shall not insist upon anything but that w$^{ch}$ is so warranted, his Ma/ will most willingly and readily condescend therunto, So that in the meane tyme they pay unto him that civile and temporall obedience which can be justly requyred and expected of loyall subjects.

'*At his Ma/ Camp, the 13 of June* 1639.'

The king delayed his particular answers unto the particulars of our petition till Saturday.

He proposed three querees unto us and craved our present answer and therafter ane answere in wryte against Saturday. The first of the querees whether we acknowledge the Kings Ma$^{tie}$ to have the sole indiction of the Assemblies, we answered y$^t$ he had the indiction *cumulative sed non privative*, and answered the objections from the Act of Parl: 1612 according as it is in our printed reasons for a generall assemblie.

The second queeree was whether he had a negative voyce at assemblie, and we having cleared y$^t$ he had not, yea not so much as ane affirmative for 40 assemblies, he urged the voyce of his assessors, w$^{ch}$ we answered as in the protestation decemb. 18.[1]

The third querce was whether he had the power of raising the assemblie, w$^{ch}$ we answered as in the s$^d$ protestation.

Upon Friday the 14 of June we drew up an answer in write to the said querees, to be presented to the King the day following.

*Answer to the Querees*

The querees proponed by his M/ ar first whether his M/ hath the sole indiction of the Generall Assemblie, Secondly,

---

[1] Protestation and Large Declaration, 386-7.

whether his M/ hes a negative voyce in assemblies, The third, whether the assembly may sitt after his M/ by his authority hes discharged them to sitt.

To all which we answer first that it is proper for the generall assemblie itself to determine questions of this kynd, and it wer usurpation in us, which might bring upon us the just censure of the generall assemblie, to give out a determination.

2. The answering of one of those thrie demands is the answering of all, for if the sole indiction belong to his M/ there neideth no question about the negative voyce and dissolving of assemblies, next if his M/ hath a negative voyce there neideth no question anent the indiction and dissolving, and if his M/ may discharge the assembly their neids no question anent the other two.

For our parts we humbly acknowledg that the Kings Ma/ hath power to indict the assemblies of the Kirk, and when in his wisdome he thinks convenient he may use his authoritie in conveining assemblies of all sorts whether generall or particular. We acknowledg also that the solemne and publick indiction by way of proclamation and compulsion belongeth properly to the Magistrate and can neither be given to the Pope nor to any forraigne power, nor can it without usurpa°n be claimed by any of his Ma/ subjects. Bot we will never think that his M/ meanes that in the case of extreme or urgent necessitie the Kirk may not by her self conveine continue and give out her owne constitu°ns for the preservation of religion.

1. Because God hath given power to the Kirk to conveine, The Sonne of God hath promised his assistance to them being conveined, and the Christian Kirk hath in all ages used this as the ordinarie and necessarie meane for uniforme establishing of religion and pietie, and for removing the evils of heresie, scandals and others of that kynd which must be, and wold bring the Kirk to be no more, if by this powerful remedie they wer not cured and prevented.

2. According to this divyne right the Kirk of Scotland hath keiped her generall assemblies with a blessing from heaven, for while our assemblies continued in strength in the doctrine, the worship and discipline, the unitie and peace of the Kirk

continued in vigour, pietie and learning wer advanced and profanity and idlenes censured.

3. The Kirk of Scotland hath declared that all ecclesiasticall assemblies have power to conveine lawfully together for treating of things concerning the Kirk and pertaining to their charge and to appoint tymes and places to that effect.

4. The libertie of this Kirk for holding assemblies is also acknowledged by parliament and ratified by Acts therof, w[ch] is manifest by the Act of Parl. holden in anno 1592 and y[t] upon the ground of perpetuall reason.

5. Because there is no ground either by Act of Assemblie or parliament, or any preceiding practise, whether in the Christian Kirk of old or in our Kirk since the reformation, wherby the Kings Ma/ may dissolve the generall assemblie, or assume unto himself a negative voyce; bot upon the contrarie his M/ prerogative is declared by act of parliament to be no wayes prejudiciall to the priviledges and liberties which God hath granted to the spirituall office bearers of his Kirk which ar most frequently ratified in parliament and especiallie in the parliament last holden by his Ma[tie].

6. By this meane the whole frame of religion and Kirk jurisdiction shall depend absolutely upon the pleasure of the Prince, wheras his Ma/ hath declared by publick proclamation in England that the jurisdiction of Kirk men in their meitings and courts holden by them doe not flow from his Ma/ authoritie notwithstanding any act of parliament w[ch] hath beene made to the contrarie, bot from themselves and their owne power, and y[t] they hold ther courts and meitings in their owne name.

Upon Saturday the 15 of June we went over againe and received from the Kings Ma[tie] as the particular answer of our desyres the answere following:

'We having considered the papers and humble petitions presented to us by those of our subjects of Scotland who wer admitted to attend our pleasure in the camp, and after a full hearing by our self of all that they could say or alleadge therupon, having comunicated the same to our Councell of both Kingdomes, upon mature deliberation with their unanimous advyce, we have thoght fitt to give this just and gracious answere :

'That thogh we cannot condescend to ratifie and approve the acts of the pretended generall assembly at Glasgow, for the reasons contained in our severall proclamations, and for many other grave and weightie considerations which have hapened both befor and since, much importing the honour and securitie of that true monarchicall governement lineally descended upon us from so many of our ancestors, yet such is our gracious pleasure that notwithstanding the many disorders comitted of late, We are pleased not only to confirme and approve our comissioners declaration given under his hand, and by our command, in the pretended generall assemblie at Glasgow anent the way taking of the service booke, booke of Canons, high Comission, and dispensing with the five articles of Perth, and y$^t$ no other oath be administred to ministers at their admission then that which is prescribed by Act of Parliament, and that all and everie one of the present Bishops and their successors may be answerable and accordingly from tyme to tyme censurable according to their merits by the generall assemblie, bot also are further graciously pleased to declare and assure that according to the petitioners humble desyres all maters ecclesiasticall shall be determined by the Assemblies of the Kirk and maters civile by the Parliament and other inferior judicatories established by law which accordingly shalbe keept once a yeare or so oft as the affaires of the Kirk and Kingdome shall requyre. And for settling the present distractions of that our ancient Kingdome our will and pleasure is that a free generall assemblie be keept at Ed$^r$ the       day of          next ensuing wher we intend God willing to be personally present, and for the legall indiction wherof we have given order and command to our Councell, and therafter a parl. to be holden at Ed$^r$ the       day of       next ensuing for ratifying of what shalbe concluded in the said assemblie, and settling such other things as may conduce to the peace and good of our native Kingdome and therin ane act of pardon and oblivion to be passed.

'And wheras we are further humbly desyred that our ships and forces by land be recalled and all persons, goods and ships restored and they made safe from invasion, we are graciously pleased to declare That upon their disarming and disbanding of their forces, dissolving and discharging all their pretended Tables and Conventicles and restoring unto us all our Castles, forts and amunitions of all sorts as lykewyse our royall honours, and to everie one of our good subjects their libertie, lands, houses, goods and meanes whatsoever taken and detained from them since the late pretended generall assemblie, we will presently therafter recall our fleet, and retire our land forces, and cause restitution to be made to all persons of their ships, goods, detained and arrested since the fors$^d$ tyme, wherby it may appeare y$^t$ our intention in taking up of armes was no wayes for invading of our native Kingdome or to innovate the religion and lawes bot meerly for the maintaining and vindicating of our royall authoritie.

' And since that heerby it doth clearly appeare that we neither have nor doe intend any alteration in religion or lawes bot that both shalbe maintained by us in their full integritie, we expect the performance of that humble and ductifull obedience w$^{ch}$ becometh loyall and ductifull subjects and as in their severall petitions they have often professed.

' And as we have just reason to beleive that to our peacable and well affected subjects this wilbe satisfactorie, So we take God and the World to witnesse that whatsoever calamities shall ensue by our necessitated suppressing the insolencies of such as shall still continue in their disobedient courses, it is not occasioned by us bot by their own procurement.'

The king prefaced this answer with a declaration that was done with the unanimous advyce of both Councels, and albeit he might cleare some expressions he could change nothing of the mater.

After we had privately advysed, we objected against the narrative and against the conclusion whilk after long dispute the king would not change.

I urged that the kings declaring y$^t$ he could not approve the acts of the pretended generall assemblie at Glasgow for the reasons contained in his severall proclamations was a direct prelimitating of the subsequent assemblie, and a declaring y$^t$

if the subsequent assemblie wer constitute of elders, as the former was, and made the same Acts againe which wer made in the former y$^t$ then his Ma/ would either raise it or not ratifie it because these wer the reasons of his former proclamations. The king answered that the devill himself could not make a more uncharitable construction or give a more bitter expression.

When I urged y$^t$ the oath of ministers according to the Act of Parliament contained canonicall obedience to Bishops, and so did declare the kings judgment and prelimite the assemblie, the king commanded me silence, and said he would speake to more reasonable men; when yet I continued shewing his Ma/ y$^t$ I was sent for to speake, and urging y$^t$ clause anent the present Bishops and their successors censurable in their persons as presupponing the nullitie of our former excom̄unication and the perpetuitie of their office he com̄anded me againe silence, and said y$^t$ still when I spake I opened my mouth.

And the king urged us to take this proclama°n to the Camp and read it their; we assured him it wold not be acceptable except his Ma/ declared y$^t$ he would quyte Bishops, and finding him a litle in a good moode we fell all downe on our knees and craved the same most earnestly that the morrow being a Sabboth day might be a day of thanksgiving for we assured him y$^t$ as long as he keiped them up against our confession of faith and acts of Assemblie he wold never winne the hearts, nor keepe peace in this kingdome, bot if he would quyte them he would have the most obedient subjects in the world; and when we demanded what good newes he reported to the rest of our numbers he smiled and bade us assure them ther was good hopes of accom̄odation and that he did not deny q$^t$ we craved bot only delayed till Munday.

When we rose, he gave to everie one of us a kisse of his hand bidding me walk more circumspectly in tyme comming.[1]

Upon his saying he would send some to the Camp to see his declaration redd I went away and advertised them therof, who wer no wayes well pleased with his declara°n.

---

[1] 'The King was much delighted with Henderson's discourse, but not so much with Johnston's. . . . He likewise was the more enamoured with us, especialie with Henderson and Lowdoun.'—Baillie i. 217.

Upon Sunday the 16 of June at sermon both thanksgiving was made for the beginning and appearance of peace and prayer sent up to God for perfecting y$^r$of, and for moving further of the king's heart.

After sermon we drew up ane draught of the declara°n as would satisfie us wanting those things which did offend us.

'We having considered the papers and humble petitions presented unto us by those of our subjects of Scotland, who wer admitted to attend our pleasure in the Camp; and after a full hearing by our self of what was offered to our royall consideration by them, having communicated the same to our Councell of both kingdomes, upon mature deliberation with their unanimous advyce, we have thoght fitt to give this just and gracious answere :

'That it is our gracious pleasure to declare and assure That according to the petitioners humble desyres all maters ecclesiasticall shalbe determined by the generall assemblie and other inferiour assemblies of the kirk, which generall assemblie shall be keiped once a yeare and oftner as the affaires of the kirk shall requyre and maters civile by the parliament and other inferiour judicatories established by law, And the parliament to be called once in three yeares or oftner as the affaires of the kingdome shall require.

'And for setling the present distractions of that our ancient kingdome our will and pleasure is that a generall assemblie be indicted and keiped at Ed$^r$, the    day of    next ensuing, wher we intend God willing to be personally present, which according to the order of that kirk shall be lawfullie constitute of ministers and elders having comission from ther severall presbiteries and burrowes and shall be free both in the maters to be treated as doctrine, worship, sacraments, government and jurisdiction of the kirk, the places and power of kirkmen and all other maters proper for a generall assemblie, as lykewyse in the maner of proceiding and in the tyme and dayes of ther sitting till maters be broght to a conclusion. And for the tymous indiction of the said intended assemblie, we have given order and command to our Councell as also it is our will and pleasure that therafter a parliament be holden at Ed$^r$ the    day of    next ensuing for ratifying of q$^t$ shall be concluded in the said assemblie and setling such other things as may conduce to the peace and good of our native kingdome, and therin ane act of oblivion to be passed.

'And since that therby it doth clearly appeare that we neither have nor doe intend any alteration in religion or lawes bot that both shall be mantained by us in ther full integritie, we expect the performance of that humble and duetifull obedience w$^{ch}$ becommeth loyall and ductifull subjects and as in their severall petitions they have often professed.'

Upon the Munday 17 of June having returned to the Camp we shew his M/ that they wer no wayes satisfied with it except his Ma$^{tie}$ declared that he should be content to quyte Bishops if the subsequent assemblie did condemne them againe, and y$^t$ he expressed in his declaration the fredome of the assemblie in the constitution or members y$^r$of, in the maters and maner of proceiding and therupon gave him the forsaid draught w$^{ch}$ the king would not use bot adhere to his owne draught, and told y$^t$ as for episcopacie he wold not prelimite his voyce, bade us propone our objections. We insisted long as befor against the two clauses of the narrative and conclusion w$^{ch}$ all the fornoone he refused to change.

When we insisted upon the expressing the friedome of the assemblie, and of his consenting to whatsoever they should determine, he wrote downe thir two lynes (we shall give way to the determinations of the generall Assemblie w$^{ch}$ we shall find agreeable to the lawes of Kirk and State). This we refused as importing both his negative voyce and y$^t$ the assemblie might not meddle with episcopacie or any other thing the king alleadged was established by law.

This fornoone at two severall tymes q$^n$ I begouth to speake the king absolutely commanded me silence.

When we urged y$^t$ the clause anent yearly generall assemblies or so often as the affaires of the kirk required may be changed that absolutely we should have yearly generall assemblies and oftener as the affaires required, The king went to a privat avisandum with both the Scots and English Councell wher through the tent we heard the Marqueis of Hamiltoun affirme y$^t$ if he consented to yearly generall assemblies he might quyte his three crounes for they wold trample over them all, and if he would follow his way he should free the assemblie of ruling elders, and if the assemblie wer constitute onlie of ministers he would paune his lyfe, honor and estate to gett his Bishops therin established and any other thing he wold desyre. We heard the Lord Chamerlaine say that this was the true state of the question, whether the two kingdomes should presently yock and by their yocking the king hasard the losse of both.

When we wer called in the clause was conceived $y^t$ we should have yearly generall assemblies and oftner, the affaires of the kirk and kingdome so requiring, wherof when some of us had conceived the sophistrie and demanded if the last words was relative to both termes of yearly assemblies and of oftner, and so whether we should want yearly assemblies if the king judged the affaires of the kirk not to require, The king shew then $y^t$ he would not grant it bot putt it over to the generall assemblie.

After dinner we renewed our objections against the two clauses qlk wer remitted till we had ended the articles of pacification qlk imediately one after one wer condescended upon having reasoned $y^t$ our meitings wer warrantable according to King James' maxime, *pro aris focis et patre patriæ*.

The King having gotten his will in all the articles at the last he condescended to hold out those words, 'for the reasons contained in his former proclamations,' and instead of expressing his whole declaration given in to the assemblie to confirme in generall 'what his Comissioner had promised in his name.'

And albeit he had once condescended to hold out the conclusion, yet fra once the Scots Councellors came in he would no wayes condescend, bot as for the legall indiction of the assemblie, after he was told $y^t$ if Bishops wer warned it wold be protested against he remitted it to the Councell, q$^r$upon the Marqueis of Hamiltoun and my Lord Treasurer declared $y^t$ they would call in generall termes all parties necessarie.

Upon Tuesday the 18 of June in the morning amongst ourselves when we wer advysing anent the declara$^o$n and articles of pacifica$^o$n we resolved upon an act amongst ourselves to declare our not passing from the assemblie w^ch the king professed he desyred not of us, even as he desyred us not to urge him to ratifie it, and wlk we required our Comissioners to intimate to the king.

*Information against all mistaking of his Ma/ declaration.*

Lest his Ma/ declaration of the date 15 June containing an answer to our humble desyres presented by our Comissioners should be eather mistaken by the well affected or willfully misconstrued by the malicious, q^rby his Ma/ justice and goodnes may be concealed, or his Ma/ good subjects may appeare to have done or admitted any poynt contrarie to their solemne oath and covenant The Generall, Noblemen, Barrons, Burgesses, ministers and officers conveined at Dunse before the dissolving of the armie have thoght necessarie to putt in wryte q^t was related to them by their Commissioners from his Ma/, to witt that as his Ma/ declared that he could not acknowledg nor approve the late generall assemblie holden at Glasgow, for which cause it is called in his Ma/ declaration *a pretended assemblie*, So was it not his Ma/ mynd y^t any of the petitioners by their acceptance of the said declaration should be thoght to disapprove or part from the same or condemne their owne proceidings as disorders and disobedient courses, and therfor as they doe intreat all his Ma/ good subjects with most submissive and heartie thanksgiving to acknowledg and confesse his Ma/ favour in indicting a frie assembly to be keiped August 6 and a parliament August 20 for ratifying of what shall be concluded in the assemblie, as the proper and most powerfull meanes to setle this kirk and kingdome, so wold they have all his Ma/ subjects to know that by accepting the said declaration and articles of pacification joyned therwith, they doe not in any sort or degree disclaime or disavow the said assemblie Bot that they still stand obleiged to adhere y^runto, and to obey and mantaine the same, and for preventing all mistaking and misconstruction that so much be made knowne to all persons and in all places wher his Ma/ declaration shalbe published, which as it is his Ma/ owne mynd expressed diverse tymes to our Comissioners, so are we assured that it will serve much for his Ma/ honour, for the satisfaction of the godly, and for the promoting of this blessed pacification, for which all of us ought earnestly to pray to God, to remember also our late oath and covenant, and to walk worthie of it, and to beseich the Lord that, by the approaching assemblie and parliament, religion and rightcousnes may be established in the land.

Afternoone we went to the king in his owne tent wher the king superscryved the declaration, made his secretaries and our Comissionars to subscryve the articles of pacification, and made our Commissioners subscryve two lynes following:

'We having considered the papers and humble petitions presented to us by those of our subjects of Scotland who wer admitted to attend our pleasure in the Camp, and after a full hearing by our self of all that they could say or alleadg y$^r$-upon, having communicated the same to our Councell of both kingdomes, upon mature deliberation with their unanimous advyce, we have thoght fitt to give this just and gracious answere:

'That thogh we cannot condescend to ratifie and approve the acts of the pretended generall assembly at Glasgow, for many grave and weightie considerations which have hapned both befor and since, much importing the honour and securitie of that true monarchicall governement lineallie descended upon us from so many of our ancestors, yet such is our gracious pleasure that notwithstanding the many disorders committed of late, We are pleased not only to confirme and make good q'soever our Commissioner hath granted or promised in our name, bot also ar further graciously pleased to declare and assure that according to the petitioners humble desyres all maters ecclesiasticall shall be determined by the assemblies of the kirk and maters civile by the parliament and other inferiour judicatories established by law which assembly accordingly shall be keipt once a yeare or as shall be agreed upon at the generall assemblie.

'And for setling the present distractions of that our ancient kingdome our will and pleasure is that a frie generall assemblie be keipt at Ed$^r$ the sixth day of August next ensuing wher we intend (God willing) to be personally present, and for the legall indiction wherof we have given order and command to our Councell, and therafter a parliament to be holden at Ed$^r$ the twentieth day of August next ensuing for ratifying of q$^t$ shall be concluded in the said assembly, and setling such other things as may conduce to the peace and good of our native kingdome, and therin an act of oblivion to be passed.

'And wheras we are further humbly desyred that our ships and forces by land be recalled and all persons, goods and ships restored, and they made safe from invasion, we are graciously pleased to declare that upon their disarming and disbanding of their forces, dissolving and discharging all their pretended Tables and Conventicles and restoring unto us all our Castles, forts and amunitions of all sorts as lykwise our royall honours, and to everie one of our good subjects their libertie, lands, houses, goods and meanes q$^t$soever taken and detained from them since the late pretended assemblie, we will presently therafter recall our fleet, and retire our land forces, and cause restitution to be made to all persons of their ships and goods detained and arrested since the aforsaid tyme, wherby it may appeare that our intention in taking up of armes was no wayes for invading of our native Kingdome, or to innovate the religion and Lawes, but meerly for the mantaining and vindicating of our royall authoritie.

'And since heirby it doth clearly appeare that we neither have nor doe intend any alteration in Religion or Lawes, bot that both shall be mantained by us in their full integritie, we expect the performance of that humble and duetifull obedience which becommeth Loyall and duetifull subjects, and as in their severall petitions they have often professed.

'And as we have just reason to beleive that to our peacable and well affected subjects this will be satisfactorie, So we take God and the World to witness that whatsoever calamities shall ensue by our necessitated suppressing the insolencies of such as shall still continue in their disobedient courses, it is not occasioned by us bot by their owne procurement.

'1. The forces of Scotland to be disbanded and dissolved within fourtie eight houres after the publication of his Ma$^/$ declaration being agreed upon.

'2. His Ma$^/$ Castles, forts and amunitions of all sorts, and

royall honour to be delivered after the said publication, so
soone as his Ma/ can send to receive them.

'3. His Ma/ ships to depart presently after the deliverie of
the Castles and with the first faire wind And in the meane
tyme no interruption of trade or fishing.

'4. His Ma/ is graciouslie pleased to cause to be restored all
persons goods and ships detained or arrested since the first of
februar last bypast.

'5. Ther shall be no meitings, treatings, convocations or
consultations of our Leiges, Bot such as ar warrantable by Act
of Parliament.

'6. All fortifications to desist and no further working
y$^r$on and they to be remitted to his Ma/ pleasure.

'7. To restore to everie one of our good subjects their
libertie, lands, houses goods and meanes q$^t$soever detained from
them by q$^t$soever meanes since the aforsaid tyme.'

This day also the king refused to come and see our armie
mustered as he had condescended the day before.

He condescended that the fortifications of Leith should be
disponed by the towne of Ed$^r$ at their pleasure, and to write
a letter to the said towne for preparing a place to the
assemblie.

Upon Wednesday the 19 of June we had sundrie disputs
anent our making or not making our declaration q$^n$ the king
published his.

We wrote letters to the Erle of Montrose as the king did
to my lord of Boyne y$^t$ we advertising them how all maters
wer setled in peace and desyring them *hinc et inde* to abstaine
from violence and hostilitie.

Lykwyse we wrote to the Lord Kirkcubright to loose his
Seige on the Kings Castle of Threve.

Upon Thursday the 20 of June we sent to the King the
Erle of Rothes and Lord Loudoun to remonstrate against the
keiping of any garizons at Barwick or fortifying of the Castle
of Ed$^r$ whilk breed great jealousie in the mynds of the people,
as also to shew unto the English lords those conditions qlk
had past in word betwixt the King and us with our modest

information against mistaking and to give an coppie of both unto sundrie of them qlk indeid my lord Chamerlaine and my Lord Holland after they had all acknowledged the truth therof and professed themselves fully cleared of the calumnies spred against us and y$^t$ they should not be so readie to come against us in tyme coming, bot craved to be advertised from our selves of all that passed heere.

'Some heads of his Ma/ treatie with his subjects in Scotland befor the English nobilitie ar sett downe heire for remembrance.

'1. For the preface and conclusion of his Ma/ last declaration althogh it contained hard expressions of the subjects in Scotland yet his Ma/ declared y$^t$ he had no such opinion of them but required the paper to stand for his credite and for a point of honour with forraigne nations, and required they should not stand with him for words and expressions so they obtained the mater.

'2. For calling of the late Assemblie pretended Seing the subjects of Scotland professed they wold never passe from the said assemblie and decrees therof, His M/ professed he did not acknowledg y$^t$ assemblie further then as it had registrate his declaration so wold he not desire the subjects to passe from the samine.

'3. Concerning the constitution of the Assemblie, It was showne his Ma/ that none could be members of the assemblie bot such as had a Comission, viz., two or thrie Ministers from everie presbiterie with a ruling elder, one from each burgh and universitie and his Ma/ Comissionar, his Ma/ contended that his assessors had vote, and upon an expression in his Ma/ declaration that referred to some reason contained in former proclamations, which wer totallie against the lawfulnes of ruling elders, It was desired y$^t$ according to the custome of this Kirk all controversies arysing should be remitted to the assemblie itself. His Ma/ had some expressions craving these to be remitted to himself, Bot being told y$^t$ it was against the constitutions of the Kirk to have any other judge bot the voyces of the assemblie wher his Ma/ or his Comissioner should be present and give the first voyce, It was concluded that the word *frie assemblie* in his Ma/ declaration did import the freedome in judging all questions arysing ther concerning constitution, members, or mater.

'4. Concerning the restitution of the Castles, as the subjects did it freelie, so did they expresse $y^t$ $w^{ch}$ might concerne the safetie of the countrie, they referred that to the tyme of the parliament, at which tyme they should signifie their desires by petition to his Ma/. As also they told it had cost much charges in fortifying and keiping therof, the representation $q^r$of to his Ma/ they referred to that tyme.

'5. Concerning the restitution of persons, houses and goods required by his Ma/, It was promised provyding the great sowmes contracted for the publick wer repayed in an equall way by all which behoved to be done either by commission from his Ma/ or by parliament; and when it was objected that much goods wer alreadie spent, the King answered that as for goods or ammunition that was spent they could not be restored bot those that ar extant must be.

'6. His Ma/ not allowing of the late assemblie for the reasons contained in his severall proclamations being excepted against as a declaration of his Ma/ judgment against ruling elders $w^{ch}$ prejudged the right constitution of a frie assemblie, his Ma/ after full hearing deleted $y^t$ clause.

'7. That part of his Ma/ declaration which beares $y^t$ no other oath be exacted of Intrants then that which is contained in the Act of Parliament, as also $y^t$ clause bearing that the pretendit Bishops, etc., shalbe censurable be the generall assemblie, being excepted against as presupposing and importing the continuance of episcopacie $w^{ch}$ we could not acknowledg as being incompatible with the confession of faith and constitution of the Kirk, his Ma/ was pleased to delete both those clauses.

'8. And it being with all instancie and humilitie prest Saturday June 15 That his Ma/ wold satisfie that maine desire of the subjects by declaring that his Ma/ wold quyte episcopacie, did answere that it was not soght in our desires, and $q^n$ it was replyed that our first desyre to have the acts of the Generall Assemblie ratified imported the same, His Ma/ acknowledged it to be so and averred that he did not refuse

it bot wold advyse till Munday the 17, at which tyme his
Ma/ being prest to give some signification of his quyting
Episcopacie, and it being plainly showne to his Ma/ that if he
wold labour to mantain Episcopacie it wold breid a miserable
schisme in this Kirk, and make such a rupture and division in
this Kingdome as wold prove uncurable and if his Ma wold
lett the Kirk and countriej be freed of them, his Ma/ wold receave als heartie and duetifull obedience as ever Prince received
of a people, his Ma/ answered that he could not prelimite
and forstall his voyce but had appointed a frie assemblie
which might judge of all ecclesiasticall maters, the constitutions q$^r$of he promised to ratifie in the ensuing parliament.'

The same morning after y$^t$ the armie wer dismissed to goe
to Dunglas the Erles of Mortoun and Kinnoule came to
publish the King's declaration.

We had a long dispute if either *verbo* or *scripto* we should
testifie our accepting therof to be not passing from the assemblie,
at length the Erle of Cassils was appointed who after the Kings
declara$^{en}$ was redd befor Colonel Munroes regiment declared y$^t$
we adhered to the assemblie and offered our information against
mistakings unto the herauld in testimonie of our adherance
therto, wherunto all the people applauded y$^t$ they did adhere
to the assemblie, and bade hang the Bishops.

This night we came to Dunglas and heard from my Lord
Rothes y$^t$ generall Rivan was to be made Captaine of the
Castle of Ed$^r$, and that the English men themselves dealt for
to have a garizon in Barwick and Carleel wherat sundrie was
offended, because they had been informed on the Tuesday
befor that the King continued all his intentions for the
establishing of Bishops, and they thoght thir wer meanes used
for y$^t$ end.

Upon Friday the 21 of June we came to Ed$^r$ wher we found
many greived with our proceidings.

We heard from the North how the Erle of Muntrose having
but twelve hundreth men at Stonehyve had derouted after the
shott of some canon my Lord Boine and Colonell Gunne and
five and twentie hundreth men with them who wer affrighted

by a barrell of powder blowing up some of them and blindfolding others, and so he chased them back to Aberdeine.

Upon Saturday the 22 of June afternoone the Castle of Ed$^r$ was redelivered with the honours and the Marqueis of Huntlie unto the Marqueis of Hamiltoun and to Generall Rivan, after sundrie shott of Canon off the Castle and off the fleet.

Upon Munday the 24 of June befornoone after the Lyon had redd the King's declaration, The Lord Lindsay in name of the Noblemen Barons Ministers and Burgesses, q$^r$of many wer upon the crosse with him declared that our acceptance therof was without prejudice to our generall assemblie wherfra the King did not desyre us to passe and q$^r$unto we do constantly adhere according to our oath' and offered unto the Lyon a coppie of our informa°n against mistakings in token therof, wherupon Mr. Harie Rollock tooke Instruments in my hands.[1]

This day we heard from the Erle of Muntrose y$^t$ he had sundrie skirmishes at the Bridge of Die, and after sundrie wer killed and hurt had taken the same and gone into Aberdeine wher his receiving of the King's lr̄es and of ours anent the peace made him stay his persute.

This day it was ordained that conforme to this ordnance, as the Erle of Cassils in the Camp the Lord Lindsay on the Crosse of Ed$^r$, so in everie burgh after the King's declaration is proclaimed, some noblemen or gentlemen in name of all the rest should give heartie thanks to his Ma$^{.}$ for his favour, bot withall declare by word that this baire acceptance of this declaration shall no wayes be prejudiciall to the late generall assemblie holden at Glasgow, q$^r$fra the King's Ma/ did not

---

[1] To ask instruments seems a more correct expression than to take instruments. 'Instruments' are the formal and duly authenticated narrative by a Notary Public of *res gestæ* of which a person interested desires to preserve a record. The practice of taking instruments is now confined for the most part to Church Courts in Scotland, as in the case where a member, who protests against a resolution of the majority of the Court, wishes to preserve evidence of his protest by obtaining from the clerk of the Court an authoritative extract of the Court's minute embodying it. He 'takes instruments' by handing to the clerk a coin (usually a shilling), in token probably of his readiness to pay the cost of the extract of the minute which he asks the Court to grant him.

desire us to passe, and q'unto we doe constantly adhere according to our oath, and therupon offer the coppie of the above written information to the Herauld.

Upon Tuesday the 25 of June we sent away my Lord Loudoun with some instructions to the King's Ma^tie as follows :
[Here the diary of 1639 ends abruptly. What follows seems to refer to the next year, 1640.]

To remember—the Lord Generall his Excellencie came out of Edg^r towards the armie upon the 25 of July the Leivetennant Generall upon the 30 of July. The armie was lying in Choulslie wood full of all sort of vans of meitt, drink, money, horsemen, baggage horse, canone horse etc.

Upon the 3 of August at a frequent meitting of the Comittie Nobilitie Barrones and officers of the armie after prayer and reassoneing our voyage to England was unanimouslie resolved, and the intentiones of the army redd approvine and divulget and some sent away both for intelligence and spreading of same. The tennor of the lr̄e followis :

Upon the 5 of August My Lord Balmerinoch and Lord Naper was sent to Lauthiane to hasten up the canone horse and that night was the busines anent the Comission of Perth

Upon the 6 of August Sir Harie Gib came to Dunse.

Upon the 7 of August the Erle of Rothes Lord Loudoun Jo^n Smyth and Mr. Ar^d Jonstoun was sent to Edg^r for to find out the wayes of getting of money and provyding of tents to the souldears, both qlk seemed unpossible for the tyme.

Upon the 8 they mett with the baillies of Edg^r and sent the elders and the deacons through the bruche, who on that day and Monoday following gottine thrie thousand pair of scheits to the souldears tents.

Upon Sunday 9 of August thair was keiped ane solemne fast

throw the haill army and in the City of Edg$^r$ qlk did contribute much to furder the money and tents.

Upon Monoday the 10 of August all the neighbours being solemnely conveined in the parliat house of Edg$^r$, after prayer and exhortatione they offere willinglie so many particular sums as amounted to ane hundredth thousand punds. This is Gods work and wonderfull in our eyes qlk requires remembrance, thankfulness, and dependence on God in new difficulties.

This day the Erle of Argyle returned to Edg$^r$ and the Erle of Rothes to the Camp wheron the haill army was mustered and sworne to the military Articles, to the great contentment of the generall officeris.

PAPERS RELATIVE TO THE

PRESERVATION OF THE

# HONOURS OF SCOTLAND

IN DUNNOTTAR CASTLE

1651-52

Edited, with Introduction and Notes, by
CHARLES R. A. HOWDEN, M.A.,
F.S.A. Scot., Advocate.

# CONTENTS

| | PAGE |
|---|---|
| ANE TRUE ACCOMPT OF THE PRESERVATION OF THE HONORS, | 112 |
| LETTER FROM GEORGE OGILVIE OF BARRAS TO THE COUNTESS OF MARISCHAL, | 118 |
| LETTER FROM THE COUNTESS OF MARISCHAL TO CHARLES THE SECOND, | 121 |
| LETTER FROM WILLIAM OGILVIE TO HIS FATHER, GEORGE OGILVIE OF BARRAS, | 123 |
| MR. JAMES GRAINGER, HIS DECLARATION ANENT THE HONORS, | 125 |
| BARRESS ALLEDGANCES ANSRED 8 NOVEMBER 1660, | 126 |
| LETTER FROM THE MINISTER OF KINNEFF TO THE COUNTESS OF MARISCHAL, | 131 |
| SIGNATURE FOR THE PATENT OF KNIGHT MARISCHAL TO JOHN KEITH, | 132 |
| LETTER FROM CHARLES II. TO THE EARL OF MIDDLETON, | 134 |
| MEMORIAL FOR THE EARL OF KINTORE, | 134 |

# INTRODUCTION

For permission to publish the following papers, the Society is indebted to the courtesy of the Earl of Kintore, whose property they are. They deal with a controversy which created some stir in Scotland in the year 1702. In that year, proceedings were taken before the Privy Council by John Keith, first Earl of Kintore, against Sir William Ogilvie of Barras and his son, in respect of a pamphlet published by them in 1701, entitled 'A True Account of the Preservation of the Regalia of 'Scotland, viz. Crown, Sword, and Scepter, From falling into the 'Hands of the English Usurpers, be Sir George Ogilvie of 'Barras, Kt. and Barronet.' This pamphlet was published as a reply to the account of the preservation of the Honours given in Nisbet's *Heraldry*, and its purpose was to show that scant justice had been done to Sir George Ogilvie, and that the chief share of credit and reward had been given to the Earl of Kintore and his mother, the Dowager Countess Marischal. Ogilvie's pamphlet, together with a number of letters relating to the siege of Dunnottar in 1651-52, and the Act and Decreet of the Privy Council in 1702, was published by the Bannatyne Club in their volume of *Papers relative to the Regalia of Scotland*, issued in 1829. The compilers of that volume, however, seem to have had access chiefly to papers upon Ogilvie's side of the controversy. The papers which are now published for the first time present the case rather from the point of view of Lord Kintore, and serve to complete the information available concerning the whole controversy. Some of them were productions in the proceedings before the Privy Council, and were afterwards by authority returned to Lord Kintore. The controversy was one of long standing. It began immediately after the Restoration. One of these papers, entitled 'Baress alledgances ansred,' is dated 8th November 1660; another, entitled 'Ane True Accompt of the Preservation of the Honours,' is undated, but is evidently a direct answer to Ogilvie's pamphlet, which, as already mentioned, was published in 1701. The legal proceedings resulted in a decreet of the Privy Council, which ordered the fining and imprisonment of Ogilvie, and the burning of his pamphlet by the common hangman.

The account of the siege of Dunnottar Castle and the preservation of the Honours has been told before. It may be well, however, in order to explain the meaning of these letters, to give again an outline of the story, more especially as one or two details which bear upon the Kintore-Ogilvie controversy have been omitted from the earlier accounts.

Charles II. was crowned at Scone on the 1st January 1651, and the Honours of Scotland, the crown, sceptre, and sword, were used in the ceremony. The coronation was followed by the invasion of Scotland by Cromwell's troops, and Charles, instead of meeting Cromwell here, determined on his expedition into England, which ended so disastrously at Worcester. It was thought necessary, therefore, to take measures to ensure the safety, during the King's absence, of the emblems of Scottish royalty. Accordingly, on the 6th of June, the day Parliament rose, the Honours were handed over by Parliament to the Earl Marischal, whose hereditary privilege it was to have their custody during the sitting of Parliament. He was instructed to transport them to Dunnottar, 'thair to be keepit by him till farther ordouris.' In obedience to these instructions, the Earl took them to Dunnottar, and concealed them there in a secret place. The command of the castle he intrusted to George Ogilvie of Barras, who was allowed a garrison of forty men and two sergeants, to be entertained at the public charge. This seems to have been practically the whole garrison at Ogilvie's command, and it was all too small to provide for the proper defence of the castle. Several times in the course of the siege which followed, Ogilvie appealed for more men, and several times he complained that nothing was done to supply him with money or provisions, and that consequently the whole cost of the maintenance of the castle fell upon the Earl Marischal's estate and upon himself. It appears that during some part of the time of Ogilvie's command, John Keith, the youngest brother of the Earl Marischal, who was then quite young, was with him in the castle.[1]

On the 28th August, the Earl Marischal and several other noblemen, members of the Committee of Estates, were surprised by a party of English horse at Alyth, and were taken prisoners. Finding that he was to be carried to London, the Earl contrived to send a messenger to his mother, the Dowager Countess Marischal, bearing to her the key of the secret place in which the Honours lay hid. Immediately on receipt of her son's message, the Countess went to Dunnottar, 'and had not stayed two hours' when she heard of the near approach of the English troops. She took the Honours from their hiding-place and gave them to Ogilvie, strictly charging him to do his utmost to secure their safety. A few days afterwards the siege of the castle began, and soon developed into a blockade.

Twice did Ogilvie receive a message from the Committee of Estates, once, before the siege began, from Aberdeen, and once, in September, from 'West end Lochtay,' demanding the Honours, that they might be removed to a place of greater safety in the Highlands. On each occasion Ogilvie conceived the warrant insufficient to free him from his trust, and refused

---

[1] See Decreet of the Privy Council, 30th July 1702, printed in the Bannatyne Club volume, 1829.

to give them up. It was afterwards maintained by Lord Kintore that Ogilvie was afraid to disobey the Committee's orders, and that it was only upon his urgent advice and persuasion that they were retained in Dunnottar.[1]

In November Ogilvie was twice summoned to surrender the castle upon honourable terms. To each summons he returned a spirited refusal. At this time only four strongholds outside the Highlands—Dunnottar, Dumbarton, Brodick, and the Bass Rock—held out for King Charles against the army of the Commonwealth.[2]

John Keith must have left the castle about the end of the year. He was probably the bearer of a letter which Ogilvie wrote to the King on the 20th December, suggesting that the castle might be relieved by sea. Charles was very anxious to relieve the castle, in which, besides the Honours, there was much valuable plate and furniture belonging to him, and he commissioned Major-General Vandruske to attempt its relief; but lack of money prevented Vandruske from obtaining a ship and the necessary means of succour, and Dunnottar had fallen before he was ready to start.[3]

For some months after Keith left him, Ogilvie continued to hold out, but his provisions began to fail, and his small garrison was exhausted. Worse than all, there were murmurings of mutiny among the defenders, and Ogilvie was compelled to drive one of the ringleaders from the castle.[4] These things pointed to the impossibility of maintaining the post much longer, and, accordingly, Ogilvie and his wife began to consider how the Honours might be saved should the castle fall. It was left to the Governor's lady to devise the means, and she purposely kept her husband in ignorance of what she did, so

---

[1] See page 135; also Decreet of Privy Council, 1702.
[2] See Gardiner's *History of the Commonwealth and Protectorate*, vol. I. p. 470.
[3] See Mr. C. H. Firth's Introduction to *Scotland and the Commonwealth* (Scottish History Society), p. xli; Cal. Clar. State Papers, pp. 124, 129, 130, 136.
[4] Colonel David Lighton; see p. 120, note 1.

that he might be able to tell the English that he did not know where the Honours were. It was not till fifteen months afterwards, when Mrs. Ogilvie was on her deathbed, that she confided to her husband the secret of their hiding-place.

The person whom she took into her confidence was Mrs. Grainger, wife of the Reverend James Grainger, minister of the neighbouring parish of Kinneff, and the two ladies between them concocted a scheme for the removal of the Honours. One day, early in March, Mrs. Grainger and her maid went to Stonehaven on some ordinary housekeeping business. Amongst other things which she brought back with her were some bundles of flax, which were carried by the maid. On her way home she passed Dunnottar, and obtained permission from the English officer to visit her friend Mrs. Ogilvie. The visit was paid, and in due course Mrs. Grainger left the castle and returned to the manse at Kinneff. But she took with her the Honours. It is said that she carried the crown in her lap, and that she was seriously inconvenienced by the courtesy of the English officer, who assisted her to mount her horse, and conducted her through the English lines. For this part of the adventure there is unfortunately no corroboration in the published documents. It is more likely that the crown was transported, as the sceptre and sword were, in the bundle of flax which the maid carried. The journey was made out without suspicion being aroused, and the Honours reached the Kinneff manse in safety.

They were then handed over to the minister, who concealed them at first, it is said, in the bottom of a bed at the manse, and afterwards secretly buried them under the pavement of the church. At the end of March, he went and informed the Countess Marischal of the removal of the Honours, and she took a receipt from him, acknowledging that they were in his custody, and stating the exact places in which they were buried.

On the 24th May the castle was surrendered to the English upon honourable terms—the last post held for King Charles.

Ten days before, Ogilvie had received a letter from the Earl Marischal, from London—a letter which seems to have been written upon compulsion—ordering him to give up the castle. The Earl did not at the time know that the Honours were safe, but the Governor, though he did not know exactly what had become of them, probably had a shrewd idea that the English would not find them in Dunnottar. One of the articles of capitulation was that the Honours should be delivered up or a good account given of them, and the English were much disappointed to find that they had been baulked of their prey.

When they were interrogated on the subject, the Ogilvies gave out that John Keith had taken the Honours from Dunnottar to Paris, and had there given them to the King. They had no satisfactory evidence of this, however, to produce, though Mrs. Ogilvie 'contrived a missive letter,' which she arranged should fall into the hands of the English, purporting to be from John Keith, acknowledging the carrying away of the Honours. The Ogilvies were accordingly arrested, and subjected to a severe examination and to some rigorous treatment, until a letter came from Keith from abroad, in which he took credit to himself for the safe removal of the Honours to Paris. This letter caused the search to slacken, and, though the English still suspected that the Honours were nearer home, Ogilvie and his wife were released on bail, after suffering about seven months of imprisonment. Mrs. Ogilvie never recovered from the hardships she had undergone, and she died some time in the summer of 1653, telling her husband on her deathbed to whose charge she had committed the Honours, and adjuring him never to disclose the secret until the King should come by his own again.

For eight years the Honours lay hid under the pavement of Kinneff Church. Secretly and at long intervals the minister visited them, and renewed their wrappings to protect them from the damp. On some of these occasions he was accompanied by Ogilvie, who provided fresh linen to wrap them in.[1]

John Keith remained in France for about two years. He then followed Middleton to Holland, but arrived there too late to join his expedition, long delayed as that had been. Middleton landed in Sutherland in February 1654;[2] Keith landed in Fife a short time afterwards. He was at once arrested by the English, but, being in disguise, he escaped, and after various adventures he joined Middleton in the north. With Middleton he remained until the skirmish at Lochgarry, in Athole, on 26th July 1654, which finally scattered the Royalist troops, and forced them to take to the hills.[3] In the course of their wanderings, Keith obtained from Middleton a receipt for the Honours bearing to have been granted in 1652 at Paris, ' tho it was trewly subscrived at Capoch in Lochwhaber.' This receipt he produced when he eventually surrendered to the English, and was questioned as to the carrying abroad of the Honours, with the result that all search for them in this country was given up.

After the Restoration, Charles was informed of the safety of the Regalia, and both the Countess Marischal and Ogilvie put in claims for the credit of their preservation. The Countess wrote to the King; Ogilvie sent his son to London. The letter of the Countess, and a letter from William Ogilvie to his father, giving an account of his doings in London, are printed here.

With regard to the quarrel that ensued, the first thing that strikes one is the pity of it. The Keiths, the Ogilvies, the Graingers, had all played their parts well, and had all deserved well of their country. There is no reason to suppose that the King was ungrateful for the service done him, and surely each might have taken his reward and been content, without launch-

---

[1] Ogilvie's Pamphlet, p. 10, Bannatyne Club volume; see *infra*, p. 131.
[2] *Mercurius Politicus*, 16th March 1654.
[3] ' Letters from Roundhead Officers,' Bannatyne Club, 1856, p. 83.

ing into unseemly squabbling and reviling of each other. It is not easy now to decide on whom the blame must fall of having begun the controversy. The Countess, in her letter to the King of 23rd May 1660, acknowledges the services both of Ogilvie and of Grainger, and seems to grudge them no reward. But then William Ogilvie goes to London to urge his father's claims, and the Countess sends a gentleman to London to see that her interests are not neglected, and trouble begins. The King seems to have been willing to act with perfect fairness. On the 4th September he writes to the Countess acknowledging her son's services and expressing his desire to reward them, but in no way committing himself against Ogilvie. On the contrary, on the 28th September, William Ogilvie received, in answer to his petition, an order upon his father to deliver up the Honours to the Earl Marischal, to whose keeping they had been committed by the Scottish Parliament. But before this order was granted, William Ogilvie, suspecting that an attempt might be made by the Countess to obtain the Honours, wrote to his father warning him to see that they were given up to no one. That such an attempt was made by the Countess is admitted.[1] But Grainger felt bound to Ogilvie, from whom he had originally received them. On the 21st July he had written to Ogilvie regarding the Honours, 'As for myself, my neck shall break, and my life go for it, before I fail to you;'[2] and on 28th September he gave Ogilvie the sceptre, and undertook, in writing, to make the crown and sword forthcoming to him on demand.[3] It is difficult to reconcile this letter and 'obligement' of Grainger's with his 'declaration' and his letter to the Countess, which are printed here. One is tempted to think that the Countess had by some means induced him to take a different view of the matter by the time that the latter were written. It is probably true that Grainger and Ogilvie went together to Dunnottar to deliver the Honours to the

---

[1] *Infra*, p. 127.   [2] Nisbet's *Heraldry*, ii. 236.   [3] *Ibid.*

Earl Marischal, but the account given in 'Baress' Alledgances Ansred'[1] of the Earl's reception of Ogilvie does not seem to be accurate. At all events, we find Grainger writing to the Countess, 'Your ladyship remembers I did ever fear that he would easily wynd himself into my Lord Marischal his favour;'[2] and Middleton writing later, 'I am struck with amasement to think that my Lord Marischal should in the least countenanced him.'[3] It was possibly in connection with the Earl Marischal's favourable treatment of Ogilvie that the family differences arose which are referred to in the King's letter to Middleton.[4]

Whatever may have been the merits of the controversy, the King seems to have acted impartially, and to have tried rather to make peace than to aggravate the quarrel. In 1660, John Keith was made Knight Marischal of Scotland, and granted a yearly pension of £400. On 5th March 1661, long after the whole matter must have been thrashed out, Ogilvie presented the Earl Marischal's receipt to the King, and, in reward for his services, received a baronetcy, with an augmented blazon of arms. He also received the promise of a pension 'how soon the King's revenues were settled,' but the promise was never fulfilled. On 11th January 1661, Parliament ordered the payment of two thousand merks Scots to Mrs. Grainger, in respect of her services in saving the Honours. At various subsequent dates new favours were shown both to Ogilvie and to Keith. In 1662, Ogilvie obtained a charter from the King, changing the tenure of his lands of Barras from ward-holding to blench, which charter was ratified by Parliament, 11th August 1669. Charles seems also, after George Ogilvie's death, to have given his son, Sir William, an appointment as Master of His Majesty's Hawks.[5] In 1677, John Keith had a further honour conferred

---

[1] *Infra*, p. 129.  [2] *Infra*, p. 132.
[3] *Infra*, p. 115.  [4] *Infra*, p. 134.
[5] See a Draft Precept (undated) making the appointment, and also a letter from Sir William Ogilvie to the Earl of Airlie, dated 22nd April 1682, both printed in the *Spalding Club Miscellany*, vol. v. pp. 205, 206.

upon him in reward for his services, and was created Earl of Kintore.

But the quarrel was not dead, and in 1701 it broke out again on the publication of Sir William Ogilvie's pamphlet. The Earl of Kintore took legal proceedings, as has been already stated, and the Privy Council seems to have adopted his version of the story in its entirety, and to have decided against the Ogilvies, who were visited with fine and imprisonment.

Of the principal actors in the story, the following brief notes may be given:

The Dowager Countess Marischal was Lady Mary Erskine, daughter of John, seventh Earl of Mar, and widow of William, sixth Earl Marischal, who died in 1635. In 1638 she married, as his third wife, Patrick Maule, who in 1646 was created Earl of Panmure. She was therefore Countess of Panmure at the time of the siege of Dunnottar, though she seems still to have been known as Countess Marischal. Lord Panmure died in 1661.

Sir John Keith, Knight Marischal of Scotland (1660), and Earl of Kintore (1677), was the fourth and youngest son of William, sixth Earl Marischal. He died in 1714.

Sir George Ogilvie of Barras, Baronet, was the eldest son of William Ogilvie of Lumgair, whose mother was a granddaughter of James, first Lord Ogilvie. In 1634 he married Elizabeth, daughter of John Douglas of Barras, fourth son of William, ninth Earl of Angus. He obtained his commission as Cornet of Horse from the Earl Marischal in 1640. In the same year he purchased the lands of Wester Barras from his wife's brother, John Douglas. He died some time before the year 1680, and was succeeded by his eldest son, Sir William, who, along with his son David, was defender in the action raised by Lord Kintore.

The Rev. James Grainger, A.M., was born about 1606,

and laureated at St. Andrews University in 1626. He became minister of Kinneff parish some time before 1646, and died at the age of fifty-seven, in April 1663.[1] His wife's name was Christian Fletcher. A tablet with a Latin inscription stands in Kinneff Church, to commemorate their services to their country.

I have to thank Lord Kintore for allowing me to publish these tattered letters and papers, which I think are not without value as bearing upon an interesting episode in Scottish history. I have also to record my great indebtedness to the Rev. Douglas Gordon Barron, minister of Dunnottar, who has read the manuscripts, and has furnished me with much information and many notes, of which I have made free use. And I have also to thank the Rev. S. Ogilvy Baker, Vicar of Muchelney, Somersetshire, the present representative of the Ogilvies of Barras, for the information he has put at my disposal regarding that family.

---

[1] *Fasti Ecclesiæ Scoticanæ*, part vi. p. 874; Hist. MSS. Com. Report, vol. viii. p. 303.

# ANE TRUE ACCOMPT OF THE PRESERVATION OF THE HONORS

The Earll Marshall being tacken prisoner at Eliot,[1] obtened leave to send a gentell man to his mother [prete]nding to give notice for a provision of monay, evry thing [being] tacken from him by the English, but his aprahencion [of] the danger of the honours was that which stuck deapest in his heart. Therfor with this gentell man he derected the key of the place wher the honours were to his mother. The next day she went to the Castell of Dunnotter, and had not stayed tuo hours, when advertised that the English were to quarter sum shouldiers n[ear] to the Castell that night, upon which being fo[rced to] flay, yet be for she stured caused to open the roum and did tack out the honours and delivred them hir self to Georg Ogalvie (Captan of the Castall by the Earll Marshall's apoyntment) and charged him, whither hie should be nesesitat to capatilat, or other ways, he should secur them, giving him asurance of all hir posible asistance in evry thing, which he chearfuly undertouk. The day foulowing the enamie marched to Aberdeen, and shortly after returning did put a garison in Fitersso, the Countas of Marshall's joyntour hous, within tuo mils of the Castell from stoping it from provison or coraspondance with the Cuntry.

Sum tym ther after the enamie having required him to surender the Castle,[2] resolved that it were the securest way to remove the honours, where being conveyed to Mr. James

---

[1] The Earl Marischal, with other members of the Committee of Estates, was taken prisoner at Alyth, on 28th August 1651, by a troop of horse from Dundee under Colonel Alured.   [2] Early in March 1652.

Granger, a preachers house did ... which he afterwards caried and put them underground in the church, as his testificat under his hand[1] doth yet declayr the perticular places they were laid in in case he should die. The castle afterward being surendred,[2] the Captan (upon bale when cald to apear) was dismised unchalinged for the honours, but having mist them, they laid him fast with his wife in Aberdeen. He being thus put too it declared that tuo or three munths befor he had cummited them to my lady Marshalls youngest son, John Keath, who had gon out of the kingdom, to be by him transported to his Magestie, who was then in France at Parise; upon which his mother did imeditly writ to him to aknoulidg and oun the tacking of them away with him, which ass sune as possible he returned the said aknowlidgment, declaring that as he carried them with him, so did deliver them by his Magisties order to Generall Midelltoun. This did tack up sum time till his answar could com, which ocasioned Georg Ogelvies confinment, but how sune his declaration was presented they did permite him to go, and set him at liberty.

The said John Keath in the meantime being as banished, who durst not return to Scotland least the English should have tacken him and so rouined him by there severity, or els, which was wors, might upon torturing him, extorted a confesion of that mater from him; so being still abroad, att last cam from France to Holand, and understanding of his Magesties commands on Generall Mideltone, who went with sum oficers from Holand to Scotland, did resolve to haserd himself in that service; and so folowing Generall Midellton and geting a veshell in Holand, landed at the Elie in Fyfe, where he was aprehended by the enamie, but being in disguis and giving himself out for a poor young merchant lad, he made his escape.

But after he cam amongest his freends, notice was had of his being in the cuntray, and sevrall parties in quest of him, he being in grait haiserd sevrall tims to be tacken, who on sevrall ocasions escapted, the sircumstances wherof were too tedious to relate. Therafter having a coraspondance with the

---

[1] Printed in Regalia Papers (Bannatyne Club), p. 40.    [2] 24th May 1652.

Marquiss of Mountross, who maried his cusian german,[1] he by his intelligence where Generall Midelltoun was, did at last joyn with him, with sum few of his friends, and constantily did remain with him in the hils till they were defeat at Lochgarioch by the English.[2]

The meanwhill the litle forse that Generall Midelltoun had with him being defate, evry man acted for himself; the Earls of Glencarne, Atholl, Montross, Sellkirk, afterwards Deuck Hamiltoune, with many other persons of quality, did capitulat, but the said John Keiths case being very hard and diferent from others, he, befor he parted with Generall Midelltoun, did desir from him a recept of the honours, at the time when King [Charles] and the said John were both at Parise, tho it was trewly subscrived at Capoch in Lochwhaber, which he did.

And therafter, after many hardships, his mother got him included by Generall Munks orders in the capitullation with my Lord Muntross, Collonal Cobet, then governor of dundie, being ordred by Generall Munke to treat with the Marquise; and after all was agried upon, Cobbeet told the said John, he had sum other thing by order of the Generall to enquir at him, which was, if he did carie away the honours abroad, as was given out, and what way he could mack it apear he did so, since it was wery much suspected that they were sum wher in Scotland. Upon which very boldly, he ouned the caring of them away, and in testamonie wherof he produced Generall Mideltons recpt daited at Paris that by the King order he had recved the honours of Scotland, to wit the crown, septer, and sourd, from John Keith, bruther jerman to the Earle Marshall of Scotland. Upon which production, Colonell Cobbet, after he red the recpt, he aknoulidged that he had acted lick a prety man, and no more to say to him; and so was included in the capulatiton. Nather was there any sherch maid by the English; which by these means above said they were absuletly preserved till the time of King Charles his

---

[1] James Graham, second Marquis of Montrose, married Isabel Douglas, daughter of William, seventh Earl of Morton, whose wife, Anne Keith, was sister of John Keith's father, William, sixth Earl Marischal.

[2] The Royalist troops were surprised and put to flight at Loch Garry in Athole on 26th July 1654.

restoration, at which time Georg Ogelvie had the impidence to send his son to London for sooth to represent to his Magesty that he had all ways the honours in his custodie, and that no person but himself, who was the only instrument of there preservation could have any pretence on that accompt.

Upon which the Countas of Marshall [being] informed [of th]is sent up a gentell man to London to inform the King of this insolance, who was graciously plesed, after the trew knowledge of the mater, not to harken to there unjust and calumius suggestions, but wrot a leter to my Lady Marshall as follows:

MADAM,—I am so sensable of the good service don to me in preserving my crown, septer, and sowrd, that as I have put marks on your sons, so I could not lett them go to Scotland, without aknowledging also my sence of your kindnes and caire in that and other things relating to my service during my absence. I do desire that these things may be delivrd to my Lord Marshall, that as he recived them, so they may be delivred by him to the inshouing Parliment, and shall only adde that on all ocasions you shall find me your afecitonat friend,

CH[ARLES].

*Whitehall, the 4th of September*, 1660.

Not withstanding of his Magistis letter [to the] Countes of Marshall, it sems that Georg Ogelvies son did not give over, having my Lord Ogelvie very much his friend, with sum others, till at last there is a letter from the Earle of Midelltoun in answer to the said Countas, by whos means the last stop was maid to his bass and fals pretintons, which is as follows:

MADAM,—I most humbly, in the first place, crave your ladyship pardon for not returning particular ansuers to your letters. Your son, my nobell friend, when he was [at] this place did . . . me that labour, and realy, Madam, I cannot on day be meste v . . . hour of time. I am both sory and ashamed that [so little a person] as Mr. Ogelvie should have put your ladyship to so [much trouble]. I confess I am struk with amasement to think that my [Lord Marischall] should in the least coutinanced him. I shall not be [wanting to put] a stop to his pretintions and serve you with ass [much faithfulness] and zeall as any servant you have, and rely it [is my] ambition to be acompted amongest the number of your servants, and I hop all my ocasions shall express that I am, Madam, Your ladyships most faithfull and obedent humbell servant, MIDELLTON.

*London, November the* 15, 1660.

Lickwise it will not be improper to insert the Ministers Declaration [under his own hand] who had the custody of these honours till the Restoration which will [clear m]uch of this afair, and is [as] follows:

Being informed that Georg Ogelvie of Barras hath his son at London, giving out that his father was the only preserver of the honours of Scotland when they were in hasard to be tacken, and that they were in his custodie ever since, tho others have been more instromentall nor he, I thought good therfor to declair the treuth, viz., That in Agust 1651 by the Countas of Marshall, the honours were delivred to Georg Ogelvie with charge to him to secure them, and he keping them in Donnoter till there was no probabilitie of longer maintining the castell, he imployed me (having suficient asurance of my loyaltie to his Magestie, and fidelitie in promis keping) to carie the honours out of the hous and secure them, and to barr sospition, I sent my wife, who brought them furth without being discovered by the enamie, tho rencountred by them in the way. This was in the begining of March 1652. And he having engadged me with all convenience I should go and aquent the Countes of Marshall therwith, in the end of March I went, and informed hir of the wholl proseder [which] she [approved] of, and was satasfied that they should remain in my [keping, taking] also my ticket of having them, expressing the perti[cular] places [whair]in they were then secured, so that I have kept them according to hir desire untill this present October 1660, the eight day of which, at my Ladys command, according to the order she had recived from his Magistie for that efect in Denotor Castell, I delivred them to the Earle Marshall befor these witneses, the Viscount of Arburthnot, the Shirof Deput of the Mairns, and sevrall other gentell men, wherupon I required a

ticket of recpt, but was defered till afterwards, since which time I am informed that Georg Ogelvie hath obteined from the Earle Marshall a recpt, and have sent [eith]er it or the doubell of it to London to be produced by his son as [if the hon]ours had bene in his custodie and by him preserved [although] it be weall knowen to his son that I had them in my [house and] keiping ever since the first delivrie of them to me. [But inde]ed the prime mean of there saftie was the declaring them [to be carrie]d of the kingdom by the Earle Marshall his brother John (which he ouned). For as it stoped the enemie from sherching for them, so it freed Georg Ogelvie from prison [an]d far[ther] trayall. In wittnes of the treuth, I have writen and subscrive[d these] presents with my hand the nynten of October 1660. (signed)     Mr. JAMES GRANGER,
Minister at Kinneff.

The originalls of the Kings letter with the Earle of Midletons, and this Declaration of the Ministers, are all in the Earle of Kintores hands to be seen.

Be all this aforsaid its hoped that the treuthe of this afair is ingeneraly [dis]covred, and that no person of honour or sense will pertack with hi[m by] giving credit to so [in]solent calumnies, wher by his false ase[rsi]ons [he re]flects most abusivly on the memory of so nobell and wo[rthy] a lady as the Countas of Marshall was knowen to be, as also upo[n the] present Earle of Kintore, who hath in all integritie declared this [to be] of facte, by which it will apear that he was the absolut and trew [instrume]nt of preserving the honours. Nay, it also reflects on the justice [and the] blesed memory of King Charles the Second, who was gracious[ly pleased] to put marks of honour on the said Earle by granting to him [the dignity] of Knight Marshall at his restoration fortie years ago, whe[re it as] the chief causes of this gift bears his preserving of the hon[ours.] As also since, he was pleased to grant him the title of Earle [of Kintore], wherin amongest other reasons that of the preservation of them is the chefest caus, and in his patant ordeans the Lord Layon to give him ane aditionall coat of arms conform to the narative of his Signiture [which] the Layon, under his seall, did grant, and gave him the croun, [septer], and sourd, all which is to be sene under the grait seale and the Layo[ns] warand for them.

Its not denyed that Georg Ogelvie did give out the honou[rs to] the minister of Kinneff, which he was ordred by the Countas [of Marshall] that in case of hazard they should be secured the best [way possible]. She was satasfied with and aproved it that they were put in [to the hands] of so honest [a] man after his cuming to hir and aquenting [hir therwith]. Upon which accompt all others conserned wold have ben ve[r]y w[ell] pleased the said Georg Ogelvie should have been rewarded by the K[ing], and it is known my Lady Marshall in a letter to his Magistie[1] did give him the caracter of a person of fedelity and secrecie in manadging [of] that afair. Yet nothing being satasfactury to him unles the absulut preservation of the honours which he most aragantly asumed to him[self] should be ludged in his pearson, so that the Countas of Marshall having informed the King of his falshood and foly, did defat all his pretent[ions]. Tho upon his first adress to the King, which he made with sum s[how of] modestie, he was maid a knight baronet, and might have got a pe[erage] if he had not so insolently indevred by his vanity and lys to put such desgrace and reprotche on the Countas of Marshall and the Earle of Kintore; wherfor it is expected that if this afair shall be represented to his Magisties Counsell, there lordships will, out of ther justice and trew vindication of the treuth, render a punishment suetabl to so great a villenny.

### LETTER FROM GEORGE OGILVIE OF BARRAS TO THE COUNTESS OF MARISCHAL[2]

*29 March,* 1652.

MADAME,—I have receauit your Ladyships and the commissione, and hes doune cuery thing ther in as ye did apoynt me. Bot treulie for that quhilk your Ladyship desyrit me to

---

[1] See p. 122.

[2] This letter was written during the siege of Dunnottar, and some weeks after the Honours had been removed to Kinneff. The Countess cannot, however, have known of the safety of the Honours at the time she wrote the letter to which this is a reply. The letter seems to show that the Countess had been

mend wes not out of any doubt or mistrust in these gentillmen, bot for your forder exonoratione quhairin busines had not takine effeck, as I desyrit Mr. Alexander to hav showne your Ladyship and them both. For thes Inglesmen sieing they hav ane absolut commissione micht hav wronged them giv they had not condisendit to euery thing they had desyrit them, and then they micht hav said ther commissione did only cary alongest uith ther inclination. Bot I salbe glad that this may giv your Ladyship and them satiesfactione, for it salbe my uttermost endevor to dou the samen and giv myselff and all that is deir to me as this is I wald submit the samen to your Ladyship and thes tua gentillmen. But I ame informit that Major-generall Deane[1] can dou nothing of any importance till he first acquent the Counsell of Estat at Lundene and hav order from them. Bot in my waik jugment it wes my Lords desyr uith Mr. Alexander Pattoune to send thes instructions to his Lordship giv your Ladyship and the rest of the frends think it guid, and them richt and wyse giv he can mak the capitulatione quhair he is, quhair he can hav ane full surtie for quhat he ends for. And in the mane tyme ye may be dalling uith Dane till ye sall heir from my Lord, quhilk may be uery quiklie giv ye wald choysit Mr. Alexander Pattone to send the doubill of thes things to him, and that it is your jugment that he sould go on that way. And giv he thinks it not fieting lat him acquent your Ladyship quhat he thinks most fieting to be doune. I crave pardoune for presumtione, bot it salbe always subjek to your Ladyships commandiments. My Lord desyrs to be carefull of the black stock and provyd the samen.[2] God knows how I sall dou the samen. For excep

---

trying to arrange some terms of capitulation with the English. Ogilvie, though very sore at the treatment he had received both inside and outside the Castle, and in low spirits about the possibility of holding out much longer, does not seem eager for the success of the Countess's negotiations. His letter is probably purposely couched in vague language.

[1] Major-General Richard Deane, commander-in-chief of the English forces in Scotland.

[2] The 'Black Stock' or Table Dormant of the Castle was a very highly valued heirloom of the Keith family. It was said to have been made of oaken planks taken from the long-ship which brought the Chatti (from whom the Keiths claimed descent) from Germany in the eleventh century. The table is still preserved in Ravelston House, Midlothian.

that quhilk your Ladyship dois in relacione to this hous, I hav non that dois so much as to countinance the samen. I hav wryttine a letter to the Sereff anent that particular and hes desyrit him to provyd and send me some nessesers quhilk can be easlie had ther sick as fishis and some salmond and some of ther mill suane, and that he wald w$^t$ (wryt) Coluberdy and Captane Martine, as they wald be ansuerabill, that they wald send me seuen or aucht gentillmen. Bot God knowis quhat obedyence wilbe gottine of this and quhat car or respect they cary to thes pepill in your absence quho hes reliveit this place. I hop the day sall cum that I sall not spair in ther faces to say so much. And nou in respect of the lest I wryt to your Ladyship anent Cornell Lichtoune,[1] hou much nied I stand of some gentill men that be faithfull and honest, bot they ar uery skars and feu frends to try them out, bot euery on having ther awne excussis. So I intreat your Ladyship to think upon this and ly tue your helping hand as ye hav euer donne befor, and for my selff I sall dou as I hav donne befor the uery uttermost of my lyff. I wald glaidlie know giv your Ladyship hes hard any thing frome your sone John as yet, for I long to heir frome him.[2] They wilbe on at your Ladyship uery schortlie, quhilk will informe you anent your barley. So giv ye think not the terms guid that is endit upon, ye may dou theruith as ye think fieting. If ye hav ane capitulatione, giv they be things disputabill that cannot be agret upon, I wald think it fieting that the frends sall sie giv they will refer the samen to my Lord and the Counsell Estat at Lundone. So my Lord may ues his awne monneyone ther uith them and I sall giv ane neu commissione to my Lord for thes poynts giv it be niedfull. I wryt to Elsick,[3] and I hav sent his letter to your Ladyship.

---

[1] David Lighton, 'who had been a colonel abroad,' was ringleader of the mutiny in the castle, and was expelled by Ogilvie. See 'Vindication' printed at the end of Ogilvie's pamphlet in the *Regalia Papers*.

[2] This reference to Ogilvie's anxiety about John Keith lends probability to the idea that he was the bearer of the Governor's appeal to the King for help. It may be that Ogilvie, knowing that his wife had removed the Honours, was already considering his scheme of imputing their removal to Keith.

[3] Sir Alexander Bannerman of Elsick, created a baronet in 1682, on account of his loyalty and sufferings during the usurpation.

I can not bot admyre hou men quho professis frendschip in siek ane busines of importance will prefer any thing to it. Bot quhat sall I say? Lou and faithfulness is remouit out of this land and kingdome, and it is Godis jugment due to us quho hes left the loue of God and loyaltie to our king. I can say no moe, bot I wish that your Ladyship may mak chois of some honest man that wilbe faithfull in the busines giv ye can not herefter persuaid him to imbres the samen, for I think it strang hou he can refuis the samen, and I find be the Lard of Morphie[1] he starts much at Elsicks unwillingnes. Always I hav submited all to your Ladyship and hes sent and subscriuit all ye desyrit me to dou, or giv Elsick cum and ane other giv he cum not that ye may put in ther name. Hoping as I ame confident ye will remember on him quho is and salbe still, Your Ladyships humbill seruant, GEORGE OGILUY.

I wish your Ladyship may keip this letter of Elsick to showe mens willingnes and ther excussis, for quhen they will not haissart ane triffell of menes they will neuir haissart lyff and fortoune. I had wryttine the gratest part of my letter or this came to my hand.

*For the Richt Honorabill my uery nobil Lady,*
*The Countes of Marschall, Thes.*

## COPY LETTER FROM THE COUNTESS OF MARISCHALL TO KING CHARLES THE SECOND

MAY IT PLEASE YOUR MAJESTIE,—Haveing received that honour of a letter from your Majestie from Collen 4th January [16]55, in which yow take notice of my desires to doe your Majestie service, which is far above my merit and short of the desire and wi[ll] I had and still hath to express that duetye which I know that I and all good people is obleiged to, if I were not bound in

---

[1] George Grahame of Morphie, who afterwards became cautioner for Ogilvie when he was liberated in January 1653.

loyalty to your Majestie, as by my birth to my dread soveraigne, yet the particular respects which yow have been pleased to put upon me both by word and writ hath tyed me so far that I esteeme myself obleiged to witness my thankfullnes in obeying any of your Majesties commaunds, though it were to the hazard of my life; and if I could express the joy I have of hearing of your Majesties being restored to what is your due by birth, would in some kynd charecter my loyalty to your Majestie, quhich is far above that which I can either say or writ.

As for the saftie of the honours I have left nothing which wes in my power to doe for the same, in which it pleased God to assist m[e], . . . ar preserved to your Majestic and your posteritie. I pray the Lord that you may long [en]joy them . . . for the way of securing of them were too tedious for a letter. Only the gentlman quho commanded the Castle of Donnotter discharged his duety verie honestlie in putting them in the hands of a persone who did show himself worthie of so great a trust.

As for the particular passages therof the bearer, Johne Keith, my sone (who by owning the carying of them beyound sea, prevented what danger a further search might have made) will give your Majestie a full relatione of all concerning the same. To which my sone, Marshall (being prisoner in the Tower of London), wes altogether ignorant untill his returne to Scotland, and then the secret wes made knowne, to his great contentment, as he will give your Majestie a further accompt, and seing that his house and familie have been loyall to their King, I must humbly entreat your Majestie to look upon them with the eye of favour, as your loyall subjects, and seing it is not necessare the honours should ly any longer in obscurity your Majestie will resolve how to dispose of them, and that I may have your Majesties warrand for obeying the same, which shall be performed by her, who shall ever continue,

Your Majesties faithfull loyall subject and<br>humblest servante.

[*Indorsed*] Copie of my Ladys Letter to the King, 23rd May 1660.

## LETTER FROM WILLIAM OGILVIE TO HIS FATHER, GEORGE OGILVIE OF BARRAS [1]

*Vestminster, in Stephens Alley, at Mr. Axtillis house, the* 15 *of September* 1660.

LOVING FATHER,—Since my last to you I have got litle doein in the businesse, and the reason is the Duick of Glocester his death and the arrivall of the Spanish embassadour have so troubled the King that none for this eight dayes darre move any businesse to his Majestic till he be a little appeased and till some dayes of mourning be past. But I am confident that the businesse about the honoures, vhich the King knowes of at length, shall goe very voll on, gif ye but keepe them undelyvered till any till ane new order come to you, and I hope ane new pension or some other commoditie besyds honour vith it. So give it vere your pleasure to come this length yourself it vold be vell vorth your paines; and give ye can not come your self, vryt to the King, and vryt your mynd to me quhat ye vold have doen, for we can not goe back vith quhat ve have already motioned and have very good hopes of, and especially the best of our friends being ingaged in the businesse. For quhen I saw that businesse vas goine vrong heire, I wrot my frendis that ye had sent me to doe for you, as I have com, and shall, God villing, continue to doe especially in this businesse vherein, give it be rightly man[na]ged I hope all that shall succeede us shall have credit of it; for all our countreymen lookes so much upon it that they say their is no Scotsman heir can say the lyk, and the King vill not let you vant ane liberall revard for it. So keepe them till I acquaint you upon any condition. And give my Lord Marschall hes surprysed you vith the Kings order befor my letter came to your hands, ye most either come or vryt to the King that he had them and hes suffered for them,

---

[1] William Ogilvie had been sent by his father to London, to present a petition to the King, asking for an order as to the disposal of the Honours. The answer to the petition was given on the 28th September, in the shape of an order on the petitioner's father to deliver up the Honours to the Earl Marischal, and to obtain his receipt therefor.

ye and your viffe, and preserved them till this tyme that ye have obeyed his Magisties order. And give ye have gotten ane receit on them ye most send it to me that I may shew it. But it vere better that ye keept them selves only till I acquaint you, unlesse they have surprysed you unvares. For I assure you your name vas never heard of in the businesse till I cam, and I hope ye vill consider the more of it and vill not abyd from this, seeing your best friends and I both am ingaged to the King to make it good that ye vas the only preserver of these honours under God. I shall heast thorow businesse as soon as I can ; but I have gotten ane strange trick played me, vhich is thus: Collonell J. Ogilvy had ane study in his chamber and I had non in myn, so he desyred me to put in my pockmantle in his closet for securities cause, as I did vith als my money in it. Vithin five dayes after he is goein home, the Duick of Glocester died and all the Court most have mourning. I vent to tell my money to see quhat I had, and did cast my compt quhat I had spent, and after I had told the money I misse fyfteen pound starlin. I tryes my man and the maid and all that vere in the house for my money. They svore they handled it not, for non got the key of the closet but the Collonells man, ane tailyor young man who had comd up to serve him for ane tym and to see and learne the fashiones. He made my clothes, and quhen he made them he not so much money as to buy candle to sow them vith till I gave it to him, as the Collonell knowes, but quhen he vent avay he did let the maid of the house see ane [le]nth excellent cloth vorth 20 shillings a yard, vith furniture [con]forme and many other things for voemen he had coft and told her he vas to carry them to France vith him. So be all probabilitie he stole the money. I desyre ye vold vryt to the Collonell to search for him to put him to ane tryall, and I doubt not but he vill be found guiltie. I vold not have need much had not this fallen out, but ye most supplie me vith some now, for I can get non here upon any tearmes, and see give ye can get my money again. For he got his maisters key often, and his maister chyded him that he vold not keepe it, as he did at last to my losse and the vay that he has opened the meale vhich I did not perceive, seeing it vos locked. He has only drawen the tackle to him and put in his hand at the end vhere the money vas in the bagge, as I did befor all the house, and has taken his pleasur. So I have vritten to the Collonell and vi . . . vyse that I vant it not. So expecting ane answer of all in [he]ast, my respectes to yourself, bedfellow and all friend being preferred, I rest, your loving and faithfull sonne to death, W. OGILVY.

*For his loving father, George Ogilvy of Barras,*
*These in all heast present.*


## MR. JAMES GRAINGER, HIS DECLARATION ANENT THE HONORS

*20th October* 1660.

Being informed that George Ogilvie of Barras hath his sonne at London giving out that his father was the only preserver of the honoures of Scotland when they were in hazard to be taken, and that they were in his custodie ever since, though others have been more instrumentall then he, I thought good therefor to declare the truth, viz.: That in Agust 1651 by the Countess of Marsha[ll] the honoures were deliuered to George Ogilvie with charge to him to secure [them], and he keeping them in Dunnottar till there was no probabilitie of longer mantein[ing] the Castell, he imployed me (having sufficient assurance of my loyaltie to his Majestie [and] fidelitie in promise keeping) to cary the honoures out of the house and to secure them. And to barre suspicion I sent my wife, who brought them forth without being discovered by the enemie, though rancountred by them in the way. This was in the begining of March 1652. And he having engaged me that with all conveniencie I should go and acquaint my Lady Marshall therewith, in the end of March I went and informed her of the whole procedour, which shee approved of, and was satisfied that they should remaine in my keeping, taking also my tickquet of having them, expressing the particular places whairin they were then secured. So that I have keeped them, according to her desire, untill this present October 1660, the eight day of which, at my Ladies command (according to the ordour shee had received from his Majestie for that effect), in Dunnottar Castell I delivered them to the Earle Marshall before these witnesses, the Visecount of Arbuthnot, the Sheriff Deput of the Mearns, and severall other gentillmen; whairupon I required a tickquet of recept, but was deferred till afterwards.¹ Since which time I am informed that George Ogilvie hath obteined from the Earle of Marshall a recept and hath sent ather it or the double of it to London to be produced by his sonne, as if the honoures had been in his custodie and by him preserved, although it be weell knoune to his sonne that I had them in my house and keeping ever since the first deliverie of them to me. But indeed the prime mean of their safetie was the declaring them to be caried off the kingdome by the Earle Marshall his brother John (which he owned), for as it stopped the enemie from searching for them, so it freed George Ogilvie from prison and farther triall. In witnesse of the truth heirof I have written and subscribed thir presents with my hand the 19 of October, 1660.

M. JAM. GRAINGER, Minister at Kinneff.

[*On back*] Edinburgh, 26 August 1702, presented by Alexander Troop, Wryter, and registrat per McKell, procurator.

Given back by act of parliament.

### BARRESS ALLEDGANCES ANSRED, 8 NOVEMBER 1660

Wheras George Ogilvie maketh severall assertiones in referrence to his part in preserving the honors of Scotland. Therfore the trueth is declared in the ensuing answeres.

1. He affirmes that allwayes since Mr. James Granger had them first in his custodie he hath had his oath never to deliver them to any persone quhatsoever but unto him.²

---

¹ Grainger actually only delivered to the Earl Marischal the crown and sword. Ogilvie had previously obtained from him the sceptre, and seems to have gone with him to Dunnottar. The Earl Marischal's receipt for the Honours was given to Ogilvie, not to Grainger.

² This statement of Ogilvie's seems to have been quite true. See Grainger's letter to him, printed in Nisbet's *Heraldry*, vol. ii. p. 236.

Answer: About the time of his Majesties arrivall in England, George Ogilvie had occasion to be with my Ladie Marshall; at which tyme she told him that she being certaine that how soon his Majestie mynded these honours, and resolved to commit them to convenient keeping, there would come some order or directione to her to deliver them to any should be intrusted. Therfore that she intended (as conceiveing it most pertinent) to remove them from Mr. Grangers house unto her own dwelling. But she promised to advertise him before she removed them. His answer wes nowayes negative, but gave his opinion, that she needed not be too sudden till his Majestie wes weell setled. According her promise, one day or tuo before she intended to send for them by a letter, she advertised Georg Ogilvie; which how soon he received he went straight to Mr. Grangers houss, and finding him in bed, in a chamber alone, he went in and, bolting the door behind him, he told him, there wes a bussines which most neerly concerned him, and quhairin if the minister helped him not, he wes for evermore ruined, and it wes within the compass of his power to preveine the danger or not; and therfore shewed him there wes a necessitie of his promise to help him to his power. By which words and the like he preingaged Mr. Granger by his solemne promise; and then told him it wes, not to deliver the honours unto any without his consent. But the nixt day my Ladie Marshall sending for them, the minister perceived himself circumveined, and much resented his simplicity.

2. That when the Committee sent their order to Mr. Granger to deliver the honours to Balmanic and James Peddee, and they to deliver them to Whitrigs,[1] that Mr. Granger offered willinglie unto him the whole honours, so to preveine the Councells order, but that he would not take them at that tyme,

---

[1] On 9th September 1660, the Committee of Estates had granted a warrant to Sir William Ramsay of Balmayne, and James Peadie, bailie of Montrose, to receive the Honours from Grainger, and to thank him in the name of the Committee, and promise him a reward for his services. On the same day they granted a warrant to Robert Keith of Whiterigs, Sheriff-depute to the Earl Marischal, to receive the Honours from Ramsay and Peadie, and to preserve them in Dunottar till the Earl's return from England. These warrants were rescinded, 28th September 1660, in consequence of the arrangements made in London for the disposal of the Honours.

wanting conveniency to cary them; except onlie the scepter; but gave him his recept on all, and tooke the ministers ticquet to deliver him the rest quhen he desired.

Answer: Georg Ogilvie haveing notice of this order of the Committee, and finding himself slighted therin, represented to the Minister that the obeying of that order would tend absolutlie to both their prejudices (although the Committee in their order had thanked Mr. Granger, and promised him reward), and advysed him to give the honours unto him before the order came; and then should he be frie from obeying it. The minister answered he would not, nor would not be any more deceived by his unhandsome policie. But while they are thus debatting there comes a servant of Whitrigs with a letter in relatione to the order, at quhich George Ogilvie took occasion to entreat the minister to doe something presentlie that so he might have something of a ground to answer the Shereff. And if he would not give him all, let him have but the scepter, and he should give him the recept of all quhich he might shew, to testifie he had delivered all. To quhich the minister condiscended upon George Ogilvies great oath to restore it whensoever he called for it, and the minister gave George Ogilvie a ticquet testifying that though George Ogilvy had given a recept for the whole, yet he had received but the scepter.

Morover when my Lord Marshall sent from Bolasheine[1] his deput and Arthur Straton of Snadown[2] with the Kings letter to my Ladie to deliver them to her sone; and her letter to Mr. Granger to deliver them to these in her sones name, Mr. Granger went to Barres requyring from him the scepter, the Kings order being come to deliver the honours; notwithstanding of his former oath, he absolutly refused to give it. So that these[2] messengers returned without receiving them; because they would not take one part without the other.

3. That Mr. James Granger went unanimouslie with him to Donnotter to deliver the honours.

Answer: My Lord Marshall haveing given a precept to

---

[1] Bolshan, in Kinnell parish, Forfarshire, at that time the property of Lord Southesk.

[2] Arthur Straitoun of Snadoune, *Scriba signeto regio*, 1629.

Mr. Granger, and ane express command to Barres, to bring in to Donnotter on Moonday the 8 October, each of them, that part of the honours quhich they had, George Ogilvie wrot to Mr. Granger to come to his house at Craigie, with the croune and sword, and that to the effect they might goe jointlie togither, and deliver all, the minister answered that he scorned to come to his house, nor would he have more to doe with him in that nor in anything else; but that seeing he had perjured himself in refuising to returne him the scepter, he would goe alone and delyver the rest by himself. Yet notwithstanding of this answer George Ogilvie, to take away any seeming of difference betuixt them in the delivery, met the minister upon the rod and so went on with him to Donnotter.

4. That he wes most affectionatly received by my Lord into Donnotter, yea even unto imbraceing.

Answer: The minister and he haveing brought in the honours all at one tyme, notice was given to my Lord, quho directed to bring them into a roome, and haveing looked upon the honours he thanked them both in generall, though more particularly the minister, and commanded the sheref deput (to quhom he had givene the charge of the houss) to lift the crowne and cary it to a closet. George Ogilvie being moved therat, snatched at the scepter and caryed it in undesired, and a certaine space therafter taryed in the dyning roome with the rest of those then attending, but received nothing afterward from my Lord but downlooking and frownes. And the nixt morning my Lord causd my Lord Arbuthnot send him word that my Lord absolutlie discharged him from any more seing his face; which he hath not since.[1]

5. That he alone hath been the onlie sufferrer, losser, and persone endangered for the preserving of these honours.

Answer: The tyme he wes prissoner (which wes the whole sume of his suff[ering]) he liberat himself from all suffering, losse or danger, by burthening my Lord Marshalls brother by his declaring to the English that he had caryed them away, which banished him for about 3 yeires, quhich tyme he wes

---

[1] With regard to the Earl Marischal's reception of Ogilvie, see *supra*, p. 109.

exposed to both hazard and want, being robbd in his travelling, my Lady, his mother, at great expenses for him, and his bills of exchange miscaryed, himself in severall hazards of taking before he could land and reach the hills of Scotland quher Generall Midltoun wes in armes, and quhen all got then capitulationes, his was hardly obtained but by much mediatione. Also Mr. Grangers wyfe wes not without much hazard in conveying them throw many of the English betuixt Donnotter and her own house.

6. Where he averres that my Lord Marshall, with good will and favour, hath given him a recept off purpose to witness that they have been in his custodie ever since they were first put into Donnotter, and also to testifie that he hath now received them compleetlie from him.

Answer: It is evidentlie cleer that my Lord Marshall being fullie assured (and it being the thing that Barres in his forsaid assertiones dare not deny) that from the day these honours were caryed out of Donnotter untill the 8 of the last October, quhich day they were delivered to my Lord Marshall, they were constantlie in Mr. Grangers particular custodie, and likwayes the major part of them being personally delivered by Mr. Granger, that part quhich Barres delivered being cuninglie wrested and perjuredlie retained for about 8 days from the man that had preserved it with the rest to that day, I say therfore it is cleer that recept hath not been givene of purpose to testifie they had been alwayes in George Ogilvies keeping, or that they were received intyrelie from him, but the reasones moveing my Lord Marshall to grant that recept, and quhich these who were solicitours for Barras to that effect, have pressed in upon him ar:

1. Because they were in Donnotter quhen Barres wes put into it.
2. Because Barres wes charged with them by my Lords mother.
3. Because he presumed haveing the scepter, to reteine it till he got some acknowledgment by way of recept, and,
4ly. Because William Ogilvies petitione wes answered with a commaund to deliver them, and take a recept theron,

which they have interpret to my Lord Marshall as a commaund on him to give one.

That they were in Donnotter when Barres was put in,

That he had ane immediat charge from my Ladie Marshall to secure them by putting them out of the houss,

That afterwards he did once or twyce visit them, and helped Mr. Granger to shift them from one place to another,

That he and his wyfe were prissoneres in Aberdean and Donnotter till they produced Mr. Johne Keiths recept,

Is all true, and all that he can truly alledge.

But all the forsaid assertiones, or that he had power to remove them from Mr. Grangers without my Ladie Marshalls warrand is arrogant truetlis.

LETTER FROM THE MINISTER OF KINNEFF TO THE COUNTESS OF MARISCHAL

*Kinneff, the 12 of November* [1660].

MADAME,—I could not of ductie [omit] to write to your Ladyship a . . . Barras is now assaying high things namelie to [a]prove . . . hes written to his Majestie anent the honoures. I do not write this . . . tion. But he told me it out of his oune mouth. I shall not insist [upon] particulars, but for preventing of any inconvenience I will relate [it in] generall, for he thought to have draune me on to concurre in his plot, [as] he feared without me he should not get things rightly gone about. But I have now given up all medling with him in that kynd. His sonne is at London and he [hes] written to him that my Lord Ogilvie is gone with him to the Kings Majestie and hes declared that his father did preserve the honoures, and affirmed that notwithstanding all that your Ladyship had written to his Majestie that they were yet in his fathers handis, and hes good hopes, as he hath written to his father, of gryt things. And if the honoures be not yet delyvered that nather any Lord or Lady in the Kingdome should

have them till he advertised them againe, evin albeit they had
a commission from his Majestie. But since that was not now
to be helped, he told me what course he should take for it,
namely that he would show a tickquet of recept subscribed be
my Lord Marshall that he had receaved the honoures from him.
I enquired where had he that, and quhen had he gotten it,
seeing I had delyv[ered] them, and he refused to give me a
tickquet of recept. O, said he, I got [it the] night before the
honoures were delyuered be my Lord Arbuthnot . . . truely
I thought it very strange. Now I did not refuse to [concu]rre
w[ith him] till I had hard all, and then I told him I would
not be deceaved [any] more with him. And your Ladyship
remembers I did ever fear that he [would] easily wynd himselfe
into my Lord Marshall his favour. Your Ladyship may
m[ake the] best use heirof your Ladyship can, for Barras is
very busie to post away letters to his sonne, for he told me he
was presently going to Newgrange to dispatch his letters. In
haist I continow, Madame, your Ladyships humbill servant in
the best service, M. JAM. GRAINGER.

MADAM,—It is eneuph [to] improve him both [of] it . . .
the honoures and at your . . . ion and . . . written the day
befor . . . the nixt week.

For the truely noble Lady, my Lady the Countesse of Marshall,
these.

[*Docquet*]. The Minister of Kinneffs Letter to the Countess of Marshall.
  12th November 1660.
Edinburgh 26 August 17  .—Presented by Alexander Troup, writer, and
  registrat per M<sup>c</sup>Kell.


SIGNATURE FOR THE PATENT OF KNIGHT MARISCHAL
TO JOHN KEITH [1]

Our Soverane Lord ordains a letter to be past under the
great scale of his antient kingdome of Scotla[nd] makeing

---

[1] 1660.

mention that his Majestie takeing to his c[onsi]deration how necessar it is for the honor of the Crown the credit of his government and service, and for the good of his subjects that all those services that . . . unto be stable and entrusted to persons of known reputation, merit and honour, and his Majestie haveing perfect knowledge of the worth and loyaltie of John Keith, brother to the Earle Marischal, quhairof he hes given good testimonie at everic occasion dureing the late troubles, and of the great service he performed in the enteir preserveing of his Majesties Royal Honors, the Crown, Sword and Scepter frome the violence and possession of these rebells that these yeeres past had overrun and possessed thameselfe of his Majesties kingdome [of] Scotland, a service n[ever to] be forgotten by succeeding generations, and which doth so justlie intitull him to some honorable employment in his Majesties service: his Majestie hath therfore of his certane knowledge mad, constit[ut] and creat, and be thir presents maks, constitutts and creats the said John Keith Knight Marischal of the kingdom of Scotland, and gives and grants unto him dureing all the dayes of his lyftyme the place and office of Knight Marischall of Scotland; with power to him to exerce and discharge the same, and to enjoy all the priviledges, benefits, dignities and others due and belonging therunto or which heirafter salbe fund to be proper and belonging unto the same. And in regard of his constant attendance at Parlaments and other occasions of his Majesties service, his Majestie hes given and granted and annexed and be the tenor heirof gives, grants, and annexeth unto the said office a yeerlie pension of          for all the yeeres of his lyftyme, to be payed out of the reddiest of his Majesties rents, customes or casualities of his Exchecker at tuo termes of the yeere, the first termes payment being at Martmes nixto come: commanding heirby his Majesties Thesaurers, principal and depute, the ressavers of his Majesties rents, and all others whome it concerns, to make exact and punctuall payment of this pension accordingly. And ordains these presents to be a sufficient warrand to the Wryter to the great scale and to the keeper of the same to wryt and exped this grant and to append the great seal therto without passing any other register or scales. London. . . .

## LETTER FROM CHARLES II. TO THE EARL OF MIDDLETON [1]

*May the 8th*, 1662.

MIDDLETON,—You are not, I am sure, a straunger to the great services were done in Scotlande by my Lady Mareshalle att a time when few or none almost durst or would owne me, therfore I need not tell you how just a sense I have of them and how desirous I am of any occasion to e[ncourage her]. Being lately in[formed] that some differences [have arisen] betwixt her, and her sone in law, the Earle of Mare[shall] (if any such shall happen) I do particularly comand you to [see] that no [wr]onge be [d]one her, but that she may enjoy what justlie she has a pretinsion too, being a person that is very much in the care of your very affectionate frinde, CHARLES R.

*For the Earle of Middleton.*

## MEMORIALL FOR THE EARL OF KINTORE [2]

When King Charles the Second went to England with the Scottish armie, by his order the Crown, Scepter and Sword wer transported to the Castle of Dunnotter to be under the care of the Earl Marischall who was allowed a leivtenent and soom souldiours for the defence of the place. The Earl imployed Georg Ogilvie, his servant, who being bred and born under him, the said George father being porter in Dunnotter and never advanced to further degrees of service, yet his soon being educat with the Earl was mutch in his favour and gave him commission to be his leivtenent when the King went

---

[1] Middleton was Commander-in-Chief of the forces in Scotland, and Commissioner to the Parliaments of 1661 and 1662. The latter was opened by him on the 8th May, the date of this letter. The Earl Marischal referred to in this letter was George, eighth Earl, the second son of the Countess, who succeeded his brother in 1661.

[2] This is a Memorial submitted to the Lord Advocate (Sir James Stewart of Coltness) preliminary to the proceedings before the Privy Council. The proceedings were taken with the concurrence of the Lord Advocate.

to England.[1]  In anno 1651 the Earl Marshall put the honours at Dunnotter in the best posture he could and lodged the Honors in a secret place in the Castle. But he being in commission with the Earles of Crafoord, Glencardin and others, mett at Eliot with meny of the Kings frinds there to consult about the affaires of the nation and government; but he with others wer surprized and made prisoners by Collonell Alured. And finding that he was to be carried to London, sent privat orders to the Countess of Marishall, his mother, to take care of the Honors. And accordingly the countess, having receaved the key, shee went to the place wher the honors wer and delivred them to George Ogilvie, the leivtenent, to care for them. Altho the Committee of States had ordered the Lord Balcarres to receiv them out of Dunnotter, yet by the good conduct of Mr. Jhon Keith, now Earl of Kintore (when very younge) and George Ogilvies earnest desire, who was affrayd to deney the Committees order, did take upon him to refuse the giving them up to the said Lord Balcarres; which fell out very happily, for if they had been given out they had been undoubtedly seased upon, the English being then master of all Scotland.

Then the English, marching northward, the Countes fears anent the honors increased, and therfor shee ordered they should be privately caried off and ane accompt sent to hir wher they wer lodged. Soom few dayes therafter the minister of Kinneff is putt upon the contryvance, who manadged it very faithfully, his wyfe and hir maid having caried the Honours in a bundle off flax to hir own house, therafter lodged them in the

---

[1] This mention of Ogilvie and of his father's position in the castle is inaccurate and partisan, though the Privy Council seems to have accepted it as true. William Ogilvie of Lumgair (George Ogilvie's father) was the second and surviving son of John Ogilvie of Balnagarro and Chapelton, a cadet of the house of Innerquharity. He was a relative of Dame Margaret Ogilvie, second wife of George, fifth Earl Marischal, and came with her, when a boy, to the Mearns. He became a great favourite of the Earl Marischal, and was employed by him in important family affairs. His father having sold Balnagarro, and his elder brother having died, he, with the balance of the price of Balnagarro, obtained a wadset of the lands of Lumgair from the Earl Marischal. It is very unlikely that he ever occupied the menial position assigned to him here. (*Barras Manuscript Papers*, in the possession of the Rev. Samuel Ogilvy Baker; Jervise's *Land of the Lindsays*, p. 403).

church, and gav the Countess of Marischall a receipt bearing the places wher they wer lodged.

The English therafter, having beseidged Dunnotter, was surrendred upon a very base capitulation as can be instructed,[1] and the leivtenent was bound to deliver the Honors or giv a rational accompt of them. And accordingly when they wer required, George Ogilvie and his wyf asserted that they wer caried abroad by the now Earl of Kintore, then Mr. Jhon Keith, and delivred to the King in Paris, but George wanting documents, hie and his wyf wer detayned prisoners till the Earl sent a declaration from France, upon which they wer sett at liberty on baill.

The Earl of Kintore having then acknowledgd under his hand the having of the Honors, and knowing the difficulties that might attend him if he should fall in the hands of his enemies he stayed abroad till Generall Midleton came over to Scotland, and therafter followed him over to Scotland. Hie endured a great many hardships, being taken in his landing in the Ely in Fyfe, but being in disguise as a young merchand lad, the English let him go. Therafter coming north he corresponded with the Marquise of Montros, who had married his cousin german, and having got some frinds with him went to the hills and joyned General Midleton and remayned still ther till they wer defeatt at Lochgarioch. And when ther was no further hopis left he fell upon a contryvance of getting a receipt from Generall Midleton, as if the Honors had been delivred to him at Paris by the Kings order. And then the Countess of Marshall by the mediation of frinds prevailed with Generall Monke to include him in the Marquis of Montroses capitulation. And being challenged by Collonell Cobbet, then governour of Dundee, who was appointed by Monke to concert the artickles off capitulation with the Marquis of Montrose, the said Cobbet told the Earl of Kintore, then Mr. Jhon Keith,

---

[1] The articles of agreement for the surrender of the Castle are printed in Appendix ii. of the Bannatyne Club volume, p. 72. The adjective 'mean' is scarcely applicable. Ogilvie and his garrison had permission to march out of the Castle 'with flying collours, drom beateing, match lighted, the distance of one mile, theare to lay down theire armes, and to have passes to goe to theire own homes, and theare to live without molestation, provided they act nothing prejudiciall to the Commonwealth of England.'

that he was ordered by Generall Monk to inquire of him if he did cary the Honors abroad, which he ouned, and upon production of Generall Midletons receipt hie was included in the capitulation with the Marquise, neither was ther ever any further enquiry made about them till the Kings restauration.

Then the Countes of Marshall wrot to the King to receiv his Majesties commands about the Honors by a very kind letter from his Majestie, with thanks for hir good service; was desired to deliver them to the Earl Marshall, and as a mark of his Majesties favour he not only made the Earl Lord Privy Seall, but gave also to Mr. Jhon Keith, now Earl of Kintore, the patent of Knight Marshall with ane considerable fee for the said office; and therafter he was created Earle of Kintore, and both thes patents, amongst his other signall services, mentions the preservation of the Honors, and the Lord Lyon is appoynted to giv him the Croun, Scepter, and Sword, as ane addition to his coat of arms.

Notwithstanding that the Honors wer thus preserved the way and manner abov mentioned, and that the King was sufficiently convinced theroff, and not only by his royall patents in favour of the Earle of Kintore, but by his privat letters to the Countess of Marishall acknowledged the same, yet the above said George Ogilvie, leivtennent, most impudently had the confidence to send up his soon to London, arrogating to himself the sole preservation of the Honors, and having adresed the Lord Ogilvy, afterwards Earl of Airly, did introduce him to his Majestie. Upon which the Countess of Marishall sent up a gentlman express, and wrote to the Earl off Midleton a true information of the wholl matter, which he very kindly represented to his Majestie, who refused to giv ear to any such suggestions. And so his pretensions being defeatt, ther was no mor of it.

Neither would the Countess of Marishall and the now Earl of Kintore bee dissatisfied with what favour the King might have bestowed on him. Nay, the Countess of Marishall in a letter to his Majestie did recommend the said George Ogilvie to his care. For its not to be deneyed, but that he knew of the careying off the Honors out of Dunnotter Castle and was kept prisoner for soom tym, till the now Earl of Kintore, then Mr. Jhon Keiths declaration from France of his having caried them abroad was the cause of the said Georges liberation. But his impudent assuming the wholl concern of ther preservation to himself and therby giving the ly both to his Majesties patents and other clear documents, for instructing the trueth of what is therin related.

Its to be observed that ther being fourty yeirs past since the forsaid George Ogilvies pretensions wer frustrate, who lived a considerable tym after the restauration, calmly thowch discontent, and that now this man, his soon, should so long after raise new dust, to the most ignominious reproach and disgrace (by his printed pamphlett) of the memory of the Countess of Marshall and now Earle of Kintore: its fitt therfor my Lord Advocatt advyse how far the Earle of Kintore may hav redress in this matter, and that Barras may be persued for printing, publishing, and dispersing of scandalous pamphlets, and that the Councill will inflict a severe censure by fining and imprisoning his person, and burning of his . . . stell printes.

JOHN ERSKINE, ELEVENTH EARL OF MAR
AND HIS SON THOMAS, LORD ERSKINE

*from the portrait by Sir Godfrey Kneller in the possession of the Earl of Mar and Kellie*

# THE EARL OF MAR'S LEGACIES
## TO SCOTLAND
### AND TO HIS SON, LORD ERSKINE
### 1722-1727

Edited from the original MS. at Alloa House, with a Biographical Introduction and Notes by

THE HON. STUART ERSKINE

# CONTENTS

|  | PAGE |
|---|---|
| Introduction, | 141 |
| Mar's Legacy to his Son, | 157 |
| Jewels, or The Legacy to Scotland, | 194 |
| Letters from the Chevalier, | 206 |
| Considerations and Proposals for Ireland on a Restoration, | 213 |
| A Scheme for restoring Scotland to its ancient Military Spirit, | 215 |
| Memorial to the Duke of Orleans, | 223 |
| A Thought with regard to Scotland, | 241 |
| Appendix, | 244 |

# INTRODUCTION

The author of the Legacy here printed for the first time, John Erskine, eleventh Earl of Mar, and eighteenth Lord Erskine, was the eldest son of Charles, tenth Earl of Mar, and Lady Mary Maule, daughter to the Earl of Panmure. He was born at Alloa in the month of February 1675, and succeeded to the earldom in 1690, and at the same time to an estate 'extremely involved, but which by good management, he in great measure retreived.'

Charles, the tenth Earl, offers some claims to notice. He raised the regiment of foot soldiers known as Scots Fusiliers, and was a Privy Councillor to Charles II. and to James VII.; but disapproving the latter's harsh and unconstitutional measures in Scotland, he broke with the King and retired abroad. When, however, the Revolution of 1688 was ingloriously and unhappily set on foot he embraced the King's interest, and as a consequence of that step, was arrested in March 1689 and sent to prison, where he died not long after his incarceration.

Of the eleventh Earl's mother, Lady Mary Maule, little that is authentic is known. It is said that she was crooked and squinted abominably; but as this statement is based on the authority of the Master of Sinclair, it must be accepted if it be entertained at all, with prodigious reserve.[1]

Charles, tenth Earl of Mar, was plagued with poverty, and during his lifetime the fortunes of the Erskines were at a very low ebb. 'Unswerving loyalty to the Royal cause,' says Lord

---

[1] The same authority asserts that Mar also was crooked. If he was so it is somewhat curious that none of the portraits of him (of which there are four or five) preserved at Alloa contain any traces of his alleged deformity.

Crawford in his book on the *Earldom of Mar*, 'the hereditary characteristic of the Erskines, throughout the great Rebellion, was punished by fines and sequestrations up to the date of the Restoration; and after that event, the debts contracted in the cause of Charles I. and Charles II., necessitated the sale of estate after estate, including the Barony of Erskine, their original honour on the Clyde, till the possessions of the family were reduced to little more[1] than the Lordship of Alloa, an ancient Erskine dependence though dignified by the supreme rights of regality. The seal was set upon these misfortunes and their decadence by the accession of John, Earl of Mar, the great-great-grandson of the Earl, restored in 1565, to the Rebellion of 1715, of which he was in fact the leader and head.'

Of Lord Mar's boyhood and youth little is known. He was educated, firstly, at Edinburgh, and secondly, at the University of Leyden in Holland. So soon as he had performed the 'grand tour' he attached himself to the powerful and influential party of the Duke of Queensberry, when his public career may be said to have begun. He took the oaths and his seat September 8, 1698, and early next year was sworn of the Privy Council of King William and Queen Mary. The young Earl remained a devoted adherent of Lord Queensberry till the latter's fall, and that of the court party in 1704 when, finding himself idle, he joined the country party in opposing the tactics of the Squadrone, and thus gained for himself the hearty support and sympathy of the Tories. When, however, the Duke of Queensberry returned to power in 1705 Mar again became his adherent, and in consequence of his zeal and fidelity in that service, was made one of the Commissioners appointed to treat of the Scottish Act of Union, being afterwards honoured with the post of Keeper of the Signet in reward for

---

[1] This is an exaggeration. At the time I am writing of nearly the whole of the great district of Mar was in the hands of the Erskines. It left them for ever in 1730, when in consequence of the appalling poverty of the family it was sold to the then Farquharson of Invercauld, and to one Lord Duff.

# INTRODUCTION 143

the part which he took in recommending that important treaty to the consideration of his countrymen. From that time forward his influence both among the Scots nation and the English Ministers began to increase, and went on developing at a very rapid rate until he was made Secretary for Scotland in the reign of Queen Anne, when he may be said to have reached the zenith of his fame.

In February 1707 he was chosen one of the Representative Peers of Scotland, an honour which was conferred on him again in 1708, 1710, and 1713, about which time also he was sworn of the Privy Council of Queen Anne. The important share he took in forcing the Union through the Scots Parliament did not, however, prevent him from speaking strongly in support of Earl Findlater's motion for the repeal of that treaty, which wa made in Parliament in 1713. This conduct Lord Mar is at some unnecessary pains to justify in the following Legacy.

'The Earl of Mar,' says Macky in his *Secret Memoirs*, speaking of the leader of the affair of 1715, 'is representative
' of one of the ancientest and most noble families in Scotland,
' hereditary guardians of kings and queens of that kingdom,
' during their minority, and hereditary keepers of Stirling
' Castle. This gentleman hath not made any greater figure
' than being of the Privy Council both to King William and
' this queen [Anne]. He is a very good manager in his private
' affairs, which were in disorder when his father died, and is a
' staunch countryman, fair complexioned, low stature, and
' thirty years old.'

The somewhat sudden and unexpected death of Queen Anne in 1714 occasioned the downfall of the Tory party. Mar, in common with many of his political friends, endeavoured at first to make his peace with the new government. In order to that end he wrote a letter to the Elector of Hanover, whilst that prince was yet on the Continent, in which his (Mar's) services to the Elector's predecessors on the throne of 'His Majesty's ancestors' were eloquently set forth, and in which much apprehension was expressed lest the colour of the Earl's political convictions should be misrepresented to the future sovereign of Great Britain. He also, it is said, 'desired to 'display his influence over the Highlanders, and for that pur-'pose procured a letter, subscribed by a number of the most 'influential chiefs of the clans, addressed to himself as having 'an estate and interest in the Highlands, conjuring him to 'assure the government of their loyalty to His Sacred Majesty 'King George, and to protect them and the heads of other 'clans, who, from distance, could not attend at the signing of 'the letter, against the misrepresentations to which they might 'be exposed; protesting that as they had been ready to follow 'Lord Mar's directions in obeying Queen Anne, so they would 'be equally forward to concur with him in faithfully serving 'King George.'[1]

The new adherents of the new Sovereign were, however, determined to follow the mistaken policy of securing the unlimited ascendency of their own party on the ruins of that of their opponents. Bolingbroke and his political friends were not long allowed to remain in suspense with respect to the nature of the sentiments entertained for them by their Whig enemies. They apprehended that they were to be pursued, hanged, drawn, quartered or outlawed without benefit of jury.[2] The well-meaning advances of Mar were coldly repulsed: he was commanded to deliver up the seals of his office, and curtly informed that his gracious Majesty King George had no further occasion for his services.

It is not to be wondered at that Mar felt the rebuff keenly, and that whilst smarting under the indignity of his dismissal, he should have allowed a burning desire for revenge to overrule the natural promptings of a somewhat cautious nature. The egregious folly of disobliging a man who could work so much mischief is perhaps the most patent, and certainly the most

---

[1] Scott's *Tales of a Grandfather*.
[2] See Lord Bolingbroke's letter to Sir William Wyndham.

disgusting, feature of Mar's dismissal, as his own procrastinating conduct and complete inability to carry the point he had in view were those of his subsequent behaviour in the field. 'Although it might be true,' says Sir Walter Scott, who was by no means partial to Mar, 'that the address was made up with the 'sanction of the Chevalier de St. George and his advisers, it 'was not less the interest of George the I. to have received with 'the usual civility, the expressions of homage and allegiance 'which it contained. . . . A monarch whose claim to obedience 'is yet young, ought in policy to avoid an immediate quarrel 'with any part of his subjects who are ready to profess allegiance 'as such. . . . It seems at least certain that in bluntly and in 'a disparaging manner refusing an address expressing allegiance 'and loyalty, and affronting the haughty courtier by whom it 'was presented, King George exposed his government to the 'desperate alternative of civil war and the melancholy expedient 'of terminating it by bringing many noble victims to the 'scaffold, which, during the reign of his predecessor, had never 'been stained with bloodshed for political causes.'

The Earl of Mar, repulsed in his advances to the new monarch, concluded, not unnaturally, from thence that, if not his ruin, at all events his permanent disgrace was absolutely determined on by the new king's political advisers. He withdrew accordingly from court, and soon afterwards set on foot the melancholy and disastrous insurrection with which his name is prominently associated in the history of our country.

At the conclusion of that ill contested and worse managed affair, Mar accompanied the Prince to France, where he enjoyed His Royal Highness's favour for a number of years. During the time that he held the chief secretary's seals, the affairs of the Prince, his master, were conducted with considerable address, if we can believe the statement of Lockhart of Carnwath (a most impartial, and in some respects even bitter, critic of Lord Mar) to that effect. His zeal and activity in the service of the unfortunate exile were apparently unbounded. Among other projects, more or less plausible, he formed one for engaging the brave and eccentric King of Sweden, Charles the XII., whose assistance he thought to purchase, by a present of oatmeal for his troops, in a plot to restore his master. Another of his schemes was that for bringing in the Duke of Argyle to the Prince's interests and service. This is said to have failed on account of Mar's jealousy of the former, but inasmuch as it was Mar himself who proposed it and endeavoured to carry it through, the assumption that he spoiled it is at least open to doubt. At all events, it is impossible to observe much of either jealousy or dislike in the friendly terms in which Lord Mar refers to the Duke in the following Legacy; nor is it likely that he would have expressly commanded his son to seek him out and secure his protection if he had entertained sentiments of dislike or jealousy regarding him.

It does not appear that Mar was much engaged in the affair of 1719, though it is certain that his advice and opinion were sought on it. The following extracts from a letter preserved in the Stuart Collection at Windsor, and printed in these pages, for the first time, may serve to substantiate this statement. 'Sire,' he says, writing from Rome to the Prince, under date February 4th, 1719, ' . . . I have often taken the libertie to
' tel y$^r$ Majesty that whenever it should please God to restore
' you to y$^r$ Dominions, that I had no designe or project of
' haveing any eminent hand in business at that time. What I
' have so much wisht for all my life will be accomplished, and
' y$^r$ Majesty will be in no want of fitt people to serve you
' in each of y$^r$ kingdoms, and who are much more capable of it
' than I, and it will be far from giveing me any grudg to
' see any you think fitt to be emploied in the most eminent
' posts of y$^r$ three kingdoms. As for the seals I have the
' honour to hold of y$^r$ Majesty at this time, you may very
' freely, without any apprehension of giveing me a mortifica-
' tion, dispose of them as soon as you land in England, not
' only those for that kingdome, but also for that of Scotland

'and Irland. I never aim'd at being thought what is comonly
'call'd to Princes a ffavourit, but my ambition is to have the
'honour, as it will be a pleasur, of being near y$^r$ person. You
'have been pleased alreddy to give me a post w$^{ch}$ entitles me to
'that, and if you think it fitt to add to it any emploiment
'w$^{ch}$ would make me to be of y$^r$ cabin councill (as it is call'd
'here) tho of ever so little business, that it may not be thought
'that after serveing you abroad in place of a minister, that I
'am quite turn'd off, I shall have all I aim at, and it would be
'in that way I wou'd end my dayes w$^t$ pleasur. As for the
'affairs of Scotland, I should have no pleasur in being im-
'mediately emploied in them, but wherein I am capable to
'give y$^r$ Majesty light or advice in them or in any of y$^r$ affairs
'in England by the little insight I have had of men and things
'there, it could be done as well as if I were [here ?] and per-
'haps w$^t$ more ease and advantage to y$^r$ Majesty. But if you
'should find either that my advice was of no use or made
'any uneasie, my not being consulted should be farr from
'makeing me so.[1]

'ffor the present intended expedition, I am reddy to serve
'y$^r$ Majesty in any way or capasity you please and that I am
'capable of, but I would presume to beg it of y$^r$ Majesty as
'a favour that I may not be sent to Scotland, tho' I wou'd
'not ask even that, did I not think that y$^r$ affairs wou'd suffer
'by it, but for all that can be done there as the expedition
'is proposed, I humblie conceive that it can be done as well
'as in the manner it was designed when you came into Italy
'had it then gone on, as if I went. There ought an ex-
'perienced officer of distinction be sent there, go who will,
'and I heartily wish the same person may who was then

---

[1] This language is so contrary to the character with which it has pleased his biographers to blacken his reputation, that one marvels that Lord Mar should have dared to hold it. Mar is usually represented as having been a greedy, needy, self-seeking courtier. It is refreshing to find him using the language of moderation and even making some sort of dim religious effort to conform to the exalted moral standard of his critics.

'design'd.[1] And He to whom y^r Majesty then gave the first
'place, is still the fittest for it. My fellow traveler[2] will be
'a good help there to him, and I doubt not but he will
'behave himself w^t that disinterested zeal he did upon the
'last occasion. In that way I can answer that all my friends
'will do all in their power as much as if I were there myself,
'as I doubt not but every man wou'd who wishes y^r Majesty well.

'What I ask is to have the honour to attend y^r Majesty as a
'Voluntier without any character or emploiment, and you shall
'have all the service of me I am capable of as much as if I had
'both and in that way, if y^r Majesty have a mind to it, I
'should think it could make no man uneasie upon my account.

'It was never my studdie to be rich, and I am now too old
'to begin to think of it. Y^r Majesty has been pleased to lay
'more honours on me alreddy than I deserve, and I can have
'nothing further or wish for that way. You will have the
'goodness, I hope, if my family by its cariage deserves it,
'to make it easie and in a way, in some measur, not to make
'those honours ashamed of its bearing them, and, for myself,
'I shall be very indifferent of opolencie.

'God grant y^r Majesty a good and safe vooage and journie
'and success in y^r project. May I be so luckie to arive in
'time to attend you in y^r expedition, but if unfortunately
'I do not, let me beg of y^r Majesty to leave directions for my
'following of you directly, where ever you go.

'As to other things, the Duke of Ormond, who has show'd
'himself so zealous in y^r service is the fittest to advise you
'and as he was the first who publickly embraced y^r Maj^s
'service who were in any business at y^r sister's death, I
'heartily wish he may have the honour and happiness to
'finish the glorious work of y^r restoration for which y^r king-
'doms wou'd be so much beholden to him and have reason to
'love him better, if that can be, than they yet do.

'I will not trouble y^r Majesty w^t any compliment, that

---

[1] Probably either Ormonde or Berwick.  [2] The Duke of Perth.

'being non of my talent, but may you be as hapie as I wish
'you, and that wou'd be more, I am sure, than any who ever
'satt upon y. thron have yet been, tho not more than you
'deserve, as y'r people will think when they have the happi-
'ness of knowing you.'

The affair of 1719[1] ended as disastrously for the Jacobites as that of 1715, and Mar was soon again employed in concerting other measures in the interests of his exiled master. From the former year to that of 1724 he had, with but few interruptions, the principal direction of the Prince's affairs, and though it would be an exaggeration to say that they flourished under his management, since nothing and nobody can be said ever to have done so that was in any way closely connected with that unfortunate personage, yet Mar conducted them well and, as far as ascertained, pleased his master as well as the majority of his party. In 1724, however, in consequence, there is strong reason to believe, of a plot between Atterbury and Colonel Hay,[2] who was afterwards created Earl of Inverness by Prince James, Mar was deprived of office. In order that my readers may fully understand the secret motives underlying this step, it is necessary that I should here digress a little.

In 1721 Bishop Atterbury had been compelled to leave England in consequence of a conspiracy against the Govern-

---

[1] An account of the Jacobite attempt of 1719 is printed in vol. xix. of the publications of the *Scottish History Society*.

[2] Colonel Hay was at one time an officer in the Scots Guards, who 'got into the Chevalier's favour by means of the Earl of Mar.' He married a daughter of Lord Stormont, and the Chevalier becoming enamoured of her, ' it was not very long before the Lord and Lady Mar were driven from Court to make room for the new favourites.' On the disgrace of Mar 'the Colonel was made Prime Minister; nobody could be introduced to an audience but by his means; no counsel was put in execution till he had first approved it ; and, in short, he governed the Chevalier and the whole court in a most absolute manner.' These extracts are taken from a book entitled *The Men of the Chevalier de St. George, on occasion of the Princess Sobieski's retiring into a Nunnery*. Hay was publicly declared secretary 5th March 1725, though it is well known he had had the principal direction of affairs for some time prior to Mar's dismission from office. He was deprived of office, April 1727. For Hay's conduct to the Princess Sobieski see Lockhart's *Memoirs*, vol. ii. p. 265. His parts, like his character, were contemptible.

ment, in which the prelate was involved, though himself and his friends stoutly maintained the contrary. It would seem that from circumstances—the most notable and at the same time the most ludicrous being that of the little white dog, which the good bishop pretended to believe had been sent into England from France by Mar for the express purpose of betraying him to the government—I say that from certain circumstances which transpired at the trial, Atterbury got a fixed notion into his head that Mar and the British Government had together and in concert conspired his banishment. This 'fire-brand of a Bishope,' as Mar calls him in the following Memorial and Legacy, accordingly left England under the impression that Mar, in addition to being his personal enemy, was a traitor to his party, in which highly explosive frame of mind he entered France, and would appear at once to have begun to endeavour to bring others to share with him the same charitable opinion.

What real grounds, however, Atterbury had for believing that Mar had betrayed him to the Government it is impossible to say, nor is he able to divulge them in his private correspondence, which has been printed. All we can say, however, in favour of Atterbury's assertion, is, that the proceedings which led to the trial and conviction of the Bishop, as well as those that followed after it, are involved in so much mystery that it would be indiscreet to affirm positively at this distance of time, that he was altogether destitute of grounds for his charges. What, on the other hand, militates most strongly against the Bishop's assumption is the fact that he was convicted of the crime with which he was charged on the slenderest evidence. The trial, in fact, was a miserable farce, an outrage upon justice; but so determined were the Government to secure a conviction that they stopped at nothing in order to make the Bishop to appear guilty. Now it would seem to stand to reason that if, as Atterbury asserted, Mar hatched a plot with the British Government to betray the Bishop to them and received money and promises of pardon for his share in it, the former would have taken very good care not to part with either their money or promises without receiving adequate value for both. In other words, it is improbable that the Government would have made so loose a compact with Mar for the betrayal of Atterbury as enabled the Bishop successfully to masquerade as irreproachably innocent at the trial, and even for many years afterwards, successfully to maintain all the appearances of a state of pious and impregnable guiltlessness.

Apart from the affair of the little white dog, to which reference has been made above, the circumstance on which the Bishop laid the greatest stress in preferring his charges of treachery against Mar was the intercepting by Government of letters addressed by Mar to the Bishop. This, however, is surely very inadequate ground on which to base reckless and wholesale charges of treachery, inasmuch as the intercepting of Jacobite letters by Government was an event of daily, if not hourly, occurrence. In a book entitled *Memoirs of the Life, Family, and Character of John, late Earl of Stair*, we are told how in 1715, ' by Lord Mar's intercepted letters which Pringle will send you,' it was said to be plain that Lord Mar 'expected the Pretender in Scotland,' yet no charge of treachery, so far as the writer is aware, was laid at Mar's door on that occasion in consequence of what was undoubtedly a common Jacobite mishap.

To take up, however, the thread of my narrative at the point at which it was dropped in order to make the above necessary digression, some time previous to his dismissal from office, but at a period not specified in the Legacy itself, Mar presented to the Prince a scheme consisting, to use his own language, of 'considerations and proposalls for the severall ' parts of the constitution and Government of Scotland upon a ' Restoration.' This scheme or 'Legacy' the Prince ' was pleased some time thereafter ' to indorse in a series of letters addressed by him to Mar from Rome. In the month of September 1723, Mar, who was at that time in Paris, writes to the Prince, who was then at Rome, saying that he is 'about a thing' which he hopes will be the best service he ever did for his master. This 'thing' which Mar was engaged upon, and which he says in his letter to the Prince he mentioned either to His Royal Highness or to Mr. Hay, was the celebrated 'Memorial to the Regent Orleans.' The history of this Memorial is a curious one. The latter was composed by Mar himself, and sent to the Regent without either the privity or permission of Prince James. The Regent, according to Mar, received it favourably, and from what is known of the former's real sentiments towards this country, there is no reason to doubt his having done so. Mar, flattered probably by the reception accorded to his Memorial by the Regent of France, sent it forthwith to the Prince his master, who, as Mar was high in his favour at the time, probably approved it also. At all events there is absolutely no evidence to show that he did not indorse it; and as the Memorial was presented in 1723, and as Mar was not deprived of office till the year 1725 it would be interesting to know what opinion the Prince held with regard to it (if he did not approve it) in the interval between those two dates. Unfortunately, however, for Mar, the Prince, if ever he approved the Memorial, which, as I have said before, there is every reason to believe he did, never expressed his approval in writing, so that when in 1725 Mar was dismissed from office, James was able to announce to the world with a clear conscience, that the secretary had been displaced on account of its treasonable nature.[1] The insufficiency, however, of this

---

[1] If the causes of Mar's dismissal constituted such clear and unmistakable evidences of his guilt it is curious that the Prince should have been at so much pains to hush up that affair. In a letter addressed to Lockhart he expressly commands his 'trustee' not to concern himself with the subject of Mar's dismissal. The less said about that affair the better, says the Prince in effect. But if Mar's guilt was so clear, what harm could have come to the Prince's affairs by the particulars of it coming to light? It is impossible to resist the reflection on these matters that the Prince was further concerned to keep the affair secret and his own part in it also than he was desirous should appear.

excuse as a ground for Mar's disgrace is plainly revealed by a reference to the Memorial itself, which, though it no doubt exceeded in some measure the principle laid down in the Legacy, approved by the Prince, yet to all practical intents and purposes was precisely the same thing. Mar was denounced as a traitor by Hay and Atterbury because he wished to induce the Prince to consent to an arrangement by which a certain number of Scottish troops should be constantly entertained in the service of the French king, and a certain number of French troops in that of the Scottish king, for the purpose of overawing England; yet if we turn to the letters of James addressed to Mar and printed in this book, we find that James readily consented to allow a certain number of Scots troops to be constantly entertained in the service of the French king, in the event of his restoration; and though Mar's proposal at the time did not embrace the larger proposition mentioned above, namely that the French king should return the compliment, as it were, and send French troops into Scotland for the purpose of augmenting the Scottish king's forces, yet if James approved the one proposition it is difficult to understand what reasonable objections he could have had to indorsing the other. His own words on the subject could not be plainer. 'In consequence 'of my letter to you of the first of Janry.' says the Prince, ' I 'think it would be for the honour and interest of Scotland that 'I should make an agreement with the King of ffrance after my 'restoration, for his entertaining a certain number of Scots 'troops in his service, w$^{ch}$ I am perswaded the Parl. will 'approve of.' It is impossible to mistake either the meaning or significance of these words, considered, as they must and should be, in conjunction with the so called 'treasonable' parts of the Memorial.

There is no doubt in my mind that Mar's removal from office was due to a conspiracy of which Hay and Atterbury were the ringleaders. The former was intensely jealous of Mar's ascendency at the Jacobite Court: the latter, as we have already seen, was the secretary's bitter enemy. The probability is that, as Mar himself states, Hay communicated either the gist or a copy of the Memorial itself to Atterbury, who, in order to revenge himself on Mar and to bring about the secretary's downfall, published the document, and caused its dissemination in Jacobite circles.[1] This skilful move had precisely the effect the wily prelate imagined it would have. It raised a storm of indignation in England against Mar, who immediately became odious to the English Jacobites, and in a short time occasioned his dismissal from office; for James, whatever may have been his real sentiments on the subject of the Memorial, had sense enough to perceive that by retaining in his service a minister who had rendered himself highly obnoxious to his English supporters he would be doing his party and interests an irremediable injury. Mar retired to Paris after his dismissal from office, where he remained till the year 1729, when he went to Aix-la-Chapelle to drink the waters for the benefit of his health, which now began to show unmistakable symptoms of an early dissolution. During his latter years he was, to his credit be it said, 'little trusted by the Jacobites'; and he would seem to have entered into some negotiations with the British Government for the purpose of procuring himself a pardon, which is not to be wondered at, considering the scurvy treatment he had received at the hands of the Jacobites and their sovereign. He died at Aix-la-Chapelle (1732) in the fifty-fourth year of his age; and was succeeded in his attainted peerage by his only son Lord Erskine, the youth to whom the following 'Jewels' and 'Legacie' were bequeathed.

Doubtless a few particulars concerning the appearance and

---

[1] There is no printed copy of the Memorial at the British Museum, nor, to the best of the writer's knowledge and belief, is there one at any other of our public libraries. The probability is that the Memorial was privately printed and circulated, and for that reason never came into the hands of the general public.

history of the valuable and interesting little volume which contains the Legacy and Memorial above mentioned will not be considered out of place in this Introduction. The book is the property of the Earl of Mar and Kellie, to whom I am vastly obliged for permission to edit it for the Scottish History Society. The whole of the Manuscript has been given with the exception of a few pages, not amounting to half a dozen in all, which, as they relate to private family affairs, would be of no interest to the public. The Legacy is written in an admirable, clear hand, in an octavo volume, bound in pale olive-green leather. A couple of small silver clasps serve to keep the volume fast, when it is not in use.

Considering the fact that the Memorial was published in London, and there circulated, though only in a private way doubtless, it is surprising that no copy of it is to be found at the British Museum or at any other of the ordinary sources of historical information. It may be, of course, that the writer is mistaken in his belief that no printed copy of the Memorial is in existence at the present time, but if this is so it cannot be laid to his charge that this conviction is the result either of indifference or idleness, for he has searched for one 'high and low,' and has found nothing to reward his pains. That the Memorial, however, or, at anyrate, the general scope and tendency of it, were known to some historians of an earlier period than the one we live in is rendered certain by the fact that allusions to it more or less vague and indefinite are to be found in one or two contemporary writings. Lockhart of Carnwath gives a short *précis* of it in his *Memoirs*, but it may well be that the allusions and criticisms of other contemporary as well as subsequent writers were based on that author's reflections. With regard to the Legacy, it is here printed in its entirety for the first time. Sir Walter Scott, however, would seem to have perused it, or to have gathered some exact particulars concerning it either from hearsay or more certain means, since he makes a reference to it in his

*Tales of a Grandfather*, wherein he takes occasion of the Rebellion of 1715 to remark that the leader of it was more successful in his schemes for improving the capital of Scotland than he was in those for the alteration of her government. By this he would surely seem either to have read the Legacy itself, or to have had imparted to him particulars concerning those parts of it which relate to the improvement of Edinburgh. When or in what manner these particulars were communicated to Sir Walter I am unable to say: they were apparently communicated to none other.

A curious incident connected with the history of the Legacy is referred to by Philadelphia, Countess of Mar, in a note written on a fly-leaf of the book. 'This book,' the Countess writes, ' was stolen out of the family at the death of John Thomas, ' Earl of Mar, who died 28th September 1828. He was the ' second Earl who had the title after the family was restored to ' its ancient titles and dignities, anno 1824. This book was ' accidentally recovered by Philadelphia, Countess of Mar, wife ' of John Francis Mar, Earl of Mar, who gave a reward for the ' recovery of it. Alloa, July 14th, 1834.' Who stole the book or in what manner it was recovered is not known. The misfortune of its theft, however, was in reality a blessing in disguise, for when Alloa House was burned to the ground at the beginning of this century the whole of the interesting and valuable collection of historical and family documents preserved in it are said to have been destroyed in the conflagration.

S. E.

# MY LEGACIE TO MY DEAR SON THOMAS, LORD ERSKINE

I

*Chillon, March* 1726.

MY DEAR TOM,—Ever since you left us I have been here in the country, and much alone, where I had time for reflection, and you may be sure my thoughts have been the most taken up about you, now when you are to enter, as it were, on a stage the first time, and a troublesome one. The world and God only knows if ever I shall have the pleasure of seeing you again.

It haveing pleased Providence so to dispose of things that I have nothing worth the while of makeing a Will or Testament for, I chose this way of biding you adieu, in case I should die without haveing an opportunity of doing it again, or by word of mouth, and if it should so please God, you will find amongst my papers here (all which I will order to be given you) a Narative of most of the incidents of my Life, all in my own hand, w<sup>ch</sup> I wrote at different times, partly to amuse myself and refresh my memorie, when I had little else to emploie me, and partly thinking it might come to be of some use to you, for whom it is only intended, and not for the publick. I still hope it may be so, and it was luckie for myself that I keept nots of some parts of my life, haveing naturally a bad memorie, since they served me in good stade o' late, when my reputation was so cruelly atacqued by my enimies.

About four years ago when I had idle time enough at Paris, I wrote the first part of the narative from as far back as I could recolect to the change of the ministry about four years before Queen Anne's death. Upon my comeing from Scotland to ffrance an. 1715 I sent to our cousin Pittodrie[1] at Aberdin, and to his Lady in his absence, two large wooden boxes or trunks pritty full of letters and other papers w$^{ch}$ had past dureing the time of my being then in that country. I know they were deliverd to him safe before the Armies came to Aberdin, and I doubt not of their haveing been well taken care of and safely preserved by him ever since, nor of their being deliverd to you when you shall come to call for them. You will find things in them not uncurious, and that may be of some use in after times, both with regard to persons and things.

There is in one of them another part of the Narative, from the above change of the Ministry, to the Elections in Scotland after K. George's comeing first over, which I wrote in my idl hours in Braemar an. 1715 dureing the time I was preparing things for what happned soon therafter, and when I was waiting returns to the orders I had sent out through the Highlands.

When I went first to Avignon, and before I came to have much business to despatch there, I emploied the time I had [to?] spair from attending the King in continueing the Narative from the Elections to my setting up the King's standard in Braemar.

ffrom the setting up the standard to the King's landing at Gravelen from Scotland, I keept a journall of the most materiall things that past where I was present. I wrote it every night before I went to bed (keeping some sheets of paper always in my pocket on purpose), but only in short notes for refreshing my memory when I should come to write the Journall full as it ought to be. The miscariage of that affair, w$^{ch}$ once had so good an appearance for restoring our King and relieving our country has made the thinking of those things ever since disagreeable to me, so that I have never been able to bring myself to enlarge that journall.

The greatest part of the originall of these notes, you'll find in one of these boxes in Pittodrie's hands, and the rest amongest my papers here, haveing been in my pocket on my leaving

---

[1] Erskine of Pittodrie.

Scotland. There is also a fair copy in Mr. Paterson's[1] handwriteing of most of the journall wrote from what I had sent of it at different times to Lord Bolingbroke in ffrance, and from that part wch I brought along wt me.

You will likewise find amongest my papers here an account of the Expedition of that body of men I sent into Argyllshire under the command of Generall Gordon, on wch my undertakeing so much depended, wrote by Mr. Campbell of Glendarull, who was an eye witness to it, and wt whom I had concerted and laid that project.

I regrait much that I have never been able to procure from some of those present (tho' I have often endeavour'd it) a particular, full, and exact account of that body of men I sent over the fforth from ffife to join the noblemen and gentlemen of the South of Scotland and North of England then in armes for the King, and of their affair in the citadall of Leith and at Seaton house, their joining the gentlemen of the South, and their march into England until the unfortunat affair of Preston, the barbaritys wch were comitted on our people after that shamefull surender, and the crull treatment the prissoners met wt, who were caried to London, and those left behind in the county prisons. I cannot tho' imagin but some one or other of these gentlemen concerned and who suffred so severely in that expedition but got off at last has wrote a particular account of it all, wch you may perhaps still chance to come by, and you should be at pains to do so, the want of wch makeing a great blank in the accounts I leave you of the attempt then made, wch never will in after times do dishonour to our country.

There is amongest my papers too an account of those things in wch I had any concern, from the King's leaveing of Gravelen to his going into Italy from Avignon an. 1716. At Geneva, where I was so long kept against my will[2] as 13 months and had so much idle time, I went on wt this Narative from the

---

[1] A prominent Jacobite; served as Secretary at War during the '15. He was a son of Sir Hugh Paterson of Bannockburn, and Lady Jean Erskine, daughter to Charles tenth Earl of Mar. His father also engaged in the '15, and was deprived of his estates.

[2] Mar was arrested by the Genoese authorities at the instance of the British Government. He was at first confined to prison, but afterwards released on *parole*.

King's going to Italy to my being arrested at that town May 1719, contrair to all right and justice.

I was some time absent from the King at his first going to Italy (he haveing been pleased to alow me to go into ffrance to meet Lady Mar [1]) so that I had not the honour of attending him from the month of ffeb. that I left him at Montebello til the month of November therafter, when I joind him again at Urbino, so that I could not be so particular as to things w$^{ch}$ past with his Maj. in my absence, and I intending only to write what I was an eye witness to, I should be excused for saying little or nothing of what happned to the King or his affairs in Spain, or while I was prisoner an. 1719, his Majesty not haveing been pleased to cary me along w$^t$ him, and I being prevented following him, as I twice endeavourd. I left at Rome two large wooden boxes or trunks scald up, in w$^{ch}$ were a great many letters and papers in relation to the King's affairs while I had the honour to serve him as Minister, of w$^{ch}$ I sent the keys from Geneve, on the King's returning from Spain, to Lady Mar, then at Rome, to be given into his Maj.s own hands, w$^{ch}$ she did, and the boxes were also deliverd to him; they properly belonging to his Maj., and I haveing but a secondary right in them, I thought it my duety to have them put into his own hands, and at the same time I wrote to him, beging upon his own account, that he would be very cautious of alowing them to be lookt into, and never unless he was present himself.[2]

Since my last comeing into ffrance, an. 1720, I not haveing the sole and principal direction of the king's officers, as when I had the honour to comand for him in Scotland, or most of the time I was about his person on this sid the sea, and consequently not being master of the papers that past concerning them, I could not well continue the Narative farther, but you will see a good deal into those affairs, and the part I acted in them, or otherways, at that time, by the letters and other papers that past betwixt the King and me and some others,

---

[1] The second Lady Mar, daughter to the Duke of Kingston. His first wife died in 1705.

[2] The letters and documents here mentioned are probably among the Stuart Papers at Windsor.

w^ch you'll find amongest my papers; where you will also find some things wrote by me concerning the unjust accusations of that firebrand of a Bishope,[1] since he was sent to ffrance for the destruction of the king's affairs.

I was to have got from my dear friend, Gene^l Dillon [2] (who had the chefe direction of the king's affairis on this side the Alpes durcing that time, and til a little after the Bishope of Rochester's comeing into ffrance), copies of severall papers to w^ch these letters to and from me relate, for makeing my collection the more compleat, so you may know where to be supply'd w^t such of them as you shall find wanting amongest my papers : you can also have from L^d Garlies [3] severall curious papers in relation to the unfortunat falling out betwixt the king and queen, etc.

All these papers as above being chifly designed for your own privat use, and to enable you upon occasion to clear up to the world some facts, w^ch may come to be necessary to be sett in a true light, you ought to be very carefull of them, and to be very sure of the people to whom you show or comunicat them. I have in all my accounts keept closs and religiously to the truth so farr as I could remember, being indifferent of the stile, and they being only designed for you, on whose descretion tho young I depend, I have been more open and free than perhaps was fit, had they been designed for the publick. I wrote the Narative always in heast, and scarce toke the time to read it over again, so it may not be very corect, and there may be some things in it too trifeling, and not fitt for such a paper, espetially about the time of my begining the world. I designed to have revised it, and writ it over corect, but laziness or some one thing or other always diverted me. If you think it worth the while, you may get our friend Mr. Ramsay, or such an one in his absence who you can trust, to put these papers in better dress, and to leave out what seems trifleing, I haveing only mentioned them to assist my memory in the threed of things w^ch happned to me in my

---

[1] Atterbury.

[2] An Irishman and an officer in the French King's service. He was a brave and good man, respected by everybody.

[3] Afterwards sixth Earl of Galloway.

younger days, so long before my putting them in writing. I name Mr. Ramsay, because of the trust I have in him, founded on the experience of his uprightness and honesty, as well as his capacity for such a thing, and I beleve the friendshipe that has been between him and me, and also his friendshipe for y$^r$ self, would make him not to grudge bestowing some time on a thing in w$^{ch}$ I am so much concerned.

I left a great many letters and copies of some papers dureing my being in public business before comeing abroad in my cabinets at London, w$^{ch}$ I suppose are still in being and safe, y$^r$ adding such of them as are worth while to what is mentioned above will make the colection more compleat.

## II

To be of some use to my native country, and to be assisting to the relise of it from the low and declining condition in w$^{ch}$ I found it was, has been my great passion, and much at my heart, ever almost since I can remember anything; and however I may have been mistaken in my notions, a view towards that has always been the rule of my actions w$^t$ regard to the publick. This shows how necessary it is to instill right notions and principales early into people, the mind beginning sooner to notice things, and to forme notions, than people are commonly aware of, and these notions formed when young are not easily effaced.

It was not without that view I entered into King William's service a few years before his death, nor into Queen Anne's on her accession to the crown, I being then at London; in which I continued the whole course of her reigne, and received many marks of her bounty and goodness. It was w$^t$ a view to that also that I was so forward for the Union of Scotland with England, which not being done at the Revolution, by the overheasty offering the crown of Scotland to King William and Queen Mary, was so much regrated by many sensible Scots people and well-wishers to their country at that time; tho I have often repented my part in that since. It was, I then conceived, the only practicable way, as things stood, for the relise of our country; and for the like reason, when I found that we continued notwithstanding of the Union to be ill treated, and conditions not keept or explain'd away, I became as much for haveing the Union broke as ever I had been earnest for its haveing been made. I was not the only man so who had been for it. My friend the Duke of Queensberry wisht as much as anybody, and had Lord Stair been alive (the great projector of the Union), I am sure he had been so too. I found the breaking of it impossible without an entire revolution, by restoring our natural king, to who's family I had always a heart likeing, and was sorry for the misfortouns happened to it, as was very natural for one come of the family I am, my predecessors haveing been so long faithful servants to it. This made me to enter into a correspondence with the king about the time of the change of ministry,[1] the last years of Queen Anne, on his first writing to me, being encouraged by some of his friends to beleve I had a warme side to his interest. But I would never engage to be concerned in any undertaking for his restoration til it should please God to remove his sister Queen Anne, til w$^{ch}$ time I told him it was his interest to have patience, as I realie believed and understood it to be. I thought I had reason to belive that the Queen and her then ministers had a mind that her brother should succeed her in the crown, there being no sense, as appeared to me, in the part they acted, unless on that bottome, though it was not to be owned. But it was to very few of them I opened my mind freely on this subject.

On the Queen's death, I entered into measurs w$^t$ those of England who favoured the Jacobit interest, and also some of Scotland, with both whom I had spoke a little on that foot before, and after concerting measures w$^t$ the King's friends at London. On my return from the elections for King George's first Parliament, I went for Scotland by the King's express and repeated orders, which he sent me by different messengers from Lorain at sundry times, as you'll see more particularly by the

---

[1] 1710.

narrative.[1] In Scotland I followed the Instructions I had received, and acted for that interest to the best of my understandings, and without any reserve or interested view; but it did not please God to give us the success we had reason to expect from so hopeful beginnings, so that the King oblig'd me to come abroad with him, where my chief studdy has been to find out ways and means for the relise of my country when an opportunity should again offer for restoring our King, so that Scotland might, on that event, be restored at the same time to the strenth, reputation, figure and independancy it had before the union of the two crowns in the person of James the 1$^{st}$ and 6$^{th}$.

The misfortouns of our country, since our king came to succeed (unfortunately for poor Scotland) to the crown of England, have proceeded from the kings always haveing been constrained by the superiour power of England, where they recided, to neglect the true interest of his ancient kingdome, when they came to clash any way, tho but seemingly, with those of England and even of Ireland. The chife ministers being alwayes English men advised accordingly, ther governing the Scots as well as the others. The Scots Ministers were only [always?] subserviant to those of England, save in the

---

[1] 'It is positively asserted by Berwick that the P. [Prince], without any intimation either to himself or Bol. [Bolingbroke], had sent orders to Mar to begin the insurrection in Scotland without further delay. [See *Marshal Berwick's Memoirs.*] The veracity and the means of information of Berwick are equally unquestionable, yet it seems difficult to credit such an extremity of falsehood and folly in James. There are several circumstances to disprove, there are none to confirm it; and on the whole I suspect that Berwick must have been misled by an excuse which Mar afterwards invented for his own rashness. James himself, writing to Bolingbroke on the 23rd of September, expresses an anxious desire that his Scotch friends will at least wait for his answer, if they cannot, as he hopes, stay so long as to expect a concert with England. [James to Bolingbroke, Sept. 23d. 1715, Appendix to Lord Mahon's *Hist. England.*] Is it not beyond belief that he should already, several weeks before, have given positive orders to the opposite effect; that he should have issued such momentous directions at a moment so unfavourable, and concealed them from his best friends and most able advisers?'—Lord Mahon's *Hist. England*, vol. i. pp. 211, 212. It would certainly appear, however, from the Narrative of Lord Mar, that the Prince acted in the manner which Lord Mahon regards as improbable. Mar, whatever ill construction it may please historians to place on his public conduct, had neither occasion nor interest to lie to his son.

time of the Duke of Lauderdale's Ministry, when Scots men's dependance was on him; but his power was more for being a Minister of England than for Scotland, and unless when it was for serveing his own ends, he minded the interests of his own country but little more than an English Minister would have done.

To find out a remidie for this evile on the event above, was my studdy and chief concern. Scotland's being restored to the same state it was in King Charles 2nd's time, and that of his brother King James w$^{ch}$ is farthest almost of what the generality of the Jacobites aime at, would be no cure, and scarce worth the fighting or contesting for, unless at the same time it were delivered or secured from being governed by English councils and councellors. I have never been one of those who were over fond of cramping and restraining the power of kings; but in this case since our King is also king of England, he will be always oblidg'd to make his principall residence there, and will never be able to help his being oblidg'd to succumb to English councils w$^t$ respect to Scotland as well as to the other parts of his dominions, until he make such concessions for that country as will put things there in a manner out of his own power and seemingly into the hands of a Scots Parliament, so that it should be necessary for the subjects of that kingdome to come to his favour and preferment by the intercession and recommendation of that Parl. which would keep them at home in place of running to London for procuring that of English Ministers.

These considerations were the occasion of my forming and laying before the king some years ago a project or sheme with regard to Scotland for the king's giveing concessions to the subjects of that country then in the time of his being abroad and not under the power and influence of the English (which would not be so were it delayed til he were restored and on his throne).

The king came into this scheme and was graciously pleased thereupon to grant such concessions for our country as I proposed, by way of Instructions to me as Lord Comissioner of his first Parliament of Scotland, upon a view there then was of an undertakeing for his restoration at that time; together with a most gracious letter relating to the whole plan or scheme. Some time thereafter upon the occasion of such another designed attempt, his Maj. was pleased to grant and send me farther Instructions to the same purpose on the representations I made him.

How these papers came since to be taken out of my hands after the Bish. of Rochester's comeing to have the chief direction of the King's affairs, and that Mr. Hay (now Lord Inverness) came to join w$^t$ him and act more like a prejudised Englishman than a Scots man, you already know, and will see a full account of amongst my papers.[1] But before I deliverid up the instructions, which by his Maj. repeated directions and orders I was (tho' most unwillingly) necessitated to do, I toke copies of them which I had attested, and I pray heaven that you may have an opportunity of makeing them be one day of service to our country, as they were intended.

There is the same reason for the king's makeing Ireland a free people and kingdome as Scotland, nor would there be any real hurt or prejudice to England by either. It would be greatly for the King's own interest and security, as well as of the Royal family, to make them both so, and independant of England and the councils of Englishmen. By so doing England would loose none of its priviledges, but unjustly oppressing its neighbour kingdomes, should that be reckoned one. It would be but justice in the king, tho those two countries had not appeared so zealous for his and his father's interest as they have done.

It would even be the interest of these his kingdomes to support the king, by their doing of w$^{ch}$ he would not be unreasonable and soly in the power of the English, as his predecessors have been since they came to that crown, for w$^{ch}$ they have dearly pay'd. It was to the Kings of England and not to the People or Parliament that Ireland submitted and they would be as much subjects to the king when out of the dependance of England as now, and have double the power to serve him. Beside Scotland, tho made entirely free, would scarce be able to keep itself so and independant, if Irland were not so too, by which it could assist them.

Upon these considerations I made a short scheme, as I had

---

[1] All these papers were destroyed in the great fire at Alloa.

made for Scotland, which is also amongst my papers. Could I have done it and sent it to the king at the time I sent that for Scotland, he would also, I have reason to believe, have entered into it.

To effectuat this as to both, it was necessary that the king should act in concert with some ffioreigne power or Prince, by whose assistance he might be the more easily restored. Ffrance was the power most proper for this, and I judged it was not impossible to make the late Duke of Orleans, who then governed that country of himself (Cardinal Dubois being dead) to see that the project was for his own and the ffrench interest, as well as for that of our King. I therefore fell to work and revised a Memoriall I had before prepaired upon this subject to have it laid before his Royal Highness. It was accordingly soon therafter presented to him by Mr. Dillon, with whom I had often talkt of the affair which he had as much at heart as I. The Duke of Orleans received it very graciously.[1] He read before Mr. Dillon the letter I wrote along with the Memoriall, in which I told him that what I did in that was unknown to the king my master; but should his R. H. realish the project I doubted not but his Maj. might be induced to send powers for treating on it with him. This I did in case the project should by any chance come to the English knowledge before the time of its being put in execution, so that they could charge nothing of it on the king, should any of them by a mistaken notion take it in ill

---

[1] This, as I have said before, is highly probable. There is every reason to believe that at one time the Regent was very favourably inclined to the Jacobite interest. 'The Regent had undertaken to set the Chevalier upon the throne, in expectation that upon the success of that attempt, the kingdom of Ireland was to have been made a settlement for his family.'—*Memoirs of the Life, Family, and Character of John late Earl of Stair*. 'Upon the whole the more one thinks of it the more one is amazed at the folly and wickedness of his [the Prince's] abettors here, and I may add at the weakness of the Regent who can be diverted by the frenzy of their madness from pursuing his own true interest.' —Secretary Stanhope to Lord Stair.—*Ibid*. p. 284. For additional evidence see a despatch from Stanhope to Lord Stair, dated March 1716.—*Ibid*. App. vol. i. p. 395. In November 1715 the Earl of Stair again found it necessary to 'memorialise the Regent in very decided terms on the support of the maintenance of the public faith of France as engaged by the articles of the Treaty of Utrecht.'—*Ibid*. p. 296.

part. But although the king was not realie privie to the Memoriall itself, yet what by the instructions he had sent me for passing such laws in Scotland upon what I had represented to him for the interest of that country and what he and Mr. Hay had wrote to me in answer to my letters, in which I had spoke of the point of Irland in generall, I thought myself enough authorized to make this first step, since this project was the only way [that?] appear'd w$^{ch}$ could bring the Duke of Orleans to quite his conjunction with King George, and [draw him?] into the king's interest; and that it was upon his Majs. own account I did it without previously acquainting him, but was to do it as soon as it was presented.

His R. H., on reading my letter, desired Mr. Dillon to make me his compliments, to assure me he would read the Memoriall with attention by himself, and recomended its being keept very secret. Mr. Dillon did not see him after for some days, and when he did it was but at his *levée* one day at Paris, where he said to Mr. Dillon in a gay, pleased way that he suposed he should soon see him at Versailes; but his sudden death a few days thereafter prevented Mr. Dillon's doing so. It is to be presumed by the way his R. H. received the letter and Memoriall, and spoke afterwards to Mr. Dillon, and its being found on his death in his own escritore, and addrest with his own hand for M. le Duc, that it was not disagreeable to him, and that he thought it of weight. What shows his approveing of it still more, was his alowing of the Duke of Ormond's comeing into Ffrance from Spain and ordering the expeding of your comission[1] immediately after his getting the Memoriall, both which had met with interruptions and lyen over for some time before.

As soon as the Memoriall was presented, I thought I could no longer dispense myself with acquainting the king with the whole, which I immediately did, and sent him a copie of the Memoriall itself and of my letter to the Duke of Orleans, but his Majs. was never pleased to write to me anything upon it since his receiveing the pacquet.

Mr. Hay was on his way to Ffrance from Italy at that time,

---

[1] Lord Erskine's commission as an officer in the French service.

but as soon as he return'd to Rome he sent a copie of the Memoriall to the Bishp. of Rochester at Paris, who spoke of it and exclaimd against it to as many as he saw. How Mr. Hay can excuse to his country his betraying a secret so much for its interest, to the man of all England the most prejudiced against Scotland, I leave to him to find out ; but I am afraid by that action alone, without mentioning many others, has done farr greater hurt to his king and country than ever it will be possible for him or all his kindred to do them service, were they ever so much inclined to it. I forgive him for the unworthie part he has acted towards me ; but I know not if the strictest rules of Christianity require our pardoning such enormous faults and prejudices to our king and opprest country. One thing I will venture to say upon this scheme and memoriall, that if ever Ffrance be induced to embrace our king's interest and endeavour his restoration, it will be upon this foot, and I shall ever be proud of haveing been the author and proposer of it, which I judge to be the best service I could do my king and country, and I am ambitious of no other inscription on my grave stone, to be remembered by posterity. You will find all these schemes and the copies of the Instructions by the king to me, my comission for being comissioner to the Parl. where they were designed to be past into laws, with the copie of the Memoriall to the Duke of Orleans and my letter, as also of that I wrote to the king with the Memoriall, lying all togither in a little strong-box, with my papers here, and I have endorsed them (not improperly, I hope) JEWELS FOR SCOTLAND.

I do not pretend that these schemes are perfect, but I hope the time will still come that there shall be a Scots Parl. acting on this bottome, which I doubt not will make the establishment and goverment of that country as much so as their situation and circumstances will allow. The attested copies of the instructions to me will show what the king was once pleased to do in favours of that country ; and it gives our countrymen a good tittle for asking him, or those who succeed to his right, the granting such concessions again, which haveing been once granted already can scarce be refused. Before the Scots go about another attempt for the Restoration, and while the king is abroad is the fit time for insisting for those concessions (or of what they may think better of that kind) being agreed to in an authentick and irrevocable maner, which will be doing good service to their king and countrie at the same time.

An establishment of this kind would make the Scots a free people and happier perhaps than they were even when under a seperat king of their own liveing amongst them, which could hardly fail were their neighbours of Ireland made free at the same time, and to be governed under the king by their own Parl. and a council of their own countrymen. As it would be much for the interest of the Royall ffamily these two countries being upon this footing, by its tying them to be ever a support to it for their own interest, so would it be their interests to support one another, and in that way ffrance would find its interest in being ever a true allie to our king and to support his whole establishment. To see these happie days, and to have some share in bringing about these advantages to my native country and posterity, has been the only thing almost that gave me any desire for liveing for some years past ; But as things now unluckily stand I cannot flatter myself w$^t$ hopes of days enough to see the accomplishment of so glorious a work ; you are young tho and may perhaps come to have that satisfaction, and heavens grant that you may. Lovers of our country ought ever to have this in view in their own mind, but not to let zeal make them go rashly about it, a reasonable caution and waiting a fitt opportunity is absolutely necessary. Such it was I judg'd when I went about that work [the Rebellion, 1715] by the kings orders, and had his Maj. come in time and those of England ansuered their engagements, both which was so reasonable to be expected that I could not doubt of it, the success would have showen I was not mistaken. What happned upon that occasion is sufficient to show our countrymen that they are not to undertake it at another time without their being well assured of the English making an attempt in their country at the same time at least the Scots do in theirs, and of haveing assistance from abroad in some proportion to the force to be against them at home on the begining of the attempt, so that they might not be swalow'd up and crushed before they could gather numbers. Any harsh usage I have mett w$^t$ from whence it was least to be expected ought not to deterr any good countryman from so good a work, the greater share any have in it, the more will be their honour and the more worthie representatives will they be of their honest old ancestors, who often endeavoured in such ways to serve their country, and the honour of doing it is a reward of itself. The more they cover their designs of this kind til the fit time come for putting them in execution, the more likely will they be to succeed, and may God Almighty direct them aright, give them success in their endeavours, and therafter the plasur of enjoying the fruits of their labours.

By the schemes above mentioned it appears how necessary it is for the Scots and Irish to be well togither. They are probablie come from the same stock and ought to look on one another as brothers. A good understanding ought to be cultivated betwixt them. They have long suffered oppression togither and from the same hands, so ought they to endeavour one another's relise and to be supporters of one another's libertys and freedome; but without designeing or attempting to return or revenge the wrongs and hardships they have lyen so long under, which would be the surest way of preserving their recover'd libertys. The king was pleased some years ago to give me a warrand for a patent of the Irish Peerage in consideration of one he had before given me of that of England being rendered of no use by the project I had laid before him and he came into for Scotland. Should you be so happie to see a restoration and things put on the footing of the project above, I would advise you to think of persuing your fortoun in Ireland rather than in England, it agreeing more with the interest of y$^r$ own country, to w$^{ch}$ you ought always to have the first and principal regard, and it will be more easie for the king, on y$^r$ deserveing well of him, to shew you his grace and favour there by grant or ȷotherways than in England. My friend Gen. Dillon, who is of that country, where he has a considerable interest, and knows my concern for it, will be ready, I am sure, to give you his advice and assistance in what relates to this (if he be alive in these days) as well as on other things, and you can not ask advice of a more worthie, sincer, honest man. If ever it come to be in y$^r$ power to be servicable to him or any of his numerous family, the friendshipe I have met w$^t$ from him ought to make you exert y$^r$ self to the utmost in doing of it, as I had not failed of doing had it been in mine power. In my schems you will see that the Highlanders are to bear a considerable part. They seem indeed to be the true remains of the old Scots, and notwithstanding of all the hardships they have mett with, are the people who can be of the greatest use for relieving our country when an opportunity offers. I must for ever acknowledge the obligations I owe them, as you ought to do, for their ready joining me even before I could produce the king's comission, which shows their zeal to their king and country and the confidence they had in me, as also for their adhering so closely to me in all the difficultys I met with at those times, a time of the greatest tryall. I hope I have not been ungratefull, haveing done all in my power to have them make the figur and lookt on as they deserved to be. There is one Highlander now gone, and the loss of him is a great one to me, as it is to his country. It is Mr. Campbell of Glendarull.[1] He had the misfortoun to have many enimies when alive, occasioned by his haveing been unluckily engaged when very young in that affair of Beaufort or L<sup>d</sup> Lovat's plot,[2] but his youth and unexperience was some excuse for it, and he hurt nobody by the part he acted therin, tho it was in his power to have done so. L<sup>d</sup> Bredalbain first recomended him to me some time before Queen Anne's death, desireing I might try, know, and prove him well before I should continue in the bad opinion I had conceived w<sup>t</sup> others of him upon comon report. That he had done so and had found him an honest, active, and sensible man, who was thoroughly acquainted w<sup>t</sup> the different humours, intersts, and inclinations of his countrymen in the highlands, w<sup>t</sup> whom he could be of good use, and that he would answer for his being a sincere well wisher to an interest to w<sup>ch</sup> he presumed and hoped I was no enimie, and that he therby shewd himself a true lover of his country. I knew L<sup>d</sup> Bredalbain to be a good judge of men and not easily imposed on, so I resolved to follow his advice as to this gentleman, forseeing I might have occa-

---

[1] A well-known Jacobite, Sinclair, in his *Memoirs*, styles him 'a very cunning fellow.' He would seem to have been much attached to Lord Mar, a circumstance which, in Sinclair's eyes, was doubtless sufficient to blacken his character.

[2] Lord Lovat's infamous outrage on the person of the mother of the Baroness of Lovat. The details of the plot are too well known to require repetition here.

sion of such an ane, and I have been farr from haveing reason to repent doing so, and after tryall puting confidence in him, w^ch therafter I did to his death. He was of great use to me in the Highlands by uniting those gentlemen and preparing things for the attempt I had in my head some years before it was put in execution for restoring our king and therby delivering our country from oppression, in w^ch when it came to be gone about he acted a very usefull and active part, and was of singular use to me in my laying measurs and schemes for that affair, as he was afterwards abroad in many things for the advantage of our country and particularly of the Highlands, as you will see by the many usefull papers he wrote on those affairs we had conversed on, that are amongest my papers here, that were of great help to me in the things I was projecting for the advantage of my country. It was pitty he had not had better education and knowen more of letters, but he had an admirable good naturall understanding, and I always found him honest, faithfull, and closs. I have knowen him often do all in his power to serve those very people who he knew were doing all they could to asperse him and do him prejudice w^t the king and me. Mr. Dillon is a witness as well as I of the usefullness he was of in the king's service since his comeing abroad, and his death was no small loss to the king, his cause, and our country, whatever he or others may think of him. Tho he be now gone, I thought I owd this small testimony to his memory, and if ever his papers come to be seen and considered by sensible people of our country, they will do him honour, and I wish it may fall in your way to be servicable to a daughter he has left behind him.

Another who was of good use in our affair in Scotland was Mr. Paterson, who served as Secretary at warr there, and I were much to blame did I not here own and attest the good and disinterested part he acted of w^ch the whole armie was witness. He has behaved himself since comeing abroad in the same way, and has suffred severely w^ch he was farr from deserveing, and it was the greater grife to me that it was perhaps partly upon the account of his atachment and honesty to me, and that it was not in my power to do anything for him. I wish you may find an opportunity of makeing that up to him, and you cannot do for honester man.

I must not here omitt good, honest, Col. Clepham,[1] who so generously left the service of the present government, where he might have been very easie, and came to me in Scotland, where I was in great want of those who understands as he does the business of a souldier. He did very good service, and it was a misfortoun to our affairs that some times for humouring of some for whom I was oblidgd to have regard, I could not follow his advice, and particularly at Sherifmoor. I have great concern and esteem for him, and you cannot do better when you have an opportunity than to do all you can to be serviceable to him and his children, w$^{ch}$ I ow him and they have reason to expect from you on my account.

I have lost another friend and cousin of yours, to my great regrait, who was very servicable to me and the affairs I was about at that time, as he has also been during our being on this side the sea, Mr. Will. Erskine,[2] brother to the Earle of Buchan. He was a very pretty fellow and deserved a much better fate than he had, but death has freed him of the uneasinesses he suffred in this world, and tho his honesty and worth makes me not doubt of his being now happie in the next, I cannot but be afflicted for the loss the cause and I have of him, and I wish heartily that it may some time or other ly in y$^r$ power and in mine to show the true value I had for him by doing for the children he has left poor behind him.

It is vt grife of heart I find myself now oblidg'd to mention here the king, but being but to you alone, my concern for my country in general, and you in particular, in a maner forces me. I heartily forgive all the unjust and unmerited treatment I have met with from him, and wish God may not lay it to his charge. Most of those who served him before me, haveing met with much the same measur, I have the less cause to complain. With all the respect to the regard due to him, I may say that he has been an unluckie man from his cradle, and is now following such courses that he is likely to be yet more unfortunat than ever providence seemed to designe he should.

---

[1] An Englishman, and mightily abused by Sinclair. He saw considerable service in the wars in the Low Countries.

[2] Captain William Erskine, deputy-governor of Blackness Castle. He married Margaret, daughter of Colonel John Erskine, deputy-governor of Stirling Castle.

I pray God that he may soon become sensible of his mistakes, and amend his unaccountable conduct and strange ways, which if he do not, he is like eer long to leave himself but very few friends, to make the restoration of the royall family and of our country by it uterly impracticable during his being in this world at least, if not to extinguish the cause.[1] And by his actings already it has but too much the appearance of his indifference, and little regard to anything of that kind. Some of his predecessors had the misfortoun to be led away by worthless favourites as he is, tho' non of them (not even K. J. 3rd of Scotland) to such a degree. There was some remedy always with them for that at home, but there is like to be non for it with him abroad, when he is blind to all that can be said to him by anybody but those who are to be complained of. God help him and honest men who have their dependance on him. When the right comes to be in his children, if they have mettle and good understanding, and that the situation of Europe then chance to be favourable, they may perhaps succeed in recovering pocession of their right; but their ffather's odd conduct may be so fresh in people's memories that it may be a heavie load upon them, and they run a great hazard, both by their education and another ffamilies being so long and well esteablished and fixt on the thron; and at best at this time there can be no prospect of it for a good number of years. What is therefore to be done in the meantime? Are those who are true lovers of their country to be idle spectators, and let it be pull'd to pieces, oppresst more and more every day, as it cannot fail of being the longer it goes on in the way it is, without endeavouring to prevent it? Are people to let their families and poor remains of their fortouns (shipwrackt for the cause) go entirely to ruin and starve, for the king's being monopolized and govern'd by insignificant favourits when honest men, lovers of their country, are not suffered to do anything for its relise, and that of their sinking families upon the king's account, and only to feed themselves with the distant and uncertain hopes of an event which is more likely never to happen than that it will? No. Sure, it is

---

[1] An allusion to the Prince's unfortunate quarrel with his consort.

impossible the laws of God, of natur, or of man can require it of them. They must do the best way they can, conforme to the circumstances in which providence has placed them and things. Their country and ffamilies require the best service always they can do in one way, if there be no opportunity of doing it in another more agreeable to their own sentiments. And if it be design'd by him who disposes of kingdomes as seemeth good to him, that things should take another turn, he will make opportunitys for bringing it about so to offer and incline peoples hearts to lay hold of them, which honest men and lovers of their country will not fail of doing, and submit to his good will and pleasur in the meantime, and how he shall think fit to dispose of them therafter.

You ow many obligations to Lady Mar, and tho she has not a way of making a show of her concern for anybody, she has been as much so about you, and realie kind as if she had born you. I doubt not of her continueing to be so when I am gone, and assisting you every way she can.

Do not repine at her, or y$^r$ sister's [1] provisions, tho they may seem too great for the esteat, as things have happned they were reasonable in the way I was at the makeing of them, and things would have answerd for the good of the ffamilie by that mariage had not unforseen accidents prevented, of w$^{ch}$ non of the least was my being oblidgd to apply Lady Mar's fortoun or portion to the paying of my debts at London, on my leaveing it, and going to Scotland by the king's comands w$^{ch}$ had not been just for me to have left unsatisfied, or a fond for doing it, nor had it been for the king's honour nor mine considering the bussiness I was going about. My being thus oblidgd to apply this money w$^{ch}$ I had designed for clearing the remaining old debts on the estate, was occasioned by my not being pay'd my appointments in Queen Anne's time, when I was one of the three principall secretarys of state for Great Britain, above six thousand pounds being still due, as it is likly ever to be. My being in the service, and in that station oblidg'd me to live at London, and in the maner I did, so that my contracting these debts there was unavoidable, and non of

---

[1] Lord Erskine's half-sister. She married James Erskine, son of Lord Grange, Lord Mar's brother.

my fault, expecting (as I had reason to do) my appointments for the clearing of them, by all w^ch you may see that L^dy Mar's money not being apply'd for clearing the esteat was more by misfortoun than anything else.

That mariage has proved happie to me. It gave me a virtuous woman of very good sense, and admirable good equall temper, that I had long loved, and who has since been an agreeable companion and kind friend in my misfortouns, she looking always on our intrests to be the same, and bearing our hard fate with a good heart, and without repining. She has behaved herself w^t such prudence both at home and abroad that she has acquired the esteem of all who know her, and since our mariage, it was the more a time of tryall of her good sense and discretion, that she is of and was bred up in a ffamily w^ch thought and acted in a very different way from me in publick affairs, but neither that nor what might be her own oppinion of those maters did not hinder her from behaveing herself as became my wife both on my going (without acquainting her) to Scotland, and the time of my being in armes there, and also on her being at Rome w^t me in the king's family, and attending afterwards on the Queen, where, in his Maj. and my absence, she met w^t such treatment from him[1] who had the direction of the king's affairs there as gave her occasion for all her temper, w^ch she likewise had at the time of the King and Queen's mariage. She never likt or inclined to medle in politicks, nor was solicitous or inquisitive to know any thing of them from me, nor did she ever offer to advise me in them, nor w^t reguard to myself or the uneasie situation I have been in for these severall years abroad, but with a true reguard to my honour preferable to any worldly interested concern. By these tryalls, and my knowing her otherways so well I may venture to assure you that notwithstanding of her education in another way of thinking as to the politicks from us, and of her being of another country, whose interest may seemingly sometimes appear to clash w^t that of ours, yet that she will never advise you to any thing inconsistant with your honour or the interest of y^r country and farr less make a bad use of any thing she may

---

[1] Colonel Hay.

chance to discover of designs for the service of it in any way. It will be y<sup>r</sup> intrest as it is your duty to be observant of her, avoiding all disputs about what may in strickness or nicity be thought to belong to you or her, as I doubt not but she will with reguard to you, and this will be the way of makeing an usefull friend of her, as well as a kind mother. . . .

Clanshipe in our country is what ought to be encouraged and keept up as much as possible, both upon account of the publick and privat intrest. You are to be at the head of one w<sup>ch</sup> tho not so numerous as those in the highlands, is perhaps as old, and has not been inconsiderable in Scotland. There are severall of our name I am oblidg'd to, and I doubt not but that all of them will be assisting to you when they see you have the intrest of y<sup>r</sup> country and familie at heart. Endeavour to keep them united, w<sup>ch</sup> is the way to make them considerable, and if you be assisting to one another, and act with good and upright intentions you may surly be so there, and consequently elsewhere, however things go, and I hope it may come to be in y<sup>r</sup> power to be servicable to them, as I intended to be, had it pleased God to have prospered my endeavours. But let not fondness for those of your own clan and kindred make you neglect those of merit, who shall deserve well of you of another. . . .

You have providence to thank that you have been more luckie in y<sup>r</sup> education than I was, and I bless God that you seem to have profited of it. May he in his goodness indue you with wisdome, w<sup>ch</sup> is what you ought to ask w<sup>t</sup> earnestness of him.

My designe of geting you placed in the ffrench service, was to keep you from being idle, and to make you by times know something of what belongs to a souldier, that you may be the fitter for service of y<sup>r</sup> king and country when an opportunity shall offer. Had the late Duke of Orleans lived, you would have been soon preferrd, but unless a young man have such a support there is little encouragment for a stranger in the ffrench service, so I leave it to y<sup>r</sup> self to consider whether to continue in it or not, and you will determine as you shall find most conduceing to the wellfair of y<sup>r</sup> affairs. . . .

Let your chife care and studdie ever be how you can be most servicable in the station in w<sup>ch</sup> Providence places you, to God in the first place, to your country in the next, and consequently to your king, and then to your ffamily and friends, in w^ch you yourself is comprehended. You ought to wait and studdy fitt opportunitys for all, and recall to your mind the great and noble things you may see in history that our ancestors the brave Scots have done in their days for the ffreedome and preservation of our country, when it was as low, and some tymes lower still than it now is, w^ch their resolution effectuated, and let us not in these latter times seem unworthie to be come of them.

You have such principalls already that I hope honesty in all your ways and dealings will be naturall to you. Do not neglect acquireing riches when you have becomeing opportunitys, but let not that be your chife view and aim, and endeavour more to be good than rich.

Being a good friend, and observant of those to whom you ow it, and are civil to you, will be of great use, pleasur and advantage, and it is the way to make others so to you; but be very cautious in the choise of y^r intimat friends, and try them by degrees before you trust them entirely, and when you have once trusted them, be as cautious of throwing them off or becomeing cool to them.

I should be glad that you were well w^t those with whom I have been in friendshipe, and it is natural to think that they will be readier to be true friends to you than others.

Those who have once been in friendshipe w^t one, and have failed one by unkindness, ill offices, or ingratitud, whether relations or others (and who has been without meeting w^t such?) forgive them as I do, but be on y^r guard with them, and knowe them thoroughly, and have new and good experience and convinceing proofs of their amendment before you trust much to them.

The situation of our affairs and the good of our family require y^r marying as soon as you can find and compass an advantagous match. The choise of a wife is perhaps the step in a man's life of the greatest consequence to him, and on w^ch his own peace, happiness, and tranquility most depends, and there is nothing w^ch shews more his good or bad sense, discretion and conduct, so that it ought to be gone about w^t great circumspection, thought, and caution. Take care you mary not for love alone, that soon goes off where there is not a foundation of other good qualitys to support it, but be sure you do not mary where you cannot love. Avoid a disagreeable woman, but be carefull that beauty temp you not to judge wrong, and a good temper and being well made in her person is much more to be wished for in a wife than beauty, so let the mind and temper charm you more than the body, and the resonableness of the body more than the beauty of the face. Where any great defect has been much or frequently in a family, espetially those distempers w$^{ch}$ run in the blood, avoid the marying into it. One in y$^r$ circumstances, espetially who has a good old family to support and keep from sinking, is oblidg'd in the choise of a wife to have great regard to convenience and the fortoun she has, but this ought not to be pushed so farr as evidently to make himself unhappie by it, Happiness not consisting in great riches but a competencie is necessary. It ought to be great and valuable considerations that should make you mary much below your own quality and degree. Non of y$^r$ predecessors have hitherto done it, but in these days there is but too little regard had to this both in England and ffrance. It is more reasonable for one to mary one of his own country than of another if a party can be found and obtaind there sutable to his circumstances, and tho her fortoun should not be quite so great as he might perhaps find elsewhere, she is to be preferd if the person of the woman please, and she be of good parents and suitable quality. After all y$^r$ care in the choise of a wife, and w$^{ch}$ you are oblidg'd to have, y$^r$ happening well, depends on God, his directions and assistance you ought to ask w$^t$ earnestness, and I hope he will be graciously pleased to take care of you and guid you aright in it. May you be no less luckie than I was in the choise of y$^r$ mother, who it was my misfortoun to loose much too airly, and tho her fortoun was but small, w$^{ch}$ was what I minded less than my circumstances required, she made it up in her good qualitys.

Tho your friends, Lords Grange and Dun, have purchest the old esteat of the ffamily for you, there is great occasion for y$^r$ looking carefully after it, all endeavours to be made to get them repay'd, w$^t$ thanks for their trouble, and its being established and fixt on your own person and then to have it well manadged and the old debts still remaining or what comes in place of them to y$^r$ tuo friends cleard and extinguished. I hope and trust that the same good providence that has hitherto so evidently taken care of us, will find out and put in y$^r$ way means to enable you to do this. I still believe, as your affairs are at present, that it will be for y$^r$ interest to dispose of the esteat in the north, as you wrote to y$^r$ unckle last year, the jurisdictions being taken away and y$^r$ unckle being under engadgments to sell the superioritys, makes the rest not worth keeping, and the money that may be got for it can be laid out to better advantage. I would still have keept there some mark of its haveing belong'd to the ffamily upon many accounts and I do not see a better way for that than what was proposed in the letter above mentioned to L$^d$ Grange.[1]

In the course of y$^r$ life, when you come to be settled and that business absolutely necessary leads you not else where, it will be y$^r$ interest to live at home as much as y$^r$ affairs in the world, and pushing y$^r$ fortoun in an honourable way, will permitte, and endeavour to take pleasur in doing so.

Alloa, the seat of the ffamily, is a fine place as any in our country and, after y$^r$ knowing of it well, it will induce you to like and improve it as I always was a doing, and if I judge right of y$^r$ disposition the more you do in that way, the fonder you will be of liveing much there.

If ever you come to be rich enough to incress the esteat, it will be your intrest and that of the ffamily to purchess near to Alloa than anywhere else and the nearer it be still the better. The esteat of Clackmanan w$^{ch}$ joins it would be the most convenient purchess you can make.

If Capt. Bruce or his son be able to keep the mantion-house and that part of the esteat of w$^{ch}$ they are now posesst, be sure not to envie them of it, but on the contrair it will be an honourable part for you to do all you can to help and conduce to their keeping of it, even tho you should make the purchess from Mr. Dalrimple (proprietor of the estate of Clackmanan), as also what you otherwise can to serve that honest, honourable, ancient family, as is becomeing one of ours who has so long

---

[1] I am unable to say what that proposition may have been, as the letter referred to is not included in either the Memorial or Legacy.

been their neghbours ; but should they unluckily not be able to keep it, or that their own convenience make them incline to dispose of it, do all you can to be the purchasser. In the case of its becomeing y$^{rs}$, the hill on w$^{ch}$ the house stands, w$^t$ the wood on the north side, if inclosed with a wall, would make a fine and beautiful Park for Red and any other kind of deer, and lying so near to the parks of Alloa would be as if it were a part of them, w$^{ch}$ it should be continued to be by you and those who succeed to you.

I was to blame, as my ffather was, for going about repairing the old House of Alloa, w$^{ch}$ was more fitt to be made a quarrie, but we were both led into it by degrees for present convenience, and never being rich enough to undertake the building of a new house all at once. That may come to be y$^r$ case too, and is likely to be so. The house is now in such a way to be made a tolerable good and agreeable one within, tho not very beautiful and regular without, with no great charge, so that it is not to be quite dispised, and I would not advise you to pull it down, unless you come to be more opulent than there is at present any appearance. By the latest Draughts and designes for it you will find amongest my drawings, you will see that it can be made, by degrees and a little at a time, convenient and agreeable w$^t$ a great deal of Loding, and not a very bad figur of an irregular one, not pretending to Archetectur, and such a one as any subject may live handsomely in, and its being to be made so by degrees will make the doing of it easie to you, without incomoding y$^r$ affairs. There is something in the old Tower, espetially if made conforme to the new designe, w$^{ch}$ is venerable for its antiquity and makes not a bad appearance, and would make one regrait the being oblidg'd to pull it down, w$^{ch}$ must be done were there a new house to be built, the gardens, avenues, and courts and the whole designe of all about it, being so farr made to answer to the old house, that a new one behoved to be built in the same place. My naturall genious running much after things of this kind, occasion'd perhaps my bestowing too much of my time that way, but it was a pritty amusement, and you may profet by it from the designs I have made and leave you for this place, and so bestow y$^r$ own time to better purpose. The Plan you caried home w$^t$ you of Alloa, is a pritty good one and the designes of the gardens and Parks were mostly made by me before my being abroad and had not much opportunity of seeing things of that natur, I altred very little when I lastly made this plan. I am farr from tying you down to it, the liberty of pleasing ones own fancy in this as in other things being what gives the great pleasur, but because I have thought so much on these designes, know the place so thoroughly, and have some knowledge and understanding of these matters, you ought to be well advised before you alter them or follow any other.

You should endeavour to live well w$^t$ all y$^r$ nighbours and in good friendshipe and intelligence. When there happens at any time what may occasion difference w$^t$ any of them, as often does, take care not to be the agressor and endeavour always to have things accomodated w$^t$ them in a friendly maner, without going to law, rather than that yealding in things not very essentiall and to be usefull to them w$^{ch}$ is the way to live agreeablie at home and to make y$^r$ own life easie.

So long as you have the esteat in Aberdineshire it will be for your advantage to visit it some times, and to pass the months of August and September in Braemar, once in tuo years is not too often: that will make you know y$^r$ people and give them occasion of knowing you, w$^{ch}$ is absolutly requiset in a highland interest espetially. It will give you an opportunity too of being acquainted with the gentlemen of the rest of the highlands and of being in concert, friendshipe, and good understanding w$^t$ them, w$^{ch}$ may come to be of service and advantage to y$^r$ country in general and y$^r$ self in particular, so it is what I earnestly recomend to you and even should you come to sell that esteat, it will still be worth y$^r$ while to visit that country sometimes, to hunt in it and keep up acquaintance w$^t$ the inhabitants, since you are to reserve a right to the huntings and being attended there, as by the scheme you sent to your unckle last year about disposeing of that esteat w$^t$ some reservations, w$^{ch}$ still appears to me the more fitt and necessary the longer I think of it.

If you be ever so luckie to recover y$^r$ hereditary right of governour, constable, and keeper of Stirling Castle, it will not be amiss for you to live sometimes there in winter as y$^r$ predecessor the

Treasurer often did, even after our king went to England and that there was no court there; but should our king come to be desirous to have all such governents w$^t$ other jurisdictions restord to the crown (as I judge were we again a free people and kingdome of ourselves it is for the interest of our country they should) be not you refractiory in quitting w$^t$ y$^{rs}$ for an adequate price, w$^{ch}$ certainly the king and Parl. would give.

Tho you should not have the Castle of Stirling to live in, you have a good shell of a house in the town, w$^{ch}$ cost your predecessor, the Regent, considerablie. It wants to be repaired w$^{ch}$ is necessar to be done and w$^t$ some alterations and additions w$^{ch}$ would not cost much would be a very good convenient house[1] for you to live in, as is proposed y$^r$ doing in the Castle should it be restord you. The principall apartment of this house has been designdly and rightly made so high up that it might overlook the town and have the prospect of the country w$^{ch}$ it has fully and is as fine an one as is to be seen anywhere. The house has a fine appearance to the street and out of regard and respect to the builder, it behoves the ffamily that is to come of him not to part w$^t$ this house or to let it go to ruin, so I recomend the preservation of it to you.

There is no liveing in the world without trust, but be very cautious of trusting entirely the sole manadgment of y$^r$ affairs to any one servant: understanding of them y$^r$ self, looking often into them, and haveing the chife direction, will make you be well served and be of great advantage to you many ways. The oftner accounts are cleard w$^t$ servants the better, and to ease you in such a troublesome task, w$^{ch}$ was ever very disagreeable to me, as perhaps it may be to you, you will do well to get a friend or two to assist you, as my brother and L$^d$ Dun used to do me.

I had two very good servants in their stations, who are both now emploied again in y$^r$ affairs, John Watson and Alexander Rait, who served me w$^t$ great affection, application, and honesty, as I doubt not of their still doing you. Be kind to them

---

[1] Much more of the building, now commonly known as 'Mar's work,' must have been standing at the period Lord Mar writes about it, as very little now remains of it. It is still the property, however, of the head of the Erskine family.

and it will be for y$^r$ advantage, I think, and ease that they agree and live well together, haveing no personall broils nor drawing different ways, w$^{ch}$ you should take care to prevent and cure if any be. I know some may not be of this oppinion, thinking when servants disagree the master is the less apt to be imposed upon and cheated, but that is not just reason in my oppinion, who hate to see people out of humour w$^t$ one another, whether inferiors or equalls, an honest man will be an honest man still and serve honestly, and so will a rogue follow his own ways and cheat you in spite of all cheques upon him.

Be kind to those who have served me or my ffather well, as I doubt not you will be to those who serve you so. It is a creditable thing to see old servants about a house or ffamily and their children taken care of and comeing into the service in their own time or after them. This has been much the custome w$^t$ our predecessors and it is too comendable to be forgot. Good servants are seldome found, but when they are, deserve to be well and kindly used and y$^r$ doing so will be a great mean of y$^r$ being well served.

Be not bookish or sedentary; use such sports, diversions, and exercises as you shall like best in a moderat way and without giveing yourself up too much to them; those on horseback or walking will be better for y$^r$ health than phisick and keep you from laziness w$^{ch}$ renders one unfit for the service of his country.

I have not observed you to be overfond of play, a great happiness, but be still on y$^r$ guard against it since it wants but a beginning and a little habitud to take too much hold of one and scarce ever fails ruining those given up to it. I do not mean tho by this that you should follow my example, since the time you can remember me, in not playing at all, w$^{ch}$ is an extream on the other side for w$^{ch}$ I am to blame; But I am too old now to learn the games of cardes, w$^{ch}$ I never likt, and this absteaning from play was occasiond by my over love of one kind of game when young, the Dice or hazard, of w$^{ch}$ I was passionatly fond and playd for a good deal of money and more than was fitt or convenient for my affairs, tho I came off with little or no loss. When one loves any game to such a degree, it is scarce to be cured without quitting of it entirely, w$^{ch}$ was the resolution I toke, first for a year, w$^{ch}$ I observed, and that toke away my itch for playing at any game of chance, that I never after had any inclination to play at any again: I somtimes tho play'd at some of the little gams of cardes and at dice too, but rarly at either and only when in a maner forced to it and for complesance to the company. A little moderat play when the company is for it is allowable and even necessary everywhere, but in ffrance there is no keeping company almost without it, and I have been often angrie w$^t$ myself for not knowing all the games of cards a little, it giveing a man an ill and acquard air in company not to do as others do in such innocent things: and when nighbours and ffriends come to see you, it looks as if you did not mind them enough or atend to what is for their entertainment, w$^{ch}$ is always disagreeable and offencive and what you should be on y$^r$ guard against.

I must not forget to mention y$^r$ musick, than w$^{ch}$ there cannot be a more agreeable, innocent amusement, and amusements of one kind or other are absolutly necessary, and the man who has a taste of non is to be pitied; But pray take care of giveing up too much of y$^r$ time to such a bewitching thing, as perhaps I did to my archetectur and designing. Amusements, tho necessary, to recreat and unbend our spirits and minds from more serious things and of moment, they ought never to make us neglect our affairs or what we may be more usefully employed about, for the service of our ffamily, generation or country, in respect of w$^{ch}$ amusements or what the Italians call virtu are but trifles.

I had the service of the Church of England sett up at Alloa, for w$^{ch}$ I made a chaple, it being nearest to my own way of thinking in those maters, a medium betwixt the bare unbecomeing nakedness of the Presbiterian service in Scotland, and the gadic, affected, and ostentive way of the Church of Rome.[1] You may be perhaps too in this way of thinking about it, and may have a mind to have that service set up again there, but be sure to choose a fitt time for it. The minister of the place will be angrie about it, but I would not fall out w$^t$ him, do

---

[1] See also the letter printed for the first time in the Appendix to this Book.

what he could, and I would not scruple going sometimes to his church and joining in the service. Endeavour in that case to keep good agreement betwixt those who frequent the one and t'other service, and never let their frequenting either be the occasion of y$^r$ kindness, dislike or neglect of any.

You know this long, constant and closs friendshipe that has been betwixt my Lord Loudon[1] and me and also Lord Stair,[2] tho differing much in publick affairs for some years past, but that should be no cause of breach of privat friendshipes, as it never was w$^t$ us, and tho the correspondance has ceased between us, I believe we are still the same to one another. I hope you shall find them friends to you too, and let it not fail on y$^r$ side.

There was a strick friendshipe, and real affection too, betwixt the late Duke of Queensberry[3] and me, as there had been betwixt our fathers. I had many substantiall obligations to the last Duke, who's memory is very dear to me. I endeavoured all I could to requitt his friendshipe to me whatever the malice of some made them say to the contrary, I never feald in the least title to him and I had been unworthie if I had. He knew this well himself, as appeard by the kindness he exprest for me on his death bed a little before his expiring, and his recomending to those who were with and had a dependance on him to have thereafter the same on me. I heartily wish and hope that the like friendshipe may be betwixt our sons.

You are no stranger to the intimacie and true friendshipe that is betwixt L$^d$ Lansdown[4] and me, he is a worthie honest man, and has less of that humour of oppressing and keeping at under our country than any of the English who has been in business I ever knew, tho I believe there is not one of them who likes their own country better nor would do more to serve it. This goodness and justness of his ought to recomend him much to all our countrymen, and I know y$^r$ esteem for him is such that there is no need of my recomending to you the continuance, and cultivating your friendshipe w$^t$ him.

---

[1] Hugh Campbell, third Earl of Loudon. He was a strong Presbyterian, and fought against Mar at Sheriffmuir.
[2] The well-known diplomatist and politician.
[3] The second Duke. He died July 6th, 1711.
[4] The well-known poet and politician.

There is another countryman of his and friend of y{rs} as well as mine, tis Ld Blanford.[1] He has a good oppinion of you and I believe loves you. He will have it in his power to be of use to you, but his friendshipe is as valuable, and as much to be courted for his vertuous good qualitys as for his high condition in the world.

You have had obligations yr self from the Duke of Argyll and Ld Islay, as yr unckle Grange informed you. Tho they and I have been often on different sides in publick affairs, yet we have been frequently on the same side too and good friends. I have had essentiall obligations myself from the Duke of Argyll, of which I am still sensible, and wish I had it in my power to return, wch I would not fail doing if ever it be. I hope they will continue their friendshipe to you, and I have too good an oppinion of your good heart to think you will ever give them or others cause to repent of the favours that have or shall be shewen to you. Our family has twice maried into theirs, so we are come of it, and as is comonly said in Scotland, Blood is thicker than water and ought to be minded.

There are other two cousins of ours who have had occasion to give proofs of their worth, honesty, and good heart. Lord Pitsligo[2] and Sr John Erskine of Alva.[3] I hope the same love and friendshipe will go on and continue betwixt you and them that was betwixt them and me, as also wt their children.

There is a gentleman in Scotland who has had a great friendshipe for me, and I for him, ever since we were acquainted when young at Edinbrugh, Robert Moray, brother to Abercarnie,[4] he is a very honest man, and it has been often my great regrait that by one thing or other it never was in my power to get something done for him for makeing his circumstances in the world more easie. Should it chance ever to fall in yr way to be servicable to him, do not, pray, fail it, upon the account of the long friendshipe that was betwixt us.

---

[1] William, Marquis of Blandford, son of Henrietta, Duchess of Marlborough, and Lord Godolphin.

[2] Alexander Forbes, fourth and last Lord Forbes of Pitsligo. He took part in the affair of '15 and subsequently in that of '45.

[3] The Erskines of Alva were a branch of the Mar family.

[4] William Moray of Abercairney, Perthshire.

Mr. Stewart of Invernity was my companion and school fellow at the coledge, and the friendshipe that was betwixt us then has never lesned since. He was also my fellow traveller and prisoner when I was arested at Geneve, and all the time of my confinement there, as you know. I am pleased w$^t$ seeing that there is also now a friendshipe betwixt you and him, so I need not, I know, say anything to you for the doing him all the service that shall be in y$^r$ power.

You know honest Mr. Symmer and Mr. Minize so well y$^r$ self, as also D$^{oct}$ Stewart, who to all I am much oblidged, that there's no occasion, I know, to recomend them to you, but forget not to make them my last and kind compliments.

You should endeavour to be at pains to have the geneologic and historicall account of our ffamily made up truely in writing, w$^{ch}$ y$^r$ unckle Grange and severall others in Scotland can help you in, and you will find amongst my papers here something of it wrote by me from such helps and lights as I could find here.

If it shall please God that I die in ffrance or anywhere else abroad, I hope you will join w$^t$ L$^{dy}$ Mar in seeing what debts I may be owing to tradspeople, servants, and otherways for liveing, cleard and satisfied. You know how farr we were from liveing extravagantly, but Lady Mar's jointure, and the interest of y$^r$ sister's mony was all we had to live on for severall years past,[1] w$^{ch}$ was neether fully nor regularly pay'd til y$^r$ unckle and cousin[2] purchest the esteat, w$^{ch}$ with the severall falls of the mony made it unavoidable for us not to run in some debt, and once being so, it was as impossible for us to live and clear that beside, when we came to be regularly payd, only by these fonds, even when the ariars of this jointure were pay'd up.

It is no great matter what becomes of a man's body when the breath of life is once out of it; But tho I should die abroad, I wish to be buried w$^t$ my ancestors at home. Wherever my death hapen, I hope I shall not be so destitut of friends to have non to take care to find some proper place where to put my body to rest and remain free from insult, until it can

---

[1] This frank confession of poverty is scarcely agreeable to the accounts of the large sums of money which Mar is said to have received from the British Government, in return of his services in betraying Jacobite secrets to the Ministers of King George.   [2] Lord Dun.

conveniently, by the advice and direction of you and such friends and relations as you shall think fit to consult, be transported to Alloa, and there, without *éclat* or giveing disturbance to any, to be decently and privatly inter'd by a few of my friends and relations.

If it shall please God so to order that you shall come to be tolerablie easie in y$^r$ affairs, w$^{ch}$ in his goodness I hope he shall, I recomend to you the haveing a Monument of Marble made and erected for the ffamily, in the Isle of the church of Alloa, over the vault or burying place, conforme to a Designe w$^{ch}$ is amongest my Drawings. This monument and the alteration of the Isle would not be very chargable, but I do not strictly tey you down to this designe for it, leaveing you at liberty to alter it according to y$^r$ own fancie w$^t$ the advice of those you may consult, who understand and have a right teast of such things, as y$^r$ acquaintance Mr. Gibb,[1] to whom pray make my compliments. I leave you also at freedome as to the inscriptions to be put on the monument, and I shall leave amongst my papers what occurs to me for them.

I shall inlarge no more here, my dear Tom, on advices to you. I hope y$^r$ own good sense and understanding will be such that you shall have no occasion for them, but those I have here given occurring to me now when my thoughts were much and concernedly taken up about you at writeing these sheets, and seeming so necessary to me for your conduct, honour, and happiness in the world, that I could not keep myself from recomending them to you. I shall conclud w$^t$ this one, To have always in y$^r$ view and endeavour to come up to merit and deserve such a character as was given by an excellent Poet,[2] tho bad yet great man, of our Predecessor the good Regent, your great grandfather's great grandfather the Earle of Mar.

'Si quis Areskinum memorit
Per bella ferocem
Parce gravem nulli
Tempore utroque Prium,' etc.

---

[1] The well-known architect. Lord Mar started him in business in London, out of gratitude for which Gibb left his children the whole of his fortune.
[2] Buchanan.

My hard fortoun haveing made me have little or rather nothing to leave you, you must accept of my papers as my Legacie, for want of a better w^ch you would have got if I had had it. And as my endeavours to serve my king, country, ffriends, Relations, and ffamily, even in the way w^ch appeard to be most honourable, just, and right (an wherein if I was mistaken I hope I shall be forgiven) has ever been my intention and chife designe, I trust to the goodness of that great exalted and eternall Being who made and governs us all, and has still provided for me, will also be graciously pleased to do so for you, who is like to begin the world w^t as many difficulties as I did, but who, I hope, shall finish his course more luckily than I am like to do, tho you cannot do it with more peace of mind, submission and resignation to the will and pleasur of our Maker than I am now readie to do, and hope in his goodness to be when it shall please him to call me out of this transitory, troublesome world. The hopes I have in you and my little girle contributing not a little to it, and I must heartily thank him for haveing blest me w^t such children, who, I beg and earnestly pray, he may alwayes have in his protection w^t our ffamily, keep it from perishing, and make it of use in his service, and in that of our king and country for many ages to come.

Now, my dear son, may all blissings on this side of time and t'other attend you and my dear Daughter. May you be an honour to y^r country, ffamily, friends, and Relations. May you be indued with parts and qualitys suetable to your station, and the part you are to act in the world, and may you live long and comfortablie. These are the earnest wishes and fervent prayers of a very affectionat, Loveing, tender ffather, who is sorry for his faults towards God and man, and hopes to die in peace and forgiveness with all the world, when it shall please the Great God Almighty to call him from it, who was so graciously pleased to creat and give him being in [the ?] world, and to call him, he hopes, to a better, Resigning and trusting his Soul to his Mercy and forgiveness, through the Merits of our blessed Lord and Saviour Jesus Christ our Redeemer. MAR.

# DIRECTIONS CONCERNING THE MONUMENT TO BE ERECTED IN THE ISLE OF THE CHURCH OF ALLOA.

*Chillon, March* 1726.

The Monument to be an obilisk of Black marble, w$^t$ a heart on the tope of which, and a flame comeing out of it of guilt brass. The obilisk standing on a Pedestall of a different colour'd marble, and Trofies of guilt brass to be on the four sides of the obilisk. Two sides to be made up of Broad swords, targets, Highland guns and pistols, powder horns and bagpipes, after the way of the Highlanders armeing. The other two sides to be of the ordinar and modern armour as now used and a comander in chifes batton.

In one place of the Tropheis to be a representation of a bundle of Papers teyd togither, and Indorsed JEWELS FOR SCOTLAND, anno 1722 and 1723.

One one side of the Pedestall, on a scutchon stuck to it, to be the armes of Mar and Erskine as is now used by me. On the side opposit, The Earle of Mar's armes w$^t$ the Earle of Panmure's impaled. On another side Earle Mar's armes w$^t$ Earle Kinnoul's impaled. And on the forth side, L$^d$ Mar's armes wt the Duke of Kingston's impaled.

The obilisk to be placed on the pedestall, the angles of the one contrair to the other, and supported on two Lyons and two grifons couchant of Brass guilt.

On the four corners of the Pedestall to be four weeping boys of white marble standing.

# THE MONUMENT

The plain field on each side or Dado of the pedestall to be of white marble, on w^ch to be cut or ingraved such inscriptions as shall be thought proper by L^d Erskine.

The Monument to be placed over the vault or Burying place, betwixt the two stairs that lead up to L^d Mar's seat in the church. A stair to be made from the door of L^d Mar's low seat into the body of the church, down to the vault or burying place, w^ch stair to be so coverd comonly w^t planks or shutters, that they can be easily taken up or opned when ther's occasion of entering into the vault.

The vault of the Isle to be taken away, for the roof to be made higher on account of the Monument, and a cupola made directly over it, w^t rooms made of each side of the Isle, all w^ch will be more clearly seen by the Designe or Drawght.[1]

---

[1] This Monument was never erected. The tower of the old church of Alloa is still standing, but little else. The modern church is close to the site of the old one.

## TO MY DEAR SON THOMAS, LORD ERSKINE

*My dear Tom,—I cannot, I think, better fill up this book than with inserting my schemes and designs for the good of our country, call'd in the forgoing sheets JEWELS, and which I may now entitle*

## MY LEGACIE TO SCOTLAND

CONSIDERATIONS and proposals for the several parts of the constitution and government of Scotland upon a restoration.

By the Restoration, the Union of the two kingdomes made in Queen Anne's time is naturally suposed to be broke, and the King has sacredly promist it in severall Declarations, so that Scotland would in that case be a free kingdome of itself, and to prevent the many inconveniences which experience has shewen to have happened in that country by the union of the two crowns in the same person (which nevertheless, if rightly improved, may be an advantage to both kingdomes), and to make some amends also for the loss of Scotland suffers by the king's reciding alwayes in England, there are severall alterations necessary to be made in the goverment and constitution of Scotland, from what it was when it had separat kings of its own reciding amongest themselves: which alterations are as much for the king's interest and advantage as for that of the People. Therfore, after the first Parl. of that kingdome's meeting and declaring itself, and the Nation free and independant of any but the king and his lawfull Heirs.

1st. To be enacted, that in all time comeing a new Parl. shall be call'd every seven years, and to be alow'd to meet at least once in two years.

2nd. That the lords of the Articles as before the Revolution be abolished, and all business to be prepar'd by comitties of Parl. as referr'd to them by Parliament.

3rd. The Act of Peace and War, as it past in queen Anne's time before the union, to be reinacted, by which the nation cannot be brought into war without the consent of Parliament.

4. To be enacted, that in all time comeing the officers of state shall be chosen and nominated by the king out of a list of three for each office to be made by Parl. and presented to his Maj., and these to hold their places no longer than seven years, but to be capable to be presented again to the king by Parl. at the end of the said seven years: and that it shall be in the king's power to change any of the said officers of state before the end of the said seven years respective, if he shall think fitt, and to put in his place one of the other two recomended to him by Parl. to the same office, or to change one officer to the post of another; and in case of Death, to name another to that post out of those recomended by Parl. for the said office or charge.

5. The Privie or Secret Council to be chosen and named in the same maner as the officers of state, and to consist of the officers of state, the three vice Precidents of the courts of justice, ten noblemen and ten gentlemen, and to hold their places as the officers of state do theirs.

6. The judges or Lords of session and justiciary court, the Barrons of Exchequer, and judges of the admiralty court, to be named by the king as the officers of State. That the Lists for the ordinary Judges to be presented to his Majesty shall be chosen by Parl. out of the first class of advocats, and these judges also to hold their places only for seven years, and be able to be deprived sooner by tryall and conviction for crimes or malversation, and in case of death the king to supply the vacancie immediatly out of lists made by Parl. for that purpose: and all those judges to be capable to be recomended to the king again at the end of every seven years. The king to name the vice Precident of the session out of the ordinary judges of that court, but his comission to be only for seven years, tho' to be in the king's power to renew it when that expires.

7. The Lords of the justiciary to be four besides the justice generall and justice clark or vice-president of the justiciary, but not of the Lords of session as now to be named, and to hold their places as the Lords of session.

8. Two Lords of session to go the circuits with each of the three classes of the lords of justiciary, for trying the lesser civil causes, not exceeding the value of      [here is a blank space]; and their sentances in these cases to be final. Likewise to have power to try all other civil causes of whatever value which shall be brought before them, but those above the value of the lesser causes to be transferable to the full session at Edinb. or else where, either by the two lords or by either of the partys. In case of the two lords determination or pronuncing sentance in any of the greater causes at the circuits, an appeal to ly open to the full session by either of the partys, as also from the full session to the Parl. The Lords of session to have no additional alowance for the circuits, and all the ordinar Lords to take the circuits by turns. Sallerys to be appointed for the necessary inferior officers to attend the Lords at the circuits.

9. The Exchequer Court to continue as it is constituted at present since the Union; but the Saleries to the Barrons to be less than those of the Lords of session, haveing less business and trouble. They to be named and to hold their places as the judges of the other courts of justice, and the chife barron or vice-precident to be named as the vice-precident of the session.

10. The court of admiralty to consist of the Lord High Admirall and two ordinary judges, to be chosen by the king out of a list made by Parl. out of the two classes of advocats, or either of them, and to hold their places as the ordinary judges as above.

11. The first class of advocats to be restricted and limited to the number of ten, and to have a fixt salary from the goverment of two hundred pounds apice, for serving the Lieges in consulting and pleading their Law-suits, which they shall be oblidg'd to do under severe penaltys, without any other reward than the sum of      [here is a blank space] from their clients every time they write an information or plead for him at the Barr of any of the Courts of justice, and

punishable if they take more than the said ffee. The said ten advocats to be chosen by the Lords of session out of the second class of advocats, as those of the first class are taken to be judges of any of the courts of justice, or fail by death or malversation.

Those of the second class of advocats to consist of Twentie, and each of them to have a fixt salery from the goverment of one hundred pounds. This number to be made up out of those who shall enter advocat, by the antiquity of their tryalls, and to have a smaller ffee from their clients than those of the first class.

No other but these thirty advocats to be alow'd to practice or plead at the Barrs of justice.

12. The Writers of the Signet to be only ten in number, and non of them to be alow'd to have more apprentices than four at one time, and no such thing as agents to be alow'd. This regulation of the coledge of justice would free the Lieges of aboundance of trouble and inconvenience, by the multyplicity of that vermine of the law who feed upon the bowels of the nation and render the people so ligitious. It would obligde most of the youth of the gentry to follow other emploiments, more useful to their country, and there would still be enough for supplying the Barr by those who would have a genious that way, and would studdy the law and enter advocats, for which there would be as above encouragement enough.

13. It is to be presumed that the nation is sufficiently weary of the sower Presbiterian Church goverment which enervates the minds of the people. Therefore it is proposed that the church goverment shall be Episcopall, but the Byshops to have no place or vote in Parliament or council, and yet their Comisarry Court shall be regulated. The Byshops to be named by the King out of lists made by Parl. of three for each Byshoprick, which lists to be made by Parl. out of lists made by the clergy in the maner that shall be regulated, of five for each Bishoprick.

14. That there shall be an act of toleration for other Protestants who have scrouples of complying with the Established Church goverment that all may have liberty of worshiping God in their own way; but the tolerated ministers

to be incapable of possessing any Parish church, until they comply with the government of the church by Byshops as established.

15. That a particular care be had to the visiting and regulating of coledges and universitys, by proper and qualified persons, the right education of youth being of great consequence to a country.

That the king and Parl. shall appoint a competent number of comissioners, out of the most eminent, learned, and most judicious men of the nation for this work, to examine into the original and present constitution, establishment, and situation of all these societys, and to consider of the most proper measures that can be taken for encouragment of usefull knowledge, such as mathematicks in its severall parts, History, the Belles Lettres, Medicin, Botany, the ground and marrow of the civill laws, and of our own municipall laws, besides Theoligie, and, in short, these profitable and liberall sciences that forme the minds of youth to the best advantage, are most conforme to natural and solid reason, and most useful in humane life, without infecting tender minds with the useless and pernicious jargon of the scools. These comissioners to make a full and impartiall report to Parl. on which such regulations to be made as shall be found most proper and practicable.

16. That the king leaves to the Parl. to reenact and confirme by a generall act such of the acts of Parl. made since the Revolution as shall be thought fitt and usefull, and to abrogat the rest.

17. That the King shall oblidge himself and actually consent to the converting all the ward holdings of the crown to Blanch or few, the vassels paying a certain price to be fixt by Parl. for such convertions.

18. An Act to be passed reviveing an old one, which declairs all mines to belong to the proprietors of the lands in which they are found, paying a tenth part of the free profits to the crown.

19. If the king shall at any time think fitt to creat a Scots peer a peer of England, his peerage of Scotland to become void and null, and those who chance to be peers of both

kingdomes at the end of the first session of the first Scots Parl. after the Restoration, to be oblidged to make their election which of them to hold; and to be declair'd incapable for any to hold both in time comeing.

20. The king to declare to Parl. at their first meeting his pleasur as to those Peers that have been made or advanced since the Revolution before they be admitted to take their places.

21. The king to agree to the restoring to the former owners the forfeiturs in King Charles 2nd and King James 7th's time, that they may continue in possession as since the Revolution, excepting such as shall not submit to his Maj$^{y's}$ goverment.

22. To be enacted that all those who hold lands of subjects shall have right to purchess these holdings from such superiors, who shall be oblidged to sell them when required, at a certain price for each kind of holding, to be appointed by the said act; and after these purchesses to hold these lands few or Blanch of the crown as the king's other vasseles.

23. To be enacted, that when the greatest part of ten vasseles of any subject shall have thus bought their holdings, the said superiors shall be oblig'd to sell to the crown their jurisdictions of justiciarys, Regalitys or Shirifships at a certain price to be appointed by the said act, and the crown to be oblidged to make such purcheses and never to alianat them again.

24. To be enacted that an Envoy or Minister on the part of Scotland (beside the Minister for England) shall be always sent by the King to reside at fforaigne courts, particularly those of ffrance, Spain, Germanie, and Holland, and to be chosen as the officers of state.

25. The garisons of Edinburgh Castle, Stirling Castle, and Inverlochie to be alwayes one hundred men each, beside the officers, and those of Dunbarton, Blackness, Dunoter, and Home Castles, 50 men each, and the citadels of Leith and Perth to be repair'd and improved.

26. That there be always two thousand or fivetien hundred regular troops kept on foot. The Highlanders to be modled into Regiaments, to the number of fivetien or sixtien thousand

men, conforme to a particular scheme for that affair, which would be the best armie of such a number for so small a charge in Europe.

The militia of the rest of the kingdome to be modled and well lookt after, conforme to a particular scheme for that purpose.

27. That three ships of war at least be always keept in pay for protecting the trade of the kingdome.

28. The general or Comander-in-Chife of the troops and militia to be named by the king out of a list of three to be made by Parl. as the officers of state, of which he to be one, and he to hold his comission as they, and to have place and vote in Parl. and council as such. He to give brevets to all the officers of the troops and militia, which the king is either to confirme by comission or ordering the generall to recomend others for the said comissions, when he approves not of those to whom the brevets had been given.

29. An agreement to be made betwixt the king and king of ffrance for five thousand men of Scots troops being always entertained in the ffrench service at that king's charge. The officers of which to have their comissions from the king of ffrance, but on the recomendation of the king of Britain and the K. of ffrance to be oblidg'd to alow the said troops or any part of them to return home at any time the king and Parl. shall think fit to recall them, six months after the said requisition.

The king of ffrance to be likewise obliged after the first three years of those troops being in ffrance, to alow one thousand of them to go home every year, upon the like number of new men being sent from Scotland to reimplace them.

30. Acts to be made for encouraging trade and particularly the ffishing, as by the particular scheme for this article.

31. Acts to be made for the encouragment of tilage in the low countrys and pastorage in the Highlands and other places not fit for tilage. The leaces or tacks of land to tennant as to the duration, etc., to be regulated by Parl., and also the distructive, oppresive, and unfrugall way of tennants' services to their masters.

32. Proper laus to be revised and made for encouraging and preserving of planting and preserving the game.

33. Provision to be made by Parl. from time to time for the necessary expences of the goverment civil and military.

It is thought that four months cess yearly, in time of peace with what may arise from the crown rents, the Customs and Excise, Post office and Ld. of sessions fixt stock, may with good managment answer the said expences.

34. An act to be made for encouraging a good corespondance betwixt the kingdomes of Scotland and Irland in relation to their trade, etc., giveing in Scotland all the priviledges of Scots men to the subjects of Irland upon the Parl. of Irland doing the same in that kingdome for the subjects of Scotland.

35. It may seem an unfavourable time for some years (til the enormous abuses in the affair of Misisipi and the South Sea Companys be forgot, which perhaps to after ages may be as hard to do, as to belive all the extravagances of that time) to recomend anything of paper credit for Scotland, but were something of that kind rightly adjusted and keept within bounds, so that the paper could not exceed more than a certain quantity, suitable, and in proportion to the specie in the nation, as by a Land Bank or some such scheme, it might be of great advantage to that country. It would raise the value of land, which would be profitable to the greatest part of Scotland. It would augment the trade and comerse of the nation, extend it farther than can be done by the small quantity of specie now in that country.

36. It is to be wished that the Metropolis were in a more convenient situation for the whole nation than that of Edinburgh, but it is too late now to think of removing it from thence on account of the insurmountable difficulties for a poor country which would attend such a work. Therefore for the universal good and comodity, all ways of improving it should be thought of, as in particular making a large bridge of three storys of arches over the low ground betwixt the Norloch and phisick garden from the High Street at Halkerston's wind to the Moultrie hill, where there might be many fine streets built as the inhabitants increast, the access to them would be easie on all hands and the situation would be agreeable and

convenient haveing a noble prospect of all the fine ground towards the sea and the ffirth of fforth and cost [coast] of ffife. One large and long street in a streight line where the long gate is now, on one side of it would be a fine opportunity for gardens down to the Norloch and on the other side towards Brughton. No houses to be on the bridge, the breadth of the Norloch, but selling the places on the ends of the bridge for houses and the vaults or arches below for warehouses and cellers, the charge of the bridge might be near defryed.

Another bridge might also be made on the other side of the toun and almost as useful and comodious as that on the north. The place where it could be most easily made is St. Mary's Wind and the Pleasants. The hollow there is not so deep as where the other bridge is proposed, so that 'tis thought that two story of arches might raise it near upon a leavell with the street at the head of St. Mary's Wynd. Betwixt the south end of the Pleasants and the Potterrow, and from hence to Bristow Street and by the back of the wall at Heriot's Hospital there is a fine situation for houses and gardens. There would be fine avenues to the toun, and outlets from it for airing, walking, etc., and by these bridges and [word omitted], Edinburgh from being a bad incomodious situation would become a very beautiful and convenient one; and to make it still more so a branch of that river called the Water of Leith might 'tis thought be brought from somewhere about the Colt Bridge to fill and run through the Norloch, which would be of great advantage to the convenience, beauty, cleanliness, and healthfulness of the toun. There would be no occasion then, from a confined situation to make the houses so monstrously high as they are now. The nobility and gentry, besides the burgesses would be encouraged to make fine buildings (stone being near); it being desirable for all or most people of condition to have Houses and be well and agreeable lodged where there affairs so often oblidge them to be, upon account of the government and courts of justice. The markets of Edinburgh now inconveniently keept on the high and main street to be removed to more convenient and proper places : Publick gardens and walks with a cour or ring for coaches to be made in St. James's Yards and Clockmill Park, for which the ground to be purchest from the Duke of Hamiltone. These would also serve for the gardens to the King's Palace of Hollyrud house, and if the hills in the Park were planted and those called Calton craigs, it would add very much to the beauty of the place.

37. The Palace of Holyrud House to be put in repair and the King's apartments to be furnisht at the publick charge, in which the comissioner to be lodged where there is one and all officers of State to have apartments in the Palace.

The toun of Leith (the port of Edinburgh) to be made easier in its priviledges, for which Edinburgh would be fully compensated by the improvements now proposed and the citadel to be repaired.

38. The chancelor being the first great and constant officer of State in the Kingdome, ffor the dignity of the govorment, a country house near the toun to be bought by the publick for him and an appartment of it to be for the comissioner when there is one. Dalkeith would be a proper place for that as would be also Pinkie, Newbotle, and Roiston.

39. The making a canal betwixt the Rivers fforth and clide would be a great improvement to Scotland as well as of great service to the trade of the whole Island, especially the Indian trade, by saveing a dangerous long passage round Britain, since by that canal the west and east sea would be joined. The way for leading this canal is from near Glasgow by Kilsyth, to the mouth of the river Carron, below ffalkirk. . . . It is computed that thirty thousand pounds sterling might do the work, but should it cost the double, it would be well bestowed and be soon repayed the profit araiseing from the canal, if there were any trade in the country. There might be also a good road easily made for transporting merchandise by land betwixt Glasgow on Clide and the fforth, by Takmedoun, St. Ninians, and the Throsk, where large barks can come up the fforth and great ships to Alloa which is but three miles lower. . . . The Merchands might have warehouses at Throsk for their goods, and from thence it is easie bringing them by water to Alloa, where they could be shift for Edinburgh, London, etc. This road would cost but a very small charge, and be of great advantage for trade and comerce and would not be useless, though the canal should come afterwards to be made.

*The appointments for the officers of State.*

<table>
<tr><td rowspan="11">Places for Noblemen.</td><td>The chancelor, who is to Preside in the Councill, Session, and Exchequer when present and to be keeper of the great Seal,</td><td>Pounds sterl.<br>2,000</td></tr>
<tr><td>The Lord Privie Seal,</td><td>1,000</td></tr>
<tr><td>The Justice general,</td><td>800</td></tr>
<tr><td>The Lord High Admirall,</td><td>800</td></tr>
<tr><td>The Principal Secretary of State, who is presumed to reside mostly out of the kingdome about the king's person, beside the profits of the signet, which to be regulated,</td><td>2,000</td></tr>
<tr><td>The Treasurer Deput or first Lord of the Treasury,</td><td>800</td></tr>
<tr><td>The general of the Mint,</td><td>800</td></tr>
<tr><td>The Lord Regester, and the fees of that office to be regulated,</td><td>800</td></tr>
</table>

The Lord Advocat, who is to be concerned in no causes but those of the crown, . . 600

(Total) 9,600

Ministers, but no officers of State, so to have no place or vote in Parl. as such or by virtue of their office.

Four comissioners of the Tresury, two to be noblemen and two of them gentlemen only and to have five hundred pounds each, . 2,000
The vice President of the Session, . . 800
The vice President of the Justiciary, . . 600
The chife Barron or vice precident of the Exchequer, . . . . 600
The fourtien ordinary Lords or judges of the Session, four hundred pounds each, . 5,600
The four Lords or Judges of the Justiciary, 300 p. each, . . . . 1,200
The Three Barrons or judges of the Exchequer, 300 p. each, . . . 900
The two judges of the admiralty Court, 100 each, . . . . . 200

|  | Pounds sterl. |
|---|---|
| The Generall Receiver of the Public Revenues and Cash-keeper, | 400 |
| The Under Master of the Mint, | 300 |
| The Ten advocats of the first class, 200 pounds each, | 2,000 |
| The Twenty advocats of the second class, 100 pounds each, | 2,000 |
| The Master of the Works, with the servants of that office, | 500 |
| The Lyon King at Arms, with the officers belonging to that office, | 200 |
| The Director of the Chancery, | 100 |
| The Knight Marischall, | 100 |
| (Total) | 17,500 |
|  | 9,600 |
| The whole expenses of the constant civil government, | 27,100 |

*N.B.*—The Ministers abroad to be added beside the charges of the under officers for the circuits.

The commissioner for holding the Parliaments to be always one of the officers of state as the king shall think fit to appoint, and his allowances as such to be twenty Pounds a day, for his whole expenses.

*The expences and charges of the Military Force of the Nation.*

|  | Pounds sterl. |
|---|---|
| The garisons, | [*Here are blank spaces in Lord Mar's MS.*] |
| The two thousand regular standing forces, | |
| The sixtien thousand highlanders, | |
| The Milicia, | |
| The general officers, | |
| The three ships of war, | |

*Lord Mar haveing sent a scheme to the king to the same purpose with the foregoing one, His Majesty was pleased some time thereafter to write, and send him the following letter and Instructions, at different times as markt by the dates:*

## COPIE OF THE KING'S LETTER TO LORD MAR from

*Rome, Jan. 1st, 1722.*

THE many instances I have had of the unparalelled zeal of my Scots subjects towards me and my ffamily, hath made me often consider of wayes and means how to settle the goverment of that my ancient kingdome upon a more advantageous and solid foundation than it hath been hitherto, to the end that when it pleases God to restore me to my Kingdomes I may be prepared to propose what may be conduceing thereto, as I shall be always ready to second my first free Parl. in every thing that may tend to the prosperity of that country as well as to the tranquility of my government.

The principles of gratitude and the tender and ffatherly affection I bear towards my people oblidge me to omitt nothing that may be any wayes for their interest and satisfaction. Providence seems now to have so disposed matters as that I hope it will not be long before my Scotish subjects have an opportunity of giveing fresh proofs of their readiness to assert and suport my just cause,[1] and in all appearance my service as well as the comon good, will soon require your personall attendance in your own country ; Wherefore I think it but

---

[1] Jacobite hopes ran high in 1722.

just that I should comunicate to you some particulars, which in my opinion, if rightly executed, may be very much for the advantage of my ancient kingdome, and I am resolved to lay them before my first free Parl. whose advice I shall be always ready to follow in any thing that may tend to the good of the nation.

I am persuaded that both you and such of my faithfull Scotish subjects as you shall think fit to comunicat my thoughts to, will have some satisfaction to observe how much they are emploied towards the providing for their future happiness, and how favourable my intentions are towards the promoting anything that may be for their good.

I need say nothing at present of what relates to the union. It is not only void in itself as haveing been esteablished by an illegal authority, but I have also in different Declarations declar'd it such, and shall be ready to repeat the same when occasion offers.

What I am now desirous of is to make that my ancient kingdome a free, independant, and flourishing People, and to that end I shall not scruple the yielding of some points which may even seem in some measure to lessen the power of this Crown.

As to my particular views and reflections I send you some of them with this in a paper apart, and shall transmitt more to you in the same maner as they ocurr to me without delay, my intention being that this Parl. immediatly after my Restoration should take the speediest means towards settling the goverment in the maner which may be most advantageous and satisfactory to the nation, and they may be assured that I shall be always ready to confirme whatever my Parl. may offer me for that effect; and I shall refer to it the reenacting and confirmeing by a generall act such acts made since the Revolution as it shall be found proper so to do.

As to the Peers created since the Revolution, the same is to to be said as to them as hath been mentioned already in respect to the Union, for haveing been created by an unlawfull authority, they are in efect no peers: I shall nevertheless consider to favour in a particular maner those of that number who shall put themselves in a condition of receiveing from me such dignitys as recompenses for loyall and honourable actions, for which they were always designed: and I shall exclud non from partakeing of my favour but such as manifestly prove themselves unworthie of it.

To conclude this letter, what I have further to add is that as in the Reflections I now send you, or in such as I may hereafter add to them, I have nor shall have nothing, but the generall good of the country in my view. It may be that I may propose some things which may more or less affect particular persons, but should that hapen I am persuaded that all concern'd will on reflection follow my example, and cheerfully yield small personall interests for considerable advantages to the comon and publick weelfare, which will esteablish a solid happiness both to my posterity and theirs.

Your interest in your country had once very near made you the chife Instrument in freeing it from oppression and slavery. May you be blessed with success in your present endeavours towards that glorious end, and may you have the honour and satisfaction of not only contributing to its delivery, but after that of haveing a particular share in the execution of my views towards its future liberty and happiness.

(*Sic sub.*), JAMES R.

In consequence of my letter to you of this date, my views are as followeth:

1st. That a New Parl. should be called every seven years, and that they meet at least once in two years.

2d. That the Lords of the Articles as before the Revolution should be abolished, and all business to be prepared by Comittes as referr'd to them by Parl.

3. That the act of Peace and War as it was passed not long before the union should be re-enacted.

4. That the officers of state, the judges of the Courts of Session, Justiciary, Exchequer, and Admiralty should be named by me out of a list of three for each vacancie to be made by Parl., and to be sent to me.

5. That the Privie Councill be chosen in the same maner as likewise the Byshops, but the last to be proposed to me by Parl. out of lists made by the clergy for that effect.

6. That all mines should belong to the proprietors of the lands in which they are, paying a tenth part of the clear profits to the crown.

7. That no man whatsoever shall be capable of sitting in both Parl$^s$. of England and Scotland.

8. That the L$^{ds}$ of justiciary shall be oblidg'd to go their circuits twice a year as they do now, and that two Lords of Session shall go their circuits with the two setts of the L$^{ds}$ of Justiciary for trying civill causes at the same time that the L$^{ds}$ of Justiciary try what is criminall, and that both one and t'other should have reasonable sallarys alow'd them.

9. That an Envoy or Minister on the part of Scotland besides the Minister of England should be always sent by the king to reside at the Courts of ffrance, Spain, Vienna, and Holland, to be chosen as the officers of State.

10. That provision should be made by Parl. for the necessary expences of the goverment, civill and military, and that the sallarys of the officers of state be also regulated by Parl.

(Sic sub.)     JAMES R.

*Rome, Jan. 1st,* 1722.

In consequence of my letter to you of the first of January, I think it would be very advantageous for Scotland,

1. That the crown should be obliged to convert all the lands holding [word omitted] of it to feu or Blench, the vassalls paying a certain price for it to be fixt by Parl.

2. That all those who hold their lands of subjects should have right to purchase their holdings from such at a certain price to be appointed by Parl. for each kind of holding, and that after such purcheses they should hold their lands of the crown with the same priviledges as the king's former vassals.

3. That when the generality of any subject's vassals have bought their holdings, the said superiours should be oblidged to sell to the crown their jurisdiction either of Justiciarys or Royalitys, at a certain price to be apointed by Parl., and that the crown should be obliged to make such purcheses and never to alianat them.

(Sic sub.)     JAMES R.

*Rome, Jan. 20th,* 1722.

In consequence of my letter to you of the first of jan. I think it would be very advantageous for Scotland,

1. That the castles of Edinburgh, Stirling, Inverlochie, Dumbarton, Blackness, and Dunnoter should be provided with sufficient garisons.

2. That there should be always two thousand Regular Troops on foot in the kingdome, and that the Highlanders should be modled into regiaments to the number of fiftien or sixtien thousand men, which last will be a small expence to the goverment.

3. That three ships of war should be constantly keept in service and pay for protecting the trade of the kingdome, and that their comanders shall be named by the king.

(*Sic sub.*)     JAMES R.

*Rome, Jan. 29th,* 1722.

In consequence of my letter to you of the first of jan. I think it would be for the honour and interest of Scotland that I should make an agreement with the King of ffrance after my restoration for his entertaining a certain number of Scots Troops in his service, which I am persuaded the Parl. will approve of.

(*Sic sub.*)     JAMES R.

*Rome, ffeb. 5th,* 1722.

Upon your going to Scotland and seeing appearance of success in the endeavours for our Restoration, you are hereby authorized to call a Parl. or Convention of Esteats of that our ancient kingdome, conform to the power given to you by our comission of comissioner, bearing date the 28 day of June 1721. To meet and to hold at such a place or places as shall seem most expedient to you, to consult on the weighty affairs of the nation and the esteablishing of our government, and particularly such other things for the good of that our king dome as are recomended to you in a letter of the 1st of January last.     (*Sic sub.*)     JAMES R.

*Rome, the fiftienth of May* 1722.

Directed: *For the Duke of Mar.*[1]

---

[1] Lord Mar was created Duke by the Prince.

In our Parl. of Scotland, which we hope is soon to be holden by you there, you are Hereby authorized and impower'd to give our consent to such act or acts as shall be past by the said Parl. for Rescinding and annulling such forfeitures as had passed in the reigns of our unckle King Charles the 2$^{nd}$, or our ffather King James the Seventh, and restoring esteats to such of the antient owners or their heirs as shall own and acknowledge our title to the crown of our dominions. (*Sic sub.*) JAMES R.

Rome, *May* 16*th*, 1722.

Addressed: *For the Duke of Mar.*

You are hereby authorized, when you are in Scotland, to institute a new Military Order of Knighthood, consisting of [here is a blank space] persons, to be call'd the Restoration Order, whereof one to be the head or Sovereigne, and to make such institutions, laws, and orders, as to you shall seem expedient, which we hereby promise to confirm: and to bestow the said order, with all the Badges of it, on such persons as you shall think fit, to the number of [here is a blank space], and particularly to the chifes of clans, as you shall find them act heartily in our service. (*Sic sub.*) JAMES R.

Rome, *May* 16, 1722.

Address'd: *For the Duke of Mar.*

At a time when I formerly designed to make an attempt on Scotland for the recovery of my Dominions, I thought it for the good of my service to send to you the following papers, viz., Comission for your being High Comissioner of our Parl. of Scotland, dated June 28, 1721.

A letter in my own hand directed to you, dated Jan. 1st, 1722.

Ten Articles of Instructions in consequence of the said letter, dated Jan. 20th, 1722.

Also three other articles of Instructions in consequence of the said letter, dated Jan. 29th, 1722.

One other article of Instruction in consequence of the said letter, dated ffeb. 5, 1722.

Also two other articles of Instructions dated May 15th and 16th, 1722,

A warrant impowering you to erect a new order of Knighthood in Scotland, dated May 16, 1722.

An order under my hand to the comander in chife of Scotland, dated Jan. 19, 1722. Together with a letter from me to the said Comander in chife, dated Jan. 19th, 1722. Together with the powers and authoritys, orders and instructions, therin contain'd, I do hereby this my letter confirm to you, and require and order you to follow and execute as they are therin specified, and hereby require all my loveing subjects to give due obedience thereunto. (Sic sub.) JAMES R.

Received at Paris by L<sup>d</sup> Mar, August 1723.

Addressed: *For the Duke of Mar.*

Lord Mar desired the king to send him the following order, as he gave to others at that time, that he might show it when the orders were given them; but that never happned, and Lord Mar's comission and comissioner was not to be made known til he should be in Scotland, except to Mr. Dillon alone, with whom all was concerted.

The generall good disposition of my faithfull subjects, of which they have given me such remarkable instances of late, has encouraged me to make an attempt at this time for the recovery of my Dominions and the relise of my opprest people, and though I have condescended to your request that you should not have the principall conduct and comand of this undertakeing upon Scotland,[1] yet I do not doubt of your readiness in giveing all the assistance you can to Generall Dillon, whom I have apointed my generall and comander in chife there, and for which intent I do hereby require and direct you to repair to Scotland, and there follow and obey such directions as you shall receive from our said comander in chife, as he shall think most for our service. Your ready complyance with what I now require of you will thereby intitle you to those marks of my favour you so justly deserve of me.

(Sic sub.) JAMES R.

Received by L<sup>d</sup> Mar at Paris, August 1723.

Addressed: *For the Duke of Mar.*

---

[1] Evidently Mar did not again wish to head a military rising in Scotland.

## CONSIDERATIONS AND PROPOSALLS FOR IRLAND ON A RESTORATION

*Jully* 1722.

1. The Parl. and kingdome of Irland to be declared in the most solemne and authentick maner ffree and Independant of all but the king himself and his lawfull heirs and successors, and Poinings Act, etc., to be anuled.

2. The Parl. to consist as now of an House of Lords and another of Comoners, and all acts and Laws to be past by the Parl. of Irland only, w$^t$ the consent of the king or his L$^d$ Livetenant, without being revised by the Councill of England, and no sentance or order of either or both houses of the English Parl. to be of any force in Irland.

3. A new Parl. to be call'd every seven years, and to meet once in two years at least.

4. No Peer of England to be capable of being a Peer of Irland unless he renounce his English Peerage.

5. All the officers of state and civill goverment to be named by the king out of lists to be recomend by Parl., of three for each office, and these to hold their places no longer than seven years, unless recomended again by Parl.

6. The Judges and Bishops to be named and hold their places in the same maner as is proposed for Scotland.

7. Not to be in the king's power to make peace or war for the kingdome of Irland but by the consent of Parl.

8. The Militia to be regulated and esteablishd by the king and Parl. conforme to the way proposed for Scotland.

9. The esteablished church of Irland and its goverment to

be as now by Bishops, Arch Bishops, etc., but liberty of contience to be alowed to all to worshipe God in their own way, and no exclusion to be on any one on account of Religion, from Parl. or any publick Emploiment.

10. A comission to be appointed by king and Parl. for regulating the affair of the fforfitours, so that all since the Revolution may be restord to their ancient properties, on such conditions as the Parl. shall by an act appoint.

11. The trade of the kingdome to be regulated and esteablished as the Parl. shall judge fit.

12. A good correspondance to be esteablished betwixt Irland and Scotland, and ways taken to encourage it, as giveing Scotsmen the same priviledges in Irland as Irish men shall have in Scotland, and the trade betwixt the two countrys to be regulated for the advantage of both.

13. An agreement to be made betwixt the king and the kings of ffrance and Spain for each of these kings' entertaining in their service 5000 Irish troups, as is proposed betwixt Scotland and ffrance.

14. Ministers or envoys from the king on the part of Irland to be keept at fforeigne courts, and recomended to the King by the Parl. of Irland, as is proposed for Scotland.

15. Twelve thousand regular troups to be keept always on oot in Irland.

16. A competent Navie or fleet to be always entertain'd for protecting the trade of the kingdome, etc.

17. Tilage to be encouraged for the better peopleing the country, and sheep walks or pastur to be restricted, by alowing only a certain and reasonable number of sheep to each tennant or farmer, conforme to the extent of his grounds.

18. The Linnen Manufactur to be regulated as found most for the interest of the country, and the propogation of Hemp (for w<sup>ch</sup> a great part of the Kingdome is exceeding proper) and the Manufacturs of sail cloath and cordage to be encouraged.

## A SCHEME FOR RESTORING SCOTLAND TO ITS ANCIENT MILITARY SPIRIT,

the only thing which can make it considerable or significant within itself or serviceable to its allies Abroad; and for esteablishing the Militia of the Kingdome upon the Restoration, and of the 26th, 28th, and 29th Articles of the generall scheme for the goverment of Scotland after that time.

If the Scots were accustomed as of old to the use of Armes, it is plain to demonstration that they could furnish and bring to the field at any time for the service of their king and country fifty thousand good men and near double that number in case of necessity, by an invasion from without or comotions within the island of Great Britain. In order to what is proposed, it is absolutely necessary to change the whole present economie of that country which has been introduced since their misfortoun of their king's resideing in England and being governed by English councills and influence. Since that time the old military spirit has been laid aside and lost, and in place of the youth of the kingdome being brought up to military exercises as in the days of yore, they have run to follow the studdy of the law, phisick, chirurgiry, etc., in hopes of raising their fortunes, and tho' not one in ten succeed that way, yet most of the gentry breed their children up with a view towards it, by putting them to what is called the Letteron[1] at Edinburgh (which is to write things relaiting to processes, securitys, and

---

[1] Letteron or Lettrin, a desk. To be bred to the Letteron, to be educated as a Writer.

by that lean on the chican of lawers), which makes them a pest to all their nighbours, their morals and honesty being ruined by it. Others send their sons to studdy the law abroad, and when they return it is lookt on as an affront if they enter not advocat, whether fitt for it or not, by which that class of men become so numerous that they are an useless load to the comon wealth and most of them still continue a burthen to their families or in a maner starve.

It is therfore proposed to discourage this way, and for that end in the general scheme for modeling the goverment on a Restoration, the number of advocats and those who follow the practice of the law is restricted to a certain moderat number, by which means the writer would be oblid'g to follow the sword when they would see encouragment given to it and no other way of employing themselves.

ffor the encouraging this project, and for haveing a numerous and well dissiplin'd Militia, the following methods are proposed for armeing and dissiplining the whole fensible men of the nation:

1. As by the generall scheme above mentioned there is to be always mentain'd in ffrance at that king's charge the number of five thousand Scots Troops, which will serve as a nursery of war for the youth of Scotland of all ranks, and afford a good mentinance for a good number of the young gentry, by being officers in that corps, the officers being to have their comissions on the recomendation of the King of Britain.

A thousand of that body of men being, by the generall scheme, to be exchanged every year after the first three years of their haveing been in ffrance, would much contribut to the putting the Militia at home into the way of exercise by those who have served abroad and return'd annually in training them up in a military way.

This would also in some years make all the Scots as ffrench men, since most of the best of them would have served five years of their youth in that country, which could not but be a very great tye betwixt the two nations.

A law to be made oblidgeing the whole gentry to send their eldest sons to serve in the Scotts troups in ffrance voluntires, at a certain age, for two or three years, besides those who have comissions in the troops there, which would not cost their parents more than keeping them at the Letteren at Edinburgh used to do, and without expence to the goverment, By which these young gentlemen would have an opportunity of good education and going to the accadimie there and makeing themselves fit for the service of their king and country when they return'd home.

There would soon rise an emulation whose children did best in this way, and those who did so would be most recomended to emploiments civil and military at home, as well as to comissions in the Scots troops in ffrance, and it would afford aboundance of good officers to be put at the head and training of the militia of Scotland.

The thousand men to be sent from Scotland yearly to relive the like number of troops from thence, not to be vagabounds, but the sons of the best sort of ffarmers and tradesmen, betwixt 18 and 25 years of age, and there would be no difficulty in finding of them, there being one thousand parishes in Scotland, in each of which the best of the youth, as above, might cast lots whose turne it should be; and they being to serve but five years, there would be soon an emulation and desire who should go, for on their comeing back and returning to their trades or former occupations, they would be more esteem'd than those who had continued at home, and even the women would prefer them for husbands, which would go a great way with the young fellows.

2. That there should be Lord Livtenants of each county or shire, who should have the comand of the Militia therof, and to have a strict eye over all the inferiour officers and oblidge them to fullfill their duty in training up all the people who are fit for armes in the military art and exercise, and assemble them as often as can be without interupting their labours.

3. The kingdome to be divided into severall districts, and over each of which to be an expert generall officer appointed who should be oblidged to make a circuit of his district at certain times to informe himself of the diligence and care of the under officers, as a cheque over the Lords Livetenants, and he also to see the people exercised by their officers and to make their report to the councill, in order to the councill's informeing the king who best deserves his royall favour and bounty.

4. That the Councill each session of Parl. lay before it the state of the Militia of the whole kingdome, to informe his majesty of it and which officers deserve best. By this means the different districts will be prompted to a noble emulation and a military spirit would soon run through the whole nation.

5. The generall officers to change their districts every third or fourth year, so that they may not look on them as their own property, and the Parl. to have a regard to the Lord Livtenants and generall officers who do their duty well, in the recomendation to the king for those who are to have civill emploiments as well as military, by which means the military service would be recompenced not only with military posts but civill, and so all the nobility and gentry would be stirr'd up and encouraged to apply themselves to the studdy of what concerns both the civill and military business, as it was in ancient Rome, where their principal men were fit both for being Legislators and captains.

6. ffor giveing the more luster, esteem and respect amongst the people to the officers of the Militia, they to have their comissions from the king himself, upon the recomendation of the comander in chife, who in the meantime is to give them Brevets as he is to do the standing forces, and severe laws to be made to prevent the soldiers being maltreated by words or blows from the officers and for the soulders giving exact obedience to their officers.

7. A Royall Military order of Knighthood to be erected and confer'd by his Majesty or the comander in chife from him, on those who shall distinguish themselves in that service. Likewise the order of St. Louis in ffrance.

8. In the proper and fair seasons of the year, the Militia to be led to the field to form camps, counterfit batles, learn the march of armies, and thereby be instructed in the three great branches of the military art.

9. The whole Militia to be regularly cloathed in their respective regiaments, which may be done without putting the state or people to any extraordinary charge. All the peasants and tradsmen, or comon people, their children and most of their servants, have a Sunday's or holyday's coat, and 'tis but

their being oblidg'd to have this coat of the livery of the regiament they belong to.

10. It is greatly for the interest of Scotland that the Highland Clans be encouraged and kept up, and their whole people armed. They are all to send to the field five and twentie goodmen upon an extraordinary occasion, but there may be easily fifetien or sixtien thousand of them modled into regiaments, if comanded by their different chiefs, which will be better than militia of any kind, and almost equall to regular troups and of much less expence. This is an advantage to Scotland in particular, and ought not to be neglected. The chiefs who can easily furnish five hundred men, to have two hundred pounds a year settled on them by the goverment, and such who cannot furnish that number to have in proportion, joining their men with other little chiefs of their nighbourhood to make up a butalion or Regiament. They to have all targets, broadswords, and fusies, and their exercise to be conforme to their armour. To be cloathed in the Highland habit with plaids, westcoats, and treus in winter, which may be of different colours and different marks on their targets, as their chiefs shall think fitt, to distinguish what regiament they belong to.

Nothing can be more advantageous to the state and to the Royall ffamily than to support such a body of Highland troops. They are generally loyall, and have a great affection for their country. They are already in the use of armes, so the more necessary til the militia of the rest of the Kingdome be traind and inurd to them. Those of the same name and clan look on themselves all as gentlemen and bretheren, and the chief as the comon father or parent from whom they all come and count their liniall descent so that they fight not only as good subjects for their king and country, but as children of the same ffamily joined in regiaments togither, which gives them an emulation to outdo one another.

In the time of war all but the chiefs to have regular pay. The yearly pensions of the chiefs will not amount to above 6000 pounds sterl., which will be no new charge to the goverment further than what has been in use to be pay'd since the Revolution to independant companys for supressing thifts and depredations (which cost at least 4000 pounds), and a regiament at Inverlochie (which cost about 13000 pounds), where there will be no occasion for so great a garison, so that instead of 17000 it will cost the goverment but about 10000 thousand to mentain always in readiness fiftien thousand good troops, that can be ledd to the field at any time for the service of the king and country, and preserve the nation at all times from robries and depredations.

11. There may be also a body of horse and dragouns form'd without much charge to the goverment. There is no Lord nor gentelman who have esteats, who have not according to their circumstances severall horse for themselves and servants beside coach and work horses that severall of them keep. They all to be oblidged to have most of these horses fit for mounting of cavalrie, which will be no more charge to them in keeping than the horses they used to keep, and not much more in the first buying. The masters and servants to be oblidged to mount these horses at certain times, and to go to the places of rendezvous where the officers for the horse should teach them the exercise and service, which officers will be often those masters themselves.

12. By the esteablishment of the Militia in this good order Edinburgh and the other great towns of the Kingdome will not find it necessary to have train'd bands or toun guards, so that expence may be better emploied in buying of horses to be given to the sons of the richest tradsmen of the different towns, and five or sixpence a day for nurishing and mentaining of them. They themselves would be willing to be at the rest of the charge for haveing the use of the horses.

By these means the noblemen, gentelmen, and Burgesses of the great towns may furnish a body of four thousand good horse or Dragouns with their officers all well mounted.

13. The ffarmers almost over all Scotland have some horses for their labour and tilage. Each ffarmer to be oblidged to have one or two of these horses fit for the horse service, which will cost but a little more at first buying than they pay at present, and they to be allowed twopence a day for each horse they so keep. This would be such an encouragment that they would do it willingly and mentain them in good condition, if they were pay'd this small pay exactly for at the

same time they would have the use of these horses for labour and tilage, and being stronger than formerly they would work the more. The ffarmers or their sons and servants to mount these horses and attend the days of *rendezvous* for learning the exercise, and they likewise to be uniformly cloathed as the foot militia by the same way.

All or most of the comons being by this to be of the militia one way or other those ffarmers or their sons would *picque* themselves on being on horseback, by which they would think themselves a kind of gentelmen, which together with the pay would make each of them run faster than another into keeping such horses; and for a further encouragment the goverment to be oblidged to pay the loss of all these horses killed in the publick service, and all the regiaments of horse (into which they should be formed) to have full pay in the time of war. ffor makeing this charge easie to the state, in place of keeping on foot three thousand regular troops, as since the revolution, after the esteablishing of the militia as above, fiftien hundred regular and standing forces may be enough to be kept always on foot, and the pay of the other fiftien hundred will according to this scheme mentain about eight thousand Dragouns among the ffarmers.

It were good to give the horsemen curasses and helmets or head-pieces (as Cromwell did, which thereafter gave them mostly the advantage over the king's forces, which they seldome had before), and it would be but the first charge of buying them to the goverment, they to whom they were given being to be accountable for them.

14. It would be of great advantage to have a Royall accademie for rideing, fenceing, danceing, and the exercise of armes esteablished at Edinburgh for the youth of the Kingdome, and it would soon become the mode and ffashion for all to go to it, in place of writeing chambers, and of much more use to their king and country.

By this project Scotland may soon save fourty or fifty thousand, have troops without engadging the publick to much newer extraordinary charges for the service of the king and country within the island, beside the five thousand in ffrance, which could soon be made up ten thousand more should there be occasion.

15. Scotland is a very proper country for breeding of good and usefull horses, so that all ways should be taken for encouraging and promoting of it there.

By the scheme a great part of the nobility, gentry, and comons would necessarily pass some of their time in ffrance, and would become as of that country, by which the ancient friendshipe betwixt the tuo nations would be renewed, fortified, and augmented.

ffrance might have also from Irland five thousand men always in its pay and service, and, upon extraordinary occasions, twenty thousand more, so that ffrance might have when she pleases fourty thousand good troops from these two countrys, which would necessarily be as faithfull to her as her own, without her paying more ordinarily and in time of peace than ten thousand.

What a source of auxiliary troops is this for a nation which is attacqued often by so many jealous neighbours! ffor a nation whose glorie and splendor is envy'd by all, ffor a nation who can scarce want any other alyance but that of the King of great Britain restored upon the foot here proposed?

# THE MEMORIAL OF JOHN, EARL OF MAR, TO THE DUKE OF ORLEANS.

COPIE OF LORD MAR'S LETTER TO THE KING AT ROME, ACCOMPANING THE COPIE OF HIS LETTER AND MEMORIALL TO HIS ROYAL HIGHNESS THE DUKE OF ORLEANS.

*Paris, Sept.* 29, 1723.

SIR,—About a month ago, I mentioned to yourself and Mr. Hay my being about a thing which I hoped would prove the best service I ever did you, and in my last by the post, I promist to give you a full account of it by this sure occasion. I think the best way of doing it is, to send you a copie of the paper itself; and it is here enclosed, with the copie I wrote along with it, to H.R.H. the Duke of Orleans, which Mr. Dillon did me the favour to deliver some days ago.

Your Maj. will see that you are no ways comitted by it, the thing being entirely from myself, and it was with a view to this that I presumed to go about it without your knowledge or alowance.

Should this project chance to come to light before the due time by any cross unforseen accident, nobody can take offence at your Maj. upon the account of it, and since I conceive it so much for the interest of my lawfull Prince and native country, any risque I can run is a pleasur.

I have had this project long in my head, and it has been matter of great regrait to me that I could not sooner lay it before the ffrench Ministry, but as long as Cardinal Dubois lived, who was so close linckt with the goverment of England, there was no venturing a thing of that kind. It has now pleased God to remove that Impediment, as I hope he soon will whatever else stands in your way. So I thought there was no time to be now lost in laying it before the Duke of Orleans, who has plainly so much interest in the thing, that it is nixt to a certainty that he will make no bad use at least of it.

It is not to be expected, let him relish the project ever so much, that he can enter immediately into the execution of it. He has been long persueing other measurs, and it will take him some time to get free of them; but being once possest of this scheme, as I hope he now will, he may find an opportunity sooner than he or we think of to relise himself of the embarasses that are now upon him, and to enter heartily into measurs for y$^r$ Maj$^s$ Restoration, which appears by this project (that I am persuaded is quite new to him) so much for his own interest and that of ffrance.

One thing I may venture to say that if any thing be capable to make ffrance seriously take to heart your restoration, it is this, and if ever they go about it, it will be on this foot, which I take to be the only solid one for the interest and security of your ffamilie.

His Royall Highness received the pacquet very graciously as Mr. Dillon tells me. He read my letter immediately before him, and said that he expected no more should be let into this affair than those mentioned in my letter, and that nobody should know of it for him, nor would he part with the papers out of his own keeping. He said that the Memoriall was long, and that he would take a time to read it by himself and think of it seriously, and would then speak of it to Mr. Dillon.

Some days after that Mr. Dillon seeing him at his levie in town, the Duke of Orleans said to him that he supposed he should soon see him at Versailles, which looks as if he had read the Memoriall and was not displeased with it, but Mr. Dillon being to go there one of these days I shall soon know what he says upon the matter, of which you shall be informed.[1]

I had wrote to the Duke of Orleans some time before, that

---

[1] Unfortunately for the success of the project, the Duke died before Mr. Dillon could see him.

haveing a designe of putting my son into the ffrench service, I beg'd a comission of Capt. Reformd for him in Links regiament. Mr. Dillon, after speaking to him of the other affair, put him in mind of this, tho' he told him he had no comission from me for so doing, as indeed he had not. His R. H. was pleased to say, after talking some time of it, that he was asham'd it had been so long delayed, but desired that he might tell me that it was agreed to, and that in time he would make up the delay. He then desired Mr. Dillon to speak of it to M. Bretuile, the secretary of war, that he might prepare the comission.

This I take to be no bad signe for the other affair, which make me much the more pleased with it.

My chife view in putting my son into the ffrench service there is to fitt him the more to be of use to you and yours, Sir, and the service of his country, where I hope he will in time distinguish himself by his endeavours for esteablishing and supporting the Royall ffamily, and be more successful than his ffather has been. But I have the satisfaction of knowing that the best endeavours I could use have not been wanting as they never shall, and I still hope that I may be so happie as to see your Maj. on your thron, and the greatest pleasur I have in life is the hopes I have of contributing still to your Restoration, and by that to the relief of our native opprest country. Soon may that time come, and that all happiness may ever attend you and yours are the constant prayers of him who is with all submission, Sir, y$^r$ Maj.$^s$ most faithful, most obedient, and most humble subject and servant, (*Sic sub.*) MAR.

P.S.—As I was writing what's above, I had a visit from Lord Southesque,[1] who is to be the bearer of this, tho he knows nothing of the contents ; and speaking of your Maj.$^s$ situation he mentioned a thing to me which I think worth the while of adding in this postscripte. It is a mariage for the Prince, your son, with the Duke of Orleans's youngest daughter, who is betwixt five and six years old. Marying great folks very young is become now to be very much the custome, and why may it not be done for the Prince as well as for others? He can

---

[1] James, fifth earl. He engaged in the affair of 1715, whereby his estates were forfeited and himself exiled.

never have a match in Europe more suitable to his quality, and the difference of their ages is so small that it is but a small objection to it. The advantages of this aliance are as great as can be, and I doubt not if it were mentioned to the Duke of Orleans by one well authorized of its being well received, and of its being a great inducement for his comeing into the scheme and project inclosed. You'll be pleased to think of it, Sir, and I shall be glad to know your thoughts on the subject.[1]

## Copie of L<sup>d</sup> Mar's letter to R. H. the Duke of Orleans incloseing the Memoriall.[2]

Monseigneur,—Je demande tres humblement pardon a votre altesse Royal de l'importuner de nouveau de mes lettres. Je ne prens la liberté de luy presenter ce Memoire, que par le desire ardent que j'ay detre en quelque maniere utile a la Nation ffrançoise autrefois l'amie et l'allie fidelle de l'Ecosse et de voir mon Prince legitime retably et ma Patrie reunie avec la ffrance d'une maniere stable et advantageuse pour l'une et pour l'autre Nation.

Je supplie instament V. A. R. de vouloir bien se donner la peine de lire ce que j'ay l'honeur de luy envoyer et je me flatte qu'elle y trouverra quelque chose de nouveau. Il contient un Project qui pourra être un jour utile a la ffrance aussy bien qua mon Prince et ma patrie.

Il nappartient qua votre A. R. de savoir les temps et les momens qu'elle voudra bien entreprendre quelque chose de cette nature, Je ne dois faire la dessus aucune question, mais je me trouverrois infiniment heureux si je voyois ariver ce jour, et si J'avois quelque part a l'execution de ce project par les ordres de V. A. R.

C'est a elle seule que je confie ce Memoire, conessant la

---

[1] It is not known what the thoughts of the Prince were; but it is not unlikely that the Duke would have consented to the match if he had lived.

[2] From the circumstance of General Dillon's having done the English of this letter and the following Memorial into French it would appear that Lord Mar was not acquainted with the French language. The aforementioned fact is doubtless quite sufficient to account for the numerous blunders which appear in Lord Mar's manuscript.

generosité de ses sentimens. Si ce projet etoit vû par quelque anglois, quoique meme naturalizé en ffrance, la chose pouroit transpirer et cela pouroit rendre la nation angloise moins zelé pour le retablissment de sa Roy legitime quelle ne l'est a present.

Je crois ce papier sûr entre les mains de V. A R. Je connois la fidelite de celuy qui la traduit et transcrit et célle du porteur est assez conue a V. A. R.

Je fais cette demarche a l'inseu du Roy mon Maitre, mais si V. A. R. goûte le project je ne desespere pas de pouvoir engager sa Majesté de l'envoyer ici des pouvois necessaires pour conclure cette affaire.—J'ay l'honeur d'etre avec un tres profond respect, Monseigneur V. A. R. le tres humble et tres obeisant serviteur.  (*Sic Sub.*)  Le Duc de Mar.

*A Paris le  Sep$^{tre}$ 1723.*

Translation of the foregoing letter from L$^d$ Mar to the Duke of Orleans:—

Monseigneur,—I humblie ask pardon of your Royal Highness for importuning you again with my letters. I only take the liberty of presenting your Highness with this Memoriall from the ardent desire I have of being in some measure servicable to the ffrench nation, formerly the faithfull friend and ally of Scotland, and of seeing my lawfull Prince restored and my country reunited to ffrance, in a maner firm and advantageous to both countries.

I beseech your R. H. to give yourself the trouble of reading what I have the honour to send you. I flatter myself you will find something new in it; it contains a project that may one day be of service to ffrance, as well as to my king and country.

It only belongs to your R. H. to know the proper time when you would undertake an affair of this nature. I am not to ask any questions upon that head; but I should think myself infinitely happie if I should live to see the day when this should happen, and I should have any share in the execution of this project by the comands of your R. H. 'Tis to you alone I confide this Memoriall, knowing the generosity of your sentiments. Were this scheme seen by any Englishman, tho' naturalized in ffrance, the business might take air, and it might make the English nation less jealous for the restoring of their lawfull king than they are at present.

I belive this paper will be safe in the hands of your R. H. I know the fidelity of him who translated and transcribed it[1] and the character of the bearer[2] is sufficiently knowen to your R. H. I make this step un-

---

[1] General Dillon.  [2] Lord Southesk.

knowen to the king my master; but if your R. H. should approve this scheme, I don't despair of prevailing on his Maj. to send the necessary powers to conclud this affair.—I have the honour of being with the profoundest respect, Monseigneur, Your R. H.'s most humble and most obedient servant. (*Sic sub.*)

Le Duc De Mar.

Copie of the Memoriall inclosed in the foregoing letter to his R. H. the Duke of Orleans from L<sup>d</sup> Mar.

*A son Altesse Royale*
*Monseigneur Le Duc D'Orleans.*

Memoire sur L'Interet de la France par raport L'Ecosse a L'Angleterre et l'Irlande.

Le Desein de ce Memoire est d'examiner s'il est de l'Interet de la France, de Retablier le Roy Jacques ou d'acquiescer a l'affermisement du Roy George et de sa Maison sur le Trone d'angleterre, etc.

Ce n'est pas sans raison que les anglois pretendent tenir la Ballance de L'Europe, dans leurs mains, et pouvoir la pancher de tel coté quils voudront par leurs forces sur mer et sur Terre.

Il ya long temps que la maison d'autiriche, et ses allies on fait une triste experience, de cette verité. Ils avaient eprouvé pendant la premiere guerre D'Holland en 1672, quil ne saffisoit pas que L'Angleterre rêtat dans la Neutralité comme elle avoit fait durant le Regne de Charles 2nd et pendant les quatre premieres années du Regne du Roy Jaques son Frere. Dans cet Intervalle, La France prit autant de villes qu'elle en assiegea, et remporta autant de victoires qu'elle donna de Battailles.

C'est ce qui determina les Imperiaux assemblés a Auxbourg a fair tout leur possible pour engager le feu Roy Jacques d'entrer avec eux dans une Ligne contre la France. Les ambassadeurs de L'Empereur, de L'Espagne et D'Hollande qui êtoient alors a Londres firent d'abord tous leurs efforts pour gagner ce Prince par les Insinuations mais voyant qu'il êtoit inflexible, Les Hollandois (comme il avoit être concerté a Auxbourg) prêterent des Troups et des vaisseaux au Prince d'Orange pour envader L'Angleterre. C'est ainsy que l'attachement du Roy Jaques pour la France luy couta en quelque façon sa couronne.

Après que ce Prince eût été, depossedé de ses etats, quel changement n'arriva pas dans les affair de France par le jonction des Troupes angloises avec celles des Imperiaux ? a quelles extremites ne fut elle pas reduite pendant le cours d'une longue guerre qui prodiga le sang de ses sujets, qui epuisa les Tresors du Roy, et qui diminua beaucoup L'etendüe de L'Empire Francois ?

Depuis l'avenement du Roy George a la couronne la paix a subsisté entre la France et la Grande Britagne parcque ce Prince n'avoit point d'autre moyen pour le maintenir sur le Trone, que par l'amitié et par la Protection d'un voisin aussy puisant que le Roy de France. Mais cette alliance est elle ou peut elle demurer long temps affermie ?

La Maison D'Autriche et les Princes Allemans son les ennemis et les Rivaux naturelles de la grandeur Françoise, Les Desire secrets et les pretextes specieux ne leur manqueront jamais pour attaquer la France sur tout tandis quelle sera Maitresse D'Alsce et de Strasbourg.

En cas dune Rupture semblable quel party prendra le Roy George ? Il est electeur de L'Empire. Il prefer sagment ses Etats Heriditaires et ceaux qu'il a nouvellement acquis en Allemagne au Royaume D'Angleterre, ou il se voit meprisé luy même et sa famile en Horreur. It est donc naturel de croire qu'il s'unira contre la France et qu'il entrainnera avec luy L'Angleterre tandis qu'il ensera la maitre.

Ce ne seroit pas de meme si le Roy Jaques remontoit sur son Trone. Ce Prince n'a acunes mesures a garder avec L'Empereur, nul lieu, nulle obligation ne l'attache a l'Allemagne, ni a acun Prince que pourvoit devinir l'Ennemy de la France mais il a un Interet puisant de cultiver l'amitie du Roy tres Chretian comme on verra bientot.

On objectera peutêtre que le Parl. d'Angleterre pourroit forcer le Roy malgré ses inclinations et ses interets de se declarer contre la France, dememe il est de son interet et de luy de ses Heritiers d'etre dans une telle situation qu'ils ne soyent jamais contraints de ceder aux humeurs capricieuses que le Parl. anglois pourroit avoir pour troubler cette unnion.

Ce Parl. a diminué l'autorité et les Prerogatives de la couroume. Il a empieté sur les droits et sur les privelcges des Royaumes d'Ecosse et d'Irland. Il a aneanty le Parl. de l'une en l'incorporant depuis peu avec le sien. Il tient depuis longues annees le Parl. de l'autre dans sa dependance. Il veut tout gouverner par ses propres councils. Les deux autres nations en gemissent, et ne cherchent qu'a secourer le joug.

De plus le peuple anglois est ennemy et rival de la grandeur Françoise autant que les Princes Allemandes. Il a été nourry pendant plusiers siecles par des guerres presque continuelles dans une haine inveterée contre la ffrance.

Voila les causes du Mal. Il parroit d'abord que le moyen le plus propre d'y remedier est d'entretenir toujours en Angleterre une armée mais rien ne servoit plus dangereux pour la maison de Stuart ne plus incompatible avec le genie anglois.

Le seul Remede efficace et salutaire est de Retablier les Royaumes d'Ecosse et d'Irlande dans leur ancienne Liberté et independance du Royaume et du Parl. D'Angleterre. Par la ces deux Royaumes egaleroient L'Angleterre en force, Il seroit de leur interet de sustenir leur Roy Legitime contre l'humeur altiere des anglois et il seroit de son Intérêt de les soutenir reciproquement.

Par la les Roys D'Angleterre seroient plus puissans, plus libres, plus maitres d'eux memes pour suivre leur Interets et leurs Inclinations et en meme temps plus obligés que jamais a conserver une union inviolable avec la France. C'est elle seule qui peut par sa force et par son voisinage maintenir sur le Trone d'Angleterre un Roy catolique et un Roy que sera toujours exposé (independament de sa religion) aux Brigues, aux caballes et aux troubles qui arrivent souvent depuis temps immemorial dance ce Royaume et qui semblent naitre comme dans l'ancienne Rome de la Forme de son gouvernment, ou sous preterite de soutenir la liberté du peuple on attaque souvent l'autorité des Roys.

Par la l'Ecosse et l'Irlande s'attacheront naturellement au Roy tres Chretien comme au guardien de leur Liberté, et de cette façon ces Royaumes luy seroient plus utiles que si lun d'eux luy appartenoit. Un Roy d'Angleterre avec trois Parl. anisey Independans dont deux auroint toujours un interet essentiel de menager la France seroit un allié tres utile a la nation Françoise laquelle seroit a jamais affranchie des craintes ou elle a toujours été de ses anciens ennemis et rivaux Les Anglois.

Par la enfin tous les Traittes Desadvantageux que la France a fait avec L'Angleterre depuis la Revolution pourient être aneantis et la France entrevoit dans tous les droits dont elle jouissoit sous le Regne de Jaques $2^d$.

Pour effectuer ce changement on propose qu'il y ait une ligue offensive et defensive entre sa Maj. tres Chretienne et le Roy Jaques et que par cette ligue Il soit stipulé :

1. Que le Roy de France fera tout son possible pour retablir Le Roy Jaques sur le Trone de ses ancêtres en luy fournissant des Troupes, des armes des vaisseaux et generalement tout ce que sera necessaire pour faire une Descent. Que le Roy Jaques sera obligé de payer et d'entretenir ces troupes a ses depens huit jours apres qu'elles seront descendües dans la grande Bretagne et que les frais de cette expedition seront rembourses par le Roy D'Angleterre aprés son Retablissement.

2. Que le Roy Jaques sera obligé par le dit Traitté de Retablir Les Royaumes d'Ecosse et d'Irlande dans leur ancienne Liberté et dans leur Independance du Royaume du Parl. et des conseils D'Angleterre pour être gouvernés dans les propres Parl de ces deux Royaumes, et quel essentiel de ces Lois sera concerté et arreté avant que les Troupes françoises quittent la grande Bretagne.

3. Que le Roy Jaques sera obligé de fournir au Roy de France cinq mille hommes des troups Ecossoises et autant d'Irlandois et meme le Double si le Roy tres Chretiene le demande, que la Roy de France sera obligé d'entretenir ces troupes à ses depens que leurs officiers receveront de luy leurs comissions, mais qu'ils seront recommandes par le Roy Jaques et par ses Heritiers legitimes et que les dites troupes auront permission de retourner dans la grande Bretagne quand le Roy D'Angleterre les demandera mais dans les temps et de la maniere dont il sera convenu avec le Roy tres Chretien par les articles du Traitté.

4. Enfin que le dit Traitté a tout ce que y aura du rapport sera ratifié et confirmé pour avoir Parlemens D'Ecosse D'Angleterre et D'Irlande avant que les troupes ffrançoises sortent de ces Royaumes.

Il seroit impossible d'executer les articles de ce traitté si on le disseroit jusqua ce que le Roy Jaques fut remonté sur son Trone. Ce Prince seroit alors entre les mains des anglois qui s'opposeroient á ce projet avec vigeur, et il n'oseroit y consentir mais tout sera facile de la maniere qu'on la proposé.

Les Anglois ne pourroient pas se plaindre avec Raison de ce que le Roy auroit recompensé la fidelité de la nation Ecosse et Irlandoise en les retablissant dans leurs premiere Independance. L'Ecosse jouissoit de cette Liberté il n'y a pas long temps et l'Angleterre est deja lasse de l'union derniere qu'elle a fait avec cette nation. Quoique les Irlandois se soumettent au Roy d'Angleterre et qu'ils luy seront toujours attachés cen'etait pas ce pendant pour être les esclaves du peuple et du Parl. anglois. Les anglois pourront ils se plaindre de ce que le Roy rend justice a deux Royaumes dont il es autant le pere que de celuy d'Angleterre. Ne peut il pas dire aux anglois qu'aprés les avoir sollicité pendant plus de Trente ans á le rappeller, ou'est effort enfin a le Retablir d'une maniere honorable et avantageuses pour la France son allie, pour ses deux Royaumes D'Ecosse et D'Irlande et pour sa Maison Royale, sans prejudice neamoins aux vrayes Libertés ni aux Loix antique du peuple anglois.

Il n'y a cun Prince etranger avec qui la France est en Liaison qui pourroit seblesser de ce Traitté, mais au contraire tous y trouverroient leurs avantages. L'Espagne sera bien aise de voir les Irlandois ses anciens amis, et ses allies redevenir un peuple libre, pour les memes raisons que la ffrance le sera de voir ses anciens amis et allies les Ecossois retablis dans leur premiere Liberté et Independance. De plus les Traittes desavantageuse faits entre L'Espagne et L'Angleterre depuis a Revolution pourroient être ancantis.

Les Hollandois Rivaux des anglois pour le commerce seroient charmés de ce project, par ce qu'il rendrait leur Negoce avec L'Ecosse et L'Irlande plus facile et plus libre. Cela paroit evidement par le chagrin que la Republique d'Hollande marqua au sujet de la derniere union de l'Ecosse avec L'angleterre.

Le Czar trouverrait ses Interets dans ce project et Il y a lieu de croire qu'il y entrevoit, et qu'il enverroit ou des troupes en angleterre selon que S. A. R. le jugeroit a propos, ou qu'il attaqueroit less etats du Roy George en allemagne dans le meme temps que la France seroit une descente dans la grand Bretagne.

Si les Suedois songeoient a leurs Interets propres plus qua ceux du Prince etranger qui le gouverne, Ils gouteroient ce projet, mais dans l'etat ou ils sont ce descin leur doit être indifferent assy bien qu'aux Danois.

L'Empereur et les Princes Allemans Rivaux de la France ne seroient pas à la verité contens de ce project parcequ'il les priveroit du secours des anglois en cas d'une Rupture avec la France. Mais ils sont trop Elignés pour en empecher l'execution si ce n'est en fflandres ou la France peut aisement les arreter sur tout puisque les Hollandois ne s'y opposeroient pas.

Si S. A. R. juge a Propos d'entrer dans ce project une grande flotte ne sera pas necessaire pour fair une descente en Angleterre. Des petits Batimens et des Batteaux de Pescheurs suffiroient pour transporter dans une seul nuit des troupes, des armes, et tout ce qu'il faut, de sorte que la flotte angloise ne pourroit pas empecher le Debarquement de ces troupes, quand elle sauroit leur dessein.

Les sujets des trois Royaumes sont generalement mecontent du gouvernement et en demandent meme en angleterre, qu'un chef, un corps des troupes et des armes pour se Rassembler et pour faire un soulevement general.

L'Ecosse est comme un seul homme pour le Roy Jaques avec un peu de secours Il s'enrendoit maitre en trois semaines et dans trois autres il pourroit envoyer de la une armee de quinze on de vingt mille hommes en Angleterre.

Les amys du Roy Jaques en Irlande n'ont point d'armes, mais avec un peu de secours, Ils pourroient en peu de temps non seulement empecher les troupes du gouvernement present de passer de là dans la G. Bretagne, mais ils seroient bientot en etat eux memes d'envoyer des troupes en Ecosse et dans l'Angleterre.

Pour executer donc le Projet en question, Il suffiroit d'envoyer cinq ou sex mille hommes en Angleterre avec vingt mille armes: Deux mille hommes en Ecosse avec quinze mille armes et quatre mille hommes en Irlande avec quinze mille armes. Le tout en monteroit qu'a Douze mille hommes et cinquante mille armes avec toutes les Munitions necessaires ce qui est un petit object pour la ffrance. Mais si l'on trouve que ce soit trop, on peut ce contenter de moins, cependant ce qu'on propose rendroit le succes assuré.

Il ne seroit pas difficile d'engager le Roy Jaques d'envoyer de Rome de pouvoirs a une ou deux personnes de confiance ny pour traiter avec eux que S. A. R. nommeroit, non seulement de ce qui est proposé, mais de tout ce qu'elle voudroit proposer de sa part ou de celle de la ffrance. Le tout pourroit se faire avec un secret impenetrable a d'une maniere si prompte que le Roy Jaques pourroit être Retably dans l'Espace de deux mois. Peu de temps aprés les articles qui regardent l'Independance de l'Ecosse et d'Irlande pourroient être ratifiés dans leurs Parl. des trois Royaumes.

Par tout cecy les desseins que S. A. R. peut avoir ne seroient ni deconcertés ni retardés, au contraire, Ils reussiroient mieux aprés le Retablissement d'un allie sur et puissant dont les vües ne pourroient être necessairement que celles de S. A. R. Quelle gloire Immortelle pour elle d'avoir achève un ouvrage que Louis le grand n'a pas pû consommer nonobstant ses efforts redoublés !

Par la S. A. R. se rendroit a jamais chere a la France, a l'Ecosse a l'Irlande, a trois nations qui y trouverroient leurs Interets, et des avantages dans tous les siecles a venir. Par là Elle se reandroit chere a la Maison Royale de Stuart, a la meilleure et la plus grande partie de la nation Angloise. Par là elle avoit seule l'honneur d'avoir reparé les injures faites a la Majesté dans la personne d'un Roy qui est comme Elle petit ffils de Henry le grand.

Sir S. A. R. croit avoir des Raisons pour ne pas entrer dans ce projet, ou pour en differer l'execution, Les amis du Roy Jaques n'ont d'autre ressourse que de l'entreprendre par eux memes, avec le concours de leur Roy qui y entrera volontiers.

L'oppression est parvenüe a son comble elle ne peut augmenter qu'en les auctissant. Le government medite a desarmer tout fait les Ecossois et a les accabler par ce nouvelles Taxes comme on a fait le Catoliques et les non jurans en Angleterre. Les Proscriptions regnent part tout, Que n'entreprendra pas un peuple desesperé, poussé a bout et resolu de perir, ou de savoir la Labité ?

S'il succombe sous poids de ses malheurs ou s'il s'en delivre tout seul, quels regrets n'aura pas La France d'avoir manqué une occasion si felicitant de former une alliance stable et advantageuse avec le Roy d'angleterre et en meme temps de se mettre a libre d'un peuple et d'un Parl. que depuis plusieurs siecles sont jaloux de la gloire de nom François.

Fin.

*N.B.*—The following paragraph of the Memoriall forgot in the copying:—Il est par consequent l'interet de La France d'avoir toujours l'angleterre, pour son allie, mais quels sont les moyens les plus surs d'affermir cette alliance.

The forgoing Memorial and letter to the Duke of Orleans haveing been sent by Mr. Hay to the Bishope of Rochester, D$^{oct}$ Attesbury, as soon as Mr. Hay returnd to the King, from the copie his Maj. had from L° Mar, it was by the Bishope's directions printed at London in ffrench and English an. 1728, dispersed there, and severall copies of it sent into ffrance at Thizy[?], intending to make Lord Mar odious to the English, without the least regard to the prejudice the publishing of it might have to the king he pretends to serve, his affairs, or the jealousies it may put betwixt the two nations.

*Translation of the foregoing Memoriall to His Royall Highness the Duke of Orleans.*

MEMORIAL touching the interest of ffrance with respect to Scotland, England, and Ireland.

THE design of this Memoriall is to examine whether it be most for the interest of ffrance to esteablish King James, or to acquiesce in the settlement of King George and his ffamily, on the Throne of England, etc.

It is not without reason that the English pretend to hold the Ballance of Europe in their hands, and to be able to incline it to what side they please by reason of their strength by land and sea.

"Tis now a long time since the House of Austria and its allies have made a melancholy experience of this truth. They found during the first Dutch war in 1672, that it was not sufficient England should remain in a state of neutrality, as she did during the reign of King Charles 2$^{nd}$, and during the first four years of the reign of his brother, King James; for in the interval France took as many towns as they beseig'd, and obtained as many victories as she fought battles.

It was this that determined the Imperialists assembled at Ausburgh to do all that was possible to engage the late King James to enter into an alliance with them against France. The ambassadors of the Emperor of Spain and of Holland, who were then at London, at first made all their efforts to gain over that Prince by insinuations; but finding that he was inflexible, the Hollanders (as it had been concerted at Ausburgh) lent troops and ships to the Prince of Orange to invade England. It was thus that the attachment of King James to France in some measure cost him his crown.

After the Prince had been disposessed of his Dominions, what a chance did there happen in the affairs of France, by the joining of the English and Imperial forces? To what extremities was she not reduced, during the course of a long war which exhausted her blood and treasure and mightily reduced the extent of her Dominions? Consequently, it is the interest of ffrance always to have England for its ally; but what are the surest means of confirming this alliance? Since the accession of King George to this crown, Peace has subsisted between ffrance and Great Britain, because that Prince had no other way of mentaining himself upon the Throne, but by the friendship and protection of so powerful a nighbour as the King of ffrance. But can this alliance remain long on a sure footing?

The House of Austria and the Princes of Germany are the natural enemies and rivals of ffrench grandeur. Secret inclinations and specious pretences will never be wanting to them for attacking ffrance, especially whilst she continues mistress of Alsace and Strasburg.

In case of a rupture what party would King George take? He is an elector of the Empire, and would wisely prefer his hereditary dominions, and those which he has lately acquired in Germany, to the Kingdom of England, etc., where he sees himself despised and his whole ffamily hated. 'Tis therefore natural to belive he would join against ffrance, and would also draw England after him [1] as long as he continued master of it.

But it would not be so if K. James should ascend the Throne. This Prince has no measurs to keep with the Emperor, no alliance, no obligation attaches him to Germany, nor to any Prince that may become au Enemy to ffrance, but he will have a powerfull interest to cultivate peace with his most Chris. Maj. as shall be shewn immediately.

It may perhaps be objected, that the Parl. of England may force the king against his inclinations and interest to declare against ffrance, examples of which have often been seen.

---

[1] The Georges were not without reason suspected of preferring their Continental to their British Dominions.

As it will be the interest of King James to hold a lasting union with France, it will also be his interest, and that of his heirs, to be in such a situation as not to be obliged to yield to the capricious humours which an English Parl. may have of disturbing that union.

That Parl. has diminished the authority and prerogatives of the crown; it has encroached upon the rights and privileges of the Parliaments of Scotland and Ireland; it has abolished the Parl. of the one and lately incorporated it with itself, and keept the Parliament of the other these many years in a state of dependancy. It governs all by its own proper councills, the two other nations groaning and only endeavouring to shake off the yoke. Moreover, the people of England are enemies and rivals of the ffrench grandeur as much as the princes of Germany; they have been bred for many ages in almost continuall wars and in an inveterat hatred against the ffrench.

These are the causes of the evil. It appears at first sight that the proper means of remedying them is to have a standing army in England, but nothing would be more dangerous to the family of Stuart nor more disagreeable to the genius of the English.

The only effectual and wholesome remedy is to Reestablish the Kingdomes of Scotland and Irland in their ancient Libertys, and free them from their dependance on the kingdome and Parl. of England.

By this means these two nations will be equall in strength to England; it will be their interest to support their lawfull King against the inconstant humours of the English, and of course it will be his interest reciprocally to support them. Thus the Kings of England, etc., would become more powerfull, more free, more masters of themselves to follow their interest and inclinations, and at the same time would be more than ever oblidged to preserve an inviolable union with ffrance. 'Tis she alone that by her strength and nighbourhood will be able to support a Catholick King upon the throne of England, and a king who will be always exposed (independent of his religion) to the cavils, cabals, and troubles which time immemorial have hapned in that kingdome, where like ancient Rome from the form of her government, when under pretence of maintaining the Liberty of the People, the Royal authority is often infringed.

Thus Scotland and Irland would be naturally attached to the most Christian King as the guardian of their Libertys; and these Kingdomes would become more beneficial to ffrance than if one of them belong'd to her. A King of England with these independent Parliaments (two of which would have an essential interest to keep well with ffrance) must be a very usefull ally to the ffrench nation who would be delivered from the fears they have long entertained of their ancient enemies and rivals the English. In fine by this method all the disadvantageous treaties which ffrance has made with England since the Revolution might be rendered void, and ffrance would rest possest of all the rights which she enjoyed in the reign of King James the $2^{nd}$.

To bring about this change, it is proposed that there be a league offensive and defensive between his most Christian Maj. and King James, and by this League it shall be stipulated :

1. That the king of ffrance shall do all that in him is possible towards the restoring King James to the Throne of his ancestors, by furnishing him with troops, armes, ships, and generally with all things that shall be necessary for a descent, and that King James shall be oblidged to pay and maintain these troops at his own expence after they shall be landed eight days in Great Britain ; and that the expence of the expedition shall be reimbursed by the King of England after his esteablishment.

2. That King James shall be oblidged by the said treatie to settle the kingdomes of Scotland and Irland in their ancient priviledges and indepandant of the kingdome, Parl., and Councils of England. To be governed at all times hereafter by laws made in the proper Parls. of those his kingdomes, and that this shall be actually agreed in and ratified before the ffrench troops depart great Britain.

3. That King James shall be oblidged to furnish the king of ffrance with 3000 Scots and 3000 Irish troops, and even double that number, if his most Christian Maj. shall desire it. That the king of ffrance shall be oblidged to mentain these troops in his own pay. That the officers shall receive their comissions from him, but shall be recomended by King James and his lawfull heirs ; and that the said troops shall be permitted to return to great Britain whenever the King of England, etc. shall demand them, but in such time as shall be agreed upon with his most Christian Maj. by the articles of the said treatie.

4. In fine, that the said Treatie, and every thing that has relation to it shall be ratified and confirm'd, and have the force of a law immutable in the three Parls. of Scotland, England, and Irland, before the ffrench troops shall depart those kingdomes.

It would be impossible to execute the articles of this treatie if it should be deferr'd til K. James shall be esteablished upon the Throne ; That Prince would then be in the hands of the English who would vigorously oppose this project, nor would he venture to consent to it ; but all would be easie in the maner here proposed. The English could not in reason complain that the King had recompensed the fidelity of the Scots and Irish nations in restoring them to their ancient independancy. Scotland enjoyed its liberty not long since, and England is already wearie of the last Union which she made with that kingdome. Although the Irish submitted to the King of England, and will be always attached to him, yet it was not to be the slaves of the people and Parl. of England. Could the English complain of the King's doing justice to two kingdomes, of which he is as much the father as he is that of England ? Might he not very well tel the English that after haveing solicited more than thirty years to be called home an offer was at length made to him to be restored in a maner honourable and advantageous to France his ally, to his two kingdomes of Scotland and Irland and to his Royal ffamily, nevertheless without prejudice to the real liberties and and ancient laws of the people of England ?

There is no foreign Prince with whom ffrance is in alliance that could be injured by this Treatie; on the contrary all would find their advantage by it.

Spain would be pleased to see the Irish their ancient friends and allies become a free people, for the same reason that ffrance would be also pleased to see her ancient friends and allies the Scots re-established in their ancient Liberty and Independancie. Moreover, the disadvantagous treaties made betwixt Spain and England since the revolution might therby be rendered void.

The Hollanders, who are rivals of the English in trade will be charmed with this project, because it would render the trafick with Scotland the more easie and free. This appears evidently by the disgust which the Republick of Holland shewd upon the union betwixt Scotland and England.

The Czar will find his interest in this scheme, and there is room to belive he would enter into it, and that he would either send troops into Britain, according as H. R. H. should judge proper, or that he would attack the dominions of King George in Germany at the same time that ffrance should be makeing a descent upon Great Britain.

If the Swedes would regard their own proper interest more than that of the foreign Prince[1] who governs them, they would relish this designe; but in the condition they are in, it may be altogether indifferent to them, as well as to the Danes.

The Emperor and Princes of Germany, rivals of ffrance, would not indeed be contented with this project, because it would deprive them of the assistance of England, in case of a rupture with ffrance; but they are too far distant to hinder its execution, except in fflanders where ffrance might easily stop them, especially seeing the Dutch would not oppose it.

If his R. H. should judge it proper to engage in this scheme, a great ffleet would not be necessary to make a descent upon England. Small barks and ffishing boats will serve to transport in one night, troops, armes, and every thing that shall be necessary, in so much that the English ffleet will not be able to prevent the sending of these forces, tho' they should be acquented with the Design.

The subjects of the three kingdomes [are?] for the most part disaffected to the present government; and even in England they require nothing but a comander, a body of troops and armes to assemble themselves and make a general riseing.

Scotland is like one man for K. James, who with a little assistance might make himself master of it in three weeks, and in three more he would be able to send an armie of 15 or 20,000 men into England.

The friends of K. James in Irland have no armes, but with a very little succour, they might be able, not only to hinder the troops of the present government from passing into Britain, but would be also in a

---

[1] The King of Denmark.

condition themselves to send troops over into Scotland and from thence to England.

To execute, therefore, the scheme in question, it would be sufficient to send 5 or 6000 over into England, with 20,000 arms; 2000 men into Scotland with 15,000 arms, and 4000 men into Irland with 15,000 arms. The whole would amount to no more than 12,000 men with 50,000 arms and all the necessary amunition, which would be a very trifle to ffrance; and if that should be thought too much, even less might serve, nevertheless what is here proposed would render the success certain.

It would be no difficult thing to engage King James to send powers from Rome to one or two persons in trust for him here, to treat with such as his R. H. should name, not only concerning what is here proposed, but of all that may be proposed on the part of his Royall Highness or that of ffrance. The whole might be conducted with such impenitrable secrecy and in so expeditious a maner, that King James might be restored in the space of two months. In a little time after, the articles that regard the Independancy of Scotland and Irland might be ratified in the Parls. of the three kingdomes.

By all this no designs which his R. H. may have will be either disconcerted or retarded; on the contrary they will succeed the better after the esteablishment of so powerfull an ally, whose views must necessarily be the same with those of his R. H. What an immortal glory will it be to his R. H. to finish a work which Lewis the great was not able to compass notwithstanding his repeated efforts! By this his R. H. will for ever endear himself to ffrance, Scotland, and Irland, three nations who will find their interest and advantages in it to all ages. By this his R. H. will endear himself to the ffamily of Stewart, and to the best and greatest part of the English nation. By this he will alone have the honour of repairing the injuries done to Majesty in the person of a king, who as well as himself, is great grandson to Henry the Great.

If his R. H. should think he has reasons not to enter into this project or to defer its execution, the friends of King James have no other expedient but to undertake it themselves with consent of their king, who will readily engage in it. Oppression is at the highest pitch, and cannot increase but by a total extirpation of them [it?]. The government threatens entirely to disarm the Scots and to load them with new taxes, as the Catholicks and nonjurors have already been in England. Proscriptions abound everywhere. When pressed to extremities, what will not a desperat people undertake, resolved to die or recover their liberty? If they sink under this weight of sufferings, or if they should alone deliver themselves, how would ffrance regret her haveing missed so glorious an occasion for formeing a lasting and advantageous alliance with the King of England, etc., and at the same time of being freed from all apprehensions of a people and Parl. who have been for many ages jealous of the ffrench name and glory.

FFINIS.

# A THOUGHT WITH REGARD TO SCOTLAND on the Foregoing Memorial to H.R.H. the late DUKE OF ORLEANS, occasioned by the Emberas appearing to the general Peace, Novemb. 1727.[1]

SHOULD there be difficultys found in the scheme in the above-mentioned Memoriall with regard to the interest of King James and the king and kingdome of ffrance by King George being so well esteablished on the thron of Great Britain and the King of ffrance being so far engaged by treaties for the support of the ffamily of Hanover there, another scheme much to the same purpose may be form'd, which might perhaps more easily be brought about; and in great measur answer the ends proposed by the Memoriall, and for the advantage of most of the powers concerned in the present dispute about the settlement of Europe.

There is ground to belive that the late King of Sweden[2]

---

[1] This paper or pamphlet is the basis of the so-called Hanover 'Plot.' Burton, the historian, has the following reference to it in his *History of Scotland* (vol. ii. p. 229): 'He (Mar) did not, however, omit such opportunities as occurred of plotting for his adopted cause when he conveniently could; and so he appears to have communicated with Sunderland, the British Minister, a plan for enlarging the Elector of Hanover's continental dominions on the condition of his consenting to a restoration—a project about which Sunderland seems to have consented to hear, from the chance so afforded him of penetrating the real designs of the enemy.' It is said on good authority that King George himself was favourably impressed with Mar's scheme.

[2] The design of bringing the King of Sweden into the Prince's measures is generally accredited to Lord Mar. Lockhart, in his *Memoirs*, says: 'There was ... a surmise that the king had some hopes of gaining the King of

in the Design he had of re-esteablishing K. James and the ffamily of Stewart, about which he was going when he was unfortunately killed, did not intend to restore him to all the Dominions his ffather, King James, was possest of, but only to part of them.

To follow out a design of this kind, the plan might be that K. James and his children should be restor'd to the kingdomes of Scotland and Irland, with some of the Plantations in America, where a great number of the natives of these two countrys are esteablished, and to leave England, with the other settlements and plantations in the East and West Indies, now belonging to that kingdome, to King George and his posterity. King James and his lawfull heirs might perhaps be happier by this than his predecessors ever were by the possession of the three kingdomes. King George and his heirs could have no reason to complain, since they would therby get the peacable and sure possession of the valuable and rich kingdome of England; and that to be confirmed to them by a renounciation by King James and his children, as King George and his should renounce to them the other two kingdomes, etc., as above, all to be guaranted by the Emperor, ffrance, Spain and Holland, and the King of Sardinia his queen and his son as next heirs in blood to King James and his children, which powers would all find their accounts by it.

England ought not in justice to complain of this division, since by it they would be more surly delivered from their fears of the Pretender, as they call him, than ever they can otherwise be. All their comerce, trade, and most of their plantations would be left to them in place of Irland (which submitted to the king and not to the people of England) the

---

Sweden to espouse his cause; and the first nottice therof to be depended upon was a letter from the Duke of Mar to Captain Straiton which he directed to be communicated to the Bishop of Edinburgh, the Lord Balmerino, and myself, wherin he signify'd that if 5 or 6000 boles of meal would be purchased by the king's friends and sent to Sweden, where there was then a great scarcity, it would be of great service to the king. But we foresaw so many difficulties in raising a sum sufficient for it, and withal so impracticable to collect and embark such a quantity of meal without being discouvered and creating some suspicion in the government, that we could not think of undertaking it with any hopes of success. (vol. ii. p. 7).

Dominions of King George in Germany would depend on them.

This division would be agreeable to the people of Scotland and Irland, who are both of one stock. A ffederal union to be esteablished at the same time between these two kingdomes, by which the laws and seperat Parliaments of both to be reserved, which would be much more advantagous to these two countrys than any kind of conjunction with England.

Neither King James nor King George will never willingly and of their own accord agree to this Division, the one thinking he has an hereditary right to the whole, and the other being in posession of all; but it would be easie for the powers above mentioned to oblidge them to it, since the people of Scotland and Irland would gladly assist in bringing it about when they see these powers interest themselves heartily in the affair, which they might do without any danger to themselves or disturbance to the affairs of Europe, but on the contrair very much for its tranquility.

THE END.

# APPENDIX

## LETTER FROM THE EARL OF MAR
## TO THE CHEVALIER

*Rome, ffeb. 5th, 1719.*

SIRE,—I think it my duty and incumbent on me at this time, when y$^r$ Majesty may be in England before I have the happiness of seeing you again, to lay before you for y$^r$ own privat use what occurrs to me by my haveing been a considerable time in business there, w$^{ch}$ gave me opportunitys of knowing things and persons that y$^r$ Majesty cannot possiblie have til some time after y$^r$ arivall, and I offer this to y$^r$ Majesty w$^t$ all submission as the best service I am capable of rendring you at this junctur.

As the Church of England and the party that goes by its name, w$^{ch}$ is now calld Torys, are the Majority of the people, so have they ever been the supporters of the Crown, and y$^r$ Majesty will find by supporting and countenancing of them that you will have a quiet and happie reine.

Y$^r$ Royall unckle King Charles found the fatall consequences, as the late King y$^r$ ffather and y$^r$ Majesty have dearly since, of his neglecting those at his restoration who had been most zealous for him and the royall cause and preferring in too partiall and eminent a way those who had been otherways in hopes by that to gain them.

Y$^r$ Majesty possesses the charactaristick of y$^r$ ffamily, Good nature, gentelness of temper and reddyness to forgive, y$^r$ showing that to those who have opposed you and forgetting the Injurys they have done to the King y$^r$ ffather and y$^r$ self when they come to alter their wayes is becomeing a great Prince, and the doing so will be I know no pain to you, but justice and equity require that those who have suffred so long for you and been instrumentall in y$^r$ service, should find the first fruits of y$^r$ favours in haveing y$^r$

countenance in the first place and being principally consulted and advised with in y$^r$ affairs, this will encourage and confirme y$^r$ friends and lessen y$^r$ enimies, w$^{ch}$ is the way to establish you and y$^r$ posterity upon the thron.

Some exceptions there must be w$^t$ regard to fitt persons and of experience and knowledge in business to be emploied under you, when there are not such to be found of the party you emploie, w$^{ch}$ is often the case there and I belive every where. And should it be so when y$^r$ Majesty comes to be restord, alow me to informe you of one who In my humble oppinion is one of the most proper to serve you as one of y$^r$ principal ministers. It is Mr. Henry Boyle, unckle to the present Earle of Burlingtone and who is now call'd L$^d$ Carleton. He has been always what they call a moderat man as to partys, but more Tory than whigg. When he was in the Secretary office in y$^r$ Sister's time, no body ever did the business better in it, and there was no body of whom that great minister, L$^d$ Godolphin, had a better oppinion. He had very good understanding and an agreeable temper and no man is easier in concert of business. He has always been well w$^t$ the Duke of Ormond, tho not of his principall advisers and I belive wou'd still be agreeable to him. Mr. Boyle was once a great friend of Mr. Primroses and it was much against his will that he quitted his emploiment at the change of L$^d$ Godolphins ministry when all those w$^t$ whom he had served were turnd out, yet he acted a very moderat part afterwards. He avoided being of the new Parl. and was very well w$^t$ Mr. Primrose and the then ministry tho not in business w$^t$ them, for w$^{ch}$ L$^d$ Marleborough and the whigg party have never yet forgiven him. It is true he has been made a Peer by George, but has never gone into their extravagant and violent measurs. He was long Chancelor of the Exchequer and sub treasurer, so is well seen in the affairs of the treasury and funds w$^{ch}$ are very intricat, and I verily belive there are not two men in England who are more capable to advise y$^r$ Majesty in those important affairs than he and L$^d$ Bingly who served in L$^d$ Oxfords time in the same post, and they could be helpfull one to another. Mr. Boyle was never one of those for bringing the power of the Crown too low and by the reputation he has generally got, the people wou'd have confidence in him that might make him very usefull to you. Upon the whole he is well worth gaining to y$^r$ intrest w$^{ch}$ I belive will be no difficult work.

As I have said, it is highly reasonable and for y$^r$ intrest that those who have appeard most zealous for y$^r$ service hitherto when y$^r$ affairs were at the lowest should be most regarded and first emploied in the eminent posts by y$^r$ Majesty. Mr. Rigg has undoubtedly a very good claim on this respect as well, as on account of his eminent parts, to have such distinguishing marks of y$^r$ favour bestowd on him in his way, as y$^r$ Majesty shall judge proper. And I hope you may be able to contrive it so that Mr. Boyle wou'd not be disagreeable to him, as I know he wou'd have been very acceptable to y$^r$ friend the Duke of Shrewsbery had it pleased God to have alowd him to see y$^r$ restoration, w$^{ch}$ he so much wisht for.

L$^d$ Bingly had always a warme side for y$^r$ Majesty, and when y$^r$ business shall once begin to go well when you come to England, as I hope in God it soon will, you want but to lay y$^r$ comands on him.

As to Scotland, I hope I may be so happie to be w$^t$ y$^r$ Majesty at furthest before the time of y$^r$ settling y$^r$ affairs there, when I shall lay my thoughts of them humblie before you, so all I will trouble y$^r$ Majesty w$^t$ at this time in relation to them is in generall, that notwithstanding of y$^r$ Restoreing that y$^r$ ancient Kingdome to its old constitution and forme of Goverment, by reliving it from the Union, w$^{ch}$ by experience has proved so grivous, yet so long as Presbitry is the esteablisht goverment of the Church there, you can never riene peacablie nor be in quiet. Esteablishing the Church there as it is in England w$^t$ the like toleration to those who cannot comply w$^t$ it, will in time make y$^r$ affairs there easie and them a happie people w$^t$ that and the encouragments y$^r$ Majesty may other wayes give them as to their trade, etc., without any loss to y$^r$ Kingdome of England; But the sooner after y$^r$ restoration you endeavour what shall be found just and reasonable that way, the more easily you will get it done, because the doing of it will in some measur depend on England.

You will have little difficulty in getting a Parliament in Scotland that will settle that country in that just way y$^r$ Majesty will propose, nor will you want fitt people to serve you there.

I know thers no occasion for my recomending the Highlanders to y$^r$ Majesty, you have seen and know them and the great atachment they have had to y$^r$ family. By encourageing of them and giveing them armes and some reasonable alowance to their chifes and superiours and preventing their being oprest by those who have jurisdictions over them until y$^r$ Majesty shall think fitt to purchess them w$^{ch}$ were much y$^r$ intrest to do, will cost but little expence and trouble, nothing in Scotland or from it can ever hurt you. It will save y$^r$ keeping any troops there but a few gards and garrisons and be of no burthen to the country.

I beg y$^r$ Majesty may pardon this presumption and may you soon have occasion for putting things, or what are better in practice.

[*Indorsed*] D. Mar. Feb. 4. and 5. 1719.

LETTERS WRITTEN BY
# MRS. GRANT OF LAGGAN
CONCERNING HIGHLAND AFFAIRS AND
PERSONS CONNECTED WITH THE STUART
CAUSE IN THE EIGHTEENTH CENTURY

Edited by
J. R. N. MACPHAIL

# INTRODUCTION

THE writer of the following letters was the only child of Duncan Macvicar and Catharine Mackenzie, his wife, and was born in Glasgow in the year 1755. Her father's family belonged to Craignish in Argyll, while her mother was on the maternal side descended from the Stewarts of Invernahyle. Three years after her birth the 77th Regiment, in which her father held a commission, was ordered to America, where she and her parents remained some ten years. In 1768 they returned to Scotland, and resided in Glasgow till 1773, when Mr. Macvicar was appointed Barrack-master at Fort Augustus, where his daughter lived till her marriage in 1779 to the Rev. James Grant, minister of the parish of Laggan, which lies in the centre of Inverness-shire. Of good Highland blood on both sides, Mrs. Grant had all along been deeply interested in everything that related to her race, and she spared no pains in becoming thoroughly acquainted with the customs, the traditions, and the language of the people among whom she now had her home. Soon after the death of her husband in 1801, Mrs. Grant removed with her family from Laggan to Woodend, near Stirling, and in 1810 she finally settled in Edinburgh, where she died in 1838, at the ripe old age of eighty-three.

In 1803 Mrs. Grant published a volume of poems, the most ambitious of which was entitled 'The Highlanders.' In 1806 this was followed by a selection from the correspondence which she had kept up with her south-country friends from 1773, when her family settled at Fort Augustus. The Highlands of Scotland were at that time an unknown land, and from their matter, as well as from their literary merit, these *Letters from the Mountains* attracted considerable attention, and secured for the writer recognition as an authority of some importance on Highland affairs—a reputation which was enhanced by the appearance in 1811 of her *Essays on the Superstitions of the Highlands of Scotland.*

One of Mrs. Grant's neighbours at Woodend was Mr. (afterwards Sir Henry) Steuart of Allanton, with whose wife—a Miss Seton of Touch—she was on terms of intimate friendship. A county gentleman of no ordinary attainments, he had the intention of writing 'An historical Review of the different attempts to restore the Stewart family to the throne, from the Revolution in 1688 to the Suppression of the Rebellion in 1745.' To Mrs. Grant, amongst others, he applied for assistance in the collection of materials, and in response to his request the following letters were written. Sir Henry Steuart, however, never succeeded in carrying out his design, and Mrs. Grant's letters, along with the other papers which he had accumulated, including *The Lyon in Mourning*, passed into the hands of Dr. Robert Chambers, to the courtesy of whose grandson and representative, Mr. C. E. S. Chambers, their publication is now due.

It is indeed rather as embodying what had already become tradition—but tradition of a very rich and special kind—than as authoritative statements of historical facts that the Society has given them a place in this volume. And in spite of many inaccuracies, some of which have been corrected in the notes, the value of such tradition, even for historical purposes, will not be gainsayed. Dr. Chambers himself made use of these letters when writing his well-known history of the Forty-five, and Mr. John Hill Burton also had access to them, as is acknowledged in the preface to his *Life of Lord Lovat*. But they are now published for the first time.

# MRS. GRANT'S LETTERS

*Melville Place, Janry. 21st, 1808.*

DEAR SIR,—I plead guilty to inexcusable delay in fulfilling my promise relative to the anecdotes, but indolence always frames excuses for procrastinating, and that with which I lulled my conscience on this occasion, was that having wrote to Miss Ferguson for Lady Stuart's reminiscences, I thought it would be a species of frugality to wait for their arrival, in case some of her anecdotes should be similar to my own, and so preclude the necessity of my writing such as she had anticipated.

She, however, has not as yet answered my letter. I have therefore confin'd myself to a branch of the subject, on which I imagine myself particularly well inform'd. You may probably think me both minute and diffuse. It may be so, but I am satisfied with being authentic and sure of my ground. Much more and much worse might be said of Lovat, but here is abundance of the dark side of human nature. We shall next bend our attention to a more luminous object while we contemplate

> 'A brave man struggling with the storms of fate.'

I shall detail the anecdotes I know of Lochiel '*con amore*,' and you may expect them very soon. But first I must know how you approve of the manner in which I have executed this part of my task. It is worth your while to look into the late Earl of Orford's reminiscences for the anecdote I refer to.[1] I have seen among Lovat's relations a little pamplet, published, I suppose, to distribute among his friends, containing an account very plainly and, I doubt not, accurately detailed, of his behaviour and conversation with his friends in the Tower, etc. It contains many interesting and curious particulars.

---

[1] *See* p. 268.

If you will take the trouble of looking over the notes on the Poem of the Highlanders,[1] which I think you have, you will find some anecdotes relative to the Prince, but those perhaps are too well known. I think I can recollect many others, but to these perhaps the same objection may lie; but from Ralia I shall expect information both curious and authentic.

Miss Colquhon has obliged me with a detail of the treacherous apprehension of the Marquis of Tullibardine, by the elder and younger Buchanans of Drumakiln. This last, by-the-bye, was married to a daughter of Murray of Polmaise.

I am astonish'd, Dear Sir, that in your search for anecdotes of the '45, you should have overlook'd a fertile source in your immediate neighbourhood. I am told Miss Lilly Wilson at Murrays Hall is a perfect magazine of that kind of knowledge, to which she had great access.

Ballacheulish,[2] who you know resided there, had the most extensive memory and the most extensive knowledge on these subjects of any person I ever knew, and he was not more knowing than communicative.

Pray be kind enough to assure Mrs. Mackenzie of my sincerest veneration, and offer my best respects to Mrs. and Miss Stuart. I inclose a line of introduction to Miss Ferguson; but can only say of Ormiston that it is four or five miles from Edr. I am, Dear Sir, with respect and regard, Your obedt. servt.,
ANNE GRANT.

DEAR SIR,—I promis'd to send you some anecdotes of Lovat and Lochiel, who were certainly the two prime movers of the northern insurrection in '45. This, if my memory does not fail me, is much in my power to do, having liv'd in great intimacy with persons to whom these extraordinary and very opposite characters were very well known.

Willing to perform the most unpleasant part of my task first, I shall begin with Lovat, who might at his outset in life

---

[1] *Vide* Introduction.

[2] John Stewart fifth of Ballachelish, married Margaret, daughter of William Wilson of Murray's Hall, near Stirling. Mrs. Grant's spelling of proper names is preserved throughout.

be styl'd a daring and unprincipl'd adventurer,[1] and who began his career of wickedness very early in a manner that would have expell'd any other person for ever from society.

Simon Fraser, afterwards Lord Lovat, was born about the year 1665. I do not recollect his first title, but his father[2] was a gentleman possess'd of some inconsiderable property in the Aird, the peculiar abode of the Clan Fraser. Tho' not very nearly related to the former Lord[3] (who left only a daughter) he was, I believe, the nearest male heir. But not having at that early period learnt to disguise the prominent features of his character, which were cunning and ferocity, his predecessor took a dislike to him, and devis'd the estate to Hugh Fraser,[4] sometime styl'd Lord Lovat, who was either his cousin or nephew (I think the latter) by the female side: this youth was then, I think, a minor studying at some university. Meanwhile Simon Fraser rais'd a number of men who had been accustom'd to follow him in all his dubious enterprises, with the intention of joining Lord Dundee in the '15,[5] tho' in hopes of securing the inheritance, he had before courted the higher powers then presiding.

I know he was not at Killiecrankie, nor do I think he was engag'd in any instance. If he had any principle of action beyond mere self-love, the exil'd family would certainly be more congenial to his early prejudices. Yet it was generally thought that this loyalty to the unfortunate serv'd merely as a pretext to add to his followers numbers whom his own personal influence could not attach to him. But having them once under his command, that undefinable magic by which he all his life

---

[1] He was not in the least an adventurer, but after his father and elder brother, the rightful heir to the title and estates of Lovat, of which the Atholl Murrays unsuccessfully attempted to deprive him. For a succinct account of this whole matter *vide* Lieut.-Col. Fergusson's introduction to *Major Fraser's Manuscript*.

[2] Thomas Fraser of Beaufort, third son of the ninth Lord Lovat and granduncle of the eleventh Lord.

[3] Hugh, eleventh Lord Lovat, by his wife, Amelia Murray, daughter of John, first Marquis of Atholl, left four daughters, of whom the eldest, Amelia, born 1686, married, in 1702, her cousin, Alexander Mackenzie, son of Roderick Mackenzie of Prestonhall. This lady and her husband long pretended right to the title and estates, a claim which continued to be maintained by their son, known as Hugh Fraser of Fraserdale, who only died in 1770.

[4] This is nonsense. [5] An obvious mistake.

sway'd the minds of those who neither lov'd or esteem'd him, made them follow his desperate fortunes. Indeed, he at this period somewhat resembl'd David when in the cave of Adullam, for 'every one that was discontented, and every one that was in debt' literally resorted to him.

The former Lord Lovat in the meantime died. The succession was consider'd as doubtful, and the doubts in such cases seldom were decided by law. The claimant who had the strongest party in the clan, especially if sanction'd by the will of the deceas'd, was generally acknowledg'd as heir. In this case the good and peaceable members of the clan were all on the side of Hugh,[1] in the absence of Simon who headed all the needy and turbulent. Hugh was receiv'd as heir to the late Lord, whose daughter he married, whose Dowager, then residing at Castle Dunie, added all her influence in his favour, and put him in formal possession of the Castle, which he relinquish'd immediately to her use, returning back to pursue his studies. Simon immediately march'd back to the Aird, resolving to take forcible possession of the estate, where he was so much dreaded that there appear'd none to oppose him, except the Dowager Lady Lovat, who refus'd him entrance to the Castle. This, however, he soon forc'd, and without respect to her age or quality (she was daughter to the Marquis of Tullibardin),[2] reveng'd himself by treating her in presence of his brutal followers in a manner too shocking and cruel for description. She immediately took refuge with her family, who were about to institute a criminal prosecution for this unheard-of outrage; to avoid this he fled to the Court of St. Germains; being well aware that his life was doubly endanger'd in Britain, as he was liable to a trial for treason on account of levying forces in the name of King James; which might have been hush'd up had not this last exploit exasperated all the Athol family and their connections, and even the public mind against him. His matchless art and assurance stood him in good stead at the Court of St. Germains, where he represented himself as a sufferer for loyalty, got into great favour, and finally was

---

[1] *i.e.* Alexander Mackenzie. The title and estates were claimed by Amelia Fraser on her father's death in 1696.

[2] Marquis of Atholl. The Marquisate of Tullibardine was not created till 1703.

trusted with secrets of the most momentous import, and sent over the year after as a secret agent to negotiate with the English adherents of the unfortunate monarch.

This mission he the more readily accepted, as important business of his own now demanded his attention at home. Hugh, the rival heir, was by this time dead, and he became undoubted successor to the family honours.[1] His credit at the Court of St. Germains was no small recommendation to him among his clan, and many thought highly of his address and abilities. Of these he was now about to exhibit a distinguish'd proof. On his way from France to England[2] (1709), where he was coming upon the mission which has been already mention'd, he was seiz'd in a French fishing-boat, with some others, and carried prisoner to London, where he was soon recognis'd in spite of his disguise, and affected ignorance of the English language. For Lovat had a countenance highly expressive of his character, and so mark'd by a peculiar style of homeliness that no one who had ever seen it could forget it.

The Earl of Godolphin was then Prime Minister. With regard to his personal virtues and public wisdom opinions have been much divided; but in respect to his utter dereliction of all moral delicacy in regard to the instruments he employ'd to obtain his political ends, I believe there has not been any difference of opinion. Never was a stronger proof of this than the present occasion afforded. This caitiff, already steep'd in crimes and treachery, and knowing his life had before been forfeit to the laws of his country, purchas'd a present immunity by discovering, without the least reserve, all the secrets entrusted to him. At the same time that he laid the lives and fortunes of so many others at the mercy of exasperated and powerful enemies, he took good care to give an exaggerated account of his own influence, power, and connections, and of the rank he was now entitled to hold in his own country; representing that the obstructions he met with in asserting his just claim had thrown him thro' desperation into the arms of the opposite faction, but that if his life was spar'd, and his income augmented without adding to the burdens of his

---

[1] Wholly inaccurate, *vide* p. 255, note 3.
[2] Lovat left this country in 1703 and did not return till 1714.

people, he would prove a grateful and useful servant to Government, and extinguish in the minds of all his friends those delusive hopes which supported their attachment to the exil'd Prince.

The English in those days were shamefully ignorant of everything relative to the Highlands of Scotland. Montrose's wars had given them some idea of Argyllshire, and a faint view of Breadalbane and Athol; but beyond that, all was to them a formless chaos, and they fear'd the more from not knowing the limits of the object that excited their apprehension. They had now got into their toils one of these monsters they least knew, and most dreaded, a Highland chieftain possessing power and property in the unknown regions of the north, and they were determin'd to derive some lasting advantage from an alliance with depravity so formidable. The sentence passed against him was not rescinded, but merely allowed to lie dormant. He had secretly a pension of three hundred a year settl'd on him, which he regularly receiv'd till the year of his death; and was permitted to return in peace, if not in triumph, to the possession of his inheritance, and of an influence which with these additional means he did not fail to extend considerably.

Meantime Godolphin made a wise and moderate use of the intelligence purchas'd at so high a price. Few if any of the English Jacobites were publicly call'd to account. They possibly ow'd their safety to their numbers, it being rather dangerous to strike at so wide a confederacy. But this artful statesman did not fail to let them know individually that they were in his power, and to watch and distrust them afterwards. This was perhaps the principal reason why the Jacobite interest in England (tho' possessing far more power and property than that in Scotland) lent such feeble aid to the insurgents afterwards.

Lovat, once settled in the abode of his ancestors, did all that a man could possibly do without reforming his life, to efface the memory of the past, and to redeem the good opinion of the neighbouring chiefs. But being by this time accounted a spy for Government, and distrusted by both parties, he had but partial success. Yet such were his numberless artifices to gain popularity, and his Proteus-like readiness to take every shape that suited the present occasion, that at length he obtain'd a degree of influence that might appear incredible when one considers that his appearance was disgusting and repulsive, his manners (except when he had some deep part to act among his superiors) grossly familiar and meanly cajoling, and that he was not only stain'd with crimes, but well known to possess no one noble or amiable quality, if we except fortitude, which he certainly display'd eminently in the last extremity. Tho' his most valuable possessions and his family seat were in the Aird, the true centre of his power and popularity was in Stratheric, a high-lying wild district between Inverness and Ft. Augustus. There he contriv'd to be really belov'd by the common people, and there he was both popular and patriotic. He very frequently resorted there, and every year spent some time regularly among them; making it his study to secure their affections, he would go easily and unlook'd for into the houses of the petty gentry, dine or stay the night with them, banish reserve by his perpetual good humour and frankness, and by a peculiar strain of jocularity perfectly suited to his audience. He came from any distance to the christening of every gentleman's first son, or the next, if it was to be call'd Simon. He us'd to walk alone on the road, and whenever he met a peasant, examine him with regard to the number of his children and state of his welfare, redress his grievances if such he had, and mingle sound advice with the ludicrous fancies and cunning blandishments which abounded in his ordinary discourse. If he met a boy on the road, he was sure to ask who he belong'd to, tell him of his consequence and felicity in belonging to the invincible Clan Fraser, and if he said his name was Simon, to give him half a crown, at that time no small gift in Stratheric. But the old women of all others were those he was at most pains to win, even in the lowest ranks. He never was unprovided of snuff and flattery, both which he dealt liberally among them: listen'd patiently to their old stories, and told them others of the King of France, King James, etc., by which they were quite captivated, and concluded by entreating that they impress their children with attachment and duty to their Chief, and they would not fail to come to his funeral and assist in the Coronach there.

At Castle Dunie he always kept an open table to which all comers were welcome, for of all his visitors he contriv'd to make some use, from the nobleman, or general, by whose interest he could provide for some of his followers, and by that means strengthen his interest with the rest; to the idle hanger-on, whose excursions might procure the fish and game, which he was barely suffer'd to eat a part of at his patron's table. Never was there a mixture of society so miscellaneous as was there assembl'd. From an affectation of loyalty to his new masters, Lovat paid great court to the military station'd in the North.[1] Such of the nobility in that quarter as were not in the sunshine receiv'd his advances as from a man who enjoy'd court favour, and he fail'd not to bend to his purposes every new connection he form'd.

In the meantime the greatest profusion appear'd at table, while the meanest parsimony reign'd thro' the household. The servants who attended had little if any wages. Their reward was to be recommended to better service afterwards, and meantime they had no other food allow'd to them but what they carried off on the plates. The consequence was that you durst not quit your knife and fork a moment, your plate was snatch'd if you look'd another way. If you were not very vigilant you might fare as ill amidst abundance, as the Governor of Barataria; a surly guest, once cut the fingers of one of these Harpies when snatching his favourite morsel away untasted. I have heard a military gentleman who occasionally din'd at Castle Dunie describe those extraordinary repasts. There was a very long table loaded with great variety of dishes, some of the most luxurious, others of the plainest, nay coarsest kind. These were very oddly arrang'd. At the head were all the dainties of the season, well drest, and neatly serv'd in; about the middle appear'd good substantial dishes, roasted mutton, plain pudding, and such like; at the bottom, coarse pieces of beef, sheep's heads, haggies, and other national but inelegant dishes, were serv'd in a slovenly manner in great

---

[1] Cf. Burt's Letters from the North of Scotland. Letter VIII.

pewter platters. At the head of the table were plac'd guests of distinction, to whom alone the dainties were offer'd. The middle was occupied by gentlemen of his own tribe who well knew their allotment and were satisfied with the share assign'd to them. At the foot of the table sat hungry retainers, the younger sons of younger brothers, who had at some remote period branch'd out from the family, for which reason he always address'd them by the title of 'Cousin.' This, and a place however low at his table, so flatter'd these hopeless hangers-on, that they were as ready to do Lovat's bidding 'in the earth or in the air,' as the spirits were to obey the commands of Prospero.

The contents of his sideboard were as oddly assorted as those of his table, and serv'd the same purpose. He began: 'My Lord, here is excellent venison, fine turbot, etc., call for any wine you please, there is excellent Claret and Champagne on the sideboard. Pray, now, Dumballoch, or Kilbockie, help yourselves to what is before you, these are Port and Lisbon, strong ale and porter, excellent in their kind.' Then calling to the other end of the table: 'Pray, dear cousin, help yourself, and my other cousins, to that fine beef and cabbage. There is whisky punch and excellent table beer.'

His conversation, like his table, was varied to suit the character of every guest. The retainers soon retir'd, and Lovat (on whom drink made no impression) found means to unlock every other mind, and keep his own designs impenetrably secret, while the ludicrous and careless air of his discourse help'd to put people off their guard, and searchless cunning and boundless ambition were hid under the mask of careless hilarity.

When he was perfectly establish'd, he form'd an alliance that completely suited his purpose. He married a daughter of the Laird of Grant[1] (about the year '22), thus connecting himself with a family of distinguish'd worth, and with another powerful clan and family by means of her sisters, one of whom was married to Sir Roderick Mackenzie of Scatwell, and the other to Grant of Ballandalloch. To this Lady, whose

---

[1] Margaret, daughter of Ludovick Grant of Grant.

modest virtues, and pious resignation deserv'd a better fate, he made a harsh and negligent husband. She liv'd but a few years after (died about 1728) her marriage, and left four children. Two sons, one of whom was the well-known General Simon Fraser, the second was a Brigadier in the Portuguese service, and afterwards among his friends in Stratheric;[1] and two daughters, the eldest of whom was married to Macpherson of Clunie, and the youngest, who died unmarried, was so deeply affected by her father's violent and impenitent death, that she mourn'd incessantly and surviv'd him but a very short time.

After the death of the first Lady Lovat, he married a Miss Campbell,[2] who was mother to the present Lovat,[3] and liv'd to a great age, having surviv'd her Lord above forty years. He went now and then to London, and got somehow introduc'd to the younger branches of the Royal Family, whom even in childhood he strove to win by the grossest flattery.

After the death of the first Lady Lovat, all restraint was thrown off at Castle Dunie. The young ladies, who inherited the modesty and piety of their mother, could not endure the profane and licentious manners of their father and his retainers, and generally resided at Scatwell, where nothing was to be seen but sanctity and decorum.

Meantime the restless and intriguing spirit of Lovat, unrestrain'd by the sentence that hung over him, was meditating another revolution and laying trains to excite that spirit in others, which he durst not discover himself. He us'd to frequent the fairs at Inverness (from about the year thirty-five to forty when he became infirm) and pay court to the meanest of the people; nay, I have heard my mother-in-law declare, that she saw him once, in the street there, embrace the Laird of Grant's piper.

Meanwhile years came on, and Lovat, long since unwieldly from excessive corpulence, lost the use of his lower limbs, and

---

[1] 'Brigadier' was a nickname given to him when a child, and not derived from any military service; *vide Transactions of Gaelic Society of Inverness*, xii. p. 382.

[2] Primrose Campbell, daughter of the Hon. John Campbell of Mamore, and sister of the fourth Duke of Argyll.

[3] Archibald Campbell Fraser, died 1815.

was carried from place to place in a litter. He had a great easy-chair, too, made for his accommodation, carried after him wherever he went. Yet this man whom few lov'd and none trusted, who was old without being venerable, and infirm without being pitied, and over whose head the axe impended, had still subtlety and address to move the whole North to his purposes, without laying himself open to detection. When the invasion was projected he gave secret orders to his son, then a lad of sixteen, studying at Glasgow College, to rouse the Frasers of Stratherick and join the adventurer[1] whenever he should arrive. Meantime he was sending to the Court of St. James' the strongest professions of loyalty and concern for the approaching danger. He knew it was in vain to tamper with his daughter, Lady Clunie, to influence her husband. That excellent person, tho' a zealous Jacobite, would never persuade him to break his oath and forsake his colours, for he had accepted a Company in the Black Watch[2] (now the 42d) and of consequence sworn allegiance to the reigning family. Lovat, however, invited two of the principal gentlemen of the Clan to Castle Dunie and so imprest their minds with regard to the probability of success, which was the only objection, that they went home resolv'd to engage their young Chief in this perilous enterprise. The conference was held at Clunie. When the Chief began to waver, his lady urg'd the dishonour and treachery of forsaking the service in which he was engag'd, on which a leading man of the Clan sternly told her, stamping with his foot, that she came there to bring heirs, not counsel. Clunie, in consequence, led out his Clan, and I have told in another place what was the result.[3]

Lovat having secretly set this great machine in motion, and having his emissaries everywhere, carrying on his plans and bringing him intelligence, lay quiet in his Castle, affecting great concern for what was going on, and railing at his son's disobedience and sedition.

When the Chevalier mov'd northward after the disastrous irruption into England, Lovat retir'd up to Stratherick to

---

[1] The Prince.   [2] His company seems to have been in Loudon's Regiment.
[3] 'A Ballad founded on Fact.' Cf. p. 276.

avoid the appearance of any understanding between him and the Prince. He had no house there, but while he stayed, resided in that of Gortulig his Chamberlain.

I have heard the daughter of this gentleman, who is still living, describe with great naïveté a scene to which she was witness the day on which Culloden was fought. Tho' the probability of success was greatly against the highlanders, they were somehow infatuated with the most sanguine expectations, all but the Prince and his veteran counsellors, who saw too well the enemies' superior advantage. Both at Stratheric and Inverness the adherents of the cause were making the most exulting preparations to receive their victorious Prince after the battle should be decided. The lady I have mention'd was then a girl of ten years old. It was decided that if the Prince conquer'd he should immediately make his way to seize on Fts. Augustus and William, and thus possess himself of the Glenmore which extends from sea to sea, and that he should consult with Lovat on his way.

For two or three days before, preparations were making for the reception of the Prince and his train. To regale them, a very ample cold collation was preparing. All the women in the vicinity were call'd in to bake cakes, and roast meat, poultry, and venison for the occasion. Such was the urgency of the time and the quantity of food dress'd, that every room in the house, even that which Lovat occupied, was us'd for culinary purposes, and fill'd with bread and joints of roasted meat.

On the fatal day of Culloden, the highlanders at first gained some partial advantage, and some one came up express to say that the fortune of the day was in favour of the Prince. The house soon fill'd with people, breathless with anxiety for tidings of their friends who were engag'd. The little girl was consider'd as an encumbrance, and order'd into a closet, where she continued a little while an unwilling prisoner. Below the house was a large marshy plain, in the centre of which was a small lake that in winter overflow'd it, but was now nearly dry. This spot the superstitious believ'd to be a rendevouz of the Fairies. All of a sudden the tumultuous noise that fill'd the house was succeeded by deep silence. The little prisoner, alarm'd at this sudden stillness, ventur'd out and saw no creature in the house, but Lovat sitting alone in deep thought. Then she ventur'd to the door, and looking down saw above a thousand people in one ghastly crowd in the plain below. Struck with the sudden shifting of the scene and the appearance of this multitude, she thought it was a visionary show of fairies which would immediately disappear. She was soon, however, undeceiv'd by the mournful cries of women who were tearing off their handkerchiefs for bandages to the wounded. In an instant quantities of linen were carried down for the same purpose, and the intended feast was distributed in morsels among the fugitives, who were instantly forc'd to disperse for safety to the caves and mountains of that rugged district. The Prince and a few of his followers came to the house; Lovat express'd attachment to him, but at the same time reproach'd him with great asperity, for declaring his intention to abandon the enterprise entirely. 'Remember' (said he fiercely) 'your great ancestor Robert Bruce, who lost eleven battles and won Scotland by the twelfth.'

The Prince made little answer, but immediately set out for a place of more safety. The first thing set about was to dispose of Lovat's great chair least it should be the means of tracing his flight. (It was loaded with lead and sunk in the lake.) He was then carried off in his litter thro' the night and lodg'd in a cave to the northward of Fort Augustus, where he might have remain'd long enough had he not been betray'd by one of his own adherents.[1] In this extremity the subtlety and craft which had ever mark'd his character were display'd in their full extent. He insisted on carrying his sword with him to this retreat. When the party from Fort Augustus came to seize him there, he affected to mistake them for a detachment from the Rebel forces, started up on his knees, and drew his sword, crying, 'Traitors, you need not hope to bring me to your purpose, I will draw my sword for my lawful sovereign, King George, as long as I live.'

This finesse did not avail, yet when he found himself caught, like an old lion in the toils, he conducted himself in a manner that would have done credit to a worthier character. No

---

[1] Another story is that he was captured on an island in Loch Morar.

complaint or reproach was heard, nor did his wonted good humour forsake him. The Coronach of the old women, on which he always laid such stress, preceded his funeral. For on seeing him carried a prisoner, they rent the air with their howlings. His old Bard follow'd the litter in which he was carried, and begg'd permission of the guard to be allow'd to kiss his hand. He stretch'd it out, and when the Bard perceiv'd it lank and fallen off by what it was formerly, he burst into tears, crying in his own language, 'Alas for the white hand and blue veins of my Master.' Tho' easy and even facetious with some of his humble friends who follow'd his march, and attended him at the inns where he stopp'd, he did not wish to be exhibited like a wild beast, to use his own words, to the people who surrounded his travelling conveyance. Governor Trapaud, who long fill'd that station at Fort Augustus, was then a Capt. and commanded the party who carried Lovat over Drimochter, being then a lively, bustling young man. He was impatient to see Lovat, who, keeping the curtains of the litter close about him, and being help'd out and in by his friends, long evaded the young officer's curiosity, who, tho' dying to see this singular personage, did not choose to force an intrusion on his privacy, but frequently peep'd into the litter to observe whether he were sleeping, hoping then to have a full view of him. Lovat, perceiving this, affected one day to snore while his friend rode slowly by. The latter, delighted to obtain at length his object, put his head into the litter and bent it over the suppos'd sleeper, who, rising with a sudden jerk, snapp'd at the nose of the terrified Capt., and then seem'd highly amus'd at his consternation, yet deign'd not during the whole journey to exchange a word with him. His behaviour while in the Tower was strongly mark'd with all the leading traits of his character. Even there he was busy, intriguing, fawning, and insolent by turns, and while his usual good humour and coarse jocularity never forsook him for a moment, he left no method untried to defeat or evade the rigours of the law, and to soften the hearts of his enemies. I have seen letters of his address'd to Prince Frederic and the Duke of Cumberland, vulgarly familiar as his usual style was, yet written with an air of simplicity not devoid of pathos, and proofs of a deeper and more refin'd subtlety than the most eloquent and polish'd productions. It was this frank and familiar simplicity that, by throwing others off their guard, had thro' life assisted him to deceive. To the desire of prolonging a life stain'd with dishonour, and which had already extended beyond the common limits of nature, he affected to be superior. All he wish'd was, as he express'd it, 'to end his days in his own country, and to attain what all his life he had most desir'd, the honour of being buried with his brave ancestors, of having all his clan in tears following his funeral, and the *Coronach* of the old women of the country over his grave.'

This same *Coronach* had certainly taken possession of Lovat's imagination in a most forcible manner. In all his petitions and conversations he recurr'd to it, and when the motives for dissimulation were extinguish'd with the hopes of life, still the long anticipated Coronach seem'd to ring in his ears, and he earnestly entreated that his corpse might be carried down to be interred in the North, still urging the same motive, and hoping no doubt that

'Their plaintive cries would sooth his hovering Ghost.'—HAMMOND.

There can be no greater proof of the strong tendency the mind has to lean at the last on the posthumous approbation even of our fellow-mortals than the solicitude which even the godless and heartless Lovat show'd to be the subject of praise and lamentation to these abject and ignorant beings. It was one of these strange caprices of human nature which made

'A perjur'd Prince a leaden saint revere,
A godless Regent tremble at a star.'—POPE.

The fancy and humour which this strange personage show'd on the brink of death, the serene dignity with which he submitted to it, and the noble sentiment he quoted from Horace, when the axe was about to fall, are well known to the public. Yet it is not perhaps equally well known that the rancour of revenge display'd itself on that awful occasion. He knew himself to have been betray'd by one whom he had long cherish'd and trusted, and in reference to this person gave out on the scaffold the Psalm expressive of bitter resentment in which

David appeal'd to the divine justice to avenge the cruelty of Doeg.

Lovat could not die uniformly great.

The Ministry, who seem'd still to smart from the wounds of the highland claymore, appear'd to consider Lovat as terrible even in death, and dreaded the influence his bones might have on his countrymen should they return to their native soil. To this purpose Horace Walpole in his *Reminiscences* records an anecdote of the Duke of Newcastle's terror and perplexity about the funeral of Lovat, which, told in his ludicrous manner, is highly amusing, and strongly marks the spirit of the times.

Thus liv'd and thus died Simon Lord Lovat, in his eightieth year, always formidable, yet always contemptible, who, had he been sincere and consistent, with the same address and ability might have been despotic among his own connections, might have sway'd the whole North with unbounded influence, and finally, might have liv'd esteem'd and honour'd, and died belov'd and lamented.

He was in a very high degree crafty, rapacious, and treacherous, subtle, cruel, and revengeful, voluptuous and addicted to every the grossest sensual indulgences, yet possessing the most perfect command of temper, and perpetual, easy, ludicrous gaiety, such as Shakespeare ascribes to Falstaff. No man was ever subject to more wounding sarcasms from his fellow chieftains and other associates, which he either bore with calm indifference, or return'd with smooth yet keen irony. But these insults were all treasur'd up in his mind, to be reveng'd on some future occasion.

Lovat's private life, even in advanc'd years, was such as would greatly disgust in description, and is really better consigned to oblivion. In the first Lady Lovat's time he us'd regularly to visit once a year at Castle Grant, and Ballandalloch, on pretence, of indulging her, but in fact to cultivate and strengthen his alliance with these families.

She never complained of him, but had always a drooping and dejected appearance. The lady he afterwards married by his recommendation liv'd with his first wife as a companion. Tho' inferior in understanding and capacity to the first Lady, Miss Campbell much excell'd her in figure and carriage; to which advantage he was at pains to direct the attention of others. At Castle Grant, he us'd to say, 'I am bringing this Lady of mine to Court to mend her carriage; is it not wonderful that she does not learn to make the most of her little person when she sees her companion's fine carriage?'

His second wife, however, had much patience and good nature, which was very severely tried. She rarely ever sat at the head of his table; and I knew a person to whom she us'd to give an account of the manner in which he us'd to feed her. Everything on the table became the prey of the attendants, except untouched birds and pastry. These were laid by in a little room of the *Hall of Hearts* of which Lovat kept the key, and reproduced till they were nearly mouldy, when they were sent up for the Lady; dinners, which if she rejected, he would go up in a rage, draw her about the room by the hair, and treat her in the most cruel manner. He continually taunted his first wife for want of beauty, and equally reproached the second with want of understanding. He seem'd, however, much concern'd at the death of the first Lady, which happen'd after the birth of her youngest daughter Sibylla. He was, however, a kind and indulgent father, and when his daughters as they grew up shew'd a disgust to the profligacy of Castle Dunie, and preferred residing generally with the only aunt they had then living, Lady Mackenzie of Scatwell, he did not resent their leaving him, but rather seem'd pleas'd with the delicacy and good principles which always govern'd their conduct. He always regretted that the first Lady was not sufficiently attended to in the lying-in which prov'd fatal to her. When his daughter, Lady Clunie (who every way much resembl'd her mother), was about to lie-in of her first child, he had the precaution to send for her to Castle Dunie, that she might have the attendance of physicians, if required, more commodiously than in that remote country. He always restrain'd the coarseness of his witticisms in presence of his daughters, whom he seem'd to regard not only with tenderness, but a degree of respect.

Sybilla, the youngest, possess'd a high degree of sensibility, which when strongly excited by the misfortunes of her family, exalted her habitual piety into all the fervour of enthusiasm.

When Lovat pass'd thro' Badenoch, where she then was with her sister, Lady Clunie, she (Sybilla) follow'd him to Dalwhinny, and there in the most pathetic manner implor'd him with floods of tears and extreme agony to avail himself of the impending stroke by withdrawing his thoughts from all earthly things, and making this danger the happy means of reconciling himself to his Saviour.

Lovat seem'd to consider all this as womanish weakness, and endeavour'd to reassure her spirits by talking lightly of the danger, and setting his enemies in a most ludicrous point of view, while he ridicul'd them with a levity of mind almost incredible in such circumstances. Sybilla departed almost in despair, pray'd night and day, not for his life, but for his soul; and when she heard soon after that he 'died and made no sign,' grief in a short time put an end to her life.

The Brigadier, as Lovat's second son[1] was call'd (I do not remember his name), was, by the Prince's influence, recommended into the Portuguese service, where he staid some years. But, being excessively attached to the country where he was greatly belov'd, he came home to visit his friends, where he became greatly attach'd to a Lady of his own name, and acquir'd rather too great a relish for the convivial mode of living and hospitality frequently carried to excess, which was then too prevalent there. He could not endure to go abroad again, and had too much honour to take the oaths to Government, which would have in that case employ'd him. With much truth, honour, and humanity, he inherited his father's wit and self-possession with a vein of keen satire which he indulg'd in bitter epigrams against the enemies of his family.

Some of these I have seen, and heard songs of his composing, which shew'd no contemptible powers of poetic genius, tho' rude and careless of polish. He sunk into a habit of dissipation, and became hopeless and careless of himself, and died belov'd and regretted by adherents of his party about the year '58, leaving his watch and what little he had to bequeath to the Lady he was attach'd to, who is still alive and unmarried. The last Lady Lovat was doom'd like her Lord to die in extreme old

---

[1] Alexander, died 1762, said by Mackenzie, *History of the Frasers*, p. 435, to have been for some time in the Dutch service. Cf. p. 262, note 1.

age a violent death. She was poison'd by a very near relation in the 100th year of her age about 16 or 17 years since.[1]

The estate of Lovat, there being now no male heir of his line remaining, will go at the death of the present Lovat to Fraser of Breiagh, a distant relation, who possesses considerable property in Aberdeenshire.[2]

It would at this distance of time be as impossible as unprofitable to detail Lovat's tricks and stratagems, exerted in his transactions with his neighbours, whom he invariably cosen'd and over-reach'd. Were Gaelic wit and humour (of all things the most volatile and evanescent) translatable, the good things said by or to Lovat would furnish a little jest-book. He indeed was like Falstaff, not only witty himself, but the cause of wit in other men, and 'all ranks did take a pride to gird at him.'

Benchar, who was very intimate with James Macpherson, the translator of Ossian (who also wrote some historical tracts), used to talk of a life and character of Lovat which he had seen in manuscript written by that author.

By what I remember of his account of this performance, Lovat's life only made part of an intended larger work, which I imagine was never publish'd. I heard, however, of its being shown to some of the Edinburgh *literati*, who observ'd that if his character of Lovat was a just one, his depravity exceeded all parallel. I imagine it was supprest in tenderness to his family. I shall be glad to hear that you receive this safely. I ought to have said that the title of the rival candidate for the honours of Lovat in the beginning of last century was Fraserdale.

I shall be glad to hear that this reaches you safely, and much regret that the indistinctness of my recollection, and the inaccuracy of my orthography, will occasion you so much trouble in arranging the facts I send you.

The want of early education is never to be got over even by those whose powers of mind urge them on

'To daring aims, irregularly great;'

---

[1] She died 23rd May 1796, *aet.* 86.—*Scots Magazine.*

[2] The Lovat estates when restored to General Simon Fraser were entailed by him. The Frasers of Brea are not included in that entail, and the family which Mrs. Grant plainly had in view was that of Strichen, sprung from the second son of the seventh Lord Lovat, who now enjoy both title and estates.

far less by a person so prest down by adverse circumstance, and a perpetual crowd of occupations as Your oblig'd obedt. Servant, ANNE GRANT.

*Melville Place, Feb. 1st,* 1808.

'DEAR SIR,—I cannot pretend insensibility to approbation such as yours, but I greatly regret that I was not made sooner sensible of my own *importance* as a narrator of facts, because in that case I should have taken some pains to correct my vicious orthography, which constant hurry and great carelessness have confirmed into habit. I should likewise have distinguished periods, and left a margin had I ever dreamt that I was doing anything more than furnishing materials for you to arrange in their own places, and digest into order in your own language. On looking over these desultory pages, however, I find they have more the air of a connected narrative than I thought. I shall consequently do all that can now be done to render it more distinct. I would not have you rely on Johnson's account of anything relative to the Highlands. A pedantic prejudice unworthy of his great mind, blinded him to all the worth and wisdom that could possibly exist among people unacquainted with the dead languages. Coarse as he was himself, the luxuries and elegancies of life had too great sway over his mind, and of self-denial he did not possess a sufficient share to know its value or assign it the proper rank among the manly virtues. Strangers to classical literature, and to modern elegance, were with him decided savages. He did not do justice to his own great powers, nor was he aware what a noble *savage* he would have been himself tho he had never seen Oxford nor had any light but that of the gospel, which shone even on these remote Isles, where ladies knew not how to make a pudding. Boswell, vain, fantastic, and credulous, often misled him without intending it. The polity of the clans, and the wisdom and humanity that appear'd in many of their customs and regulations, could only be known by a person acquainted with the language and residing among them. Tales of wonder are always told to strangers, and it is in the fury of exasperated passions that the wild and wonderful originates. The ancient state of the Isles (where tales too true were told him) was calculated to cherish a vindictive and sanguinary spirit. Before the Bruce and Baliol contention, which swallow'd up the regulations, the arts, the learning, and the very national spirit, as well as national records of this ancient and comparatively enlightn'd kingdom, all predatory incursions came from the North, and spent their first fury on these Islands. Even in time of peace, they were often attack'd by Norwegian pirates, so often indeed that all their possessions were precarious. And many submitting to those invaders, while others preserved their loyalty. These different parties, exasperated to savage severity at each other, bequeath'd the most rancorous feuds to their successors. The Lord of the Isles, courted by both the kings of Norway and Scotland, became himself a rebel and a pirate, and threw his force into each scale by turns. He even set up for an independent Prince in later times, encourag'd by those long minorities at once bloody and feeble, which prevented Scotland from ever recovering its primitive importance, and by strengthening the hands of a turbulent aristocracy, render'd the talents and the virtues of her last race of Monarchs of little avail to themselves or their country. This way of telling you what you already know much better than I do, is not meant for your information, but merely to serve for a basis to some details and reflections I mean to trouble you with hereafter. There is nothing in which the ignorance of the learn'd and the folly of the wise appears more in than the absurd and imperfect accounts given of a people who are so well worth knowing more of, were it but for the singularity of being without any defin'd head or pretension to independence, for so many centuries a people by themselves, with manners, customs, and language entirely distinct from those of their rulers. Can anything, for instance, be more contradictory than to see the very same writers, who at one time represent the clans as hordes of ferocious barbarians who blindly rush'd on to pillage and to slaughter at the bidding of their chiefs, without the least moral sense to distinguish good from evil, but merely actuated by passive obedience and love of plunder? To see these writers immediately after record of the same people instances of fidelity, disinterestedness, and true

s

magnanimity that do honour to human nature? Is virtue, 'that self-given, solar ray of pure delight,' a paroxysm, or how were so many people of all ranks at one critical period affected with this paroxysm, who were before strangers to native probity and generous feeling?

To return to Dr. Johnson's anecdote of Lovat, half of it is true. Did you not discover under the decent terms which I made use of what was the nature of the crime perpetrated by Lovat, of which the Dowager Lady Lovat was the object? She was not to this miscreant the object of any passion, but the most rancorous hatred, being a woman advanc'd in years,[1] and in some degree deform'd on the shoulders or back. Her personal disadvantages were balanc'd by worth and understanding, and by the high alliances she brought to her family, for the house of Athol was greatly look'd up to in the north. The motive of this crime and the public mode in which it was perpetrated have no parallel in the history of mankind, but one to which I refer you, 2nd Samuel chap. 16th ver. 22nd. If I do add any more particulars of Lovat's shocking life, I think they will be best inserted as notes, not to break the unity of what has been done. I cannot comprehend how Lovat's letters were dated at Beaufort;[2] I should suppose it Beaulieu, for so he affected to style his residence, which was a very mean tho' defencible building, call'd by the country people Castle Dunie. The spot on which it stood was call'd Lamamonach, or the place where Monks dwelt, a monastery of French Monks, call'd the Abbey of Beaulieu, having stood there. They gave the same name to a beautiful small river which, descending from Strath Glas, pass'd close by this mansion and discharg'd itself into the Firth below Inverness. The Airds is perhaps only a popular term by which the district occupied by the estates of Lovat, Relick, Belladrum, and other old families of the Frasers, is distinguish'd. It is a beautiful and fertile spot, lying immediately below Inverness, on the north side of Kessock ferry. It is bounded on the south by Inverness, on the west by Strath Glas, on the north by Ross-shire, and

---

[1] She was only thirty-four, and that a marriage was actually gone through seems beyond dispute.

[2] Beaufort near Beauly.

on the east by the Firth. Airds in the Gaelic means heights, in contradistinction to hills and mountains, and is here applied to a stretch of high yet verdant ground which runs parallel to the sea thro' this district.

Of General Fraser, whom I remember and [whose] character I well knew, I can say little, that is, he differ'd from his father only as a chain'd-up fox does from one at liberty. A slight veil of decorum was thrown over the turpitude of his heart and conduct, and he was a well-bred, shrew'd, plausible man and a good enough soldier. His impudence and craft were not inferior to his father's, tho' less obvious. He was prosecuted in England for seducing, under the most aggravating circumstances, the wife of his friend, Major Santlow from Boston. At the remarkable trial of Alexander Stuart,[1] Acharn, falsely accused of the murder of Glenure in 175', he pled at the bar (to which he was educated after being out in the '45) for the prosecutor, and was wonder'd at for his assurance in alluding to that circumstance, saying thus, 'On an occasion which I ought to blush to mention,' and then went on with great coolness descanting upon the 'unnatural rebellion' and the crimes thence arising. He was too much a man of sense and of the world to forsake the straight path openly, yet no heart was ever harder or no hand more rapacious than his. One instance shall suffice. When the General's estate was restor'd to him the whole country broke loose into the most rapturous joy at having once more a head to the Clan. Songs and bonfires were made over all the Aird and Stratheric, and he return'd home from his foreign campaigns like a belov'd Prince to his faithful subjects. All this I saw and heard, being then the '74 or thereabouts. In the '76 he rais'd a 2d battalion to his Regt. to go out to America. There was very little time for this, and to fill up this Corps suddenly he promis'd high bounties, which were to be paid when they reach'd headquarters at Glasgow, and solemnly assur'd many that they should be dismiss'd after standing the review. The wretch'd creatures were all cheated and deceiv'd, and from their want

---

[1] The reference is obviously to James Stewart (Seumas-a-Glinne), whose misfortunes form the basis of Mr. R. L. Stevenson's *Kidnapped* and its sequel *Catriona*.

of letters and the English language could obtain no redress.
These poor people were follow'd by numbers of wretched
women, who, barefoot and half cloth'd, were invoking the
divine vengeance on their perjur'd chief. Mrs. Donaldson,
daughter to Colonel Gordon Graham, and married to Major
Donaldson of the 42d, was then with her husband at Glasgow.
General F. gave a public dinner to the 42d and their ladies
in return for one he had receiv'd from them. He call'd on
Mrs. Donaldson, and with great politeness escorted her to
the Inn where they din'd. She assur'd me she had very near
fainted by the way, and was indispos'd for days after, and I
have not known a firmer-minded woman, but thus it was.
She understood the Gaelic language—a circumstance of which
the General was not aware. While she leant on his arm as
they proceeded along they were follow'd by the wretch'd wives
and mothers of these men whom he had betray'd into the
service and cheated of their bounty. These, perishing with
hunger and cold, pour'd forth 'Curses both loud and deep' in
their native tongue with all the emphasis of rage and anguish,
praying that he would never see heaven, etc. All this he
heard with an unmov'd countenance, thinking she did not
understand it, and talk'd to her the whole time in the gallant
and disenga'd manner. Meanwhile the clothing of his Regt.
was so poor in quality and so scrimp in make that the poor
men were starving. Now this man was suddenly enrich'd,
was old, and had no family; moreover, he despis'd his heir,
the present Lovat, and had he treated his people with common
justice they would adore him. Yet I speak much within the
truth. I would not wish to be known to say this on account
of his widow,[1] to whom I was oblig'd for civilities when last in
London, as well as to the Lyttleton family. Lady Lyttleton
is her sister. I will endeavour to recollect dates by circumstances, but the persons to whom I was most indebted for
intelligence dated one thing by another, and never mentioned
the year of the Lord. Immediately after the poem of the 'Highlanders'[2] you will find one call'd 'A Ballad founded on fact.'

---

[1] He died 1782, having married Catherine, second daughter of John Bristowe of Quiddenham Hall, Norfolk.

[2] *Vide* Introduction.

This fact is the burning Clunie's Castle, and in the notes at the end you will find a sketch of that transaction, to which I will, if you wish it, add many curious particulars. Lovat was eighty years old when he suffer'd. In the succession of this family it has pleas'd providence to

'Change nature's law and curse his race with fools,'

but these are now extinct, and the estate goes to a distant branch. I am in haste after all this prolixity, Dr. Sir, yours respectfully, ANNE GRANT.

I have sent to Dr. Gleg, and write to Inverness tonight for the pamphlet of the Tower transactions. I shall observe your directions punctually.

Lochiel will be soon forth coming, but I must not be heard of as an anecdote-monger on this occasion.

*Melville Place, Febry. 3d,* 1808.

DEAR SIR,—How shall I excuse myself for breaking thro' both your injunctions and my own resolutions with regard to the accuracy and distinctness necessary to make what I say intelligible? You would pity me if you knew how extremely nervous the occurrences of the last year have render'd me. A large family in a small house create so many interruptions that it is impossible to write with composure. When I saw you I hop'd to have been able to spend two or three weeks at Jordanhill, where I could have my mornings to myself and perform the little task you set me in quiet. The rambling anecdotes I send you are merely for your own amusement, and to help you to form some judgment of the highland character. If any part of them illustrates your subject, you are heartily welcome to use it. But I should think them too detach'd for your purpose.

You see I have proceeded but a short way in my account of that admirable character Lochiel, to which, by-the-bye, I think that of Sir Evan Du no improper prelude. Do not think I have been embellishing his daughters. Were I not afraid of appearing fabulous, I could tell you many more singular particulars about them.

The present Fassfern,[1] whom I knew very well, is nephew to Donald of Lochiel, and knows all that can be known of his own family. But then he communicated many interesting particulars to John Hume,[2] and was, I believe, very much displeas'd at the manner in which that writer garbl'd the intelligence entrusted to him. I doubt, under these circumstances, whether he (Fassfern) would have comprehension or liberality enough to answer more inquiries on the same subject, at least in writing.

Many years ago, when I liv'd at Ft. Augustus, I had a friend whose brother, in consequence of my intimacy with her, was very well known to me. He had had a classical education, a great thirst of knowledge, and a violent enthusiasm for highland poetry, music and antiquities. Of the Rebellion few of our contemporaries knew so much. His father was out with the Prince, and his uncle, Macpherson of Fleigherty, march'd a company with him to Derby.

This person was also a great collector of scarce papers relating to the events of former times, and I am much of opinion had once in his possession a manuscript memoir of Sir Evan of Lochiel,[3] which exists somewhere among his descendants.

This gentleman married and settl'd in the country. But his affairs being embarrass'd, about ten years since he set about to amuse his melancholy by publishing an old manuscript history in his possession, of Sir Eneas Macpherson,[4] the hero of his clan, but relinquish'd the design, justly fearing the subject would not have sufficiently general interest. He then went into the army, and has been long a Capt. in the 22d, and Brigade Major. When I was in London last, he came up from Colchester and saw me very frequently.

---

[1] Ewen Cameron, created a baronet in 1815 in recognition of the conspicuous gallantry of his son, the well-known Colonel John Cameron of the 92nd Highlanders, who fell at Quatre Bras.

[2] John Home, author of *Douglas* and *The History of the Rebellion in* 1745.

[3] Probably that published by the Abbotsford Club in 1842, cf. Preface, p. xliii.

[4] Æneas, second son of William Macpherson of Invereshie, 'a learned advocate and antiquary of the reign of Charles II., who received the honour of knighthood,' and the author of a history of his clan still extant in MS., *penes* Cluny Macpherson.

I have the pleasure to hear since that he has distinguish'd himself at Copenhagen, and reap'd some solid advantages in consequence.

Now this Major Macpherson is the person of all others of whom I could best depend on for ability and inclination to furnish me with anecdotes regularly dated in chronological order. I do not spare my own pains, they will be mere dry facts, and if you prefer my mode of narrating them, I will with great pleasure arrange them for you.

I should scarce have time to hear from him here, being to set out for London in a fortnight, but if you are satisfied with my account as I can give it (for I really have no regular dates) I will transmit all I know immediately. If, on the contrary, you prefer the more accurate and circumstantial detail, which I may be able to give with the Major's assistance, and perhaps write more legibly amid the leisure and repose, which I hope for at Sunbury, tell me, and I shall so arrange it, but let me know immediately.

My authorities for the facts I have given and mean to give you, are very good ones. I knew well two granddaughters of Lochiel's, sisters of the late Clunie, who were our next neighbours at Laggan. I was very intimate, too, with Miss Margaret, daughter to the unfortunate Dr. Cameron, Lochiel's brother. A lady so distinguish'd for the homeliness of her person and the superior qualities of her mind, that I am sure Mrs. Stuart must have known or heard of her. My mother, too, remembers much of the Lochiels, whose memory she adores. I retain Lovat to make a correction of importance. Sir Robert gave him the pension, but it was Godolphin who examined him in the year nine, when he was taken coming from France. It was for Killicrankie and not for Panmure[1] that he rais'd his troops. At this latter period the noose was about his neck, and he made a merit of forbearance. On this he got the pension. Macpherson of Benchar, who knew the whole race, was my particular acquaintance. When Lovat's daughter was married to Clunie, a young woman came home as a humble companion with her from Castle Dunie, who, being uncommonly sensible and well principl'd, was always retain'd in the family, and was so useful by her

---

[1] Lord Panmure was 'out' in the '15.

fidelity and ingenuity during the nine years which Clunie lay conceal'd in the country, that the family ever after had the highest value for her, and treated her more like a relation than a dependant. This person went to France afterwards with this unfortunate family, and return'd with Mrs. Macpherson after Clunie's death. When the estate was restor'd, Clunie built a house for her and settled a pension on her. She was a very distinct, intelligent person, and from her I heard more of the fate of the exiles in France, as well as of the Lovat family, than from any one, except, indeed, my mother-in-law, who was nearly related to Lady Lovat, and saw her often after her marriage.

I shall endeavour to enclose the account I receiv'd from Miss Colquhoun of the manner in which the Marquis of Tullibardine was betray'd by Drumakiln.—I am, dear Sir, With sincere good wishes towards all your family, Your faithful, humble servant, ANNE GRANT.

I write so rapidly that I run my periods together unconsciously. I shall send you memoirs of the Brigadier, the only honest man of the family, with those of his father.

### MEMOIR RELATIVE TO THE MARQUIS OF TULLIBARDINE.

About three weeks after the battle of Culloden, the Marquis of Tullibardine[1] came across the moors and mountains, thro Stratheric and Lochaber, in search of a place of safety and repose, he being a very infirm old man, and so unfit for travelling on horseback, that he had a saddle made on purpose somewhat like a chair, in which he rode in the manner ladies usually do.

When he came down towards Loch Lomond, he was quite worn out, and recollecting that a daughter of the family of Polmaise (who were connected with his own) was married to Buchanan of Drumakiln,[2] who liv'd in a detach'd peninsula

---

[1] The eldest son of the first Duke of Atholl. He had been attainted for his share in the '15, and the estates and titles were settled by Act of Parliament on the next heir.

[2] *i.e.* to the eldest son of the old laird.

running out into the Lake, thought on these accounts that this place might be suitable for a temporary refuge.

He was attended by his French secretary, two servants of that nation, and two or three highlanders who had guided him thro' the solitary passes of the mountains. Against the judgment of these faithful attendants, he bent his course to the Ross, for so the house of Drumakiln is called. I should have mention'd that the old Laird of Drumakiln was still alive and in the house with his son. The Marquis, after alighting, begged to have a private interview with his cousin. He told him he was come to put his life into her hands, and what in some sense he valued more than life, a small casket, which he deliver'd to her, entreating, whatever became of him, that she would keep that carefully, till demanded in his name, it containing papers of consequence to the honour and safety of many other persons. In the meantime, the younger Drumakiln rudely broke in upon them, and, snatching the casket from her hand, said he would secure it in a careful place, and went out. This casket was never more seen. It was suppos'd to contain family jewels.

Meantime the French secretary and the servants were (they arrived in the evening) watchful and alarm'd, seeing the father and son walking in earnest consultation, and observing horses saddl'd and despatch'd with an air of mystery, and every one seeming to regard them with compassion. All this time the Marquis was treated with seeming kindness. While he partook of some refreshment, some of the children running in, cried out, 'Mamma, we never saw such odd men as the Marquis's.' 'How are they so odd?' answer'd the mother. 'They are all greeting and roaring like women.' This incident, the lady (who was a person of mean capacity) afterwards told her neighbours as a strange instance of effeminacy in these faithful adherents.

At night the secretary went secretly to his master's bed-side, and assur'd him there was treachery. He answer'd he could believe no gentleman capable of such baseness, and at any rate, was incapable of escaping thro' such defiles as those they had pass'd. Told him in that case it would only aggravate his sorrow to see him also betray'd, and advis'd him to go off immediately, which he did.

Early in the morning a party from Dumbarton, summon'd for that purpose, arriv'd to carry the Marquis away prisoner, who bore his fate with calm magnanimity. The fine horses he brought with him were detain'd, and he and one attendant who remain'd were mounted on sorry horses belonging to Drumakiln. The officer who commanded the party taunted that gentleman in the bitterest manner, and the commander of Dumbarton Castle treated his noble prisoner with the utmost respect and compassion, but regarded Drumakiln with the coldest disdain.

Very soon after young D— mounted the Marquis's fine horse (his servant riding another which had belong'd to that nobleman) and set out on a visit to his father-in-law, Polmaise.

When he alighted he gave his horse to the groom, who, knowing the Marquis well, instantly recognis'd him. 'Come in, poor beast,' said he, 'times are chang'd with you since you carried a noble and worthy Marquis, but you shall always be welcome here for his sake.' D— ran in to his father-in-law, complaining that his servants insulted him. Polmaise made no answer, but turning on his heel, rung for his servant to bring out that gentleman's horses.

After this, and several similar rebuffs, the father and son began to shrink from the infamy attach'd to this proceeding. There was at that time only one newspaper publish'd at Edinburgh, conducted by the well-known Ruddiman.[1] To this person the elder Drumakiln address'd a letter or paragraph to be inserted in the newspaper, bearing that on such a day the Marquis of Tullibardine surrender'd to him at his house. This was regularly dated at Ross.

Very soon after the father and son went together to Edr., and waiting on the person appointed to make payments of this nature, demanded the reward.

It should have been before observ'd, that Government were

---

[1] *The Caledonian Mercury.* In the issue of April 29, 1746 the following paragraph appears: 'By a letter in Town from the West, there is advice that the Marquis of Tullibardine with five others, and —— Mitchell the young Pretender's governor had surrendered themselves and were confined in Dumbarton Castle. That the Marquis was in a very bad state of health, and it was thought could not live many days.'

by this time not at all desirous to apprehend the Marquis, tho' his name was in the first heat inserted in the proclamation.

His capture, indeed, greatly embarrass'd them, as it would appear cruel to punish, and partial to pardon him. To return. The official person desir'd them to return the next day for the money. Meanwhile he sent privately for Ruddiman, and examin'd him with regard to the paragraph already mention'd.

He found it on his file, in the old Laird's handwriting, and deliver'd it to the commissioner. Next day the Lairds were punctual to the assignation. The commissioner deliver'd the paragraph in his own handwriting folded up to the elder culprit, saying, 'There is an order on the treasury which ought to satisfy you,' and turn'd away from him with mark'd contempt. Soon after the younger Laird was found dead in his bed, to which he had retir'd in usual health. Of five children whom he left, it would shock humanity to relate the wretched lives and singular and untimely deaths. Of them, indeed, it might be said—

> 'On all the line a sudden vengeance waits,
> And frequent hearses shall besiege their gates.

And they were literally consider'd by all the neighbourhood as caitiffs

> 'Whose breasts the furies steel'd
> And curst with hearts unknowing how to yield.'—POPE.

The blasting influence of more than dramatic justice or of corroding infamy seem'd to reach every branch of this devoted family. After the extinction of the direct male heirs, a brother, who was a Capt. in the army, came home to take possession of the estate. He was a person well respected in life, and possess'd some talent, and much amenity of manners. The country gentlemen, however, shunn'd and dislik'd him on account of the existing prejudice. Anything may be endur'd but contempt. This person, thus shunn'd and slighted, seem'd to grow desperate, and plung'd into the lowest and most abandon'd profligacy. It is needless to enter into a detail of crimes which are hastening to desir'd oblivion. It is enough to observe that the signal miseries of this family have done more to impress the people of that district with a horror at treachery and a sense of retributive justice than volumes of the most eloquent instruction could effect. On the dark question relative to temporal judgments, it becomes us not to decide, yet it is of some consequence in a moral view to remark how much all generous emulation, all hope of future excellence, is quench'd in the human mind by the dreadful blot of imputed infamy. It is not mere wisdom or philosophy, or anything less than the most exalted consolations of Christianity that can support the mind in such a state.

The last wretched Drumakiln, whose death too much resembl'd his life, left a daughter on whom, having first legitimated her, he settled his estate. She is married to Hector M'Donald, Esqr., of Boisdale. She labours with much success to redeem the character of the family.

*Melville Place, Febry. 11th, 1808.*

DEAR SIR,—The high praises with which you grace efforts so broken and imperfect as mine, if not merited, are at least encouraging, and have produc'd a discovery entirely new to me. Like Moliere's Bourgeois Gentillhome who had made prose all his life without knowing it, it appears that I have been as unconsciously philosophising, for I never suspected that the depth of my reflections entitl'd them to be accounted Philosophical.

However inadequate any feeble aid of mine may be to that purpose, I rejoice to think you are about to open a rich mine of materials for elucidating our views of human nature that has been too long trod underfoot with stupid negligence, while we have been compassing sea and land to bring from Africa and Otaheite, pictures of man degraded by tyranny and gross ignorance, or debas'd by voluptuous sensuality.

Lions, unluckily, are no painters, and highlanders are no philosophers, at least the peculiarities in the manners and traditions of their own country have always appear'd too familiar to themselves to excite much wonder or reflection. And it has not occurr'd to them how much amusement and instruction others might derive from the contemplation of a state representing man unpolish'd and unlearn'd, yet courteous, humane, and in full possession of his native energies.

I am so delighted with the prospect of seeing this desideratum rescued from oblivion that I too long delay the information which it is the intention of this letter to communicate.

Dr. Macpherson's treatise on highland antiquities is accounted a valuable work.[1] It was publish'd previously to the translation of Ossian, and much approv'd by the Edr. *Literati*. He brought to the [task] great literary integrity, strong powers of mind, sound and extensive learning, and the most extensive knowledge of his subject. Highland antiquities were his darling pursuit, and the solace of a life spent in solitude and study after the early death of a belov'd wife. No character, no authority stands higher than his. I should have told you that he was minister of Slate in the Isle of Sky, and father to Sir John Macpherson, a learned, worthy, and amiable man, once governor of our Indian possessions after the return of Hastings.[2] His other son is now minister of Slate; he, too, is a learn'd man, has an unequal'd memory and a rich fund of anecdote, but being wealthy, proud and indolent, he turns his time and talents to no account, but lives always surrounded by buffoons and parasites who are by turns the objects of his satirical wit and indiscriminate bounty and hospitality. Yet this lounger is, from that very circumstance, possess'd of materials that would be valuable in other hands. Traditionary remnants of the wit and wisdom, the wars and policy of their ancestors making up great part of these people's conversations, if I saw him I could draw much out of him, but he is far too lazy to write.

He is, however, in possession of a treasure that will perish with him if not soon rescued from his hands. He has a great quantity of papers by him, the materials of a great work which his father had in contemplation on his favourite subject.

Sir John had a kindness for a good old man who had been domestic tutor to him and his brother, and who, being very

---

[1] *Dissertations on the Ancient Caledonians*, etc., by the Rev. John Macpherson, D.D.

[2] For an account of his somewhat remarkable career, *vide Dictionary of National Biography*.

unfortunate in life, officiated latterly as schoolmaster at Laggan. He was very much about us. At length Sir John, fearing he might want some comforts which his advanc'd age requir'd, wrote to him to go to Slate and spend the rest of his days in his brother's family, where he (Sir John) had a good right to make a guest welcome. Knowing the independent spirit of our old friend, Sir John contriv'd on this occasion to make himself the oblig'd person, requesting that Mr. Evan Macpherson would employ his time in revising and arranging the manuscripts left by the deceas'd Dr. Macpherson, a task which he (Sir John) had often in vain solicited Martin (his brother) to perform.

Mr. Evan, who was very well fitted for this employment, set out with a determination to engage in it immediately on his arrival. To his great grief, he saw his friend's manuscripts lying in a clos'd up lumber room below old chests, etc.

Martin, highly piqued at seeing this task transferr'd to our friend, would not suffer him to touch them, and there they lie to this hour I am persuaded. Mr. Evan, disliking the society with which his old pupil was surrounded, return'd, as he express'd it, to die near us, which happen'd a year after, in 101, and much genuine worth and valuable knowledge died with him.

I shall very likely meet Sir John in London. My distress and hurry prevented it last year when he was ask'd to his friend, Sir Walter Farquhar's,[1] to meet me at dinner, but I could not come. I know both brothers very well; a sister of Sir John's having been married to a brother of Major Macpherson's whom I formerly mention'd. If you would write me a letter saying you had been inform'd that some manuscripts relative to a subject you wish'd to illustrate remain in possession of Dr. Macpherson's family, and that you are sure a liberal and enlighten'd person, such as Sir John is well known to be, will not, on a proper representation, withhold them from such a purpose, etc., etc.

Now if you will send a letter of this nature address'd to me at Mr. Hall's, Edr., where I propose being next week, I shall,

---

[1] Son of the Rev. Robert Farquhar, minister of Chapel of Garioch in Aberdeenshire, and an eminent London physician.

by shewing or sending it to Sir John, induce him, I doubt not, to lay his commands on Martin to give up the manuscripts for your use. I know he would willingly oblige me from a circumstance which occurr'd when I was last in London. James Macpherson's Introduction to the history of Great Britain contains materials suited to your purpose, well arrang'd and express'd. A petulant and flimsy book [1] (wrote as a refutation of many of Johnson's assertions in his tour) by Macnicoll, the minister of Lesmore, contains nevertheless many amusing and well authenticated anecdotes. I forget its title, but every gentleman in Argyleshire has a copy of it.

One Alexander Campbell,[2] from Rannoch, has lately publish'd a poem, to which he gives the title of 'The Grampians left desolate,' which I suppose has no extraordinary merit, but the notes on which, I am told, are replete with such traditional intelligence as you wish for. There are manuscript histories of families which at any [rate] contain some dry facts worth knowing: Clanranald's,[3] for instance. Mr. Henry Mackenzie [4] could procure you the archives of the Grant family. The Montrose papers too might be useful. An introductory essay such as you mention would doubtless add great interest to your subject. I mistook if I spoke of being 6 weeks in England. I fear I must be there till August, but will from thence gladly communicate all I know, having the command of office franks.

I have a correction and an addition to make with regard to Lochiel's daughters. There was not of that set married to Auchalder, but there were two married in this country, one to Wright of Loss, the other to Macgregor of Bohawdie.[5] Adieu, dear Sir. I shall write once more from Edr. with some anecdotes, and am in the meantime, Yours, etc., etc.

Anne Grant.

Lord Selkirk, as you well know, has written a book on emigration, and that with much candour and apparent

---

[1] *Remarks on Dr. Samuel Johnson's Journey to the Hebrides*, by the Rev. Donald MacNicol.   [2] Born at Tonbea 1764, died 1824.

[3] *i.e.* *The Black and Red Books of Clanranald*, now published in *Reliquiæ Celticæ*, vol. ii.

[4] *The Man of Feeling*. He married Penuel, daughter of Sir Ludovick Grant of Grant.   [5] Cf. p. 321 note.

benevolence, in which he draws from false premises very true and just conclusions. In the appendix of this book you will find some information which I know to be authentic.

Thoughts[1] on the attachment of the clans to their chiefs—On filial piety—On enthusiasm—On the superstitions of the highlands, their origin and effect, illustrated by authentic anecdotes—On the consequences of certain immortalities as the system of life was affected by them—On the obscure and mystical, yet fervid and exalted ideas of the Deity and the worship He requires which pervaded the minds of highlanders of every rank.

Highland villains trembling at futurity like Shakspear's—Morality founded on sentiment, assuming by degrees a systematic form in a country undisturbed by conquest or foreign wars, where the essentials of Christianity had their due influence, and where certain lessons of practical piety were deliver'd from father to son with increas'd effect thro' successive ages—Peculiar effects produc'd on the imagination and the heart by cherishing with unusual care the memory of the departed, dwelling on their sayings and actions, and mixing them as it were with their surviving friends in an inexplicable manner.

Lastly, on the utter impossibility of preserving in any other situation the spirit and character of a people so localiz'd, and bound by so many ties of fancy, memory, affection, and tradition to the strong featur'd land of their nativity.

Debas'd by an innate sense of degradation when driven to mingle with the mob of other countries with whom they have nothing in common. This spirit, if at all preserv'd beyond the limits of their native mountains, is chiefly found to exist in a body of highlanders devoted to arms, who, having no new abode or acquir'd localities to efface those so long endear'd to them, and going out in bodies from different clans, cherish both that martial ardour and that pathos of patriotism which is their peculiar [possession].

Strongly exemplified in the deservedly celebrated 42d Regt., which, as a body corporate, is worthy to have a little history

---

[1] The first portion of this letter is missing.

transmitted of its achievements, its sufferings, its fidelity and magnanimity in several trying and distinguish'd instances.

On the additions, or cognomens, of the chiefs.

On the badges, Marches, Tartans, etc., which distinguish'd the clans.

Singular origin of the Macraws.[1]

Remarkable difference of character and manners between the different clans.

Honourable strictness among the chiefs in adhering to a promise once solemnly given, instanc'd in the manner in which Glenmoriston acquir'd Dalentay, etc., etc.

Characteristic peculiarities.

There are many singular and interesting anecdotes worth preserving relative to the escapes and adventures of these persons who were attainted, such as Ranald Ratray of Ragnagalion in Castle Ratray, Stirling of Craigbarnet, Macdonald of Teindrich, the convicts sent to Maryland, etc., etc.

These are hints whereon to found queries. Now, I am so confus'd, and the materials crowded into my lumber garret of a memory so disarranged, that I could not without some such finger-posts find my way thro' my own recollections.

Will you, if you wish for such aid of materials as I can give, demand in the order you see fitting my thoughts and recollections on each of these subjects, these letters you may afterwards arrange in the way you can best connect them.

I am going to give you a little anecdote illustrative of the history of woman. Drumakiln (the last), of whose infamous life and shocking death I had occasion lately to speak, seduc'd a well brought up and rather superior young woman belonging to the lower class, to live with him. She had three beautiful and promising children who were her consolation under the remorse that prey'd on her mind.

---

[1] Probably referring to the story told by Dr. Johnson. The 'Macraes,' he says, 'were originally an indigent and subordinate clan, and having no farms nor stock were, in great numbers, servants to the Maclellans who, in the war of Charles I., took arms at the call of the heroic Montrose and were in one of his battles almost destroyed. The women that were left at home being thus deprived of their husbands, like the Scythian ladies of old married their servants, and the Macraes became a considerable race.'—*Journey to Western Islands*, p. 91.

When the eldest was seven and the youngest scarce three years old, they were all swept away by a scarlet fever or some other complaint. Agonis'd with grief and penitence, the young woman retir'd to her father's house, and to perpetuate for an example or warning to others her transgression and its punishment, erected a stone in the churchyard of Luss with the following inscription,

> 'Under this stone lie three children
> John, Helen, and William Buchanan,
> Who by the sin of their wicked parents,
> John Buchan[an] and Helen Stuart,
> Were brought to this world,
> And to punish these sins
> And preserve them from such,
> Were early taken out of it, Anno Domini,' etc., etc.

This now is precisely the meaning and very near the words of the epitaph, which I think is still more forcibly express'd.

Think of the power of early good impressions and the strength of the mind that could thus sacrifice all ordinary feelings and considerations to set up this perpetual memorial of her own disgrace for the eventual benefit of others.

I am here in Rose Street with my old friends and shall not set out for London for a week. You will please address any commands you have for me in the meantime here under cover to James Shearer, Esq., Surveyor of the Post Office, who has lately connected himself in a manner with me by marrying a young friend of ours.—I am, with the most affectionate wishes towards all your family, Dear Sir, Yours faithfully,

ANNE GRANT.

*Brompton grove,* 17 *March* 1808.

DEAR MADAM,—I was truly sorry that it was not in my power to have had the happiness of being of your party at my friend Sir Walter's dinner. When you return to town I will have much satisfaction in waiting upon you; and by that time our friend the Duchess of Gordon will be here.

Nothing could give me more satisfaction than to aid your friend Mr. Stuart in his literary pursuits: his brother-in-law, Mr. Seton at Delhi, is one of the most respectable characters in the public service in India. A true Caledonian; having had the advantages of foreign education and all admired by the people of India for his superior attention to business and his perfect probity. You should inform Mr. Stuart that when I was at Rome in 1792, I had access to read a MS. copy written by Prince Charles, of the History of his Campaigns in Scotland in 1745, etc. It was communicated to me by the keeper of the Stewart Papers in Cardinal York's possession; and on condition that I should neither take a copy of it or make any extracts from it. I obtained permission to the Duke of Sussex, then in Rome, to peruse it upon the same conditions. It is, I think, possible to obtain that MS., now that Cardinal York is no more, and if the intercourse with Rome were open I would write to my friend Cardinal Erskine upon the subject.

As to the manuscripts and papers that my father has left, I do not believe that they could be of much use to Mr. Stuart. I left those relative to his deportation with the late James Macpherson of Ossian memory, and it was from them chiefly that he wrote his own *Introduction to the History of Great Britain*.

What you observe relative to the state of society, of which we have seen the last characteristic shades in our native country, is perfectly just. Many causes combined in favour of that state of society: the spirit of true poetry which kept the memory of noble actions, as that of the best affections of the heart, in continued admiration; the hospitality which formed the intercourse of the chiefs and their family connections; the opportunities which the cadets of those families had of seeing foreign countries and serving in the armies of France, Germany, and Italy, always anxious to return to their native soil with a good name, together with an emulation between the different clans to surpass each other in acts of liberality and renown. These and other causes gave the manners of the last century in our highlands and islands much of the old early Grecian character mixed with the loyalty and spirit of chivalry. You remember the great Lord Chatham's words, 'I sought merit where it was to be found! I found it in the mountains of the north, a bold and a hardy race,' etc.[1]

The antient music of our songs was the great inspirer of

---

[1] The idea of raising Highland regiments, usually attributed to Pitt, was really due to Duncan Forbes of Culloden.

the whole organisation of society in those days, and it is a fact elucidated by the oldest Italian history of music, that it was the music of the old songs of our hills which James, one of our Scots kings, was supposed to have composed, and which the Italians called the new species of music 'lamentabile et lacrimabile,' yes, long before the days of David Rizzio.

There is a singular characteristic difference between our finest and most pathetic music and that of Italy. With us it is generally a plaintive lamentation relative to the *past*, with the Italians it is all invocative of future happiness as in Serenas, etc.

Letters gave early instruction to our native land, and the good old schoolmaster, Evan,[1] whom you so justly esteemed was one of the last schools of these good effects. Our clergy in the highlands were above all the ranks of society there exemplary and useful members of instruction. The *Literati* who formed the select instructors of Scotland about seventy years ago, united and reanimated the spirit of highland as of the lowland renown of our country in its capital; and hence perhaps the rise and prosperity of the British Empire with Scots migration in the east and the west and even at its capital in a very considerable degree. English prejudices were thus done away, and Ireland is now in train of joining the works and deeds of her ancient genius to the mass of British renown. Do you, dear madam, continue to give us so classically the best ideas of the merits and renown of our Caledonian ancestors, and like a daughter of Ossian, you will most effectually aid your country and the ardour to defend it against our enemies and our own commercial and civilisation dangers you see how sincerely I by these observations would wish you to continue your poetical amusements, and how anxious I would be to aid your friend Mr. Stuart in his useful pursuits. —I have the honour to be, dear Madam, Your most faithful and most humble servt. JOHN MACPHERSON.

*P.S.*—What you have written about Mr. James Macpherson and Ossian, etc. etc. is most correct and founded upon my early knowledge of that subject. My old friend Mr. Grant

---

[1] Cf. p. 286.

of Coriemony never forgave his being completely taken in by the *Wish of the Aged Bard*, which you have so much improved in the translation of it into superior verses. Honest Evan Macpherson copied it, and as he valued himself on spelling Gaelic perfectly, he gave it its complete appearance of antiquity to Coriemony's eyes. You have, I hope, read the poem of your namesake, Charles Grant, Esq., junr.,[1] which won the prize, on the Restoration of Learning in the east. Admirable!

*Sunbury, Middlesex, March* 20, 1808.

DEAR SIR,—I was disappointed at not hearing from you when I left Edinburgh, from a fear that your headache had been worse than usual, or some of you indispos'd. I went up with an old friend and her husband, who had return'd from India last year, and was now oblig'd to return to London, and too delicate to bear the land journey. There was a large party of us, who knew each other very well, and were glad to be together. We came up in four days, and our passage was on the whole a pleasant one. It is not possible for me to express how much I was hurried for nine days that I staid in London, by the kindness of my friends, who wish'd me during that little time to see everything, and be introduc'd to numberless people. Among these kind friends, it's but just that I should mention Sir W. Farquhar's family, Mr. Fielding of the Palace, Mr. Hatsell of the House of Commons, his brothers and family, and, finally, the Bishop of London.[2] The attentions of Mr. Charles Grant's family were still more gratifying, and may in some respects be more important to me. I have no one of new people that is new to me who has so charm'd me by her attentions and by her manners as the Honble. Mrs. Stuart, who is married to the Primate of Ireland,[3] and is a daughter of that Penn[4] who now represents the Legislator and founder of Pensylvania and Philadelphia, but all this is egotism quite from the purpose. Your business was never a moment

---

[1] Afterwards Lord Glenelg.      [2] Dr. Beilby Porteus.
[3] The Hon. W. Stuart, fifth son of John, third Earl of Bute, became Archbishop of Armagh and Primate of all Ireland.
[4] Sophia Margaret Juliana, daughter of Thomas Penn of Stoke-Pogis.

out of my mind. The friend I came up with is a Niece of Major Macpherson's. I wrote directly on my arrival; he is in a distant quarter, the name of which I forget. He answer'd me immediately; but says that it will take him some time to recollect and look thro' his papers before he can send me any intelligence worth transmitting; yet expresses himself delighted that the cause is in so good hands. Having appointed to be here at a certain day, I broke away from London rather abruptly, which hurried me exceedingly. Yet I must return for a few days in April, and shall then meet, perhaps, the Major, if he comes to see his niece embark at any rate. I shall hear from him again, but that is not near so well. Excessive fatigue and exertion, with the addition of a great cold, make me write a very stupid letter, but I hope my head will clear when [there is an improvement in] the weather, which even in these Elysian shades is bleak and cold. I daily defer'd writing to Sir John,[1] from an expectation of dining with him at Sir W. Farquhar's, who hop'd to induce him to break his resolution against dining out. He is indeed a very great invalid, but you may see how zealous he is to promote your undertaking, which I hope nothing less than ill health will induce you to relinquish or defer.

I speak my very conscience, and do not mean a compliment, when I say you are the fittest person I think in the Kingdom for this undertaking. When I say this, it is because I know there is no highlandman existing that can bring to it the prerequisites of learning, Antiquarian and Genealogical knowledge and habitual elegance and purity of style, besides vigour of mind, join'd as it seldom is with unwearied application. Were there an existing highlander possessing all these indispensables, who was at the same time a gentleman with full command of time, that highlander would be still better adapted to the work, but there is no such being. I need not tell you that in this case you are only an architect. It is not to be suppos'd that you shall create the marble and the mortar, 'tis enough that you polish and arrange. How humbly and how gladly would I drive a wheelbarrow to the undertaking, with all the materials I could collect, but this must be a work of time and

---

[1] Sir John Macpherson.

patience. I pick'd up some anecdotes from a relation at Edr., which I will try to detail hereafter. Now I think of it, Dr. Stuart at Luss might be useful. He is a modest man, a good scholar, and, I should think, no bigot to Whiggism. Pray let me hear from you soon, to know how your undertaking thrives. I am charm'd beyond measure with the family and their mode of living here. I write Mrs. Stuart soon. Excuse headache, etc., and believe me, dear Sir, yours with esteem,

Anne Grant.

*Windsor*, 14 *June* 1808.

Dear Sir,—I am sure you must by this time consider me as a great trifler, and begin to lose all dependence on my professions of zeal in the cause you are engag'd in, and of industry in gathering together antiques for the cabinet you are, I hope, busily constructing. I must begin my vindication by telling you a secret. At the request of particular friends I have been since the beginning of this year busily engag'd in preparing for the press Memoirs of a deceas'd worthy well known in her time not only all over the Continent, but to all the distinguish'd persons who in her day led the British army to the Canadian frontier.[1] But I shall refer for particulars to the Memoirs themselves, which will very soon appear; by very soon, I mean before Christmas, for the delay of printers you know to be notorious. The conveniency of getting these Memoirs quietly arrang'd where my attention would not be every moment call'd off by family cares was one motive for my accepting Sir John Legard's in[vitation], and yet I find difficulty, by dint of early rising, etc., to attend closely even for a few hours in a day to my subject, the kindness of many excellent people making many demands on my time. I was oblig'd to return for a fortnight to London to see several of my old acquaintance from America, who being near relations or intimate friends of my rever'd Patroness, whom I am now commemorating, can furnish me with anecdotes. One of my motives in returning to London was to meet Major Ewan Macpherson, who wrote to me that he deferr'd his communica-

---

[1] Madam Schuyler.

tions till we should meet, and I being at any rate going to London, wish'd to time my return there so as to meet him. He was at that time suddenly appointed to some office which attach'd him to the troops now in Sweden; call'd for me twice and mist me; I sent to him, but found he was gone off express to the place of debarkation. You cannot imagine how much I was disappointed. I wrote to Sir John Macpherson some weeks ago, and that uncourtly knight, tho' he always talks of me to the Farquhars and others in terms of the warmest friendship, did not condescend to answer my letter; possibly he may have wrote north to his brother Martin and waits his answer, and in that case he may wait long enough, for Martin is the very Prince of Procrastination. I am quite of your opinion with regard to Sir John's epistolary talents; they are certainly of the lowest order, and yet he govern'd India well, and is a kind-hearted, benevolent man. He is asthmatic and in very bad health. I was strongly tempted to call on him lately. I went by invitation, as you may suppose, to Fulham, the Bishop of London's Palace, May 20th, and staid four days, and there I saw more of the great and the noble than ever I imagin'd it could fall to my share to meet with. It is delightful to see the filial respect and attachment which many of the nobility seem to entertain for that venerable and amiable prelate. He was recovering from a serious illness, and from one o'clock to five every day there was a constant succession of visitors of the first rank, both eminence of merit and station. But all these matters I hope to recount at leisure at Allanton on my return, when I hope to be admitted to pass a fortnight there. For you see there will be no such thing as returning at once to my native obscurity after having sail'd like a paper kite so far out of my element. I am charm'd with the Bishop, and cannot say enough had I leisure of Mrs. Porteous. I am to have the privilege, for such I account it, of passing a little more time with them before I leave England. You will think me a perfect fugitive when you find this dated from Windsor. But the house from which I write, were I not bound down by prior engagements, has a more legitimate claim on my time and attention than any one in England. It is that which belongs to Miss Grant, alas now the only representative of the old Arndilly family. She and I have corresponded for two years past, and she was the cordial friend of my dear Charlotte, and has been in many respects a most useful friend to me. She lives here very much confin'd by her attention to two declining nervous sisters, but is a person highly valued for worth, judgment, and singular benevolence. She is cousin to Lady    , and was her guide and monitor, while the state of her mind admitted of influence. It will be a sufficient testimony of Miss G.'s merit to say that she was the valued friend of the late Mrs. Eliza Carter, and many other eminent persons, and that the Princess of Wales greatly wish'd to have her about the young Princess. I came up here a day before with Isabella, but was hurried about seeing the place. I wish I had leisure to stay a little longer where I have met with so much affectionate kindness and so many objects of real interest. But I cannot indulge myself in a longer holiday from my book, and must return to-morrow. I find my task so often broke in that I have vow'd to suspend correspondence till it is done. But this is a holiday at any rate, and here I get a frank, which only now and then occurs at Sunbury. I wish at leisure to charm Mrs. Stuart by telling her of the fervent devotion of the good old King, whose morning prayers in his private Chapel I have attended at 8 for three days past. I have, notwithstanding my constant application, which is really fatiguing, wrote to the Highlands for anecdotes. I should be zealous on your account tho' I did not care for the work, and zealous for the work's sake tho' I did not care for you. Excuse the hasty and homely expression by which I describe this double stimulus. Our Rector at Sunbury is a Scotchman, and does us great credit as our countryman. Dining in his house last week I was awhile in his study, and happening to open the Statistical Accounts, all which he has, I lighted on that of an old acquaintance, Mr. Grant's co-presbyter, who mentions his having many papers in his hands that give light regarding the history of the family of Lochiel, which it appears he did not give to John Hume, who would scarce have asked the favour, keeping very shy of his old brethren. Fearing to overload this frank, which I got after I had folded my letters, I shall merely request you to cover and forward it to Killmallie, free, if possible, the within note. I am thus hurried for fear the man should die, and being that he is (I whisper this) a kind of gander, I cannot explain matters to him as I would to a person of more comprehension, and therefore simply ask the favour for myself. I am quite jealous that Mrs. Stuart has not wrote to me, and beg you will not [omit] to mark in her pocket book to remember to forget.[1] Miss Stirling of Kippendavy—I forget this moment Miss Steuart's cousin—was at Sunbury with Lord Glenbervy one day lately. They were Sir John's mother and sisters that you saw at York. Convey the expression of my sincere veneration to Mrs. Mackenzie, and bid Miss Steuart cherish the memory of her sincere wellwisher and your oblig'd servant,

ANNE GRANT.

### MEMOIR OF THE FAMILY OF LOCHIEL.

DEAR SIR,—It is in tracing the history of Man when he has ceas'd to be a savage, and when his faculties, by a certain degree of moral culture, amid the benefits of social order, have begun to unfold. In short, it is in the patriarchal ages, before the coercion of laws and the tyranny of customs have transform'd him into an artificial being, that we can study nature undebas'd by ferocity, and undisguis'd by refinement.

Of these patriarchal ages, however, there are few memorials, because they were necessarily illiterate ones. Somewhat of the substance we see preserv'd in the sacred records, and somewhat of the shadow reflected in the compositions of the earlier poets of every nation.

In those rugged and barren districts of our own country, which, shelter'd by mountains that shut out both the conqueror and the legislator, retain'd traces of primitive manners long after they were effac'd in all other places. Some remains of ancient attachment, confidence, and simplicity, subsisted even within the last century, among wide extended families, who lov'd their head more than they fear'd him, and whose ardent and faithful attachment was the result and the reward of paternal kindness and protection, ever vigilant and unwearied.

---

[1] *Vide* Peter Pindar's 'Birthday Ode':—

'*Mem.*
'To remember to forget to ask
Old Whitbread to my house one day.'

It may be thought absurd to assimilate societies so warlike as these with the patriarchal modes of life. But it must be remember'd that their habitation was not assign'd in those fertile meadows and extensive plains, where the primitive herdsmen tended their flocks amidst peaceful abundance. They became hunters from necessity, and the transition from the hunter to the warrior is a very short one. He who braves danger in the forest will not shun it in the field; and he who goes always arm'd, will not readily submit to injury or insult. The hunter Esau, who pursued the sylvan chase thro' the forest of Mount Seir, was bred in the same pastoral tent, and under the same patriarchal dominion, with the shepherd Jacob, who fed his flocks in the adjoining plain, and seem'd equally solicitous to obtain the paternal blessing. Yet harden'd by his manner of life, he was sturdy and self-righted, and evidently an object of terror to those who had injur'd him, tho' the sequel shows him generous as brave.

The interior of this mountainous district, which afforded shelter to those primitive hunters, was by the hand of nature parcell'd out into subdivisions, the limits of which were defin'd most distinctly, and easily defended.

In every narrow vale, where a blue stream bent its course, some hunter of superior prowess, or some herdsman whom wisdom had led to wealth, and wealth to power, was the founder of a little community, who ever after look'd up to the head of the family as their leader and their chief. Those chains of mountains which form'd the boundaries of their separate district had then their ascents cover'd with forests, which were the scene of their hunting excursions. When their eagerness in pursuit of their game led them to penetrate into the districts claim'd by the chief of the neighbouring valley, a rash encounter was the probable consequence, which laid the foundation of future hostilities.

These petty wars gave room to a display of valour and conduct in the chiefs, and produc'd a still closer cohesion and mutual dependence among their followers. These hasty animosities were soon hush'd into peace, yet often renew'd. The consequence was that the clans became expert in arms, cautious, vigilant, and enterprising. They form'd alliances, offensive and defensive, cemented them by intermarriages between the chief families of the confederating clans, govern'd their followers by a kind of polity not ill-regulated, and the chief had the power of life and death over all his large family (for such he consider'd his clan), but this was very sparingly us'd. In cases of long feud and much mutual exasperation, a chieftain might be cruel to his enemies, but never to his friends. To their own people they were invariably clement and indulgent. Nor were these paternal rulers in any sense so despotic as they have been represented; so far otherwise, that of all monarchs they were the most limited, not being permitted to take a step of the least importance without consulting their *friends*. By this expression was meant the elders of their tribe, including relations so distant, that in any other country they would not be recognis'd as such. But then in this council of elders, those who were not regarded as prudent and sagacious persons had no weight. It can scarcely be imagin'd by us, who depend not so much on the wisdom of our sages, how nicely they weigh'd and discriminated the degrees of intellect, and how carefully the wise or witty sayings of these oracles were treasur'd up and deliver'd down to posterity. The poor laird could neither marry or give in marriage, raise a benevolence or levy war without the full consent of these counsellors, who, unless he happen'd to be a man of uncommon talents, govern'd him much more than he did them. He led out the tribe no doubt, but then they led out the families of which the tribe consisted, and unless perfectly satisfi'd with the ground of quarrel they would not move.

The celerity with which they sometimes appear'd in the field, was rather a proof of the unanimity of the clan than the despotism of the chief.

Of the bold exertion of control us'd by these mountain Hampdens, I am about to give a well-known instance.

Sometime in the last years of the 16th century, there was a Laird of Grant, who was either in mind or body so enfeebl'd that he was not able to maintain the requisite authority, even in his own immediate family. His eldest son, of whom the renown'd Prince Hal seems to have been a prototype, was call'd Laird Humphry. He was remarkable for ready wit, personal graces, bodily strength, and superior skill and dexterity in all athletic games and exercises, but he was volatile, unprincipl'd, profuse and licentious. He gather'd up among the youth of the country a train as far as possible resembling himself, and thro' Strathspey and Murray, where the family had then large possessions, nothing was to be heard of but the excesses of Laird Humphry and his dissolute attendants. Having drank all the claret in Murray, and borrow'd and run in debt till no one would trust them, he then return'd to his own country, and honour'd every house by turns with a visit, which lasted till he and his banditti had left nothing eatable or drinkable within the walls, besides polluting them with vice and intemperance. The elders in this extremity held a council, the result of which was, that if they did not immediately remove this pest, their importance and dignity as a clan was at an end. On this great occasion they laid not only their wits but their purses together, bought up Laird Humphry's debts, and laid him up in prison at Elgin, where he was confined till his death many years afterwards, the next heir in the meantime discharging all the functions of a chieftain. Now the chief justice, by whom the heir-apparent was imprison'd, show'd no greater firmness, and ran no greater risk.

I could give a hundred instances of the freedom of speech allow'd the subject in these suppos'd arbitrary dominions, but shall confine myself with a very modern one within my own knowledge.

There remain yet more vestiges of this dominion of the affections in the lesser Hebrides than in any other part of [the] highlands.

The Macniels of Barra have possess'd that island without a rival or competitor for time immemorial, and it is a very singular circumstance in the history of that family, that nineteen Roderick Macniels [1] in succession have inherited that estate without any of them having a brother; the lady always had one son, who continued the family, but never had more. Thus there was in the family of Barra a great dearth of hereditary counsellors, yet every islander was ready in his own humble, or rather familiar, way to proffer advice.

---

[1] This is not so.

About twenty years ago Barra, without asking the consent of his islanders, came to Lochaber to solicit the hand of the beautiful and amiable daughter of Cameron of Fassfern, nephew to the banish'd Lochiel. Among the rowers that brought his boat from Barra was an old man of the lower class, who had been perhaps his father's foster-brother or one of the island sages.

A few days after his arrival he was walking with other gentlemen in the street of Maryburgh,[1] when old Ronald call'd out in his native tongue, 'Rory, do you hear? I say, Rory.' 'Yes, I hear you very well, but am engag'd at present.' 'But wait, Rory, is it indeed true what I hear of your marriage?' 'Be quiet, I have gentlemen with me; I will speak with you again.' 'Nay, but Rory, dear Rory, be cautious, 'tis the mother of your children you are seeking; you do not need money; but is she prudent and modest, tell me that, Rory?' And all this in a loud voice in the open street. I should have premis'd that Barra is a well-bred, respectable, worthy man, whose appearance and manners might claim distinction wherever he is seen. The man's freedom was not the grossness of vulgar familiarity, nor Barra's forbearance the want of dignity. It was the earnestness of affectionate simplicity on the one side, and the condescension of true greatness of mind on the other. There is a volume of character in this simple anecdote.

Yet simplicity in that sense which precludes penetration into human character, and occasional stratagem and finesse, made no part of the highland manners. They were often necessitated from their manner of carrying on their hunting or predatory excursions, to be like Arviragus,

> 'Subtle as the fox for prey,
> Like warlike as the wolf for what they eat'; (SHAKESPEARE)

while their peculiarly social mode of living together, the address necessary to conciliate and adjust jarring interests among allied clans, and the habit of making all private considerations subservient to the good of the community, sharpen'd their native sagacity and enlarg'd their minds. Meantime

---

[1] Now Fort-William.

their excessive delight in poetry, music, and the tales in which the heroic deeds of their ancestors were preserv'd, communicated to their imaginations a tender and romantic enthusiasm, which gave a high and peculiar colouring to their affections and their virtues. Without entering into any discussion of the disputed question relative to the antiquity or authenticity of their boasted Ossian, it is undeniably certain that remains, undoubtedly genuine, of poems compos'd by the bards attach'd to certain great families, within these three or four centuries, still exist sufficient to do honour both to the genius and the virtues of this secluded people.

These remains are peculiarly valuable for the high strain of heroic generosity and pure morality which breathe thro' them and entitles the Mountain Muse to praise,

'Beyond all Greek, beyond all Roman fame.'

It is to be observ'd to the honour of those untaught bards that their wild strains of eulogy and lamentation never fail'd to wait upon departed merit, however deprest or unfortunate. No highland worthy ever died 'uncelebrated or unsung.'

The gallant Marquis of Montrose, tho' no highlander himself, had often led the clans in alliance with his family to victory, and finally to defeat. He who was indeed

'The courtier's, scholar's, soldier's eye, tongue, sword,
The observed of all observers'— (*Hamlet*)

had not a single chaplet hung upon his hearse but those woven by the hands of his faithful mountaineers. Their plaintive and pathetic strains have flow'd abundantly, and the *Shion shuil Ghreumach*—the wine blood of the Grahame, a common figure, to express generous and high descended blood, in the Celtic poetry—shed at the cross of Edinburgh, still wakes the throb of indignant sympathy in every highland cottage. Of this accomplish'd Hero, who was himself an elegant and classical poet, no one tuneful memorial is to be found in the English language; yet he has departed in the light of his renown, and his name lives in the song of the bards.

There were two great principles held in the utmost reverence in the Highlands on which much of the peace and order of society depend everywhere. In the first place, the violation of an oath, or even a promise once solemnly made, was regarded with unspeakable horror. Then the conjugal union was held so sacred that infidelity was scarcely heard of, and the criminal, when such there was, universally detested.

This picture of Highland society may appear a flattering one: yet those best acquainted with the subject will allow it to be a sketch very faithfully drawn. No doubt there are shades and some very dark ones. When the sword and balance are not plac'd under legal sanctions in appropriate hands, the irregular efforts of daring individuals to execute summary justice or redress dubious wrongs produce dreadful effects.

Of these I shall give one or two striking instances. When feuds ran high between contending clans, their last resort for security was to fortify a small island in one of the lakes with which that country abounds. Then by bringing in all the boats on the approach of an enemy they were secure from all danger. The south side of Loch Ness is call'd Strath Erick, from some powerful Dane who once attempted to force that pass, and was oppos'd by Cuming, head of that clan.[1] This Cuming, being mortally wounded, sat down to rest on the top of a high mountain, over which the military road has been since carried. There he expir'd, and there still remains a cairn or rude monument of stones erected to his memory, which is perpetuated by the name of the mountain, *Suie Chuiman*, the seat of Cuming. Descending from the mountain you arrive at a little plain beside the Tarfe, where the warrior was interr'd. This is call'd *Cillchuiman*, the tomb of Cuming, and is now the site of Fort Augustus. This district belong'd to the Frazers, who, being often at war with the Macintoshes and Macdonalds, their neighbours, felt the want of an island to secure their families in when they went on expeditions. They, like the Venetians, made an artificial one in a small bay of Loch Ness by sinking piles of wood and then heaping up stones. Part of this artificial island still remains, and is call'd the Cherry Isle, from some trees of that kind planted on it. There, too, are to be seen the remains of a castle once

---

[1] The Cumyns at one time seem to have included Lochaber as well as Badenoch in their vast possessions.

belonging to the Lovat family. In this lonely fortress, some time about the middle of the fifteenth century, Lovat left his three daughters while he went out on some warlike excursion. One of these young ladies was very beautiful, and was belov'd by Lovat's neighbour to the westward, Macdonald of Glengary. Not liking her family, however, he did not make open proposals, but strove privately to win her affections. This dishonourable attempt was repuls'd with due indignation. Resentment and dislike to her family now prompted this recreant lover to take an unmanly revenge by slandering the object of his passion.

Appriz'd of this the injur'd fair one sent a message in the most private manner to Glengary by her foster-father, acquainting him that on the following night she should send her attendants different ways, and alone in the castle wait to receive him at midnight.

Glengary gladly complied with the assignation, yet did not go unarm'd. For this the damzels were prepar'd. The entrance to these castles generally led to a kind of hall on the ground floor, to which three or four steps of a descent led down. In the dusk of the evening the old man, by direction, kill'd a bullock and spread the new-flay'd hide, with the inside outwards, upon these steps. Whenever the expected lover set foot on this slippery descent he slid backwards, as was intended. The old man, who waited at the bottom with a Lochaber axe, sever'd his head in a moment from his body. The lady who offer'd this victim to her violated fame did not long enjoy her triumph undisturb'd. The deed (in which the perpetrators gloried) was soon known.

The Macdonalds led their force against Lovat, overpower'd and took him prisoner. They carried him into the deepest recess of a thick wood, where swarms of flies were attracted by the close sultry heat. There they bound him to a tree, and opening his mouth as wide as possible fixed a stick to prevent its closing, that he might be chok'd by the insects which would in these circumstances fly into it. In this extremity some one propos'd to spare his life on condition that he would take the *great oath* to relinquish the estate of Abertarph to the Glengary family. They, the Glengary family, enjoy'd it till the late General Frazer purchas'd it back in '76.

Abertarph is that picturesque district water'd by the rivers Tarph and Oich, in which Fort Augustus lies, and which extends westward from the head of Loch Ness to Loch Oich by Invergarrie house.

Lovat on this occasion departed from his dignity as a chief. According to the receiv'd notions he was not allow'd to part with territory for the preservation of his life.

The clans possess'd unequal shares of power and numbers, yet the prevalence of mind was here strongly mark'd. A clan which had been rul'd by a succession of wise and brave leaders soon deriv'd such consequence from the abilities of its chiefs as made it greatly preponderate in the scale of political importance over others more numerous and possessing more territory.

Among these, that of the Camerons was particularly distinguish'd. Many gentlemen of this name possess'd property, such as Dungallan, Callart, Glendissery, Clunes, etc. etc., but all acknowledg'd Lochiel as their chief, and literally resign'd their lives and fortunes in whatever cause he adopted. A succession of able and honourable men supported the credit of the clan, and by judicious and respectable marriages created useful connections to the family. Perhaps even our frugal country did not afford an instance of a family who liv'd in so respectable a manner and show'd such liberal and dignified hospitality on so small an income.

Their authority, supported by the general confidence in their personal virtues, was indisputed. Yet justice requires that even this generous clan and their successive gallant leaders should not receive unqualified praise.

The clan, with very little scruple of conscience, were wont to make excursions in search of prey, which they denominated a spreath.[1] They were, however, more honest and more decorous than the Elliots or Armstrongs of the border. Their chief never headed their excursions, never shar'd their prey, and severely punish'd them when they trespass'd on the bounds of any ancient ally of the family. To this effect there is a letter among the archives of the Grants, written with all the

---

[1] Probably a confusion of *creachadh*, a foray, with *spreidh*, cattle.

air of ceremonious dignity which one sovereign might be suppos'd to use in addressing another.[1]

It seems there had been an alliance by marriage between the chiefs of the two clans, in consequence of which a close friendship subsisted between the tribes. A band of the Camerons set out to make depredations on the inhabitants of the east coast. They had to cross the island from sea to sea (their way lying thro' Badenoch and Strathspey) before they arriv'd at their destination. Returning thro' the dark passes of the mountains with a heavy prey of cattle the Grant herdsmen saw, or thought they saw, some of their own cattle among them. These they reclaim'd: a scuffle ensu'd, for it was a point of honour with highlanders to rescue their cattle from depredators at the extreme risk of life, else they were for ever disgrac'd. The skirmish between these enrag'd combatants was so sharp that some lives were lost on the part of the Grants. The Laird of Grant wrote to his *Right traist* Cousin Lochiel, representing how utterly impossible it was to put up with this flagrant violation of the friendship subsisting between the clans without due satisfaction for the injury receiv'd.

Lochiel in answer assur'd his good cousin of his great concern for the injury his people had sustain'd. 'We would not willingly,' says he, 'that any of our men should skaith the lieges in your bounds, they only went forth to make a spreath upon the land of Murray, whence all men take their prey.'

A Cameron of the lower [order] was condemn'd, and I believe executed to appease the wrath of the Clan Grant; he did not suffer for taking cattle at the risk of his life from those whose business it was manfully to defend their property. Far less was he condemn'd for defending himself when attacked. His crime was violating the arm'd neutrality and breaking the ancient league, offensive and defensive, subsisting between the clans.

The Lochiels had for some generations been men of a commanding appearance, robust, athletic make, and dark hair and

---

[1] The letter referred to is seemingly one from Allan Cameron of Lochiel to Sir James Grant of Freuchie, dated 18th October 1645. Cf. *Chiefs of Grant*, vol. ii. p. 76.

complexion. So many deeds of fame had been achiev'd by chiefs of this complexion, equally brave and fortunate, that superstition began to note it as a lucky one, and finally it was foretold by gifted seers that a fair Lochiel should never prove a fortunate one.

In the year 1675 was born Ewan du, or dark-hair'd Evan, who was fated by his courage, fidelity, generosity, and loyalty, to eclipse all his predecessors.[1] He was singularly belov'd by his people; and besides the virtues of his heart, and the powers of his understanding, possess'd that vigilance, prompt exertion, and determin'd firmness, which peculiarly fitted him for those military employments in which he afterwards distinguish'd himself. He very early display'd his attachment to the abdicated monarch, having led a considerable body of Camerons to the assistance of Viscount Dundee, at the Pass of Killiecrankie.[2] Here his courage and conduct went near to turn the fortune of the day. How this conduct came to be overlook'd by Government, at the very time that Glencoe, who was just at Lochiel's door, became the object of such signal vengeance, does not appear. Nor can it at this time be easily accounted for. His popular character, and powerful connections, might make it seem worth while to conciliate him; but if that was the intention, it does not appear to have succeeded.

Some time after, about the end of King William's reign, his son John went privately to France. He was an intelligent man, of frank and pleasing manners, who had more knowledge, and had associated more with his superiors than was usual for the chieftains of those days. There is reason to suppose that it was about this time that he became acquainted with the Duke of Berwick, who had a great friendship for him.

About this time too, Barclay of Urie, well known as the acute and able apologist of the Quakers, was also in France at that time, when probably commenc'd the acquaintance which

---

[1] Eoghainn Dubh was really born in 1629, and died at the age of ninety in 1719. He married (1.) Mary, daughter of Sir Donald MacDonald of Sleat; (2.) Isabel, daughter of Sir Lachlan Maclean of Duart; (3.) Jean, daughter of David Barclay of Urie.

[2] At Killiecrankie he carried the royal standard. For a description of his appearance, vide Macaulay's *History of England*, chap. xiii.

soon after produc'd a matrimonial alliance between the families of Urie and Lochiel.[1]

This marriage was an additional proof of the gallant chief's independence of mind and deserved [all praise].

In the meantime every effort was made by the ruling powers at home to detach Lochiel from his allegiance to the abdicated monarch.

Great offers were made him on the part of Government. He was to have a pension of £300 a year, which was to descend to his son (whom they were particularly anxious to lure back to Scotland), and to be Governor of Fort William.

This generous chieftain, however, was above temptation. While Government were thus vainly negotiating with him, a very different kind was carrying on between Sir Ewan and another distinguish'd chief.

Alaster Du (Dark Alexander) of Glengarrie, whose territories border'd on those of Lochiel, and whose castle was situated on Loch Oich, not many miles from Achnacarrie, is still celebrated in the poetry and traditions of his own country, for wisdom, valour, and magnanimity.[2] He was the head of a very powerful tribe styling themselves Macdonells, in contra-distinction to the Macdonalds of the Isles, whose claim of superiority they always resisted, claiming to be a distinct family descended from the ancient Earls of Antrim in the north of Ireland. Indeed, the bards and sennachies of the house of Glengarrie did not fail even here to claim precedence, alleging that the family of Antrim deriv'd of them. Be this as it may, the Glengarrie family had at this time reach'd the acme of their power and popularity. An immediate predecessor of the renown'd Alaster had added literary and civic honours to the wild wreathes that had flourish'd round the brows of his ancestors. He had in consequence of his talents and attainments been created a Lord of Session, at a time when no little power and consequence was attach'd to that office.[3] He went

---

[1] Robert Barclay of Urie, the Apologist, born 1648, educated at the Scots College, Paris, returned to Scotland 1664, died 1690.

[2] Cf. Macaulay's *History of England*, chap. xiii.

[3] The reference is probably to Æneas Macdonell, ninth of Glengarry, who was raised to the peerage in 1660 as Lord Macdonell and Arros. No Glengarry was ever a Lord of Session.

afterwards to Italy, where he acquir'd a taste for architecture; and on his return built the Castle of Invergarrie (part of the walls of which still remain undemolish'd) on the model of an edifice of the same kind which had attracted his attention at Padua.

The heroic Alaster du succeeded to all the honours and all the popularity of his predecessor, and in sincere, however misplac'd loyalty to the house of Stuart, equall'd his neighbour Sir Evan.

Both men of abilities, integrity, and candour; and both stimulated by an ardent zeal for the cause which to them appear'd just. All the rivalry so usual between neighbouring clans was swallow'd up by the powerful sentiment which united them.

They concerted all the plans of their political measures or military operations together, and led their united clan to guard the hard-disputed Pass of Killiecrankie, where Glengarrie had a brother kill'd, and several Camerons of note fell victims to their principles. After this hard struggle the two chieftains returned to their respective abodes. Glengarrie, for some reason which does not now distinctly appear, was more obnoxious to Government than Sir Ewan, who very composedly occupied the house of Achnacarrie, tho' it was not very defensible and stood near the garrison; while Glengarrie found it necessary to retire for some time. His followers being at that time uncivilis'd, and less amenable to regular discipline than the Camerons, had probably by their ravages provok'd a more aggravated hostility.

He retir'd for some time among the woods and mountains of Glengarrie, remaining sometimes for days together in a small wooded island of Locharkaig, where tradition says they contriv'd a stratagem to elude the threaten'd vengeance of Government, which was afterwards put into execution with a dexterity and resolution equal to the subtlety and secrecy with which it was plan'd. It is said that some young men belonging to the most powerful families in England had come down with a certain regiment then lying at Fort William, to see the country, and take a share in the desultory warfare then carried on. These youths were accounted cadets or volunteers. Of such many were attach'd to every regiment in those days, who got a soldier's pay if they chose to accept it, were consider'd as pupils in the art of war, at liberty to retire if they chose, and eligible, being often persons of family, to fill the vacancies which war or disease occasioned among the subalterns. This regiment was now about to occupy the garrisons of Stirling and Dumbarton, and was most probably succeeded by some other regiment. These who had been amusing themselves with their fowling pieces on the way to the Black Mount, were engag'd with each other in conversation, and bringing up the rear with some of the staff, and little dreading an assault in desolate regions where there are no inhabitants but a few wandering herdsman, and in a country which they consider'd as completely subdued.

Two hundred well-arm'd and light-footed highlanders, however, lay conceal'd in the heath and bushes in a narrow pass, confin'd on one side by a steep mountain, and on the other by a small lake by the path, for road there was none, that led towards Teyandrem [1] or the Black Mount. When the rear of the regiment to which these youths were passing fearlessly thro' the deep solitude, as they thought it, of this savage district, the highlanders sprung so suddenly from their ambuscade, that before they could recollect themselves sufficiently to have recourse to their arms for defence, these dexterous partisans had snatch'd away their prey. This consisted of eight or ten young men of the description above mention'd, and a few more of less note, whom in their indiscriminate haste they had swept away with the rest.

There were some shots fir'd in the confusion which produc'd little effect besides alarming the regiment.

This sudden and mysterious disappearance of their young *élèves* excited the utmost concern and perturbation among the superior officers. They could not possibly define the purport and tendency of this manœuvre; that so many people should venture their lives in this bold enterprise against unequal odds was very wonderful, if the intention were merely to carry

---

[1] Tyndrum.

away a few prisoners, and thus incense a power able to crush them in an instant.

What they knew of the sagacity and forecast of the chieftains and their habit of acting in concert on emergencies, forbid them to indulge the supposition of its being a mere predatory attack, the dictate of revenge or sudden caprice. Utterly at a loss for the motive of this well-concerted stratagem, they were equally puzzl'd how to act in consequence of it. To pursue them was useless, being entirely ignorant of their route. To divide into parties was unsafe in what now clearly appear'd to be a hostile country. To spoil and ravage the country while uncertain from what district or clan this unseen blow came, was to shake the wavering allegiance of some, and kindle others into fatal desperation.

After revolving all things in their minds, it appear'd to them most probable that this plan was the result of that smother'd hostility which their own rashness and insolence had fomented, and that the intention was to engage them in a pursuit which should afford advantage to some large arm'd body lurking in the fastnesses for that purpose, to rush upon them and destroy them when involv'd in those intricate and dangerous passes which were only safe for the natives.

Afraid to pursue the aggressors, and asham'd to communicate to Government the result of a transaction from which they deriv'd so little credit, it was determin'd they should march silently on and suspend all measures of retaliation till they had some sure grounds to go on, by discovering the real aggressors and the tendency of this outrage. At Dumbarton they found a letter address'd to the commander of the corps, informing them 'that certain chiefs of clans who had no objections to King William's ruling in England, considering that nation as at liberty to choose its own rulers, but that they never could consistent with oaths they had repeatedly sworn on their arms and by all that is holy, take an oath to any other sovereign while any of the family at St. Germains continued to exist. That they, however unwilling to perjure themselves or to hold their lands in daily fear, subject to the insults of the petty instruments of power and to the groundless accusation of treason to the ruling powers, were willing to live quietly under the present rulers as long as their conscience was not forc'd, nor their possessions disturb'd.'

These last, they said, they and their followers were resolv'd to defend from aggression with the last drop of their blood. But in the meantime, to prevent as far as possible encroachments which might drive them into hostilities with a government, which, tho' they did not acknowledge, they meant not hereafter to disturb, they had taken hostages to insure their safety, and these they would never part with till Sir Evan and Alaster Du had obtain'd assurances that while they liv'd peaceably on their lands they should not be disturb'd for their principles, nor for any part they had formerly acted when government was so little settled or establish'd that no man obeying the Sovereign to whom he had originally sworn allegiance, could be said to disturb the peace of a country for the mastery of which rival Sovereigns seem'd contending.

This proposal was accompanied with a strong and pathetic remonstrance on the folly and danger of alienating and finally exasperating clans powerful from their union and from the inaccessible country they inhabited, by treating them with continued harshness and distrust, and making the tenderness of their conscience and their fidelity (while it could be available) to their unfortunate exil'd Sovereign, a pretext to lay them at the mercy of 'every petty petling officer' who might think fit to experserate them into hostility that he might treat them as rebels. They quoted the late horrid massacre of Glencoe as justifying this measure of precaution, and threaten'd if their petition was rejected to take refuge with their prisoners in France and proclaim to all Europe the impolicy and cruelty of the treatment which had been the means of driving them there.

This remonstrance and petition for immunity, after being secretly and carefully perus'd, was despatch'd by a private express, not to the council (the king being then for the last time abroad), but to the relations of the young captives who were deeply interested in the success of the negotiation, and whose wives and sisters, at a time when the generality of even well inform'd people were shamefully ignorant of the manners and character of the Scottish mountaineers, might apprehend that their kinsmen might be not only kill'd but eaten by these remorseless savages, as they consider'd them.

Besides these private considerations, the aspect of public affairs was more favourable for the success of such an 'arm'd neutrality' than at any former period. William had outliv'd his queen, and with that popularity which her gentle and gracious manners attracted, and which was repell'd by his cold and forbidding ones, he was visibly declining in health, and the honours due to him as a patriot hero (whose very ambition was sanctified by the noble end he uniformly pursued) had not their due influence in a country, torn by the factions which divided a jealous aristocracy and a turbulent populace.

William's love of power was all directed to that single object, which had been the ruling passion of his life, the preserving the liberties of Europe from the encroachments of France.

If he was eager amidst all his affected indifference to obtain the dominion of this island, it was that he might turn all its resources against the common enemy. Thus engross'd by his military pursuits and foreign politics, it was little to be expected that he should take an intimate concern in those dark corners of his dominions where an 'Imperium in Imperio' still subsisted that eluded or resisted the ordinary regulations of civil government. These he left to the great officers of state in that turbulent kingdom, which foreigners were too ignorant, and natives too knowing to govern aright. By too knowing, I mean that they knew too well the confederacies and relative interests of their own tribes and factions to rule impartially.

Meanwhile, William, who had never been much lov'd, now childless and declining, was less fear'd than formerly. All eyes were turn'd towards the court of the Princess of Denmark, who, in herself, mild, pious and estimable, deriv'd additional popularity with the adverse party, from the coldness subsisting between her and the king.

The consequence which she deriv'd from being the recognis'd successor to the crown, was considerably augmented by her being the mother of a son to whom the nation fondly look'd up as the descendant of their ancient line of monarchs, born in their own country, and bred up in those religious and political principles for which they had suffer'd and sacrific'd so much.

The partisans of this court, which had already obtain'd considerable influence over the minds of the people, were not inclin'd to regard with much severity a stratagem which a late tragical event had in some degree authoris'd, and after a secret negotiation, the grounds of which, it is said, were never communicated to the king, both Sir Evan and Glengarrie were assur'd of safety for the future, and impunity for the past. The youths went home pleas'd with their treatment and the amusements which had been devis'd for them in their retreat.

The credit of this fact rests merely on the country tradition, and the silence concerning it in the publications and records of these times is accounted first, by the shame which the commanders of the regiment felt at being thus surpris'd and outwitted by an inferior number of those whom they had been accustom'd to style barbarians and treat as such.

Those on the other hand who had been urg'd by their concern for the safety of their relatives to bring about this treaty without assigning their motives, were equally interested in concealing it.

Sir Evan and Glengarrie [lived] peaceably unquestion'd all the ensuing reign, which was a very happy one for these and the neighbouring chieftains who were no longer forc'd to meet clandestinely in their favourite island, and whose friendship for each other continued undiminish'd thro' life. Few chieftains have been so much belov'd and admir'd in life, or so sung and celebrated after it as these memorable friends, who still live in the lays of their native bards.

The Keppochs, a highland family of the name of Macdonell or Macdonald, I am not sure which, have been long distinguish'd for valour and for genius, to which I might add the personal advantages of grace and beauty. Sheelah or Julia, an eminent poetess of this accomplish'd family, who was married to Gordon of Belderno, was contemporary with these mountain heroes.[1] In her youth she must have known them

---

[1] Well known in Gaelic as Sileas na Ceapach. She married Alexander Gordon of Beldorney.

well, Keppoch being in the close neighbourhood both of Invergarrie and Achnacarrie.

Her family, if I mistake not, were cadets of Glengarrie,[1] and in the numerous lyrics that owe their birth to her prolific muse, much of the history of that family and even of that period, may be trac'd, for after her connection by marriage with the Gordons, the virtues and valour of that powerful tribe, and the vicissitudes to which its heads were subjected are by turns the object of eulogy and lamentation.

The enthusiasm with which her character was deeply ting'd, seems to have been not only poetical, but heroic, patriotic, and in a very high degree devotional. She was a Catholic too, and took every advantage that a religion so pompous and picturesque offer'd, to embellish her poetry with the peculiar imagery it afforded. The hymns and sacred rhapsodies of Sheelah are still the consolation and delight of all pious highland Catholics. Of her monody on the death of the renown'd Alaster Du, or at least of one of the many poems she consecrated to his memory, follows an extract literally translated, and selected more for its singularity than any superiority of poetical merit:

> 'Dark Alexander of Glengarrie,
> Thou art departed and we remain forlorn.
> Thou wert our guard, our comfort, and our ornament,
> Thou wert admir'd of lovely women,
> Thou wert the pleasure of heroic men,
> Thou wert as among metals as the most pure gold,
> Thou wert as the noblest Lyon among the beasts,
> Among the birds as is the Eagle of strongest wing,
> As is the shapely Salmon of bright scales among the fish,
> As is the moon among Stars,
> Or the fair-hair'd sun amidst revolving planets,' etc. etc.

The parallel betwixt Alastar Du and every object of transcendent worth is carried much further, and concluded with some very tender and pathetic retrospections of the past and sublime anticipation of the future.

But it is time to leave our poetess and our hero to return

---

[1] They were not. The family of Glengarry are said to be descended from the marriage of John first Lord of the Isles with Amie MacRuari, Lady of Garmoran; the family of Keppoch from his marriage with the Princess Margaret, daughter of Robert II.

to the more immediate subject of this Memoir. Sometime in the latter years of the reign of King William, Sir Evan had the satisfaction of seeing a marriage take place betwixt his son John and the beautiful and estimable daughter of Barclay of Urie, the apologist for the Quakers.[1]

It is well known that the doctrine so abhorr'd and revil'd of passive obedience and non-resistance makes a part of the tenets of this primitive and inoffensive sect. They were (perhaps on that very account) patronis'd by James the Second, and always retain'd a kindness for the abdicated family. This is the only point of agreement I can possibly see between a meek and simple Quaker, and a lofty and ambitious highland chieftain. But John, the son of Sir Evan, tho' obscured in some measure by the too near brightness of his illustrious parent (and his own voluntary exile in his early days) was possess'd of superior qualities of mind and innate worth sufficient to induce so good a judge as Barclay to consider him worthy of his alliance. Sir Evan cordially approv'd of this marriage, which was indeed every way respectable. This was an additional proof of the old chieftain's good sense, for it was in those days an unheard-of thing for a highland chief to marry without the consent of his whole clan. When he did marry it was generally the daughter of some neighbouring great man, acquainted with the language and manners of that country.

This singular choice of the younger Lochiel, however, soon met the sanction of general approbation. Before the ancient chief, full of years and honours, slept with his fathers, he had the comfort to witness the happiness his son deriv'd from this marriage, and to see him live very respectably and altogether undisturb'd in the seat of his ancestors. This serene aspect of matters continued unruffl'd during the whole reign of Queen Anne, a Princess whose memory the highlanders hold in the highest veneration on account of the tranquillity and plenty they enjoy'd during her reign, which was advantageously contrasted with the former and subsequent periods. Indeed King

---

[1] It was Sir Ewen himself who married as his third wife Jean, daughter of Colonel David Barclay of Urie, and sister of Robert Barclay the Apologist. John Cameron of Lochiel married Isabel, daughter of Sir Alexander Campbell of Lochnell.

William was most unjustly made accountable for the famine (a very severe one of seven years' continuance) which depopulated some inland districts of the highlands during his reign. The scarcity was extreme everywhere in those pastoral countries which at best produce very little grain. But on the seaside the supply of marine productions of various kinds afforded constant relief, for not only fish but the algae and other seaweeds afforded sustenance to this distress'd people. If poor King William was blam'd for a famine which was consider'd as a visitation on his public and personal sins, tho' the suffering devolv'd wholly on others, the singularly rich crops which land too long left fallow afforded in the times of *good* Queen Anne were in a great measure attributed to her pious prayers. It was in short all over the highlands a period of peaceful abundance, still held in grateful remembrance, during which the Whig Lyon endur'd and sometimes even fondl'd the Tory Kid. And had the Duke of Gloucester liv'd the distinction of parties would in a great measure have been obliterated by the mild sway of this benevolent Princess. I only speak of parties as they existed in the highlands.

The Quaker lady meantime acquir'd the language of the country, and became distinguish'd for prudence, activity, and affability; no chieftainess could be more popular. One great defect she had, however, which was more felt as such in the highlands than it would have been in any other place. She did not, as a certain resolute countrywoman of hers was advis'd to do, 'bring forth men children only.' On the contrary, she had twelve daughters in succession, a thing scarce pardonable in one who was look'd up to and valued in a great measure as being the suppos'd mother of a future chief.[1]

In old times women could only exist while they were defended by the warrior and supported by the hunter. When this dire necessity in some measure ceas'd the mode of thinking to which it gave rise continued, and, after the period of youth

---

[1] This is nonsense. By his three wives Sir Ewen had altogether fifteen children, of whom eleven were daughters. Jean Barclay was the mother of seven daughters and one son, who was her eldest child. John Lochiel's children consisted of one daughter and seven sons, the eldest of whom was Donald, the 'Gentle Lochiel' of the '45.

and beauty was past, woman was only consider'd as having given birth to a man.

John Lochiel's mind was above this illiberal prejudice. He fondly welcomed his daughters and caress'd their mother on their appearance as much as if every one of them had been a young hero in embryo. His friends and neighbours us'd on these occasions to ask in a sneering manner, 'What has the lady got?' To which he invariably answer'd, 'A lady indeed.' This answer had a more pointed significance there than with us, for in the highlands no one is call'd a lady but a person married to the proprietor of an estate. All others, however rich or high born, are only *gentlewomen*. How the prediction intentionally included in the chief's answer was fulfill'd will hereafter appear.

Besides the family title, every highland chieftain has a patronymic deriv'd from the most eminent of their ancestors, probably the founder of the family, and certainly the first who conferr'd distinction on it. Thus Argyle is the son of Colin, Breadalbane the son of Archibald, etc.; and the chief of the Camerons was always styl'd son of Donald Du, Black Donald, whatever his name or complexion may be. This dark complexion, as well as the appellation deriv'd from it, became, it would appear, hereditary in the family, and at length it became a tradition or prophecy among the clan that a fair Lochiel should never prosper.

After the birth of the twelve daughters, to the great joy of the clan, an heir appear'd, but their satisfaction was not a little check'd on finding the ill-omen'd laird was as fair as any of his sisters. Tho' fair, however, he was not effeminate, but added to the dignity of appearance and muscular strength which distinguish'd his ancestors a singularly mild and engaging countenance. He was call'd Donald.[1] Archibald, afterwards known as the hard-fated Dr. Cameron, and John, denominated Fassfern, from the possession he held, were born soon after. The proud prediction of their father was soon amply fulfill'd with regard to the daughters of this extraordinary family, which centred in itself so much beauty, merit,

---

[1] The 'Gentle Lochiel.

and good fortune that their history unites the extravagance of romance with the sober reality of truth.

The fair Quaker made not only an excellent wife but a most exemplary mother. Her daughters were better educated than the generality of young women in these remote corners, and tho' little or nothing was to be expected with them, the fame of their engaging appearance soon attracted admirers from all quarters.

There was little or nothing to be expected with them, or indeed with any highland damsel, but the great point was to be well born and well allied. Now, tho' no people on earth set more by high descent than the highlanders in choosing a wife, ancestry was not the sole consideration. They were much persuaded that the qualities of the mind as well as personal and constitutional defects or advantages were hereditary. They were therefore anxious to a degree, scarce credible to modern refinement, to avoid the risk of inherited faults or blemishes. To express the thing in their own homely manner, the Lochiel maidens were consider'd as of an excellent breed, and when the eldest and one or two of her sisters were well married the additional attraction of forming good alliances drew admirers to the younger branches of the family. They seem'd indeed like the Sibyl's leaves, to rise in value as they decreas'd in number. The younger ones were taken away almost in childhood, and the youngest of all, who was allowedly the most beautiful, was actually married to Cameron of Glendissery in the twelfth year of her age, and after his death to Maclean of Kingarloch, so that she was successively the wife of two heads of families.[1]

The least beautiful of this tribe of beauties, who, however, possess'd a commanding figure and superior understanding, was Jean, afterwards married to Clunie,[2] the chief of the clan Macpherson. She had the advantage over her fairer sisters of being celebrated in English, or rather Scotch verse, being the reputed heroine of the popular and pathetic song known by the name of 'Lochaber no more.'

---

[1] Christian, who married Glendessary, was Jean Barclay's eldest daughter.

[2] Lachlan Macpherson of Nuid who succeeded to the chiefship in 1722. Their eldest son Ewen, the Cluny of the '45, married Janet Fraser of Lovat.

The poet, who in strains at once tender and heroic, laments his departure from Lochaber and consequent separation from his Jean, is said to have been an officer in one of the regiments station'd at Fort William. The marriages of these admir'd sisters derive a certain political importance from their forming links of a chain which their father, from his popularity and power of mind, was enabled to draw in any direction, and to which his son afterwards, by the combin'd power of affinity and ability, communicated the same momentum.

In this view it is worth while to trace each distinct head of this powerful confederacy which associated so many noted families by the ties both of kindred and opinion into one mass of disaffection to Government and strong mutual attachment.

The sons-in-law of John Lochiel were, 1st. Cameron of Dungallon. 2nd. Barclay of Urie. 3rd. Grant of Glenmoriston. 4th. Macpherson of Clunie. 5th. Campbell of Barcaldine. 6th. Campbell of Auchalader. 7th. Campbell of Auchlyne. 8th. Maclean of Lochbuy. 9th. Macgregor of Bohaudie. 10th. Wright of Loss. 11th. Maclean of Ardgour; and, 12th. Cameron of Glendissery.[1] It is singular that all these twelve ladies became the mothers of families, and made good wives and mothers, insomuch that their numerous descendants still cherish the bonds of affinity now so widely diffus'd, and still boast their descent from these female worthies.

Thus powerful in new form'd connections, and happy in the midst of an admirable family, Lochiel liv'd in tranquil comfort till the death of Queen Anne, ominous to all Tory visions of felicity, again brought troublous times, and once more brought the fidelity of the Jacobite chiefs to the severest test. Some of the Scotch nobility, who languish'd to see Scotland once more in reality an independent kingdom, nourish'd in the minds of the chieftains a hatred to English dominion. This

---

[1] This list is very inaccurate. First of all, it refers to the daughters, not of John, but of Sir Ewen. Moreover, there were only eleven, not twelve, of these ladies. Then, none of these married Campbell of Achlyne, Maclean of Lochbuy, or Wright of Loss; while there is no mention of the marriage of Katharine Cameron to William Macdonald, Tutor of Sleat, or of her sister Marjory to Macdonald of Morar. Macgregor of Bohandie also is better known under the name of Drummond of Balhaldy. Cf. also p. 287. Barclay of Urie was Robert, the grandson of the Apologist.

had indeed been too often delegated into the hands of cruelty and rapine, to be in any degree popular; and tho' the scourges of the land who had thus abus'd authority were themselves Scotchmen, still the English rule was blam'd for the unparallel'd miseries of the country during the intermediate period between the accession of James the First and the Union. There still lurk'd in the minds of the less instructed Scotch a strong desire of being govern'd by a king of their own, who should reign in Scotland only, and to whom that kingdom should not be merely a secondary object.

This dislike to English sway was greatly exasperated by the cruel abandonment of the settlement of Darien, which gave the lieges of the low country a dislike to King William's person and government, equally strong and better grounded than that which the highlanders had conceiv'd, in consequence of the famine, when they imagin'd themselves starv'd to atone for his personal transgressions.

This eager wish for unattainable, or at best precarious and tributary independence, was lull'd to sleep by the lenient counsels and military triumphs that render'd the reign of their belov'd Queen glorious abroad, and comparatively tranquil at home, and she had the additional merit of having a grandfather born in Scotland, and to all these merits the passion for a direct line of succession for some time gave way. The leaders of the party did not fail to whisper to the chiefs that this pious princess was too conscientious to let her dominions descend to a stranger, and had made provision in her settlements to prevent such an alienation, as they consider'd it, of the crown.

Nothing could equal the astonishment of these deluded chiefs when they found that the dreaded foreigner was in actual possession of a crown of which they knew their inability to dispossess him.

To restore their ancient race of monarchs to the separate crown of Scotland was their fondest wish. This visionary project was never adopt'd by the Jacobites at large, who were too well inform'd to suppose it either practicable or eligible, but it serv'd as an engine to excite the zeal of bards and sennachies, who were still numerous in the Highlands, and in whose poetry strong traces of this very project may still be found.

The insurrection of the year fifteen, kindl'd from the embers of the unextinguish'd hopes of the Jacobites, is too well known to require any detail here, and was too ill conducted to do much credit either to those who kindl'd or those who extinguish'd it. Lochiel,[1] however, as far as fidelity is honourable, had merit in his adherence to his principles, having much to lose, and little to expect from a change. Before he went to the field of Sheriff Muir, which decided the contest, without leaving to either side the honours of victory, he arrang'd matters so as to be prepar'd for the worst. The frequency of feuds and civil wars in Scotland during those long and feeble minorities, equally fatal to the independence of the throne and the liberties of the people, had taught the Barons to practise all the finesse and stratagem render'd necessary by a state of perpetual change and uncertainty. The son and father, for the general advantage of the clan, often affected to take different sides, that the estate might in any event be preserv'd to the family. Lochiel did not exactly follow this example, but he left his affairs so arrang'd, and under such careful guidance, that in case of the worst that could be fear'd, his estate and affairs might be protected. He had a powerful band of sons-in-law to give aid and counsel to the heir, now nearly of age, and I think at college.

Donald, the younger Lochiel, having no concern in the rising, of which he was purposely kept in ignorance, was not liable to be question'd on that account. Tho' he was carefully educated in the family principles, a reflective mind and much acquir'd knowledge, remov'd him far from that headlong rashness which pursues the end without duly considering the means. Conscious that the honour and interest of the clan were safe in the hands of such a son, the elder Lochiel [1] (now consider'd by Government as a proscrib'd rebel), after hovering for some [time] in Braemar and Badenoch and the intermediate districts, join'd General Gordon, and follow'd the fortunes of the unfortunate adventurer to France, after his ill-advis'd landing

---

[1] John is meant, though Sir Ewen did not die till 1719. Cf. p. 308 note 1.

and coronation at Scone. He was now consider'd too powerful to be conniv'd at, and of too much consequence to be forgiven, had he even been willing to submit. He resided chiefly at the court of St. Germains, where he enjoy'd a high degree of favour and confidence, particularly with the Duke of Berwick, and tho' he seem'd to renounce Scotland till a change of Government should render his return eligible, he at different times made private visits to his native country, where he could remain, if not publicly, at least safely, as long as it suited his inclination, having sons-in-law in every district ready to protect him, besides the most dutiful and amiable of sons, who consider'd himself as merely holding his possessions in trust for his father. To all the noble and generous qualities display'd in the age of chivalry by his brave ancestors, Donald of Lochiel united a gentleness of manners and elegance of mind to which those unpolish'd warriors were strangers. He married about the year '28 a daughter of Sir James Campbell of Auchinbreck, of which marriage the present Lochiel is descended. Of this lady it is sufficient praise to say that she was every way a suitable companion for her husband.[1]

Donald, tho' no less attach'd to the abdicated family than his predecessors, found it expedient for the general good to submit quietly to the ruling powers, but never took the oaths of allegiance to the reigning family. Nothing could be a greater proof of the esteem in which he was held by all parties than his being indulg'd in this tenderness of conscience so near a military station.[2]

In the many private visits which the elder chieftain made to his son, it cannot be doubted that there was a kind of tacit agreement that what they esteem'd 'the good old cause' should be supported when occasion became ripe. Donald, however, a patriot and a person of deep reflection, lov'd his king well, but his country still better. Nor would he be persuaded to risk the safety of that country by any prospect of personal advantage. Ambition, 'that last infirmity of noble minds,' had no great power over his. John Lochiel had look'd too

---

[1] Their family consisted of three sons and four daughters.
[2] Fort-William.

near into the court of France to depend much upon it; and to the sound judgment of his son it seem'd obvious that an attempt unsupported by powerful aid from abroad would be unavailing. Indeed it was evident that without foreign aid, and the hearty co-operation of the English Jacobites, any further attempts to reinstate the exil'd Prince would only end, as the former had done, in a desperate display of unavailing courage and fidelity, and the utter ruin of his Scotch adherents.

John Lochiel the exile deriv'd much consequence from the influence he possess'd over his numerous progeny. The sons of his daughters[1] were in some instances become the heads of families, and all look'd up to him for light. The slightest intimation of his will would have been sufficient to set his family confederacy in motion, but the chief saw too clearly to hazard the fate of so many, without well weighing the consequences, and his son's wisdom, early ripen'd by the cautious and critical part he had to act, forbade all precipitance.

In this state of matters he was appris'd of an intended descent on Scotland, which was to be powerfully supported by the French, and no less effectually seconded by the English Jacobites. It was necessary to be well assur'd of this before any steps could be taken in a country aw'd by garrisons and known to be disaffected. But while Donald was thus anxiously waiting for certain intelligence of their plans, what was his astonishment to hear of the young adventurer's landing in the wilds of Moidart, a savage district on the sea coast, in that neighbourhood where his standard was first display'd. After remaining there in concealment for a few days, he came to Auchnacarrie.[2]

Lochiel strongly express'd his sorrow and concern at seeing him so ill provided, and so slenderly attended. He strongly dissuaded him from showing himself till more suitable preparation should be made for his reception, and till a force should arrive on the coast strong enough to encourage and support.

Full of the ardour of youth and presumption of sanguine hope, the Prince remain'd unmov'd by the chieftain's arguments, and began to reproach him with a circumspection and

---

[1] Should be 'sisters.' Cf. p. 318 note.
[2] The Prince landed at Borradale on 25th July 1745. He met Lochiel there, and does not seem to have visited Auchnacarrie at that time.

coolness incompatible with genuine attachment, and which tended to damp the zeal of his more courageous followers. Seeing no persuasion could deter the leader from prosecuting this rash adventure, he arrang'd his papers and affairs, as a man setting out on a journey from whence he was not to return, and with ominous sadness collected all his force, and having once embark'd in this perilous enterprise, he exerted himself with as much determin'd courage and eager perseverance as if it had been undertaken with his entire approbation. The sequel, it is well known, fully justified his objections, and the intermediate narrative of public transactions includes the account of the gallantry, clemency and good faith which distinguish'd his conduct during the course of that unhappy contest. Had not his judgment so far contradicted his wishes, he might have given still more effectual aid to the cause which a vain waste of blood and courage adorn'd without strengthening it. He sacrific'd himself and his followers, but could not be induc'd to persuade his brothers-in-law to engage in a cause so hopeless. Most of these, however, wish'd well to it, and some in consequence of previous impressions join'd it.

This chief was wounded in the leg in the battle of Culloden, and afterwards convey'd by some faithful followers to a shealing in the gloomy and unknown recesses at the west end of Loch Erroch. In the meantime, the house of Achnacarrie was burnt and plunder'd, as well as the Castle of Glengarrie, and the district inhabited by Lochiel's followers ravag'd with unsparing cruelty; the details of this would be painful to humanity. Attracted by the fame of the advantages gain'd by the highlanders at Falkirk and Prestonpans, John of Lochiel came over from France and landed on the coast of Lochaber, a very short time before the final blow which scatter'd irretrievably his adherents.[1] He return'd in the same vessel after taking a last look of the scene of his past authority and happiness. He return'd, I know not on what account, privately to Scotland a few years after, and died in Edinburgh.[2]

---

[1] He was present with the reinforcements which marched from Perth to Falkirk before the battle.

[2] Mackenzie's *History of the Camerons* says he died in exile at Newport in Flanders in 1747 or early in 1748.

It is hard to say what could particularly exasperate the conquerors at a character so distinguish'd for mildness and probity as that of Lochiel,[1] yet his blood seem'd to be sought after with the most rancorous perseverance. It was known that his wound made escape from the country difficult, if not impossible, and a considerable reward was offer'd for apprehending him. In the plunder of the house of Achnacarrie, a picture was found drawn for Lochiel, and accounted a good likeness. This was given to a party of the military, who were despatch'd over Corryaric in search of the unfortunate invalid. On the top of this mountain they met Macpherson of Urie, who being a tall, handsome man, of a fair and pleasing aspect, they concluded to be the original of the portrait they carried with them. This anecdote I had from Urie himself. He was a Jacobite, and had been *out* as the phrase was then. The soldiers seiz'd him, and assur'd him he was a d——d rebel, and that his title was Lochiel. He in return assur'd them that he was neither d——d nor a rebel, nor by any means Lochiel. When he understood, however, that they were a party in search of Lochiel, going in the very direction where he lay conceal'd, he gave them room finally to suppose he was the person they sought. They return'd to Fort Augustus where the Duke of Cumberland then lay, in great triumph with their prisoner. Urie, as he expected from the indulgence of some about the Duke, was very soon set at liberty; and this temporary captivity had the wish'd-for effect of giving the younger Lochiel time to recover of his wounds and leave the kingdom. In his flight to France he was accompanied by his lady, the faithful and affectionate associate of his exile. His son was left under the care of his brother Fassfern,[2] being then a mere infant.[3] A daughter, Donalda, was afterwards born in France, but attach'd herself so fondly to her father that at his death,[4] which happen'd

---

[1] Donald nineteenth of Lochiel.

[2] John Cameron of Fassifern married Jean Campbell of Achallader, and their eldest son, Ewen, afterwards Sir Ewen, was the father of the well-known Colonel John Cameron of the 92nd Highlanders who fell at Quatre Bras.

[3] He was born in 1732.

[4] He died 26th October 1748, so the daughter cannot have been then fourteen if born after the '45.

when she was about fourteen, she pin'd away with grief and never recover'd. Lochiel was what is call'd colonel of a reform'd regiment in the French service; and having a peculiar faculty of attaching the affections of those among whom he liv'd, was particularly belov'd among his new friends as well as among the associates of his exile, and held in great respect by the unfortunate adventurer.

These unhappy exiles were for a while amus'd with fleeting projects; in consequence of one of these Lochiel and Clunie went to visit their Prince at a retreat on the upper Rhine, to which he had retir'd after his cruel and perfidious imprisonment at the Castle of Vincennes.[1]

They found him sunk in that lassitude which often succeeds long protracted agitation and smother'd sorrow. He was accompanied by Miss Walkinshaw and her daughter, afterwards Duchess of Albany. In this child and her mother his whole affections seem'd to centre. This was very mortifying to the two chiefs by whom that lady was consider'd as a spy for the English court. They left him after a short visit, under the dominion of his Delilah, and return'd hopeless and dejected. From this time Lochiel's health began to decline. Exile, terrible to all, was to him embitter'd by a separation from vassals so faithful and attach'd, and friends so numerous and so worthy as fell not to the lot of any other man.

Nor was the attachment of those affectionate followers altogether unavailing. The estate of Lochiel was forfeited like others, and paid a moderate rent to the crown, such as they had formerly given to their chief. The domain formerly occupied by the laird was taken on his behoof by his brother. The tenants brought each a horse, cow, colt, or heifer, as a free-will offering, till this ample grazing farm was as well stock'd as formerly. Not content with this they sent a yearly tribute of affection to their belov'd chief, independent of the rent they paid to the commissioners for the forfeited estates. Lochiel's lady and her daughter once or twice made a sorrowful pilgrimage among their friends and tenants. These last receiv'd them with a tenderness and respect which seem'd augmented by the adversity into which they were plunged.

---

[1] As the Vincennes incident took place after Lochiel's death, and before Cluny's arrival in France, the statement in the text cannot be literally correct.

Lochiel died, as was generally thought, of a broken heart, about the year [1748].

His daughter soon follow'd him, and his wife did not long survive this amiable exile, who seems to have something peculiarly estimable and endearing in his character. So much was he belov'd in life, and so tenderly lamented by his tribe and party. Being a man of deep feeling, his fate was thought to be accelerated by the vindictive cruelty which pursued his kindred. The violent death of Dr. Cameron [1] and the banishment of Fassfern, who both fell victims to the rancour of party, no doubt embitter'd, if they did not shorten his remaining days. It was a melancholy winding up of this catastrophe that his only son should fall a victim to the ill judg'd, tho' affectionate attachment of this generous tribe, yet so it was.

The young Lochiel,[2] tho' what the Scots call a landless laird, was cherish'd with enthusiasm by all the Camerons as the representative of their ancient chiefs. His friends, however, did not choose that he too should become a victim in a lost cause. They gave him a very good education, and at an early period procur'd for him a commission in the British army.

At an early age he married; and Government being soon after engag'd in levying men for the American War, found it convenient to use the agency of the attainted chiefs for that purpose. They, notwithstanding their poverty and privations, retaining an unbounded influence over the minds of their clans.

Lochiel was offered a company in General Fraser's regiment, the 71st,[3] provided he could raise it among his clan. This he soon and easily did, and march'd to Glasgow at the head of it, in order to embark on board some vessels then lying at Greenock under orders to sail for America.

While the regiment was about to embark, Lochiel was taken

---

[1] Dr. Archibald Cameron's judicial murder did not take place till 1753.

[2] On Donald's death his eldest son was John, who died in Edinburgh in 1762, unmarried and predeceased by his brother James. 'The Young Lochiel' here mentioned is accordingly Charles the third son. He married a Miss Marshall in 1767 and died in 1776.   [3] Cf. p. 275.

ill with the measles, which assum'd rather an alarming appearance, and for the present prevented his embarking with his company. Finding the oldest lieutenant about to assume a temporary command, they positively refus'd to stir, asserting 'that they had not engag'd with King George but Lochiel, that they would follow him wherever he went, but would obey no other leader.' Finally, in the Green of Glasgow, they made a circle round the adjutant, laid down their arms, and [positively] refus'd to take them up again till order'd by their chief. Lochiel, who lodg'd near the scene of [this disorder],[1] was soon inform'd of all those particulars. Tho' ill in bed, and very feverish at the time, he got up, dress'd, and with his sword in his hand went down and harangued his people; representing to them that unless they went on board their conduct would be imputed to disaffection, and thus become ruinous and disgraceful to him, and that he hop'd to overtake them at Greenock before they embark'd. They took up their arms, huzza'd their chief, and immediately resumed their march. Enfeebl'd by his effort and exhausted by agitation, Lochiel again took his bed and died in a very few days after, in consequence of going out in a raw misty day of November, when he was so unequal to that exertion.

Most of this devoted company perish'd in the contest which follow'd, and during which Fraser's regiment was thrice renew'd, and lost 2400 men. The present Lochiel is the son of this last chief, and to him the estate was restor'd sometime about the year '85.

*Jordanhill, Decr. 24th*, 1808.

---

[1] He was ill in London at the time, and at once hurried to Glasgow.

# INDEX

ABERDEEN, 47, 96, 103, 112, 113, 131.
Aberlady, 53, 55.
Abertarf, 305, 306.
Achnacarrie, 309, 310, 316, 325 and *n*, 326, 327.
Admiralty court, 196, 208.
Advocates, proposed regulations for, 196.
Aird, the, 255, 256, 259, 274, 275.
Airlie, earl of, 137.
Allhamstoks. *See* Auldhamstocks.
Alloa house, 156, 166 *n*, 181-183.
Alured, colonel, 112 *n*, 135.
Alyth (Eliot), 103, 112 and *n*, 135.
*Ane True Accompt of the Preservation*, etc., 102.
Angus, William, 9th earl of, 110.
Annandale family, 3.
Anne, queen, 317, 318, 321.
Applegirth. *See* Jardine.
Arbuthnot, viscount, 116, 126, 129, 132.
Argyll, Archibald, earl of, 19, 45, 46, 59, 76, 98; letter to, from the earl of Holland, 37.
—— John, duke of, 146, 188.
Armies to be dissolved, 91.
Arnot, sir John, of Berswick, lord provost, 4.
—— Marion, 6.
—— Rachel, 4, 6, 7.
Articles of pacification signed, 90.
Arundel and Surrey, Thomas Howard, earl of, 71 and *n*, 77.
Athol, earl of, 114.
Atterbury, Francis, bishop of Rochester, 149-151, 153, 154, 161, 169.
Auldhamstocks, 53, 63.
Avignon, 158, 159.
Axtillis, Mr., 123.
Aytoun, 43, 46, 47, 57.

BAILLIE, ROBERT, principal of Glasgow university, 8, 14, 18, 19.
—— —— of Jerviswood, 10-13.
Baker, rev. S. Ogilvy, 111, 135 *n*.
Balcanqual, Dr., dean of Durham, 71 *n*.
Balcarres, lord, 135.
Ballacheulish. *See* Stewart, John.
Ballandalloch, 268.
Balmayne. *See* Ramsay, sir William.
Balmerino, lord, 52, 59, 97, 242 *n*.
Balnagarro, lands of, 135 *n*.
Bannerman, sir Alex., of Elsick, 120 *n*, 121.
Barclay, colonel David, of Urie, 317 *n*.
—— Jean, 317 and *n*, 318 and *n* -320.
—— Robert, of Urie, 308, 309 and *n*, 317 *n*.
—— —— grandson, 321 and *n*.
*Baress alledgances ansred*, 102, 109.
Barra, 53, 56.
—— island of, 301.
Barras. *See* Ogilvie, George.
—— lands of, 109.
Bass Rock, 104.
Beaufort, 274 and *n*.
Beaulieu abbey, 274.
Belladrum, 274.
Berwick, 14, 42, 44, 50, 68, 92, 95.
—— duke of, 164 *n*, 308, 324.
Bingly, lord, 245, 246.
Birks, near Berwick, 32.
Bishops, 64; abolition of, 76, 85, 87, 95; to be answerable to general assembly, 83, 94; ministers' oath of obedience to, 85; all the people 'bade hang the bishops,' 95.
Blacader, laird of. *See* Home, sir John.
Black mount, 311.
Blackness castle, 199, 210.
'Black stock,' the, or table dormant of the castle, 119 *n*.

Blandford, William, marquis of, 188 and *n.*
Bolingbroke, lord, 144 and *n*, 159, 164 *n*, 166.
Bolshan, Forfar, 128.
Bolton (Bontin), 53.
Borthrik, Mr., 63.
Bothans, 53, 56.
Boyle, Henry. *See* Carleton, lord.
Boyne, lord, 92, 95.
Braemar, 158, 183.
Breadalbayn, lord, 172.
Bressey, Benjamin, 11.
Bretuile, M., French secretary of war, 225.
Bridge of Dee, 96.
Bristowe, Catherine, wife of general Fraser, 276 *n.*
—— John, 276 *n.*
Brodick, 104.
Bruce, captain, 181.
—— sir William of Stenhouse, 5, 7.
Buchanan of Drumakiln betrays the marquis of Tullibardine, 254, 280-284.
—— captain John, of Drumakiln, 283, 284, 289, 290, 294.
Burnet, Gilbert, bishop of Salisbury, 4, 9.
—— Robert, lord Crimond, 5.
Burntisland, town of, letter to, from Hamilton, 59, 60.

CALLART, 306.
Cameron of Dungallon, 321.
—— of Glendessery, 306, 320 and *n*, 321 and *n.*
—— of Lochiel, memoir of the family of, 298-330.
—— Allan, of Lochiel, 307 *n.*
—— Dr. Archibald, 319, 329 and *n.*
—— Charles, of Lochiel, 329 *n*, 330 and *n.*
—— Christian, 320.
—— Donald, of Lochiel, 278, 318 *n*, 319, 323-329.
—— Donalda, 327 and *n.*
—— Ewen, of Fassifern, 278 and *n.*
—— sir Ewen, of Lochiel, 308-318 and *n*, 321, 323 *n*; MS. memoir of, 278 and *n.*
—— Jean, 320.
—— John, of Fassifern, 319, 327 and *n*, 329.
—— —— colonel, 278 *n*, 327 *n.*
—— —— of Lochiel, 253, 254, 277, 308, 317 and *n*, 318-326 and *n.*
—— —— of Lochiel, son of Donald, 329 *n.*

Cameron, Katherine, 321 *n.*
—— Margaret, 279.
—— Marjory, 321 *n.*
Campbell of Auchalader, 287, 321.
—— of Auchlyne, 321 and *n.*
—— of Barcaldine, 321.
—— of Glendaruel, 159, 172 and *n.*
—— Alexander, his *Grampians left desolate*, 287 and *n.*
—— Isabel, 317 *n.*
—— sir James, of Auchinbreck, 324.
—— Jean, of Achallader, 327 *n.*
—— Primrose, second wife of lord Lovat, 262 and *n*, 269, 270.
Camsfield, 54.
Capoch in Lochaber, 107, 114.
Carlaverock, 55.
Carleton, Henry Boyle, lord, 245, 246.
Carlisle, 42, 95.
Caroline, queen, 10.
Carter, Eliza, 297.
Cassilis, earl of, 95, 96.
Castle Dunie, 256, 260, 262, 269, 274.
Castle Grant, 268, 269.
Charles I. of England, 65, 66, 68, 70, 77, 80, 90; his dislike of presbytery, 21; his ecclesiastical policy, 22, 23; accepts responsibility of service-book, 28; prepares army against Scotland, 32; his demands and arguments, 48, 78, 82; his *Large Declaration*, 71 and *n*; his *Declaration*, 86, 90, 91, 95; Scots remonstrate with, 92.
Charles II. of England, 104, 107, 108, 114, 117, 125, 127, 131, 136, 137; hates Wariston, 18; coronation of, 102; desires the Honours be delivered to earl Marischal, 115; letter from, to countess Marischal, 115; letter to, from countess Marischal, 121; commands Ogilvie to render Honours to earl Marischal, 123 *n*, 128; makes John Keith knight marischal, 132; letter of, to earl of Middleton, 134.
Charles XII. of Sweden, 146, 241 and *n.*
Charslie wood, 97.
Cherry isle, Loch Ness, 304.
Clackmannan, 181.
Clanranald family, 287 and *n.*
Clepham, colonel, 174 and *n.*
Closeburn, 54.
Clunes, 306.
Cobet (Cobbeet), colonel, governor of Dundee, 114, 136.
Cockburn, Adam, of Ormiston, 9.

## INDEX

Cockburnspath, 46, 47, 53.
Coke (Cooke), John, secretary, 68, 70.
Coldingham, 47, 57, 59.
Coldstream, 47.
College of justice, 36, 48, 67.
Cologne (Collen), 121.
Colquhoun, miss, 254, 280.
—— sir James, of Balvie, 9.
Coluberdy, 120.
Committee of estates, 103, 127, 128.
Commissioners (Scots), subscribe articles of pacification, 90.
Commonwealth, army of the, 104.
Congalton, Patrick, of Congalton, 5.
*Considerations . . . for Irland on a Restoration*, 213.
Conzier, Mr., 56.
Corryaric, 327.
Court of session, 196, 208.
Covenant, national, 13, 25, 26.
Covenanters, 33, 69; acquit the king but accuse the bishops, 27; desire a free general assembly, 28; their discussions with Hamilton, 29; forbid king's proclamation to be read, 32.
Craig, Elizabeth, wife of James Johnstone, 4, 5, 7 *n*, 12.
—— sir James Gibson, 33.
—— Margaret, 6, 8.
—— sir Thomas, of Riccarton, 4, 5.
Craigie, 129.
Craignish, 251.
Cramond, 52.
Crawford, earl of, 135.
Crechtoun, James, 54.
Cromwell, Oliver, 19, 102.
Culloden, battle of, 326.
Cuming clan, 304 and *n*.
Cuninghame, lady Catherine, 9.
—— Francisa, 9.
—— sir James, of Glengarnock, 9.
—— William, 35.

Dalentay, 289.
Dalhousie, earl of, 35, 46, 55.
Dalkeith, 47, 55.
Dalrymple, Mr., of Clackmannan, 181.
Dalziel, lord of, 69.
Darien settlement, 322.
Deane, major-general, commander-in-chief of English forces, 119 and *n*.
Declaration read before Munroe's regiment, 95. *See also* Charles I.
Dickson, David, 58, 59.
Dillon, general, 161 and *n*, 167, 168, 171, 173, 212, 223-225, 227 *n*.
*Directions concerning the Monument to be erected in the church of Alloa*, 192.

Dirleton, 53, 55.
Donaldson, major, 276.
Douglas, Archibald, 3.
—— Elizabeth, 110.
—— Isabel, marchioness of Montrose, 114 *n*.
—— John, of Barras, 110.
Drumakiln. *See* Buchanan.
Drumlanrig, lord, 54.
Drummond of Balhaldy, 321 *n*.
—— general Wm., of Cromlix, viscount Strathallan, 10.
Dubois, cardinal, 167, 223.
Duff, lord, 142 *n*.
Dumbarton, 104, 199, 210, 311.
Dumfries, 52-55.
Dun, lord, 180, 184, 189.
Dunbar, 35, 42, 43, 46, 53.
Dundee, 114, 136.
Dunfermline, earl of, 63-70.
Dungallan, 306.
Dunglas, 46, 51, 63, 95.
Dunnottar castle, 102-108, 116, 118 *n*, 119 *n*, 122, 125, 126 *n*, 127 *n*, 128, 129, 130, 131, 136 and *n*, 199, 210.
Duns, 46, 47, 49, 50, 58, 61-65, 89, 97.
Durie, lord, 59, 76.

East Lothian. *See* Haddington.
Edinburgh, 24, 47, 48, 58, 83, 86, 90, 95, 97; committee of, 49, 57; letters to the committee of, 43, 44, 62; contributions of, to the army, 47, 97; provost and bailies of, 52, 56; Mar's proposals for the improvement of, 201-203.
—— castle, 92, 95, 96, 199, 210.
Elders, ruling, question of, 30, 93.
Elie, Fife, 113, 136.
Eliot. *See* Alyth.
Elsick. *See* Bannerman (Alex.).
Elsinford, 53.
Erskine, cardinal, 291.
—— of Pittodrie, 158.
—— lord, 42, 51.
—— John. *See* Mar, earl of.
—— sir John, of Alva, 188 and *n*.
—— lady Mary, countess marischal, 110.
—— Thomas, lord, 157, 168 and *n*.
—— captain William, 174 and *n*.
—— barony of, 142.
—— family of, 142 and *n*.
Ethrington, 43, 44, 49.
Exchequer court, 196, 208.
Eyemouth (Haymouth), 43, 44, 46, 47, 57.

# INDEX

FARQUHAR, sir Walter, 286 and *n*, 290, 293, 294.
Farquharson of Invercauld, 142 *n*.
Ferguson, miss, 253, 254.
Fetteresso (Fitersso), countess of Marshall's jointure house, 112.
Fielding, Mr., 293.
Fife, 48, 52, 54.
Findlater, earl of, 143.
Fishery laws of England and Scotland, 2.
Fisherraw, 55.
Fishwick, 49.
Fleming (Phleeming), lord, 51, 61.
Flether, Christian, 111.
Forbes, Alexander. *See* Pitsligo, lord.
Foresterseat, lady, 8.
—— lord, 5, 12.
Forfeited estates, 199, 211.
Fort Augustus, 327.
Forth and Clyde canal, 203.
Fort-William, 302, 310, 324.
Foster's regiment, 48.
Foulis, James, baron of Colinton, 4 *n*.
Fraser, Alexander, second son of lord Lovat, 262 and *n*, 270 and *n*.
—— Amelia, 256 *n*.
—— Janet, of Lovat, 320 *n*.
—— Simon. *See* Lovat, lord.
—— general Simon, son of lord Lovat, 262, 271 *n*, 275, 276 and *n*.
—— Sybilla, daughter of lord Lovat, 269, 270.
—— Thomas, of Beaufort, 255 and *n*.
Frasers of Brea, 271 and *n*.

GALLOWAY, earl of, 54.
Garlies, lord, 161 and *n*.
Garvald (Garvitt), 53, 56.
General assemblies, 30, 76, 81, 82, 86-88, 93, 94.
—— —— (Glasgow), 31, 70, 83, 84, 85, 89, 93, 96.
Geneva, 159 and *n*, 160, 189.
George I., 144.
George III., 297.
Gibb, Mr., architect, 190 and *n*.
Gibson, sir Alex., of Durie, 6, 8.
Gile, sir Harie, 97.
Gleg, Dr., 277.
Glenbervy, lord, 298.
Glencairn, earl of, 114, 135.
Glencoe, massacre of, 313.
Glendessery. *See* Cameron.
Gloucester, duke of, 123.
Godolphin, lord, 245, 257, 258, 279.
Gordon, duchess of, 290.
—— general, 159, 323.

Gordon, Alexander, of Beldorney, 315 and *n*.
Gortuleg, 264.
Goswick, 42.
Graden, lady, 13.
Grahame, George, of Morphine, 121 and *n*.
—— colonel Gordon, 276.
Grainger, rev. James, minister of Kineff, 105, 108, 109-113, 116, 117, 126 and *n*, 129, 130, 131, 135 ; his declaration anent the Honours, 116, 125 ; his action anent the Honours, 125-128 ; letters from, to countess Marischal, 131.
—— Mrs., conveys the Honours from Dunnottar, 105, 109, 116, 125, 130, 135.
Grange, lord, 180, 181, 188, 189.
Grant of Ballandalloch, 261.
—— of Coriemony, 292.
—— of Glenmoriston, 289, 321.
—— laird of, 301.
—— miss, of Arndilly, 296, 297.
—— Mrs., of Laggan, 251, 252; letters from, to sir Henry Steuart, 253-271, 277, 284, 288 and *n*, 293, 295 ; letter to, from sir John Macpherson, 290.
—— Charles, 293 and *n*.
—— rev. James, 251.
—— sir James, of Freuchie, 307 *n*.
—— Margaret, wife of Simon, lord Lovat, 261 and *n*, 268.
—— family, 307.
Gravelines, 158, 159.
Gunne, colonel, 95.
Guthrie, rev. James, 7, 17.

HADDINGTON, 35, 43, 46, 52, 53.
—— earl of, 63.
Hamilton, marquis of, 23, 27, 32, 78, 87, 88, 114 ; letter from, to captain Watson, 59 ; letter from, to town of Burntisland, 60 ; answer from Burntisland, 60 ; intercepted letter of, to lord Ogilvie, 68.
—— sir Patrick, 63.
Hatsell, Mr., 293.
Hay of Dunfermline, 16.
Hay, colonel, secretary to the chevalier, 149 and *n*, 153, 154, 166, 168, 169, 177, 223.
—— Alexander. *See* Foresterseat, lord.
—— Helen. *See* Wariston, lady.
Hemp, cultivation of, in Ireland, 214.
Henderson, Alexander, 25, 31, 42, 58, 76, 85 *n*.
Hepburn, (Hebroun) Adam, 63.
—— sir Adam, of Humbie, 10.
—— Thomas, 10.

# INDEX

Henryson, Edward, 4 *n*.
—— sir Thomas, lord Chesters, 4 *n*.
Heriot, Agnes, wife of James Foulis, 4 *n*.
—— Helen, 4 *n*.
—— Robert, of Lymphoy, 4 *n*.
Highlands, proposals for the formation of highland regiments, 219, 246, 291 *n*; English ignorance of the, 258, 272, ; characteristics of highlanders, 288; highland music, 291; manners and customs, 298-304; highland poetry, 303; highland forays, 306, 307; famine in, 318.
Holland, 107, 113.
—— earl of, 39, 42, 46, 48, 49, 61, 64, 93; letters from, 37 and *n*; letters to, from the Scots army, 39, 42.
Home or Hume, captain, 51.
—— earl of, 46, 49, 51, 52, 63.
—— George, of Graden, 11.
—— sir John, of Blacader, 39, 40, 43, 46, 48.
—— John, 278 and *n*, 297.
—— castle, 199.
Honours of Scotland, 102, 105, 106, false receipts of, 107; delivered to charge of Ogilvie, 112, 116; in charge of Mr. James Grainger, 125; buried by him, 112, 113; how conveyed from Dunnottar, 133, 135; said to have been sent to Paris, 114; countess of Marischal's account of, to king, 121, 122; dispute between Grainger and Ogilvie anent, 128, 129.
Humbie, 53, 56.
*Humble desires of H.M.'s subjects*, 70.
Hume. *See* Home.
Huntly, marquis of, 32, 96.
Huton, 59.

Inchcolme, 35.
*Information against all mistaking of H.M. declaration*, 89, 96.
Inglis, James, of Ingliston, 5.
Innerwick, 53.
Invergarrie, castle, 310, 316.
Inverlochy castle, 199, 210, 220.
Ireland, schemes for the government of, 166, 167 and *n*; a good understanding between Ireland and Scotland desirable, 201; proposals for, on a restoration, 213; Irish troops for service in France, 231; independence of, 231, 232, 234.
Islay, lord, 188.

Jackson, John, 5.
James vi., his attempts to restore episcopal government, 22; on the king's negative voice in parliament, 75 *n*.
Jamesone, George, his portrait of Wariston, 33.
Jardine of Applegirth, 54.
Jedburgh, 46, 51, 61.
Johnson, Dr., criticisms on, 272, 289.
Johnston of Hilton, Berwickshire, 3 *n*, 5.
—— lord, 46, 54.
—— Alexander, 8, 9.
—— Archibald, Wariston's grandfather, merchant of Edinburgh, 3, 4.
—— Archibald, of Wariston. *See* Wariston, lord.
—— —— son of Wariston, 8.
—— Beatrix, 5.
—— David, 7 *n*.
—— Elizabeth, 10.
—— Euphan, 12.
—— Gavin, 3.
—— Helen, 11.
—— James, merchant of Edinburgh, 4, 7 *n*, 12.
—— —— 5.
—— —— secretary for Scotland, 1, 9, 10, 17.
—— —— son of the secretary, 10.
—— —— of Beirholm, 3.
—— Janet, 5, 7, 11.
—— Joseph, 5,
—— Margaret, 11.
—— Rachel, 5, 10, 11.
—— Samuel, advocate, of Sciennes, 4, 6.
Jordanhill, 277.
Justiciary court, 196.

Keith, Anne, countess of Morton, 114 *n*.
—— John, earl of Kintore, 101, 103, 104, 106, 107, 109; created earl of Kintore, 110, 114, 117, 118, 120 and *n*, 122, 126, 129, 131-138; his adventures abroad and in Scotland, 131, 136.
—— Robert, of Whiterigs, 127 and *n*, 128.
—— William. *See* Marischal, earl.
Kelso, 37, 42, 51, 52, 57, 59, 61.
Ker, lord, 46, 58.
Killicrankie, battle of, 308 and *n*, 310.
Kilmallie, 298.
Kinneff, 117, 118 *n*, 131, 111.
—— church, 105, 106.

Kinneff, minister of. *See* Grainger, rev. James.
Kinnoul, earl of, 95.
Kintore, earl of. *See* Keith, John.
Kintyre, 19.
Kirkcaldy, 52.
Kirkcudbright, lord, 52, 54, 92.
Knighthood, military order of, 211, 212.
Knight Marischal of Scotland, office of, 133.

LAG, laird, 54.
Laggan, 251.
Lamamonach, 274.
Lambingtoune, 52.
Lansdown, lord, 187 and *n*.
*Large Declaration concerning the late tumults*, 71 *n*.
Laud's liturgy, Charles's copy of, 28 *n*.
Lauder, 61.
Lauderdale, duke of, 165.
*Legacie to Scotland*, 151, 155, 156, 194-205.
Legard, sir John, 295.
Leith, 35, 45, 48, 159, 199, 203; fortifications of, 33, 92; privileges of, 203.
Leslie, general Alexander, 33, 35, 42, 46, 51-53, 58, 61, 63.
—— Robin, 63 *n*, 64.
Letter sent to the shires of Scotland from Dunbar, 35.
Letteron, 215 and *n*.
Lighton, col. David, 104 and *n*, 120 and *n*.
Lindsay, lord, 35, 43, 46, 96.
Linen manufacture of Ireland, 214.
Lochaber, 280.
'Lochaber no more,' 320, 321.
Locharkaig, 310.
Lochend, 40.
Loch Erroch, 326.
Lochgarry, 107, 114 and *n*, 136.
Lochiel. *See* Cameron.
Loch Lomond, 280.
Loch Ness, 304.
Lockhart of Carnwath, 145, 152, 155.
London, 103, 108, 127 *n*, 131, 135; tower of, 122.
Lord advocate, 138.
Lord chamberlain, 88, 93.
Lorraine, 163.
Lothian, earl of, 42, 46, 51, 57-59, 61, 63.
Lothians, the, 54, 97.
Loudoun, earl of, 25, 35, 43, 55, 70-72, 78, 85 *n*, 92, 96, 97.
—— Hugh, earl of, 187 and *n*.
Lovat, lord, 305, 306.

Lovat, Archibald, lord, 262 *n*.
—— Hugh, lord, 255 and *n*, 256.
—— —— of Fraserdale, 255 *n*, 256 *n*.
—— Simon Fraser, lord, 172 and *n*, 253, 254, 255 and *n*: his outrage on the dowager lady Lovat, 256, 274; at the court of St. Germains, 256; a Jacobite agent in London, 257; transfers his services to the government, 257, 258; his popularity in the highlands, 259; his hospitality at castle Dunie, 260, 261; marriage of, 261; his second marriage, 262; intrigues for a rising in the north, 263; his interview with prince Charles after Culloden, 265; taken prisoner, 265 and *n*; his behaviour in the Tower, 266, 267; character of, 268; MS. account of his life, 271.
—— dowager lady, 256, 274 and *n*.
—— master of, 263.
—— estates, 256 and *n*, 257 and *n*, 274, 305.
Lumgair, lands of, 135 *n*.
Lyon king of arms, 96, 117, 137.
Lyttleton, lady, 276.

MACDONALD of Glengarry, 305, 316 *n*.
—— of Morar, 321 *n*.
—— of Teindrich, 289.
—— Æneas, of Glengarry, 309 *n*.
—— Alexander, 309-316.
—— Hector, of Boisdale, 284.
—— Julia, 315 and *n*, 316.
—— William, tutor of Sleat, 321 *n*.
MacGregor of Bohaudie, 287, 321 and *n*.
M'Kell, procurator, 126, 132.
Mackenzie, Alexander, 255 *n*, 256 *n*.
—— sir Alexander, of Coul, 11.
—— Catherine, 251.
—— Henry, 287 and *n*.
—— Roderick, 11.
—— —— of Prestonhall, 255 *n*.
—— sir Roderick, of Scatwell, 261.
—— lady, of Scatwell, 269.
Maclean of Ardgour, 321.
—— of Kingarloch, 320.
—— of Lochbuy, 321 and *n*.
Maclellans, the, 289 *n*.
MacNicol, rev Donald, his *Remarks on Johnson's journey to the Hebrides*, 287 and *n*.
Macniels of Barra, 301, 302.
Macpherson of Benchar, 271, 279.
—— of Cluny, 263 and *n*, 277, 280, 320 and *n*, 321, 328 and *n*.
—— of Fleigherty, 278.

# INDEX

Macpherson of Urie, 327.
—— sir Eneas, 278 and *n*.
—— Evan, schoolmaster, 286, 292, 293.
—— major Evan, 278, 279, 294, 295.
—— James, 271, 287, 291, 292.
—— John, D.D., 285 and *n*.
—— sir John, 285-289, 294, 296, 298; letter from, to Mrs. Grant, 290.
—— Lachlan, of Nuid, 320 *n*.
—— Martin, minister of Sleat, 285-287, 296.
Macraes, the, 289 and *n*.
Macvicar, Duncan, 251.
Mar, Charles, tenth earl of, 141.
—— John, seventh earl of, 110.
—— —— eleventh earl of, 141 and *n*, 150-152 and *n*, 154, 163; sketch of his career, 142-149; extract of letter from, to the chevalier, 146; his *Legacie* to his son, Thomas, lord Erskine, 157-191; his *Memorial to the Regent Orleans*, 152 and *n*, 153, 154 and *n*, 167 and *n*, 168, 169; sent into Scotland to effect a rising, 164 and *n*, 170, 176; opposed to the union, 163, 165; his 'Scheme ... for the government of Scotland,' 151, 165, 194-205; his *Directions concerning the monument to be erected in Alloa church*, 192, 193 and *n*; his *Legacie to Scotland*, 194-205, letters to, from the chevalier, 206-211; letters from, to the chevalier, 223, 244; his *Memorial to the Duke of Orleans*, 223; letter from, to the duke of Orleans, 226.
—— lady, 160, 176, 177, 189.
—— John Thomas, earl of, 156.
—— lady Mary, 141.
—— Philadelphia, countess of, 156.
Marischal, dowager-countess, 101, 103, 105, 107, 108, 110-122, 125, 127, 131, 135-138; letter to, from Middleton, 115; letter to, from the king, 115; letter to, from George Ogilvie, 118; letter to, from Grainger, 131; letter from, to Charles II., 121; letter in favour of, from Charles II., 134.
—— earl, 46, 109, 112, 115, 122, 123 and *n*, 126 *n*, 128, 129-132, 137; parliament delivers Honours to his custody, 102; taken prisoner, 103, 112, 135.
—— George, fifth earl, 135 *n*.
—— —— eighth earl, 134 and *n*.
—— William, sixth earl, 110, 114 *n*.
Marlborough, lord, 245.

Maryburgh. *See* Fort William.
Martin, captain, 120.
Maule, Patrick, earl of Panmure, 110.
Maxwells, the, 52.
May, isle of, 35.
Mearns, the, 135 *n*.
Meldrum, Robert, Leslie's secretary, 58, 61, 63 *n*.
*Memoranda for Lords Rothes and Loudon*, 72-76.
*Memorial of John Earl of Mar to the Duke of Orleans*, 152 and *n*, 153, 154 and *n*, 155, 167 and *n*, 168, 169, 223, 228.
Menzies (Minize), Mr., 189.
Merse, the, 49, 51.
Middleton, general, 107, 109, 113, 114, 116, 130, 136, 137; letter from, to the countess Marischal, 115; letter to, from Charles II., 134.
Midlothian, 52.
Military order of knighthood, 218.
Militia for Scotland, 216-221.
Ministers, of Scotland, letter from the army to, 45.
Monk, general, 114, 136, 137.
Montebello, 160.
Montgomery, lord, 35, 55.
Montrose, James, first marquis of, 32, 33, 35, 46, 55, 92, 95, 96, 303.
—— James, second marquis of, 114 and *n*, 136.
—— papers, 289.
Moray, Robert, 188 and *n*.
—— William, of Abercairney, 188.
Morham (Norhame), 53, 56.
Morison, Helen, 6.
Morphine, laird of. *See* Grahame.
Morton, earl of, 12, 63, 95, 114 *n*.
Munro, col., 41 and *n*, 46, 51-54, 57, 61.
Murray, Amelia, 255 *n*.
—— sir Patrick, 52, 53.
Musselburgh, 47, 55.

Napier, lord, 59, 97.
National covenant. *See* Covenant.
Newcastle, duke of, 268.
Newgrange, 132.
Newhaven, 48, 52.
Nicholson, sir Thomas, 76.
Nidsdaile, lord, 54, 55.
Nisbet, James, 6.
—— sir John, of Dirleton, 6.
—— Patrick, lord Eastbank, 6.
North Berwick, 51, 53, 55.

Officers of State, 15, 204, 205.
Ogilvie, David, 110.

## INDEX

Ogilvie, sir George, of Barras, 101-119 *n*, 121-123, 125-132, 135 *n*, 137, 138; letter from, to countess Marischal, 118; letter to, from his son William, 123.
—— Mrs., 104-106, 136.
—— John, of Balnagarro and Chapelton, 135 *n*.
—— dame Margaret, second wife of George, fifth earl Marischal, 135 *n*.
—— lord, 68-69, 110, 137.
—— sir William, of Barras, 101, 108-110, 123, 124, 126, 130, 131.
—— letter from, to his father, 123.
—— William, of Lumgair, 110, 135 *n*.
Oliphant, John, 51.
Orford, earl of, 253.
Orleans, duke of, 178; Mar's *Memorial* to, 152 and *n*, 153, 154 and *n*, 167 and *n*, 168, 169, 223; letter to, from Mar, enclosing the *Memorial*, 226.
Ormiston, 56, 254.
Ormond, duke of, 148, 168, 245.

PANMURE, lord, 110, 279 and *n*.
Paris, 106, 107, 113, 114, 136.
Parliament of Ireland, proposals for, 213.
—— of Scotland, 66, 75, 77, 91.
Paterson, Mr., 159 and *n*, 173.
—— sir Hugh, of Bannockburn, 159 *n*.
Patton, Alexander, 118.
Paxton, 59.
Peadie (Peddee), James, bailie of Montrose, 127 and *n*.
Pencaitland, 53, 56.
Penn, Sophia Margaret Juliana, 293 *n*.
—— Thomas, of Stoke-Pogis, 293 *n*.
Perth, five articles of, 6, 22, 83; commission of, 97; citadel of, 199.
—— duke of, 148 *n*.
Phanles, captain George, 56.
Phleeming. *See* Fleming.
Pitsligo, lord, 188 and *n*.
Pittodrie. *See* Erskine.
Porteus, Dr. Beilby, bishop of London, 293, 296.
—— Mrs., 296.
Poulett, John, baron, 9.
Presbyterian church government, 197.
Preston, battle of, 159.
—— John, of Fentonbarns, lord president, 6.
Prestongrange, lord, 6.
Prestonkirk, 53, 55.
Prestonpans, 55.
Primrose, Mr., 245.

Privy councils, 24, 67, 84, 102, 110, 195, 208.
Proclamations, 32, 38, 41, 57, 66, 67, 69.

QUEENSBERRY, duke of, 142, 163, 187 and *n*.

'RAINBOW,' the, in Leith roads, 59.
Rait, Alexander, 184.
Ramsay, Mr., 161, 162.
—— sir William, of Balmayne, 127 *n*.
Ratray, Ranald, of Ragnagallon, 289.
Ravelston house, Midlothian, 119 *n*.
'Reasons and grounds of our humble Desires,' 76, 77.
Rebellion of 1715, 145, 323; causes of its failure, 170.
—— of 1719, 146, 149.
—— of 1745, 254, 363, 364.
Records of the kingdom, 16.
Regalia, papers relative to the, 101.
Registers of general assembly recovered by Wariston, 16 *n*.
Relick, estate of, 274.
Renton, laird of, his charter kist, 49.
Ridpath, George 1 and *n*.
Rigg, Mr., 246.
Ripon, treaty of, 14.
Rivan, general, 95, 96.
Rollock, Harie, 96.
Rome, 160.
Rothes, earl of, 25, 35, 52, 55, 56, 70, 72, 77, 92, 95, 97, 98.
Ruddiman's *Caledonian Mercury*, 282 and *n*, 283.

SAFE conducts, 68, 69.
St. Giles, riot in, 1637, 24.
Saltoun, 53, 56.
Santlow, major, 275.
Scatterraw, 42, 52.
Scatwell, 262.
Schuyler, madam, 295 and *n*.
Scone, ceremony of coronation at, 102.
Scotland, letter to noblemen of, from the earl of Holland, 37; letter to the shires of, from the army, 45, 50; Mar's scheme for the government of, 194-205, 208; scheme for restoring the ancient military spirit of, 215.
Scots army, 41, 43, 46, 47, 58, 62, 63, 65, 66, 71, 92, 95, 97; provisions for, 46, 47, 53, 55, 56; money coined for, 56; letter from, to Edinburgh committee, 62.
—— fusileers, 141.

# INDEX 339

Scots troops for France, 200, 210, 216, 231.
Scott, Walter, of Highchester, earl of Tarras, 10.
Seaton house, 159.
Selkirk (Selchrig), letter from, 51.
—— earl of, 114, 287 *n.*
Service book, 24, 28 and *n*, 83.
Seton, Mr., of Delhi, 290.
—— miss, of Touch, 252.
Sharp, James, archbishop of St. Andrews, 8.
Shearer, James, 290.
Shrewsbury, duke of, 246.
Silver to be coined, 56, 57.
Skene, sir James, of Curriehill, 5, 7.
—— sir John, of Curriehill, 5.
'Some heads of H.M. treatie,' 93.
Southesk, lord, 63, 128 *n*, 225, 227.
Spott, 53.
Stair, lord, 163, 167 *n*, 187.
Stenton, 53, 56.
Steuart, sir Henry, of Allanton, 252; letters to, from Mrs. Grant of Laggan, 253-271, 277, 284, 288, 293, 295.
Stewart of Inveruity, 189.
—— Dr., 189.
—— Alexander, trial of, 275 and *n.*
—— sir James, of Coltness, lord advocate, memorial to, 134.
—— John, 59.
—— —— of Ballachelish, 254 and *n.*
—— sir John, of Coldingham, 57.
—— sir Lewis, advocate, 6.
Stirling, 59; castle of, 183, 184, 199, 210, 311.
—— of Craigbarnet, 289.
—— miss, of Kippendavy, 298.
Stonehaven, 119 *n.*
Straiton, captain, 242 *n.*
Stratheric, 259, 263, 264, 275, 280, 304.
Strath Glass, 274.
Straton, Arthur, of Snadown, 128.
Stuart, Dr., at Luss, 295.
—— hon. Mrs., 293 and *n.*
—— Charles Edward, 225, 325 and *n*, 328; his meeting with Lovat after Culloden, 265; MS. history of his campaigns in Scotland, 291.
—— Helen, 290.
—— Henry, cardinal of York, 291.
—— James Francis Edward [the chevalier], 145, 152 and *n*, 154, 159; extract of letter from the earl of Mar to, 146-149; approves of the earl of Mar's scheme for the government of Scotland, 151, 165, 166; sends Mar into Scotland, 163, 164 and *n*, 170, 176; letters to, from Mar, 223, 244; letters from, to the earl of Mar, 206-211.
Stuart, hon. W., primate of Ireland, 293 and *n.*
Suna, island of, bought by Wariston, 19.
Sunbury, 279, 297.
Supplication with the king's majesty, 64.
Sussex, duke of, 291.
Swinton, Helen, wife of Edward Henryson, 4 *n.*
—— John, of that ilk, 4 *n.*
Symmer, Mr., 189.

TANTALLON CASTLE, 35 and *n.*
Tarfe, the, 304.
Teviotdale, sheriff of, 42, 46, 58, 70.
Threve, siege of, 92.
*Thought (a) with regard to Scotland on the Memorial,* 241.
Traitors cannot be declared by proclamation, 67.
Tranent, 53, 55.
Trapaud, governor of Fort Augustus, 266.
Traquair, high treasurer, 23, 88.
Troup, Alexander, writer in Edinburgh, 126, 132.
Tuesden, Mr., 51.
Tullibardine, marquis of, 254, 256 *n*; account of his betrayal by Buchanan of Drumakiln, 280-284.
Tweed, the, 43, 59.
Tyndrum, 311.
Tynninghame, 53, 55.

UNION of England and Scotland, 2, 142-143, 162, 163, 165, 194, 207, 246.
Urbino, 160.

VANDRUSKE, major-general, 104.
Vane, sir Henry, 51.
Verney, sir Edmund, 65 and *n*, 66, 68.
—— sir Ralph, 32.
Vincennes castle, 328 and *n.*

WALKINSHAW, miss, 328.
Walpole, sir Robert, 10, 279.
Wariston, Archibald Johnstone, lord, 5, 8 *n*, 12-14, 25, 26, 31, 58, 61, 71, 72, 76, 78, 85, 97; birth and education of, 7, 8; his papers and diary, 1, 2; his character and opinions, 13-16; his long prayers,

16, 17; hated by Charles II., 18; frames the national covenant, 13, 25; Scots commissioner at pacification of Berwick, 14; accepts office from Cromwell, 19, 20; silenced by the king, 85, 87; execution of, 12, 13, 17, 18; portrait of, 33.
Wariston, lady, 8, 12.
Wariston's close, Edinburgh, 12.
Watson, captain, letter to, from Hamilton, 59.
—— John, 184.
Waughtone, 52, 53.
Wemyss, sir John, of Bogie, 11.
Wester Barras, lands of, 110.
Westminster assembly, 1643, 14.
Westnisbitt, 49.
Wetherburne, laird of, 51, 57.
Whitadder (Quhitteter), river, 59.

Whitehall, 115.
Whiterigs. *See* Keith, Robert
Whittinghame, 56.
Whittington, 53.
Whytekirk, 53, 55.
William III., 314, 318, 322.
Wilson, Lilly, 254.
—— Margaret, 254 *n.*
—— William, of Murray's Hall, 254 *n.*
Winnercom, captain, 36.
Woodend, 251.
Worcester, battle of, 102.
Wright of Loss, 287, 321 and *n.*
Writers to the signet, proposed regulations for, 197.

YESTER, lord, 35, 56.
York, 32.

# Scottish History Society.

## THE EXECUTIVE.

*President.*
THE EARL OF ROSEBERY, K.G., K.T., LL.D.

*Chairman of Council.*
DAVID MASSON, LL.D., Historiographer Royal for Scotland.

*Council.*
ÆNEAS J. G. MACKAY, Sheriff of Fife and Kinross.
Sir JOHN COWAN, Bart.
J. BALFOUR PAUL, Lyon King of Arms.
G. W. PROTHERO, Professor of History in the University of Edinburgh.
J. R. FINDLAY.
P. HUME BROWN, LL.D.
J. FERGUSON, Advocate.
Right Rev. JOHN DOWDEN, D.D., Bishop of Edinburgh.
Professor Sir THOMAS GRAINGER STEWART, M.D.
J. R. N. MACPHAIL, Advocate.
Rev. A. W. CORNELIUS HALLEN.
Sir ARTHUR MITCHELL, K.C.B., M.D., LL.D.

*Corresponding Members of the Council.*
C. H. FIRTH, Oxford; SAMUEL RAWSON GARDINER, LL.D.; Rev. W. D. MACRAY, Oxford; Rev. Professor A. F. MITCHELL, D.D., St. Andrews.

*Hon. Treasurer.*
J. T. CLARK, Keeper of the Advocates' Library.

*Hon. Secretary.*
T. G. LAW, Librarian, Signet Library.

# RULES

1. The object of the Society is the discovery and printing, under selected editorship, of unpublished documents illustrative of the civil, religious, and social history of Scotland. The Society will also undertake, in exceptional cases, to issue translations of printed works of a similar nature, which have not hitherto been accessible in English.

2. The number of Members of the Society shall be limited to 400.

3. The affairs of the Society shall be managed by a Council, consisting of a Chairman, Treasurer, Secretary, and twelve elected Members, five to make a quorum. Three of the twelve elected Members shall retire annually by ballot, but they shall be eligible for re-election.

4. The Annual Subscription to the Society shall be One Guinea. The publications of the Society shall not be delivered to any Member whose Subscription is in arrear, and no Member shall be permitted to receive more than one copy of the Society's publications.

5. The Society will undertake the issue of its own publications, *i.e.* without the intervention of a publisher or any other paid agent.

6. The Society will issue yearly two octavo volumes of about 320 pages each.

7. An Annual General Meeting of the Society shall be held on the last Tuesday in October.

8. Two stated Meetings of the Council shall be held each year, one on the last Tuesday of May, the other on the Tuesday preceding the day upon which the Annual General Meeting shall be held. The Secretary, on the request of three Members of the Council, shall call a special meeting of the Council.

9. Editors shall receive 20 copies of each volume they edit for the Society.

10. The owners of Manuscripts published by the Society will also be presented with a certain number of copies.

11. The Annual Balance-Sheet, Rules, and List of Members shall be printed.

12. No alteration shall be made in these Rules except at a General Meeting of the Society. A fortnight's notice of any alteration to be proposed shall be given to the Members of the Council.

# PUBLICATIONS

OF THE

# SCOTTISH HISTORY SOCIETY

*For the year* 1886-1887.

1. BISHOP POCOCKE'S TOURS IN SCOTLAND, 1747-1760. Edited by D. W. KEMP. (Oct. 1887.)

2. DIARY OF AND GENERAL EXPENDITURE BOOK OF WILLIAM CUNNINGHAM OF CRAIGENDS, 1673-1680. Edited by the Rev. JAMES DODDS, D.D. (Oct. 1887.)

*For the year* 1887-1888.

3. PANURGI PHILO-CABALLI SCOTI GRAMEIDOS LIBRI SEX. — THE GRAMEID: an heroic poem descriptive of the Campaign of Viscount Dundee in 1689, by JAMES PHILIP of Almerieclose. Translated and Edited by the Rev. A. D. MURDOCH.
(Oct. 1888.)

4. THE REGISTER OF THE KIRK-SESSION OF ST. ANDREWS. Part I. 1559-1582. Edited by D. HAY FLEMING. (Feb. 1889.)

*For the year* 1888-1889.

5. DIARY OF THE REV. JOHN MILL, Minister of Dunrossness, Sandwick, and Cunningsburgh, in Shetland, 1740-1803. Edited by GILBERT GOUDIE, F.S.A. Scot. (June 1889.)

6. NARRATIVE OF MR. JAMES NIMMO, A COVENANTER, 1654-1709. Edited by W. G. SCOTT-MONCRIEFF, Advocate. (June 1889.)

7. THE REGISTER OF THE KIRK-SESSION OF ST. ANDREWS. Part II. 1583-1600. Edited by D. HAY FLEMING. (Aug. 1890.)

# PUBLICATIONS

### *For the year* 1889-1890.

8. A LIST OF PERSONS CONCERNED IN THE REBELLION (1745). With a Preface by the EARL OF ROSEBERY and Annotations by the Rev. WALTER MACLEOD. (Sept. 1890.)

   *Presented to the Society by the Earl of Rosebery.*

9. GLAMIS PAPERS: The 'BOOK OF RECORD,' a Diary written by PATRICK, FIRST EARL OF STRATHMORE, and other documents relating to Glamis Castle (1684-89). Edited by A. H. MILLAR, F.S.A. Scot. (Sept. 1890.)

10. JOHN MAJOR'S HISTORY OF GREATER BRITAIN (1521). Translated and Edited by ARCHIBALD CONSTABLE, with a Life of the author by ÆNEAS J. G. MACKAY, Advocate. (Feb. 1892.)

### *For the year* 1890-1891.

11. THE RECORDS OF THE COMMISSIONS OF THE GENERAL ASSEMBLIES, 1646-47. Edited by the Rev. Professor MITCHELL, D.D., and the Rev. JAMES CHRISTIE, D.D., with an Introduction by the former. (May 1892.)

12. COURT-BOOK OF THE BARONY OF URIE, 1604-1747. Edited by the Rev. D. G. BARRON, from a MS. in possession of Mr. R. BARCLAY of Dorking. (Oct. 1892.)

### *For the year* 1891-1892.

13. MEMOIRS OF THE LIFE OF SIR JOHN CLERK OF PENICUIK, Baronet, Baron of the Exchequer, Commissioner of the Union, etc. Extracted by himself from his own Journals, 1676-1755. Edited from the original MS. in Penicuik House by JOHN M. GRAY, F.S.A. Scot. (Dec. 1892.)

14. DIARY OF COL. THE HON. JOHN ERSKINE OF CARNOCK, 1683-1687. From a MS. in possession of HENRY DAVID ERSKINE, Esq., of Cardross. Edited by the Rev. WALTER MACLEOD. (Dec. 1893.)

*For the year* **1892-1893.**

15. MISCELLANY OF THE SCOTTISH HISTORY SOCIETY, First Volume—
    THE LIBRARY OF JAMES VI., 1573-83.
    DOCUMENTS ILLUSTRATING CATHOLIC POLICY, 1596-98.
    LETTERS OF SIR THOMAS HOPE, 1627-46.
    CIVIL WAR PAPERS, 1645-50.
    LAUDERDALE CORRESPONDENCE, 1660-77.
    TURNBULL'S DIARY, 1657-1704.
    MASTERTON PAPERS, 1660-1719.
    ACCOMPT OF EXPENSES IN EDINBURGH, 1715.
    REBELLION PAPERS, 1715 and 1745. (Dec. 1893.)

16. ACCOUNT BOOK OF SIR JOHN FOULIS OF RAVELSTON (1671-1707).
    Edited by the Rev. A. W. CORNELIUS HALLEN.
    (June 1894.)

*For the year* **1893-1894.**

17. LETTERS AND PAPERS ILLUSTRATING THE RELATIONS BETWEEN CHARLES II. AND SCOTLAND IN 1650. Edited, with Notes and Introduction, by SAMUEL RAWSON GARDINER, LL.D., etc.
    (July 1894.)

18. SCOTLAND AND THE COMMONWEALTH. LETTERS AND PAPERS RELATING TO THE MILITARY GOVERNMENT OF SCOTLAND, Aug. 1651—Dec. 1653. Edited, with Introduction and Notes, by C. H. FIRTH, M.A. (Oct. 1895.)

*For the year* **1894-1895.**

19. THE JACOBITE ATTEMPT OF 1719. LETTERS OF JAMES, SECOND DUKE OF ORMONDE, RELATING TO CARDINAL ALBERONI'S PROJECT FOR THE INVASION OF GREAT BRITAIN ON BEHALF OF THE STUARTS, AND TO THE LANDING OF THE EARL MARISCHAL IN SCOTLAND. Edited by W. K. DICKSON, Advocate. (Dec. 1895.)

20, 21. THE LYON IN MOURNING, OR A COLLECTION OF SPEECHES, LETTERS, JOURNALS, ETC., RELATIVE TO THE AFFAIRS OF PRINCE CHARLES EDWARD STUART, by the Rev. ROBERT FORBES, A.M., Bishop of Ross and Caithness. 1746-1775. Edited from his Manuscript by HENRY PATON, M.A. Vols. I. and II.
    (Oct. 1895.)

## PUBLICATIONS

*For the year* 1895-1896.

22. THE LYON IN MOURNING. Vol. III. (Oct. 1896.)
23. SUPPLEMENT TO THE LYON IN MOURNING.—ITINERARY OF PRINCE CHARLES EDWARD. With a Map. Edited by W. B. BLAIKIE. (Jan. 1897.)
24. EXTRACTS FROM THE PRESBYTERY RECORDS OF INVERNESS AND DINGWALL FROM 1638 TO 1688. Edited by WILLIAM MACKAY. (Oct. 1896.)
25. RECORDS OF THE COMMISSIONS OF THE GENERAL ASSEMBLIES (*continued*) for the years 1648 and 1649. Edited by the Rev. Professor MITCHELL, D.D., and Rev. JAMES CHRISTIE, D.D. (Dec. 1896.)

*For the year* 1896-1897.

WARISTON'S DIARY AND OTHER PAPERS—
    FRAGMENTS OF THE DIARY OF SIR ARCHIBALD JOHNSTON, LORD WARISTON, 1639. Edited by GEORGE M. PAUL, W.S.
    PAPERS RELATIVE TO THE PRESERVATION OF THE HONOURS OF SCOTLAND IN DUNNOTTAR CASTLE, 1651-52. Edited by CHARLES R. A. HOWDEN, Advocate.
    THE EARL OF MAR'S LEGACIES TO SCOTLAND AND TO HIS SON LORD ERSKINE, 1722, 1726. Edited by the Hon. STUART ERSKINE.
    LETTERS WRITTEN BY MRS. GRANT OF LAGGAN CONCERNING HIGHLAND AFFAIRS AND PERSONS CONNECTED WITH THE STUART CAUSE IN THE EIGHTEENTH CENTURY. Edited by J. R. N. MACPHAIL, Advocate. (Dec. 1896.)
    *Presented to the Society by Messrs. T. and A. Constable.*

JOURNALS AND PAPERS OF JOHN MURRAY OF BROUGHTON, PRINCE CHARLES' SECRETARY. Edited by R. FITZROY BELL, Advocate.

ACCOMPT-BOOK OF BAILIE DAVID WEDDERBURNE, MERCHANT OF DUNDEE, 1587-1630. With Shipping Lists of the Port of Dundee, 1580-1630. Edited by A. H. MILLAR.

*In preparation.*

JOURNAL OF A FOREIGN TOUR IN 1665 AND 1666 BY JOHN LAUDER, LORD FOUNTAINHALL. Edited by DONALD CRAWFORD, Sheriff of Aberdeenshire.

THE POLITICAL CORRESPONDENCE OF JEAN DE MONTREUIL WITH CARDINAL MAZARIN AND OTHERS CONCERNING SCOTTISH AFFAIRS, 1645-1648. Edited from the originals in the French Foreign Office, with Translation and Notes by J. G. FOTHERINGHAM.

SCOTLAND DURING THE PROTECTORATE, 1653-1659; in continuation of SCOTLAND AND THE COMMONWEALTH. Edited by C. H. FIRTH.

SIR THOMAS CRAIG'S DE UNIONE REGNORUM BRITANNIÆ. Edited, with an English Translation, from the unpublished MS. in the Advocates' Library, by DAVID MASSON, Historiographer Royal.

A TRANSLATION OF THE STATUTA ECCLESIÆ SCOTICANÆ, 1225-1556, by DAVID PATRICK, LL.D.

DOCUMENTS IN THE ARCHIVES OF THE HAGUE AND ROTTERDAM CONCERNING THE SCOTS BRIGADE IN HOLLAND. Edited by J. FERGUSON, Advocate.

RECORDS OF THE COMMISSIONS OF THE GENERAL ASSEMBLIES (*continued*), for the years 1650-53.

REGISTER OF THE CONSULTATIONS OF THE MINISTERS OF EDINBURGH, AND SOME OTHER BRETHREN OF THE MINISTRY FROM DIVERS PARTS OF THE LAND, MEETING FROM TIME TO TIME, SINCE THE INTERRUPTION OF THE ASSEMBLY 1653, ON THE PUBLIC AFFAIRS OF THIS DISTRESSED AND DISTRACTED KIRK, WITH OTHER PAPERS OF PUBLIC CONCERNMENT, 1653-1660.

PAPERS RELATING TO THE REBELLIONS OF 1715 AND 1745, with other documents from the Municipal Archives of the City of Perth.

THE DIARY OF ANDREW HAY OF STONE, NEAR BIGGAR, AFTERWARDS OF CRAIGNETHAN CASTLE, 1659-60. Edited by A. G. REID from a manuscript in his possession.

A SELECTION OF THE FORFEITED ESTATES PAPERS PRESERVED IN H.M. GENERAL REGISTER HOUSE AND ELSEWHERE. Edited by A. H. MILLAR.

A TRANSLATION OF THE HISTORIA ABBATUM DE KYNLOS OF FERRERIUS. By ARCHIBALD CONSTABLE.

DOCUMENTS RELATING TO THE AFFAIRS OF THE ROMAN CATHOLIC PARTY IN SCOTLAND, from the year of the Armada to the Union of the Crowns. Edited by THOMAS GRAVES LAW.

MACFARLANE'S GENEALOGICAL AND TOPOGRAPHICAL COLLECTIONS IN THE ADVOCATES LIBRARY. Edited by J. T. CLARK, Keeper of the Library.

# Scottish History Society

LIST OF MEMBERS

1896-1897

# LIST OF MEMBERS

ADAM, SIR CHARLES E., Bart., 3 New Square, Lincoln's Inn, London.
Adam, Robert, Brae-Moray, Gillsland Road, Edinburgh.
Adam, Thomas, Hazelbank, Uddingston.
Agnew, Alex., Procurator-Fiscal, Court-House Buildings, Dundee.
Aikman, Andrew, 27 Buckingham Terrace, Edinburgh.
Aitken, Dr. A. P., 57 Great King Street, Edinburgh.
Aitken, James H., Gartcows, Falkirk.
Alexander, William, M.D., Dundonald, Kilmarnock.
Allan, George, Advocate, 56 Castle Street, Aberdeen.
10 Anderson, Archibald, 30 Oxford Square, London, W.
Anderson, John, jun., Atlantic Mills, Bridgeton, Glasgow.
Andrew, Thomas, Doune, Perthshire.
Armstrong, Robert Bruce, 6 Randolph Cliff, Edinburgh.
Arnot, James, M.A., 57 Leamington Terrace, Edinburgh.
Arrol, William A., 11 Lynedoch Place, Glasgow.

BAILLIE, RONALD, Advocate, 11 Albany Street, Edinburgh.
Bain, Walter, 19 Burns Street, Ayr.
Baird, J. G. A., M.P., Wellwood, Muirkirk.
Balfour, C. B., Newton Don, Kelso.
20 Balfour, Right Hon. J. B., Q.C., 6 Rothesay Terrace, Edinburgh.
Ballingall, Hugh, Ardarroch, Dundee.
Barclay, George, 17 Coates Crescent, Edinburgh.
Barclay, R., Bury Hill, Dorking.
Barron, Rev. Douglas Gordon, Dunnottar Manse, Stonehaven.

## LIST OF MEMBERS

Begg, Ferdinand Faithfull, M.P., 13 Earl's Court Square, London, S.W.
Bell, A. Beatson, Advocate, 2 Eglinton Crescent, Edinburgh.
Bell, Joseph, F.R.C.S., 2 Melville Crescent, Edinburgh.
Bell, Captain Laurence A., R.N., 1 Eton Terrace, Edinburgh.
Bell, Robert Fitzroy, Advocate, 7 Ainslie Place, Edinburgh.
30 Bell, Russell, Advocate, Kildalloig, Campbeltown.
Beveridge, Erskine, St. Leonard's Hill, Dunfermline.
Black, James Tait, 33 Palace Court, Bayswater Hill, London, W.
Black, Rev. John S., LL.D., 3 Down St., Piccadilly, London, W.
Blaikie, Walter B., 6 Belgrave Crescent, Edinburgh.
Blair, Patrick, Advocate, 4 Ardross Terrace, Inverness.
Bonar, Horatius, W.S., 15 Strathearn Place, Edinburgh.
Boyd, Sir Thomas J., 41 Moray Place, Edinburgh.
Brookman, James, W.S., 16 Ravelston Park, Edinburgh.
Brown, Professor Alex. Crum, 8 Belgrave Crescent, Edinburgh.
40 Brown, J. A. Harvie, Dunipace House, Larbert, Stirlingshire.
Brown, P. Hume, LL.D., 19 Gillespie Crescent, Edinburgh.
Brown, William, 26 Princes Street, Edinburgh.
Brownlie, James R., 10 Brandon Pl., West George St., Glasgow.
Bruce, Alex., Clyne House, Sutherland Avenue, Pollokshields.
Bruce, James, W.S., 59 Great King Street, Edinburgh.
Bruce, R. T. Hamilton, Grange, Dornoch, Sutherlandshire.
Bryce, Right Hon. James, M.P., 54 Portland Place, London, W.
Bryce, William Moir, Dunedin, Blackford Road, Edinburgh.
Buchanan, A. W. Gray, Parkhill, Polmont, N.B.
50 Burns, Alan, B.A., Advocate, 7 Melville Crescent, Edinburgh.
Burns, John William, Kilmahew, Cardross.
Burns, Rev. Thomas, 2 St. Margaret's Road, Edinburgh.
Bute, The Marquis of, Mountstuart, Isle of Bute.

CALDWELL, JAMES, Craigielea Place, Paisley.
Cameron, Dr. J. A., Nairn.
Cameron, Richard, 1 South St. David Street, Edinburgh.
Campbell, D. S., 63 High Street, Montrose.
Campbell, Rev. James, D.D., the Manse, Balmerino, Dundee.

## LIST OF MEMBERS

Campbell, James A., Stracathro, Brechin.
60 Campbell, P. W., W.S., 25 Moray Place, Edinburgh.
Carmichael, Sir Thomas D. Gibson, Bart., Castlecraig, Dolphinton, N.B.
Carne-Ross, Joseph, M.D., Parsonage Nook, Withington, Manchester.
Carrick, J. Stewart, 12 Blythswood Square, Glasgow.
Chambers, W. & R., 339 High Street, Edinburgh.
Chiene, Professor, 26 Charlotte Square, Edinburgh.
Christie, J.,
Christie, Thomas Craig, of Bedlay, Chryston, Glasgow.
Clark, George T., Talygarn, Llantrissant.
Clark, James, Advocate, 4 Drumsheugh Gardens, Edinburgh.
70 Clark, J. T., Crear Villa, Ferry Road, Edinburgh.
Clark, Sir Thomas, Bart., 11 Melville Crescent, Edinburgh.
Clouston, T. S., M.D., Tipperlinn House, Morningside Place, Edinburgh.
Cochran-Patrick, R. W., LL.D., of Woodside, Beith, Ayrshire.
Constable, Archibald, LL.D., 11 Thistle Street, Edinburgh.
Cowan, George, 1 Gillsland Road, Edinburgh.
Cowan, Hugh, St. Leonards, Ayr.
Cowan, J. J., 38 West Register Street, Edinburgh.
Cowan, John, W.S., St. Roque, Grange Loan, Edinburgh.
Cowan, Sir John, Bart., Beeslack, Mid-Lothian.
80 Cowan, William, 7 Braid Avenue, Edinburgh.
Craik, James, W.S., 9 Eglinton Crescent, Edinburgh.
Crawford, Donald, Advocate, 17 Melville Street, Edinburgh.
Crole, Gerard L., Advocate, 30 Northumberland St., Edinburgh.
Cross, Robert, 8 Rothesay Terrace, Edinburgh.
Cunningham, Geo. Miller, C.E., 2 Ainslie Place, Edinburgh.
Cunynghame, R. J. Blair, M.D., 18 Rothesay Place, Edinburgh.
Curle, Alex. Ormiston, B.A., W.S., 32 Melville St., Edinburgh.
Curle, James, W.S., Priorwood, Melrose.
Currie, James, 16 Bernard Street, Leith.
90 Currie, Walter Thomson, of Trynlaw, by Cupar-Fife.
Currie, W. R., 30 Burnbank Gardens, Glasgow.

Cuthbert, Alex. A., 14 Newton Terrace, Glasgow.
DALGLEISH, JOHN J., Brankston Grange, Bogside Station, Stirling.
Dalrymple, Hon. Hew, Lochinch, Castle Kennedy, Wigtownshire.
Davidson, Hugh, Braedale, Lanark.
Davidson, J., Solicitor, Kirriemuir.
Davidson, Thomas, 339 High Street, Edinburgh.
Davies, J. Mair, C.A., Sheiling, Pollokshields, Glasgow.
Dickson, William K., Advocate, 19 Dundas Street, Edinburgh.
100 Dickson, Wm. Traquair, W.S., 11 Hill Street, Edinburgh.
Dinwoodie, Miss E., Millbank, Moffat.
Dixon, John H., Inveran, Poolewe, by Dingwall.
Doak, Rev. Andrew, M.A., 15 Queen's Road, Aberdeen.
Dodds, Rev. James, D.D., The Manse, Corstorphine.
Dods, Colonel P., United Service Club, Edinburgh.
Donaldson, James, LL.D., Principal, St. Andrews University.
Donaldson, James, Sunnyside, Formby, Liverpool.
Douglas, David, 10 Castle Street, Edinburgh.
Dowden, Right Rev. John, D.D., Bishop of Edinburgh, Lynn House, Gillsland Road, Edinburgh.
110 Duff, T. Gordon, Drummuir, Keith.
Duncan, James Barker, W.S., 6 Hill Street, Edinburgh.
Duncan, John, 8 Lynedoch Place, Edinburgh.
Dundas, Ralph, C.S., 28 Drumsheugh Gardens, Edinburgh.
Dunn, Robert Hunter, Belgian Consulate, Glasgow.

EASTON, WALTER, 125 Buchanan Street, Glasgow.
Ewart, Prof. Cossar, The University, Edinburgh.

FAULDS, A. WILSON, Knockbuckle, Beith, Ayrshire.
Ferguson, James, Advocate, 10 Wemyss Place, Edinburgh.
Ferguson, John, Town Clerk, Linlithgow.
120 Ferguson, Rev. John, Manse, Aberdalgie, Perth.
Findlay, J. Ritchie, 3 Rothesay Terrace, Edinburgh.
Findlay, Rev. Wm., The Manse, Saline, Fife.
Firth, Charles Harding, 33 Norham Road, Oxford.

Fleming, D. Hay, 16 Greyfriars Garden, St. Andrews.
Fleming, J. S., 16 Grosvenor Crescent, Edinburgh.
Flint, Prof., D.D., LL.D., Johnstone Lodge, Craigmillar Park, Edinburgh.
Forrest, James R. P., 32 Broughton Place, Edinburgh.
Forrester, John, 29 Windsor Street, Edinburgh.
Foulis, James, M.D., 34 Heriot Row, Edinburgh.
130 Foulis, Thomas, 27 Cluny Gardens, Edinburgh.
Fraser, Professor A. Campbell, D.C.L., LL.D., Gorton House, Hawthornden.

GAIRDNER, CHARLES, Broom, Newton-Mearns, Glasgow.
Galletly, Edwin G., 7 St. Ninian's Terrace, Edinburgh.
Gardiner, Samuel Rawson, LL.D., 7 South Park, Sevenoaks, Kent.
Gardner, Alexander, 7 Gilmour Street, Paisley.
Garson, William, W.S., 60 Palmerston Place, Edinburgh.
Gartshore, Miss Murray, Ravelston, Blackhall, Edinburgh.
Geikie, Sir Archibald, LL.D., Geological Survey, 28 Jermyn Street, London, S.W.
Geikie, Prof. James, LL.D., 31 Merchiston Aven., Edinburgh.
140 Gibson, Andrew, 3 Morrison Street, Govan.
Gibson, J. C., c/o James Forbes, 18 Coltbridge Terrace, Murrayfield, Edinburgh.
Gibson, James T., LL.B., W.S., 37 George Street, Edinburgh.
Giles, Arthur, 107 Princes Street, Edinburgh.
Gillespie, Mrs. G. R., 5 Darnaway Street, Edinburgh.
Gillies, Walter, M.A., The Academy, Perth.
Gordon, Rev. Robert, Mayfield Gardens, Edinburgh.
Goudie, Gilbert, F.S.A. Scot., 39 Northumberland St., Edinburgh.
Goudie, Robert, Commissary Clerk of Ayrshire, Ayr.
Gourlay, Robert, Bank of Scotland, Glasgow.
150 Gow, Leonard, Hayston, Kelvinside, Glasgow.
Graeme, Lieut.-Col. Laurence, Fonthill, Shaldon, Teignmouth, Devon.

Graeme, Lieut.-Col. R. C., Naval and Military Club, 94 Piccadilly, London.
Grant, William G. L., Woodside, East Newport, Fife.
Gray, George, Clerk of the Peace, Glasgow.
Green, Charles E., 18 St. Giles Street, Edinburgh.
Greig, Andrew, 36 Belmont Gardens, Hillhead, Glasgow.
Gunning, His Excellency Robert Haliday, M.D., 12 Addison Crescent, Kensington, London, W.
Guthrie, Charles J., Advocate, 13 Royal Circus, Edinburgh.
Guy, Robert, 120 West Regent Street, Glasgow.

160 HALKETT, MISS KATHERINE E., 3 Pitt Street, Camden Hill, London, W.
Hall, David, Crookedholm House, Hurlford, Ayrshire.
Hallen, Rev. A. W. Cornelius, The Parsonage, Alloa.
Hamilton, Hubert, Advocate, 55 Manor Place, Edinburgh.
Hamilton, Lord, of Dalzell, Motherwell.
Hamilton-Ogilvy, Henry T. N., Prestonkirk.
Harrison, John, 8 St. Andrew Square, Edinburgh.
Hedderwick, A. W. H., 79 St. George's Place, Glasgow.
Henderson, J. G. B., Nether Parkley, Linlithgow.
Henderson, Joseph, 11 Blythswood Square, Glasgow.
170 Henry, David, 2 Lockhart Place, St. Andrews, Fife.
Hewison, Rev. J. King, The Manse, Rothesay.
Hill, William H., LL.D., Barlanark, Shettleston, Glasgow.
Honeyman, John, A.R.S.A., 140 Bath Street, Glasgow.
Howden, Charles R. A., Advocate, 25 Melville Street, Edinburgh.
Hunter, Colonel, F.R.S., of Plâs Côch, Anglesea.
Hutcheson, Alexander, Herschel House, Broughty Ferry.
Hutchison, Rev. John, D.D., Afton Lodge, Bonnington.
Hyslop, J. M., M.D., 22 Palmerston Place, Edinburgh.

IMRIE, MRS. T. NAIRNE, 34 Ann Street, Edinburgh.

180 JAMESON, J. H., W.S., 3 Northumberland Street, Edinburgh.
Jamieson, George Auldjo, C.A., 37 Drumsheugh Gardens, Edinburgh.

Jamieson, J. Auldjo, W.S., 14 Buckingham Ter., Edinburgh.
Johnston, D., Glenholm, 204 Newhaven Road, Edinburgh.
Johnston, David, 24 Huntly Gardens, Kelvinside, Glasgow.
Johnston, George Harvey, 22 Garscube Terrace, Edinburgh.
Johnston, George P., 33 George Street, Edinburgh.
Johnstone, James F. Kellas, 431 Union Street, Aberdeen.
Johnstone, J. T., 20 Broughton Place, Edinburgh.
Jonas, Alfred Charles, Poundfald, Penclawdd, Swansea.

190 KEMP, D. WILLIAM, Ivy Lodge, Trinity, Edinburgh.
Kennedy, Neil J., Advocate, 71 Great King Street, Edinburgh.
Kermack, John, W.S., 13 Glencairn Crescent, Edinburgh.
Kincairney, The Hon. Lord, 6 Heriot Row, Edinburgh.
Kinnear, The Hon. Lord, 2 Moray Place, Edinburgh.
Kirkpatrick, Prof. John, LL.D., Advocate, 24 Alva Street, Edinburgh.
Kirkpatrick, Robert, 1 Queen Square, Strathbungo, Glasgow.

LAIDLAW, DAVID, Jun., 6 Marlborough Terrace, Kelvinside, Glasgow.
Lamb, A. C., 3 Lansdowne Place, Dundee.
Lang, James, 9 Crown Gardens, Dowanhill, Glasgow.
200 Langwill, Robert B., The Manse, Currie.
Laurie, Professor S. S., Nairne Lodge, Duddingston.
Law, Thomas Graves, Signet Library, Edinburgh, *Secretary.*
Leadbetter, Thomas, 2 Magdala Place, Edinburgh.
Leslie, Colonel, of Kininvie, Banffshire.
Livingstone, M., 47 Braid Road, Edinburgh.
Logan, C. B., D.K.S., 12 Rothesay Place, Edinburgh.
Lorimer, George, 2 Abbotsford Crescent, Edinburgh.
Low, James F., Seaview, Monifieth.

MACADAM, J. H., 95 Leith Street, Edinburgh.
210 Macadam, W. Ivison, Slioch, Lady Road, Newington, Edinburgh.
M'Alpine, William, 11 Archibald Place, Edinburgh.
Macandrew, Sir Henry C., Aisthorpe, Midmills Road, Inverness.
M'Bain, J. M., British Linen Bank, Arbroath.

## LIST OF MEMBERS

Macbrayne, David, Jun., 17 Royal Exchange Square, Glasgow.
M'Candlish, John M., W.S., 27 Drumsheugh Gar., Edinburgh.
Macdonald, James, W.S., 4 Whitehouse Terrace, Edinburgh.
Macdonald, W. Rae, 1 Forres Street, Edinburgh.
Macdougall, Jas. Patten, Advocate, 39 Heriot Row, Edinburgh.
M'Ewen, W. C., W.S., 2 Rothesay Place, Edinburgh.
220 Macfarlane, Geo. L., Advocate, 3 St. Colme Street, Edinburgh.
Macgeorge, B. B., 19 Woodside Crescent, Glasgow.
MacGregor, John, W.S., 10 Dundas Street, Edinburgh.
M'Grigor, Alexander, 172 St. Vincent Street, Glasgow.
Macintyre, P. M., Advocate, 12 India Street, Edinburgh.
Mackay, Æneas J. G., LL.D., 7 Albyn Place, Edinburgh.
Mackay, Eneas, 43 Murray Place, Stirling.
Mackay, Rev. G. S., M.A., Free Church Manse, Doune.
Mackay, James F., W.S., Whitehouse, Cramond.
Mackay, James R., 37 St. Andrew Square, Edinburgh.
230 Mackay, Thomas, 14 Wetherby Place, South Kensington, London, S.W.
Mackay, Thomas A., British Linen Bank House, Inverness.
Mackay, William, Solicitor, Inverness.
Mackenzie, A., St. Catherines, Paisley.
Mackenzie, David J., Sheriff-Substitute, Wick.
Mackenzie, Thomas, M.A., Sheriff-Substitute of Ross, Tain.
Mackinlay, David, 6 Great Western Terrace, Glasgow.
Mackinnon, Professor, 1 Merchiston Place, Edinburgh.
Mackintosh, Charles Fraser, 18 Pont Street, London, S.W.
Mackintosh, W. F., 27 Commerce Street, Arbroath.
240 Maclachlan, John, W.S., 12 Abercromby Place, Edinburgh.
Maclagan, Prof. Sir Douglas, M.D., 28 Heriot Row, Edinburgh.
Maclagan, Robert Craig, M.D., 5 Coates Crescent, Edinburgh.
Maclauchlan, John, Albert Institute, Dundee.
Maclean, Sir Andrew, Viewfield House, Balshagray, Partick, Glasgow.
Maclean, William C., F.R.G.S., 31 Camperdown Place, Great Yarmouth.
MacLehose, James J., 61 St. Vincent Street, Glasgow.

Macleod, Rev. Walter, 112 Thirlestane Road, Edinburgh.
Macphail, J. R. N., Advocate, 53 Castle Street, Edinburgh.
M'Phee, Donald, Oakfield, Fort William.
250 Macray, Rev. W. D., Bodleian Library, Oxford.
Macritchie, David, 4 Archibald Place, Edinburgh.
Main, W. D., 128 St. Vincent Street, Glasgow.
Marshall, John, Caldergrove, Newton, Lanarkshire.
Martin, Francis John, W.S., 9 Glencairn Crescent, Edinburgh.
Marwick, Sir J. D., LL.D., Killermont House, Maryhill, Glasgow.
Massie, James, 6 Inverleith Avenue, Edinburgh.
Masson, David, LL.D., Gowanlea, Juniper Green.
Mathieson, Thomas A., 3 Grosvenor Terrace, Glasgow.
Maxwell, W. J., Terraughtie, Dumfries.
260 Melville, Viscount, Melville Castle, Lasswade.
Melville, Rev. Dr., Culfargie, Polwarth Terrace, Edinburgh.
Mill, Alex., 9 Dalhousie Terrace, Edinburgh.
Millar, Alexander H., Rosslyn House, Clepington Rd., Dundee.
Miller, P., Dalmeny Lodge, Craiglockhart, Slateford.
Milligan, John, W.S., 10 Carlton Terrace, Edinburgh.
Milne, A. & R., Union Street, Aberdeen.
Milne, Mrs., Viewlands, Perth.
Mitchell, Rev. Prof. A. F., D.D., St. Andrews.
Mitchell, Sir Arthur, K.C.B., M.D., LL.D., 34 Drummond Place, Edinburgh.
270 Mitchell, James, 240 Darnley Street, Pollokshields, Glasgow.
Moncrieff, W. G. Scott, Advocate, Weedingshall House, Polmont.
Moffatt, Alexander, 23 Abercromby Place, Edinburgh.
Moffatt, Alexander, jun., M.A., LL.B., Advocate, 45 Northumberland Street, Edinburgh.
Morison, John, 11 Burnbank Gardens, Glasgow.
Morries-Stirling, J. M., Gogar House, Stirling.
Morrison, Hew, 7 Hermitage Terrace, Morningside.
Muir, James, 27 Huntly Gardens, Dowanhill, Glasgow.
Muirhead, James, 2 Bowmont Gardens, Kelvinside, Glasgow.

Murdoch, Rev. A. D., All Saints' Parsonage, Edinburgh.
280 Murdoch, J. B., of Capelrig, Mearns, Renfrewshire.
Murray, David, 169 West George Street, Glasgow.
Murray, Colonel John, Polmaise Castle, Stirling.

Nicolson, A. B., W.S., Westbourne House, Union Street, Aberdeen.
Norfor, Robert T., C.A., 11 Hope Terrace, Edinburgh.

Ogilvy, Sir Reginald, Bart., Baldovan, Dundee.
Oliver, James, Thornwood, Hawick.
Orrock, Archibald, 17 St. Catherine's Place, Edinburgh.

Panton, George A., F.R.S.E., 73 Westfield Road, Edgbaston, Birmingham.
Paton, Allan Park, Home Cottage, Roseneath St., Greenock.
290 Paton, Henry, M.A., 15 Myrtle Terrace, Edinburgh.
Paton, Victor A. Noël, W.S., 33 George Square, Edinburgh.
Patrick, David, LL.D., 339 High Street, Edinburgh.
Paul, J. Balfour, Advocate, Lyon King of Arms, 30 Heriot Row, Edinburgh.
Paul, Rev. Robert, F.S.A. Scot., Dollar.
Pearson, David Ritchie, M.D., 23 Upper Phillimore Place, Phillimore Gardens, London, W.
Pillans, Hugh H., 12 Dryden Place, Edinburgh.
Pollock, Hugh, Craig-Ard, Langside, Glasgow.
Prentice, A. R., 18 Kilblain Street, Greenock.
Prothero, Professor, 2 Eton Terrace, Edinburgh.
300 Pullar, Sir Robert, Tayside, Perth.
Purves, A. P., W.S., Esk Tower, Lasswade.

Ramsay, William, 10 Frederick Street, Edinburgh.
Rankine, John, Advocate, Professor of Scots Law, 23 Ainslie Place, Edinburgh.
Reichel, H. R., Principal, University College, Bangor, North Wales.
Reid, Alexander George, Solicitor, Auchterarder.

## LIST OF MEMBERS

Reid, John Alexander, Advocate, 11 Royal Circus, Edinburgh.
Renwick, Robert, Depute Town-Clerk, City Chambers, Glasgow.
Richardson, Ralph, W.S., Commissary Office, 2 Parliament Square, Edinburgh.
Ritchie, David, Hopeville, Dowanhill Gardens, Glasgow.
310 Ritchie, R. Peel, M.D., 1 Melville Crescent, Edinburgh.
Roberton, James D., 1 Park Terrace East, Glasgow.
Robertson, A. Ireland, 31 Sciennes Road, Edinburgh.
Robertson, D. Argyll, M.D., 18 Charlotte Square, Edinburgh.
Robertson, John, Elmslea, Dundee.
Robson, William, Marchholm, Gillsland Road, Edinburgh.
Rogerson, John J., LL.D., Merchiston Castle, Edinburgh.
Rosebery, The Earl of, K.G., Dalmeny Park, Linlithgowshire.
Ross, T. S., Balgillo Terrace, Broughty Ferry.
Ross, Mrs., 7 Grange Terrace, Edinburgh.
320 Ross, Rev. William, St. Mary's Manse, Partickhill, Glasgow.

SCOTT, REV. ARCHIBALD, D.D., 16 Rothesay Place, Edinburgh.
Scott, John, C.B., Seafield, Greenock.
Shaw, David, W.S., 1 Thistle Court, Edinburgh.
Shaw, Rev. R. D., B.D., 21 Lauder Road, Edinburgh.
Shaw, Thomas, M.P., Advocate, 17 Abercromby Pl., Edinburgh.
Sheriff, George, Woodcroft, Larbert, Stirlingshire.
Shiells, Robert, National Bank of Neenah, Neenah Wisconsin.
Simpson, Prof. A. R., 52 Queen Street, Edinburgh.
Simpson, H. F. Morland, 80 Hamilton Place, Aberdeen.
330 Simpson, Sir W. G., Bart., Balabraes, Ayton, Berwickshire.
Simson, D. J., Advocate, 3 Glenfinlas Street, Edinburgh.
Sinclair, Alexander, Glasgow Herald Office, Glasgow.
Skelton, John, Advocate, C.B., LL.D., the Hermitage of Braid, Edinburgh.
Skinner, William, W.S., 35 George Square, Edinburgh.
Smail, Adam, 13 Cornwall Street, Edinburgh.
Smart, William, M.A., Nunholm, Dowanhill, Glasgow.
Smith, Andrew, Broompark, Lanark.
Smith, Sir Donald A., K.C.M.G., Glencoe, Argyllshire.

Smith, G. Gregory, M.A., 9 Warrender Park Cres., Edinburgh.
340 Smith, Rev. G. Mure, 6 Clarendon Place, Stirling.
Smith, Rev. R. Nimmo, LL.D., Manse of the First Charge, Haddington.
Smith, Robert, 9 Ward Road, Dundee.
Smythe, David M., Methven Castle, Perth.
Somerville, F. R., Glencorse Cottage, Morningside Park, Edinburgh.
Sprott, Rev. George W., D.D., The Manse, North Berwick.
Stair, Earl of, Oxenfoord Castle, Dalkeith.
Steele, W. Cunninghame, Advocate, 69 Gt. King St., Edinburgh.
Stephen, Rev. William, Parsonage, Dumbarton.
Stevenson, J. H., Advocate, 9 Oxford Terrace, Edinburgh.
350 Stevenson, Rev. Robert, M.A., The Abbey, Dunfermline.
Stewart, Donald W., 62 Princes Street, Edinburgh.
Stewart, Major-General Shaw, 61 Lancaster Gate, London, W.
Stewart, R. K., Murdostoun Castle, Newmains, Lanarkshire.
Stewart, Prof. Sir T. Grainger, M.D., 19 Charlotte Sq., Edinburgh.
Strathallan, Lady, Machany House, Perthshire.
Strathern, Robert, W.S., 12 South Charlotte St., Edinburgh.
Strathmore, Earl of, Glamis Castle, Glamis.
Sturrock, James S., W.S., 122 George Street, Edinburgh.
Sutherland, James B., S.S.C., 10 Windsor Street, Edinburgh.

360 Taylor, Benjamin, 10 Derby Crescent, Kelvinside, Glasgow.
Taylor, James Pringle, W.S., 19 Young Street, Edinburgh.
Taylor, Rev. Malcolm C., D.D., Professor of Church History, 6 Greenhill Park, Edinburgh.
Telford, Rev. W. H., Free Church Manse, Reston, Berwickshire.
Tennant, Sir Charles, Bart., The Glen, Innerleithen.
Thoms, George H. M., Advocate, 13 Charlotte Sq., Edinburgh.
Thomson, John Comrie, Advocate, 30 Moray Place, Edinburgh.
Thomson, Rev. John Henderson, Free Church Manse, Hightae, by Lockerbie.
Thomson, John Maitland, Advocate, 3 Grosvenor Gardens, Edinburgh.

Thomson, Lockhart, S.S.C., 114 George Street, Edinburgh.
370 Trail, John A., LL.B., W.S., 14 Belgrave Place, Edinburgh.
Trayner, The Hon. Lord, 27 Moray Place, Edinburgh.
Tuke, John Batty, M.D., 20 Charlotte Square, Edinburgh.
Tweedale, Mrs., Milton Hall, Milton, Cambridge.
Tweeddale, Marquis of, Yester, Gifford, Haddington.

UNDERHILL, CHARLES E., M.D., 8 Coates Crescent, Edinburgh.

VEITCH, G. S., Friarshall, Paisley.

WADDEL, KATHERINE, 37 Monteith Row, Glasgow.
Walker, Alexander, 64 Hamilton Place, Aberdeen.
Walker, James, Hanley Lodge, Corstorphine.
380 Walker, Louson, Westhorpe, Greenock.
Walker, Robert, M.A., Tillydrone House, Old Aberdeen.
Wannop, Rev. Canon, Parsonage, Haddington.
Warrender, Miss, Bruntsfield House, Edinburgh.
Waterston, George, 56 Hanover Street, Edinburgh.
Watson, D., Hillside Cottage, Hawick.
Watson, James, 40 Barscombe Avenue, Streatham Hill, London.
Waugh, Alexander, National Bank, Newton-Stewart, N.B.
Williamson, A. C., Advocate, 6 Moray Place, Edinburgh.
Wilson, Rev. J. Skinner, 53 Albany Street, Edinburgh.
390 Wilson, John J., Clydesdale Bank, Penicuik.
Wilson, Robert Dobie, 38 Upper Brook Street, London, W.
Wood, Alexander, Thornly, Saltcoats.
Wood, Mrs. Christina S., Woodburn, Galashiels.
Wood, Prof. J. P., W.S., 16 Buckingham Terrace, Edinburgh.
Wood, W. A., C.A., 11 Clarendon Crescent, Edinburgh.
Wordie, John, 45 West Nile Street, Glasgow.

YOUNG, A. J., Advocate, 60 Great King Street, Edinburgh.
Young, David, Town Clerk, Paisley.
Young, J. W., W.S., 22 Royal Circus, Edinburgh.
400 Young, William Laurence, Solicitor, Auchterarder.

## LIST OF LIBRARIES

Aberdeen Free Public Library.
Aberdeen University Library.
All Souls College, Oxford.
Antiquaries, Society of, Edinburgh.
Athenæum Club, 107 Pall Mall, London, S.W.
Baillie's Institution Free Library, 48 Miller St., Glasgow.
Belfast Library, Donegall Square North, Belfast, Ireland.
Berlin Royal Library.
Birmingham Free Library.
10 Bodleian Library, Oxford.
Boston Athenæum.
Boston Public Library.
Cambridge University Library.
Copenhagen (Bibliothèque Royale).
Cornell University, Ithaca, Michigan, U.S.A.
Dollar Institution.
Dundee Free Library.
Dresden Public Library.
Edinburgh Public Library.
20 Edinburgh University Library.
Free Church College Library, Edinburgh.
Free Church College Library, Glasgow.
Glasgow University Library.
Gray's Inn, Hon. Society of, London.
Harvard College Library, Cambridge, Mass.
Inverness Free Library.
Leeds Subscription Library.
London Corporation Library, Guildhall.
London Library, 12 St. James Square.
30 Manchester Public Free Library.
Mitchell Library, Glasgow.
National Liberal Club, London.
National Library of Ireland.
Nottingham Free Public Library.
Ottawa Parliamentary Library.
Paisley Philosophical Institution.
Peabody Institute, Baltimore.
Philosophical Institution, Edinburgh.
Procurators, Faculty of, Glasgow.
40 Reform Club, Pall Mall, London, S.W.
Royal College of Physicians, Edinburgh.
St. Andrews University Library.
Sheffield Free Public Library.
Signet Library, Edinburgh.
Solicitors, Society of, before the Supreme Court, Edinburgh.
Speculative Society, Edinburgh.
Stonyhurst College, Blackburn, Lancashire.
Sydney Free Library.
Toronto Public Library.
50 United Presbyterian College Library, Edinburgh.
Vienna, Library of the R. I. University.

www.ingramcontent.com/pod-product-compliance
Lightning Source LLC
Chambersburg PA
CBHW030404230426
43664CB00007BB/743